MW00788350

GENEALOGIES OF MAHĀYĀNA BUDDHISM

Genealogies of Mahāyāna Buddhism offers a solution to a problem that some have called the holy grail of Buddhist studies: the problem of the "origins" of Mahāyāna Buddhism. In a work that contributes both to a general theory of religion and power for religious studies as well as to the problem of the origin of a Buddhist movement, Walser argues that that it is the neglect of political and social power in the scholarly imagination of the history of Buddhism that has made the origins of Mahāyāna an intractable problem. Walser challenges commonly-held assumptions about Mahāyāna Buddhism, offering a fascinating new take on its genealogy that traces its doctrines of emptiness and mind-only from the present day back to the time before Mahāyāna was "Mahāyāna." In situating such concepts in their political and social contexts across diverse regimes of power in Tibet, China and India, the book shows that what was at stake in the Mahāyāna championing of the doctrine of emptiness was the articulation and dissemination of court authority across the rural landscapes of Asia.

This text will be of interest to undergraduate and postgraduate students and scholars of Buddhism, religious studies, history and philosophy.

Joseph Walser is Associate Professor of Religion at Tufts University, USA.

GENEALOGIES OF MAHĀYĀNA BUDDHISM

Emptiness, Power and the Question of Origin

Joseph Walser

Routledge
Taylor & Francis Group
LONDON AND NEW YORK

First published 2018
by Routledge
2 Park Square, Milton Park, Abingdon, Oxon OX14 4RN

and by Routledge
711 Third Avenue, New York, NY 10017

Routledge is an imprint of the Taylor & Francis Group, an informa business

© 2018 Joseph Walser

The right of Joseph Walser to be identified as author of this work has been asserted by him in accordance with sections 77 and 78 of the Copyright, Designs and Patents Act 1988.

All rights reserved. No part of this book may be reprinted or reproduced or utilised in any form or by any electronic, mechanical, or other means, now known or hereafter invented, including photocopying and recording, or in any information storage or retrieval system, without permission in writing from the publishers.

Trademark notice: Product or corporate names may be trademarks or registered trademarks, and are used only for identification and explanation without intent to infringe.

British Library Cataloguing-in-Publication Data
A catalogue record for this book is available from the British Library

Library of Congress Cataloging-in-Publication Data
A catalog record for this book has been requested

ISBN: 978-1-138-95555-4 (hbk)
ISBN: 978-1-138-95556-1 (pbk)
ISBN: 978-1-315-66626-6 (ebk)

Typeset in Gentium Plus
by Apex CoVantage, LLC

To my parents on both sides of the ocean, whose love and wisdom made me who I am.
And to Radha, Tara and Rohan who are the reason for everything I do, every day.

CONTENTS

Acknowledgements xi

PART I
Genealogies of Mahāyāna **1**

1 Introduction: on origins and genealogies 3

2 Mahāyāna in retrospect: from my house to the Dalai Lama (looking back from 2017 to 1930) 11
Assessing the essence 20
Tibet as Buddhist: tracing the lines of power 21
Emptiness and the analytic of power 25
Inculcating dispositions to authority: the Kālacakra *31*

3 Mahāyāna in the republic, Mahāyāna in the empire: tracing "religion" from republican China to the early Qing Dynasty (1920s – 1723) 40
Religion vs. superstition in 20th-century East Asia 41
The Fin de Siècle *turning point 44*
The Qing imperium and the usefulness of Mahāyāna 48
The Yonghegong Temple in Beijing and the political work of monuments 48
Emperor Qianlong: the tantric initiate and the tantric state 53
Tantra, emptiness and the reincarnate emperor/lama, or why it's never too late to have a venerable past 57
Yongzheng emperor and the great Ming debate 60

4 The image of emptiness across the landscape of power (China: 11th century BCE – 15th century CE) 72
The ancestor image 75
The image of emptiness: Di, space and the celestial pole 76
The image of the earth and control of the cults 85
Exorcism and the state: when possession is nine-tenths 88
Religion in the service of taxation 90
Buddhist exorcism and the heart of Mahāyāna 91
Conclusion 93

5 Buddha Veda: an Indian genealogy of emptiness (20th century – sixth century CE) 99
Emptiness and power in Orissa: from Mahima Dharma Sampradāya to Jagannātha of Puri 100
Buddhism and Brahmanism in Maitrīpa (ca. 1010–1097 CE) 105
Bhāviveka's sixth-century Mahāyāna 111
Bhāviveka, Mahāyāna and Yogācāra 116
Bhāviveka, Mahāyāna and Brahmanism 118
Preliminary conclusion 123

PART II
The genealogy of the *Perfection of Wisdom* **127**

6 What did the text of the *Perfection of Wisdom* look like? 129
The versions 129
The quest for the ur-sūtra 130
The core pericope 134
The ending 137
Subhūti's non-apprehension 138
The Mindlessness section and its relation to the Irreversibility section 143
The message of the original Perfection of Wisdom *149*
Mahāyāna 151
Bodhisattvas 152
What's missing? 154

7 Mahāyāna Sūtra as palimpsest: discerning traces of the *Tripiṭaka* 158
Beyond "origin" as mere advent 158
Heteroglossia and textual rationale 160
Intertextuality and adaptation in Buddhist literature 162
The Non-Apprehension section and its intertexts 163

Sermon on selflessness? 164
Nominalism? 166
Cessation of cognition 168
Selflessness . . . but differently 170
The perfected as untraceable 172
Fearlessness 177
Abhidharma *echoes* 181
Conclusion: the perfection of wisdom 183

8 Palimpsest II: brahmanical writings on the *Tripiṭaka* 190
The importance of incoherence 190
The context of abhidharma *literature?* 192
The context of other schools? 195
The context of luminous thought and varieties of unaware thought 195
The context of acitta *neither existing nor not existing as anti-Brahmanical dependent-origination* 198
The context of absence of mental construction (avikalpa) 200
Nirvikalpa 202
Brahmanical intertexts and their implications 205

9 Placing early Mahāyāna 222
Placing the Perfection of Wisdom *in the early Mahāyāna suite* 223
Mañjuśrī's Inquiry Concerning the Office of the Bodhisattva Sūtra 226
Placing the early Perfection of Wisdom 229
Mistaken sounds 232
Subhūti's araṇavihāra*: preaching or penetration?* 234
Emptiness, Brahmin nuns, tulkus *and the power of possession* 238
Putting it together 240
Conclusion 242

10 On sites and stakes: meditation on emptiness and imperial aspirations 246
Shifting contexts, shifting interpretations 248
The Uṇṇābhabrāhmaṇasutta *and the* Bṛhadāraṇyaka Upaniṣad *on cosmic foundations* 251
The Horse Sacrifice 256
Piling the Fire Altar and legitimation regress 259
Buddhist Brahmins 262
On power and reproduction 263

Sovereign echoes: on manhood and celibacy, on thrones and crowns 265
Buddhist brahmodyas *as court debates* 268
The Mahāyāna genealogy from the Vedas to the sutras to Tantra to Zen 269

Bibliography 274
Index 289

ACKNOWLEDGEMENTS

I came to this project – or shall I say the project came to me – in a somewhat roundabout fashion that may explain my particular interest in emptiness in the development of Mahāyāna. Sometimes the best gift one scholar can give to another is a robust criticism. In my first book, *Nāgārjuna in Context*, I outlined what Mahāyāna would have looked like on the ground, as it were, in second-century India. After its publication, Richard Nance wrote a review on H-Net Buddhism in which he (rightfully) takes me to task for not distinguishing Nāgārjuna's Mahāyāna articulation of emptiness from ideas of emptiness that were being used in early Buddhist canonical texts more generally. Pointing to *Saṃyutta Nikāya* IV.85 and *Paṭisambhidāmagga* II.10, he concludes that, "If Nāgārjuna was indeed attempting to smuggle new wine in old bottles, he may have done his job too well – the new wine is arguably indistinguishable from the old."[1]

I suppose that like anyone who is reading such statements in the first review of their first book, my heart sank. I knew that early Mahāyāna authors were up against some kind of opposition. Otherwise, why would the Perfection of Wisdom in 8000 Lines state that if you were to even hear of the fate of someone who doubted the authenticity of its teachings, you would vomit boiling blood and die from fear. But Nance had correctly pointed out that I hadn't really distinguished Nāgārjuna's Mahāyāna version of emptiness from the discussions of emptiness found in canonical (and therefore presumably non-Mahāyāna) texts such as the *Saṃyutta Nikāya* or the *Paṭisaṃbhidhāmagga*, and consequently I could not account for why there might have been resistance to it. The worst part was that I wasn't even sure I even *knew* the difference between the Mahāyāna version of emptiness and its non-Mahāyāna counterpart. How could I not know something so simple and yet so fundamental to my project?

Naturally, I turned to other scholarship on early Mahāyāna to try to fill the gap in my education. After a few months of reading, I began to suspect that no one else really understood the distinction either. What I really needed was a book that explained Mahāyāna's distinctive take on the doctrine of emptiness, who came up with it, why it mattered and finally, why anyone would have objected to it. In short, I was looking for a book that explained what was at stake in the doctrine of emptiness and how those stakes might have differed from the interests of Buddhists who did not identify with the Mahāyāna or their interpretation of emptiness. What were the distinctive social and political interests that formed the crucible for the strand of Mahāyāna Buddhism that espoused the doctrine of "emptiness"? Were these interests lay or monastic? Were they sectarian or geographical? Since I was unable to find a book that answered these questions to my satisfaction, I decided I had to write one.

What is contained in these pages is my attempt at an answer. As I bring the project to completion, I am painfully aware that any attempt to trace out the genealogy of Mahāyāna will necessarily be only fragmentary. This book will strike some as attempting to cover way too much ground and will strike others as not covering nearly enough. Both are correct. To provide the "big picture" I have had to delve into many areas in which I am by no means an expert. In taking up these topics, I am not trying present myself as an expert in these fields but rather am trying to draw attention to scholars whose delightful work had not yet been conscripted into the project of discussing the trajectory of Mahāyāna. Because I have attempted to provide a wide context for Mahāyāna, I have had to call on the help of many scholars – many of whom wrote extensive critiques on chapters that never made it into the book. That said, this book would have never come to be without the extensive feedback – positive and negative – of many people. In particular, I would like to thank Bhikkhu Anālayo, James Apple, John Powers, Daniel Stuart, Todd Lewis, Roger Jackson, Jan Nattier, Anne Mahoney, Brian Hatcher and especially Eve Mayer and Paul Harrison for their extensive feedback on specific chapters. Harrison in particular provided me with extensive and robust criticisms of the book, as only he can. Many (though definitely not all) of these criticisms I have taken into account, and I think the book is better for it. I have also benefitted from some lengthy conversations with John Dunne and Stephen Hodge. My work on the *Split Manuscript* would not have been possible without lengthy discussions with the Kharoṣṭhī Club at University of Washington in general and with Richard Salomon, Timothy Lenz and Jason Neelis in particular. For all my insights into genre theory and textuality, I would like to thank Wyatt Phillips at Texas Tech University who introduced me to the wonderful world of genre theory. And for being a regular sounding board for my thoughts on critical theory and its implications for the field of Buddhist studies, I would like to thank Ananda Abeysekara. I owe a huge debt of gratitude to my editor, and to Rebecca Shillabeer at Routledge, who saw the book to its completion. I would also like to thank Tara Kola, who read and commented meticulously on each of these chapters and made a herculean attempt to render them intelligible to an English-speaking audience. If I got anything right, it is due to these scholars. Any errors or infelicities are, of course, my own. Consider them a gift to other scholars, that they might further their own careers in criticizing me.

And to Mike Levy, a friend of mine who is a music producer who reads scholarship on Buddhism just because he finds it interesting, let me say that I wrote this with you in mind. Finally, I would like to thank my wife Radha, who supported me through this over-long process, and my children, Tara and Rohan, whose patience has been sorely tested over the past 13 years of writing this book.

Note

1 Nance (2006).

PART I

Genealogies of Mahāyāna

1

INTRODUCTION

On origins and genealogies

This book addresses two separate but related problems in Buddhist studies. The first concerns the genealogy of what comes to be known as the "Great Vehicle," or Mahāyāna Buddhism, the Buddhism comprising many of the traditions found in China, Korea, Vietnam and Japan including Zen, Pure Land and Tantric forms of Buddhism. The second problem concerns the political and social history of the two ideas associated with the name Mahāyāna. The first is that everything is to be characterized as "emptiness" (*śūnyatā*). The second, which is alternately presented as a corollary of the first, as an independent thesis or as the antithesis of the first, is that mind is the ultimate temporal and ontological source of all that we perceive. The mind-centered thesis is sometimes assumed to come later than the doctrine of emptiness and is referred to as the doctrine of "mind-only" (or "*vijñāpti-mātra*" – the alternate name for the Yogācāra School).

The question that this book seeks to address is, *where* did these ideas originate and *how* were they woven into the developments of the schools we know of as Mahāyāna. More importantly, *why* did anyone think that these ideas were important enough to perpetuate and invest considerable resources to reproducing across diverse geographic, cultural and historical contexts? The questions of where, how and why are related, although imperfectly. Despite the messiness of the available data from the early period, some scholars have seen the advent of Mahāyāna and especially its doctrines of emptiness and mind to be a kind of religious "revolution"[1] that was ultimately responsible for partitioning Buddhism into Mahāyāna and non-Mahāyāna. While most scholars are careful in how they characterize Mahāyāna, even the most anti-essentialist treatment will nevertheless include a discussion of the special relationship between Mahāyāna and the doctrines of emptiness and "mind-only" that constitute the seminal doctrines of Mahayana's two main schools, the Mādhyamika and Yogācāra. We are thus led to conclude that it was something about these two ideas that started the revolution. Let me state my conclusion at the outset: there was no Mahāyāna revolution, and this is a book about it.[2]

Ever since I was a graduate student, the question of "the origin of Mahāyāna" was often referred to in quasi-religious terms. It was the "holy grail" of Buddhist studies, a kind of "Great White Whale" that had eluded some of the biggest names in Buddhist scholarship. Yet, by the late 1990s it seemed something more like the quest for cold fusion or the search for the Yeti – an impossible task and one whose motivations were suspected as being suspiciously "Protestant"[3] anyway. The consensus – repeated often in not-so-hushed tones at conferences if not always in print – seemed to be that Mahāyāna began at some point around the beginning of the Common Era but that all of its first exemplars had been destroyed, leaving us with nothing but second- and third-generation versions of Mahāyāna. Mahāyāna's origins were therefore permanently out of reach and nothing more could (or should) be said about it.[4] I myself have been warned on more than one occasion to stay away from the topic. And yet problem of "the origin of Mahāyāna," while being relegated to something of an academic curiosity, still nags. Professors in countless university classes on Buddhism introduce their sections on Mahāyāna by making apologetic remarks to the effect that we simply do not know how or why it began. So, chalk it up to Protestantism or simply to the fact that I think origins are fascinating in their own right, this book is my attempt to answer the question of the origins of Mahāyāna Buddhism by addressing its genealogies and historical configurations of power.

I believe that the place to begin the discussion is not with a summary or critique of past attempts to figure out the origins (which would be redundant for the specialist and would try the patience of the non-specialist), but with a broad theoretical observation of some pitfalls others have run into. One of the major problems that has been discussed by several scholars is that, in order to determine the origin of something we need to have a precise sense of what *it* is. But to say what Mahāyāna is at the outset of the investigation lures the researcher surreptitiously into the trap of what Paul Williams calls "the essentialist fallacy."

> The importance of appreciating doctrinal diversity applies not just to Buddhism as a whole but to the Mahāyāna itself. There is a fallacy which I shall call the 'essentialist fallacy.' It occurs when we take a single name or naming expression and assume that it must refer to one unified phenomenon . . . giving rise to the feeling that because we use the same word so there must be some unchanging core . . . Because the expression 'Mahāyāna' (or its equivalent in the local language) has been used by Buddhists from perhaps as early as the first century BCE to the present day, from India through Tibet, Central Asia, Mongolia, China to Japan, Far East Asia and the Western world, so it must refer to some identifiable characteristics which we can capture in a definition.[5]

Essentializing religion is an easy trap to fall into, and I myself have been guilty of it on occasion.[6] I have no hard evidence for saying so, but I think that academic scholars of religion tend to reify religion even slightly more than practitioners of religion. This may have something to do with the way that religion is packaged for us. In the academic study of religion, we encounter religion in discrete units. At university, we can purchase a course on "Buddhism," which will have a very different content than one on "Christianity." Our textbooks are devoted to either "standalone" religions or treat a number of religions in which each religion is dedicated its own chapter (as in the genre of "world religion" textbooks). If genres create a horizon of expectations for the consumption and interpretation of information, then we can say that the way that "religions" are apportioned and sectioned off in religious studies textbooks creates the expectation that religions are discrete units of largely doctrinal propositions that are mutually exclusive. Religions, then, are kinds of boxes into which the scholar sorts people, doctrines and rituals. Boxed up in this manner, when something is "Mahāyāna" then it should be distinct and opposed to its other, which is said from one angle to be "Theravāda," or "Sectarian Buddhism," or from another angle said to be "Hinduism," "Brahmanism," Daoism, etc.

But the apparent discreteness of religious categories (which tends to be less pronounced in other academic genres, such as history) falters when we begin to look at the specifics of the religion involved. In order for a religion to be distinguishable from something else, it needs to display enough uniformity across instances to be identified as "religion *x*" in the first place. But this leads us to the uncomfortable question of *who* is deciding which examples will define the category? In the case of Mahāyāna, we could take the easy way out and say that a Mahāyānist is anyone who self-identifies as a Mahāyānist (on the rare occasion when the question would be posed). But then what? Can we really relate the name to any single set of propositions? On the one hand, in the 14th century, the famous Tibetan scholar/monk Jey Tsongkhapa asserted that the litmus test for Mahāyāna is *bodhicitta*, which he understood to be the mind motivated by compassion. But if this is Mahāyāna, then how do we reconcile this with other self-identifying Mahāyānists? What about self-identifying Mahāyānists of the "Mahāyāna sect" that (at least in official histories) terrorized the Chinese state of Wei in 515 CE. The latter did not appear to hold compassion to be a central feature of Mahāyāna. According to the *History of the Wei Dynasty*:

> [The *śramaṇa* or monk Faqing from Jizhou called himself] *Dacheng* [大乘 or Mahāyāna]. [Faqing taught his followers] that one who has killed one man will be a bodhisattva of the first stage, while killing ten men will make him a bodhisattva of the tenth stage. He also mixed narcotic drugs and ordered his followers to take them. [As a result the minds of his followers became disturbed such that] fathers, sons, and brothers did not recognize each other and had nothing in mind but killing. Thus, his crowd killed the magistrate of Fucheng, devastated the district of Bohai and killed the officials . . . [T]he evil hordes became even stronger. Everywhere they slaughtered and destroyed monasteries and cloisters. They butchered the monks and nuns, and burned the sacred scriptures and images declaring: 'The new Buddha has appeared who will eradicate the old demons.'[7]

Here, we find a group of allegedly 50,000 people identifying with the name "Mahāyāna," led by a monk teaching them to pursue a bodhisattva path of 10 stages but presumably *not* thereby holding up compassion as an important part of that Mahāyāna. Williams is aware of this problem, and from his introduction we could get the impression that the only historically stable feature of Mahāyāna is the name itself, while what the name denotes is a moving target. This unstable and contested vocabulary contributes to the difficulties scholars face in creating their own narratives and analyses.

If we push the anti-essentialist argument a bit further, however, it turns out that our inability to place our collective fingers on the identity of Mahāyāna over time has something to do with the temporality of concepts themselves. And here we find that the question of what Mahāyāna is at any point in time cannot be so easily extricated from the question of origins. First of all, we cannot begin with a *definition* of Mahāyāna in order to then discern its origin. As Nietzsche pointed out long ago, once we latch onto 'definitions,' we have already stepped outside of history.

> [A]ll concepts in which an entire process is semiotically concentrated elude definition; only that which has no history is definable At an earlier stage, on the contrary, this synthesis of "meanings" can still be disentangled, as well as changed; one can still perceive how in each individual case the elements of the synthesis undergo a shift in value and rearrange themselves accordingly, so that now this, now that element comes to the fore and dominates at the expense of others, and under certain circumstances one element . . . appears to overcome all the remaining elements.[8]

In other words (to paraphrase Quentin Skinner) Mahāyāna doesn't have a definition, it has a *genealogy*. But as Nāgārjuna himself might point out, genealogies don't *have* origins – they *produce* them retrospectively. It is for this reason that have titled this book *Genealogies of Mahāyāna Buddhism* and not *Origins of Mahāyāna Buddhism*. Although I will address the issue of origins, the temporality of the very idea of origin[9] must always incorporate that for which it is an origin. In other words, the origin must encompass quite an expansive "present" in order to be an origin *of* something, of an essence, of that without which it could not be considered an origin at all. Conversely, to pick out the "origin" among the sea of possible data requires us to appeal to a state of affairs which by our own admission is not yet fully there at the temporal point of origin. It is thus an atemporal or transcendent "Mahāyāna" that we would bring to bear on every historical case to discern the alleged "origin" of Mahāyāna in order to judge it to be an "origin" in the first place. We can't say that a thing or an event *is* an origin; rather it *becomes* an origin. Put more simply, every origin is produced by the genealogy that looks back to it and is not simply the product of the factors that lead up to it.

In order to have a more accurate view of what is going on, we need to understand words "Mahāyāna" and "origin" to be prepositional. "Mahāyāna" is never just a static value floating out there in the wild – it is always Mahāyāna *for somebody* (or a community of somebodies). By extension, an "origin" is not independent of the completed thing for which it is an origin. Gavrilo Princip may have shot Archduke Franz Ferdinand on June 28, 1914, but was not deemed to have started something called "World War I" until 1939. Even then, the phrase "World War I" would not have had the same significance to an El Salvadoran or Venezuelan that it would have had to a German or a Brit.

If the origin cannot truly be an origin until its putative essence appears, *then origins can only be seen retrospectively from their purported effects.* Though it would be nice if we had "the original"[10] of all our Mahāyāna sutras, a second- or third-generation copy will also do, because later generations are already looking back to later editions in their own genealogies of their tradition. What determines the object as an "origin" is precisely the viewer's ability to hold it up to the fully formed object. The "origin" has to be defined from the perspective of the completed product, not from the standpoint of its putative producer. In the case of things that fit into existing categories, such teleological thinking generally causes us few problems. I can start to build a house and end up with a house that looks pretty much like what I started to build. But when we are producing a new category like a religion, a set of tokens that *had* been understood to fall into one category must now be known to be another. In other words, the origin has to be understood as part of something old before it can be understood as the beginning of something new.[11] This is something of a commonplace in religious studies: Christianity was Judaism – right up until it wasn't.

Interrogating the origins of a religion, in fact, provides a uniquely non-essentializing vantage point precisely because it calls into question the reified categories by directing attention to the humans who are coming to think in these categories and the very practical payoffs for doing so. In shifting the focus from the category "Mahāyāna" onto the pragmatic concerns of those who used it, we can begin to get a clearer, if more complicated picture of what was at stake in Mahāyāna and its seminal teachings.

Given the retroactive nature of origins, I have designed this book to be an historical presentation of Mahāyāna, but in reverse chronology. In doing so, I begin with my own subject position as a middle-aged white guy living in the Northeast of the United States (i.e., the demographic that still heads to bookstores to find out about stuff). I don't want to give the impression that there is anything particularly interesting about my subject position; I only bring it up to point out that the starting point for my inquiries into Mahāyāna's origins, though hardly unique, is both specific and *contingent*. A Shin Buddhist from Kyōtō might (and hopefully will) write a very different and equally valid genealogy of Mahāyāna. The categories of Mahāyāna available to those of my ilk in bookstores, meditation centers and college classes will be inflected through the specific set of institutional constraints particular to the 21st-century American Northeast. Once we examine those conditions, we can then explore how other, earlier categorizations of Mahāyāna were conditioned by different sets of circumstances. Our deployment of the category will be different from their (no less contingent) use, while nevertheless being related to it. The genealogical contingency in either case should not be looked at as a flaw since the genealogy of any vantage point on Mahāyāna Buddhism will be a legacy, not an invention. Moreover, diverse contingent positions tend to converge as we go backwards, even as the terrain becomes increasingly unfamiliar to contemporary expectations.

The book falls into two parts. In the first half of the book, I will start with the most readily recognizable exemplar of Mahāyāna by folks of my ilk: the 14th Dalai Lama. As the chapters progress, I trace a number of genealogical threads of his Mahāyāna backwards to a particular threshold in first-century India marked by the *Perfection of Wisdom in 8,000 Lines* with special attention to the social and political repercussions of Mahāyāna along the way. While it would be far beyond the scope of this book (not to mention the abilities of its author) to give a complete account of the history of Mahāyāna in Tibet, China and India – much less to delve into the Mahāyāna histories of Korea, Vietnam or Japan – the first half of the book is intended to provide representative snapshots of ways that Mahāyāna and the doctrine of emptiness functioned socially and politically in these different contexts. The second half of the book investigates the factors (Buddhist and non-Buddhist) that might have led to the creation and circulation of the *Perfection of Wisdom in 8,000 Lines* itself – a work which becomes a kind of Mahāyāna prototype.

In many ways, this book will provide a kind of counter-narrative to the usual account of Mahāyāna's development as presented in other fine works such as Paul Williams' *Mahāyāna Buddhism: The Doctrinal Foundations.*[12] While Williams' text is a great overview of Mahāyāna doctrine, he sticks rather closely to a structure similar to what is found in the Tibetan "presentation of the tenets" genre. This tells us something about the distinctions that Buddhists have made between different sects and schools of Mahāyāna, but tells us little about why anyone would want to keep it around, fund it or defend it with troops. In other words, Williams doesn't give the reader much of a sense of the political and social use of the ideas that come to be identified as Mahāyāna. And to anyone living in Asia prior to 1900, the political usefulness of Mahāyāna would likely have been more obvious than it is today.

I begin, then, in the next chapter with the current (the 14th) Dalai Lama to discuss ways that the Mahāyāna distinction is taught in Western meditation centers. I then connect these teachings to the pragmatic political position of the Dalai Lama himself as it has been laid out by the Central Tibetan Administration. Again, following the pragmatic and its relationship to the doctrines, I attempt to show how and why the Mahāyāna doctrine of emptiness and the primordial mind have increasingly come to be cast as "apolitical" as part of their rather new framing as "religion." In Chapter 3, I go back to a time when Mahāyāna *was* understood to be central to the project of empire-building during the reigns of the Yongzheng and Qianlong emperors (17th and 18th centuries). Chapter 4 traces the use of the image of emptiness backwards in Chinese history to a time before Buddhism, in order to argue that emptiness and to some extent the primordial mind were an important component of "internal colonialism" even before Buddhism got there. Both emptiness and mind will be shown to code authority across dynasties, partly because each was to some extent detachable from any particular religion. I go on to argue that the malleability and fungible nature of the image of emptiness and mind made it useful to bring independent village cults into the imperial regime. Having traced the vicissitudes of emptiness and empire (or at least the aspirations to it) from the US to Tibet all the way back to ancient China, I turn in Chapter 5 to India, which provided the original context that fostered Mahāyāna and its ideas of emptiness and mind. In this chapter, I show how each of the political processes revolving around the image of "emptiness" (*śūnyatā*) outlined in the previous chapters were operative in India right up until the late 19th century. Going back to the time of the yogi Maitrīpa (11th century) and the monk Bhāviveka (sixth century), I then show that the *Perfection of Wisdom* – and especially its first chapter – were understood to be prototypical for the Mahāyāna doctrine of emptiness and mind-only. Yet at least in the sixth century these ideas were rejected by some as being too Brahmanical – a point that will take on more significance when I argue that the *Perfection of Wisdom* may in fact have been written by Brahmin Buddhists for circulation within Brahmanical communities.

Whether dealing with Tibet, China or India, one of the recurring themes of each of the chapters of Part I is the *Perfection of Wisdom*. Tibetan, Chinese and Indian Buddhists understood the themes of emptiness and mind-only to be grounded in a number of canonical texts, with only a handful of titles recurring through this long history. One of the earliest of these canonical touchstones is the *Perfection of Wisdom*, and whether or not it was the earliest, it *becomes* the prototype of Mahāyāna in the political genealogy that I have traced. The chapters of Part II examine the genealogy of the core section of the *Perfection of Wisdom* in which these doctrines appear to have been formed. I argue that the ideas of this original core were not really revolutionary but in fact hewed quite closely to a certain strand of thought in the early Buddhist canon itself. Chapter 8 shows that certain elements, while having affinities with canonical texts, appear to also be influenced by a certain strand of Brahmanical thought, especially that of the Kṛṣṇa Yajurveda Maitrāyaṇī branch – which may have been part of the reason why there was some resistance to the Mahāyāna. I argue that one of the interests in the Brahmanical composition of the *Perfection of Wisdom* was to present a workable Buddha-centered version of *brahman*/Prajāpati as a companion to the yogas that Brahmin Buddhist communities had been practicing all along. Chapter 9 argues, based on a number of linguistic and paleographic factors, that the *Perfection of Wisdom* was probably composed near the royal seat outside of Mathura sometime in the latter part of the first century CE by a Sarvastivādin monk who was born and raised a Maitrāyaṇī Brahmin. Finally, in Chapter 10, I argue that the adoption of the doctrines of emptiness and mind-only by Buddhist Brahmins was part of a larger strategy to become permanent religious adjuncts to the court (similar to a court priest or *purohita*). Such a Buddhist Brahmin could offer the regime legitimacy through a demonstrated knowledge of emptiness and mind as the cosmic foundations that had become a key feature of the relatively new coronation liturgies of the Horse Sacrifice.

What these chapters show is that there are a limited set of themes that recur in different combinations across time and space, coalescing around the term "Mahāyāna," namely: 1) emptiness, 2) mind-only, 3) nondiscriminating or non-cognizing awareness, 4) "perfection of wisdom" and 5) *bodhicitta*. Tracing the genealogy of ways that people have distinguished Mahāyāna from other things will show that sometimes one of these five is called on and sometimes all of them are. Sometimes several of these features are understood to have equal Mahāyāna standing, sometimes some are subordinated to others, and sometimes they are understood to be opposed to one another. In the first half of the book, I show that a distinct, if somewhat hazy trajectory of Mahāyāna distinctions can be traced back to a vanishing point on the horizon marked by the first few pages of the *Perfection of Wisdom in 8,000 Lines*. In the second half, I show that much of what becomes distinctively Mahāyāna has been considered to fall within "Buddhism" all along, albeit largely within Brahmanical communities of Buddhists at a time prior to a hard and fast distinction between Buddhism and Brahmanism.

Notes

1 E.g.: "Emerging somewhat mysteriously around the first century of the Common Era, the revelatory Prajnaparamita literature signals a gentle revolution in Buddhist thinking, a vast maturing in the Buddhist mind and heart after five hundred years of intensive meditation and realization which followed the passing of the founder, Shakyamuni Buddha." Lex Hixon "Mahayana: The Gentle Revolution" in Mother of the Buddhas." See also, Garfield 2015; Cole 2009; Murti 1955.

2 Adapted from Stephen Shapin (1994), p. 1.

3 Schopen (1991) argues that searches for origins seek a pristine apostolic community in which the "true" Mahāyāna lies, in contradistinction to its subsequent contamination.

4 The idea that the search for origins of Mahāyāna are thwarted by the fact that we are dealing with second- or third-generation texts whose originals are now lost begins with an aside made by Harrison (1995) – where the comment was qualified and made regarding a single text. This comment was then amplified by Jonathan Silk (2002), who generalizes Harrison's remark (and adds a number of other arguments) to apply to Mahāyāna in general. I address the problems behind these assertions in Chapters 7 and 8.

5 Williams (2009), p. 2.

6 My tendency to assume that Mahāyāna was an identifiable thing separate from non-Mahāyāna opened me up to Nance's critique.

7 Seiwert and 西沙馬 (2003), p. 111.

8 Nietzsche (2010), p. 80.

9 For a recent discussion of this problem as it applies to Buddhist studies, see Abeysekara (2018).

10 I am not sure whether "an original" is ever more than a figment of our imagination. I have been writing this book for 13 years. I have thrown away roughly four times the amount of material that I eventually included in the book. I discarded those rough drafts for a reason, and yet they were genuinely precursors to the final version. If someone were to peer into my drafts folder, which files would they designate "the original"?

11 For a lengthier treatment of this issue, see Walser (2015).

12 Williams (2009).

2

MAHĀYĀNA IN RETROSPECT

From my house to the Dalai Lama (looking back from 2017 to 1930)

I would like to begin this particular journey of a thousand miles about two blocks from my doorstep. Wanting to find out about Mahāyāna Buddhism, I head off to my nearest Barnes & Noble. Being a bit mystified as to where exactly I am going to start my search for the origins of Mahāyāna, I go downstairs to the "Eastern Religions" section to look for a book commensurate with my intellectual capacities. *The Complete Idiot's Guide to Buddhism* and *Buddhism for Dummies* seem well suited for the purpose, and I flip through them to find out what Mahāyāna is. Gary Gach's *Complete Idiot's Guide* tells me that Buddhism is divided into Theravāda Buddhism and a Mahāyāna that consists of Pure Land, Zen and the "Lotus Schools" of Nichiren, Sokka Gakkai, etc. It also explains that Tibetan Buddhists divide Buddhism into "Theravada, Mahayana and Vajrayana, though the latter might be considered Mahayana with a tantric twist."[1] More generally, he states that Mahāyāna has five characteristics: "1) innovation, 2) devotion, 3) emptiness-based wisdom, 4) populism and 5) skillful means."[2] Landaw and Bodian's *Buddhism for Dummies* also lists five characteristics of Mahāyāna: 1) the compassionate bodhisattva replaces the arhat as the ideal, 2) all beings (monastic and non-monastic) can achieve Buddhahood, 3) "Buddhahood is an enduring principle that exists throughout the universe," 4) "the nature of all existence is essentially non-dualistic," and 5) "progress along the spiritual path involves recognizing the innate perfection of the present moment just as it is."[3] In both books we find these somewhat ahistorical characteristics of Mahāyāna embedded in a larger historical narrative of the development of Mahāyāna.

In the general trajectory of the historical narrative, if not in all the details (despite their self-deprecating titles), the *Idiot's Guide* and *Buddhism for Dummies* are really not all that different from other surveys of Buddhism such as Snelling's *Buddhist Handbook* or Harvey's *Introduction to Buddhism* or even Williams' *Mahāyāna Buddhism: The Doctrinal Foundations*. In all of the introductory texts I surveyed on my trip the story is basically the same. Mahāyāna is said to begin sometime between first century BCE and first century CE in India with the writing of anonymous Mahāyāna sutras. Then starting in the second century, the twin schools of Nāgārjuna's Mādhyamika (with its doctrine that not only are individuals selfless, but that all things are selfless in the sense that they are empty of their own nature) and Asaṅga's Yogācāra (with its doctrine that everything is mind-only) arise. These ideas travel to Tibet, China, Mongolia, Korea, Japan and Vietnam where they manifest as Vajrayana, Zen or Pure Land.

Along the way, we are introduced to a number of other Mahāyāna teachings. For example, the Buddha has three bodies: the "Dharma Body" (emptiness itself), the "Enjoyment Body" (which is how that Buddha appears to the meditator) and the "Manifestation Body," which is the physical manifestation of the Buddha that appears in history. We are told that Mahāyānists understand themselves to be "bodhisattvas" headed for full Buddhahood in order to save others because they have "*bodhicitta*," usually rendered as the compassionate mind that marks the beginning of the path to Buddhahood. To attain final Buddhahood, they must practice and attain six perfections – the perfection of giving, morality, energy, patience, concentration and the perfection of wisdom. Finally, in texts discussing Tibetan Buddhism we are told that the culmination of many meditations lies in the experience of the "mind of pure light."

What is curious to me as I ponder the historical narrative of the arc of Mahāyāna's development (other than the fact that many of these books shy away from stating how or why it began) is the fact that the tale is one of religious ideas arising one after another like a string of pearls stretching from one end of Asia to another with no reason for its existence and perpetuation other than its utility for human liberation. None of these books really discuss any political repercussions of Mahāyāna or mention the specific, pragmatic interest that emperors, magistrates and gentry might have had in it. And indeed, none of the books that I found at the Barnes & Noble thought it necessary to justify why their depiction of Mahāyāna was so apolitical. That Buddhism pertains most naturally to one's private life appears to simply be taken for granted.

Johannes Bronkhorst, writing for a bit more academic audience, does address this issue head on.

> Mahāyāna was not a new sect (*nikāya*). Monks who chose the path to Buddhahood remained members of the same monastic community and continued to submit to the same monastic rules. On the doctrinal level there were initially no points of dispute either. And why should there be? Doctrine and order were not at stake. Strictly speaking, nothing was at stake, for only a personal motivation was involved. Undoubtedly, the adepts of Mahāyāna studied the same texts as the other Buddhists, and from the point of view of Buddhist doctrine, one would hardly expect the birth of Mahāyāna to produce significant changes.[4]

I will grant that none of the Mahāyānists I know are leaders of any modern nation – much as I might wish otherwise. I will also grant Bronkhorst that an individual could take up Mahāyāna from motivations that we might call "private." But if we confine our analysis of Mahāyāna exclusively to the realm of internal, private experiences and motivations, then what should we say about major political leaders throughout history who not only practice Mahāyāna traditions but in fact represent them? If Mahāyāna were first and foremost a *private* concern, then wouldn't we have to see the politicization of Mahāyāna as a deviation? Something seems off about this.

Returning to the Barnes & Noble "Eastern Religions" section, I notice that the books are arranged alphabetically. This alphabetical arrangement makes multiple works attributed to a single author stand out visually on the shelf in a way that single works do not (this being only my second book, I notice things like that). One large and therefore very visible cluster of books whose author crushes my own literary output is that of Tenzin Gyatso, better known as the 14th Dalai Lama. Although I have run into a number of Americans who are not quite sure whether the Dalai Lama is Hindu or Buddhist,[5] among middle-aged white American self-identified Buddhists, if anybody would represent Mahāyāna, it would be the Dalai Lama. Asking whether the Dalai Lama is a Mahāyānist is probably the closest a Buddhist can come to the obviousness of "Is the Pope Catholic? Does a bear . . .?" (you get the idea). And yet, no one can deny that (until recently) the Dalai Lama was also a political leader *because of his status within Mahāyāna institutions.* In the remainder of the chapter, I will show how the doctrines stated to characterize Mahāyāna in the above surveys appear in specific contexts within the Dalai Lama's own discussions and will then show how those contextualized doctrines have played out politically for him over the course of the 20th and now 21st centuries. I will argue that the political formations of Mahāyāna cannot simply be passed off as a deviation from some set of canonical doctrines. The truth is far more complicated than that.

That said, I look among the numerous books in the Dalai Lama cluster and pick a title that seems to auspiciously represent his views: *The Essential Dalai Lama* (2005). The book is an anthology of English-language writings and lectures[6] given by the Dalai Lama mostly from the 1980s and 1990s. In browsing through the book, I find a distinct picture of Mahāyāna emerge, not by way of any systematic definition or narration, but from the assumptions that he assumes his audience brings to his lectures. *The Essential Dalai Lama*, then, is as good a place as any to outline an understanding of Mahāyāna generated in conversation between the Dalai Lama and his Euro-American and Indian audiences in the context of dharma lectures.

The first of these understandings, however, is that the teachings given by the Dalai Lama are Mahāyānist not only because they are Mahāyāna doctrines, but also because of their uniquely Mahāyānist source. In the preface, the editor Rajiv Mehrotra tells us that their author is regarded as ontologically unique and uniquely Mahāyānist.

> Though the Dalai Lama himself is at pains to stake no such claim, describing himself as merely a "simple Buddhist monk," millions of his followers, both Tibetans and others, regard him as a "Living Buddha," a reincarnation of the compassionate Avalokteshvara, the fourteenth incarnation in the line of Dalai Lamas, Bodhisattvas who choose to reincarnate to provide temporal leadership to Tibetans and to serve and teach all humanity.[7]

Now, I am told[8] that Tibetans generally don't refer to the Dalai Lama as any kind of Buddha, (one finds the phrase "living Buddha" more often in Chinese discussions of the Dalai Lama) nor, as Mehrotra notes, has the Dalai Lama himself ever referred to himself as such. Tibetans tend to distinguish between Buddhas and bodhisattvas and the Dalai Lama is an incarnation of the bodhisattva Avalokiteśvara. Mehrotra's assertion of the Dalai Lama's Buddhahood, has a genealogy of its own and should alert us to the fact that the discourse conventions of these dharma talks and the anthologies consumed by Indian and Euro-American audiences operate with relative autonomy to the life world of many Tibetans both in and out of exile. This is not to say that the discourses are independent of prior Buddhist tradition, but merely that they tap into its resources in specific ways to address specific concerns of several audiences simultaneously. This fact makes the discourses somewhat more contingent than one would expect in an explanation of "doctrine". But one of my contentions in this book is that pointing out the contingent or discursive specificity does not diminish a work's importance, it merely locates the horizon of its action. Turning to the section of that book called "Buddhist Perspectives," I find a lengthy discussion about the Greater Vehicle and its distinction from other vehicles.

> As you all know, the usual explanation is that there are two vehicles of Buddhism, the Lesser and the Greater, that is, the Vehicle of the Hearers and the eremitic Buddhas [Hinayana] and the Vehicle of the Bodhisattvas [Mahayana]. The Greater Vehicle is in turn divided into the Greater Vehicle of the Sutras and the Greater Vehicle of the Tantras. The system of the Four Noble Truths, which forms all Buddhists' basic belief structure, necessarily follows this division into two vehicles.
>
> . . . Without the practices associated with the Four Noble Truths, or the way of the thirty-seven aids of the Awakening taught in the texts of the Lesser Vehicle, it is impossible to truly practice the spirit of Awakening of the Greater Vehicle, which is benevolence and compassion. I mean great compassion.
>
> . . . prejudices have occurred in Tibet between the Greater Vehicle of the Tantras and the Greater Vehicle of the Transcendences (the six transcendent virtues). The adepts of the transcendent virtues did not look favorably upon the tantras. For their part, the adepts of the tantras had scarcely any respect for the Vehicle of the Transcendences, especially where discipline was concerned.[9]

The Dalai Lama's discussion here assumes that his audience already knows that there is a Mahāyāna Buddhism (the Greater Vehicle) whose members are known as "bodhisattvas" that is distinct from Hīnayāna (a pejorative term meaning "Lowly Vehicle"), whose members are designated as either "Hearers" or "eremitic Buddhas." Although he is somewhat cursory regarding the content of either vehicle in this lecture the Dalai Lama associates the Lesser Vehicle with the "practices associated with the Four Noble Truths (the truths of suffering, the arising of suffering, the cessation of suffering and the path leading to the cessation of suffering) or the way of the thirty-seven aids of the Awakening."[10] Mahāyāna, in turn, is characterized by the "spirit of Awakening" (presumably this translates *bodhicitta*), by which he means the mind so filled with compassion that it motivates the practitioner to aspire to Buddhahood – thereby making the aspirant a "*bodhisattva*" – or Buddha-to-be. Although he does not say so explicitly here, most Tibetan versions of the stages of the bodhisattva path (or Mahāyāna path) to Buddhahood begin with the cultivation of compassion before setting off toward the realization of emptiness or the mind of clear light.

Beyond compassion, Mahāyāna itself is divided into two sub-vehicles in this essay: the Mahāyāna of the Sutras, or exoteric sermons of the Buddha and the Tantras, or esoteric Buddhist teachings. At a later point, he specifies the Mahāyāna Sutra vehicle as the "Greater Vehicle of the Transcendences." In context, this can only be the Mahāyāna of the *Pāramitās* - indicating a class of Mahāyāna sutras whose prototype would be the *Prajñāpāramitā* or *Perfection of Wisdom*. One of the Dalai Lama's points in presenting these distinctions appears to be that, although some Buddhists appeal to these distinctions to denigrate what they see to be "lower" vehicles,[11] "this prejudice was a defect and an error."[12] He argues that, in fact, the vehicles relate to one another architectonically as foundation and superstructure. The Four Noble Truths of the so-called Lesser Vehicle are not rejected or replaced by subsequent vehicles, but simply "made more profound and clearer" with each addition. In all, the Dalai Lama presents us with a structure of Buddhism whose foundation is the Four Noble Truths and Thirty-Seven Limbs of Awakening and whose upper echelons are comprised of Mahāyāna sutras such as the *Perfection of Wisdom* and tantric practices culminating in the tantric teachings of the "clear natural light of the mind."

Shifting metaphors somewhat, he explains the progression from Lesser Vehicle to the Mahāyāna Sutra Vehicle to the Mahāyāna Tantra Vehicle by referring to each vehicle as successive "turnings of the wheel of dharma." The rubric of the three wheel turnings was made famous by a relatively early Mahāyāna sutra, the *Samdhinirmocanasūtra*, dating from the early centuries of the Common Era.[13] However, in that sutra the three turnings are interpreted to be: 1) the teachings for the non-Mahāyānist disciples (*śrāvakas*), 2) the Mahāyāna bodhisattvas who practice the "Perfection of Wisdom" and finally 3) the Mahāyānist Yogācāra or "mind-only" bodhisattvas. By adapting the three "turnings" to the Lesser Vehicle, Perfection Vehicle and Tantric Vehicle scheme, the Dalai Lama makes the case that the Buddha turned the wheel a second and third time (the Mahāyāna, *Perfection of Wisdom* and Tantric teachings respectively) so as not to limit his teaching to the Thirty-Seven Limbs of Awakening of the first turning.

But he then adds a few more distinguishing marks of Mahāyāna, which is where the essay gets a bit complicated (a fact not helped by a somewhat awkward translation):

> In the philosophical systems of the Greater Vehicle, what was taught by the Buddha in the texts of the Lesser Vehicle advances in breadth and depth. For example, the texts of the Lesser Vehicle concern only our

> Instructor Shakyamuni. . . . on the Diamond Throne [i.e. under the Bodhi Tree at Bodh Gaya, India], he undertook the way of juncture [yoga?]; and he became an authentic and perfect Buddha as he emerged from this diamond-like contemplation [*vajropama samādhi*?] or way of cessation. These texts teach that it was only during the second part of his life that he was a Buddha. However this may be, here it is a matter simply of what is called a supreme body of apparition, [*nirmāna-kāya*?] not other bodies of the Buddha. In the Greater Vehicle, the system of three or four bodies of the Buddha prevails. In the Greater Vehicle of the Transcendences [the *Pāramitā*], the Buddha will teach the system of the four bodies. He will explain how the four bodies are realized [by practitioners] in the tantras.[14]

The Dalai Lama begins by saying that the difference between vehicles is also marked by different conceptions of the Buddha himself. The so-called Lesser Vehicle teaches that Śākyamuni only becomes "Buddha" after he becomes enlightened on the "diamond-throne" under the Bodhi Tree at Bodh Gaya. By contrast, the Greater Vehicle, in its *Perfection of Wisdom* literature, has a doctrine of three bodies. According to the classical theory, the Buddha has three bodies: the Dharma Body (*dharma-kāya*), which is emptiness or the ultimate reality itself; the Enjoyment body (*sambhoga-kāya*), which is the body created by a Buddha or celestial bodhisattva such as Avalokiteśvara as the result of past merits; and the Manifestation body (*nirmāna-kāya*), which is a kind of body magically produced by the Enjoyment body in order to teach sentient beings. Sometimes the Dharma Body is, as the Dalai Lama notes, divided into two, leaving us with four bodies: the Essence body (*svābhāvikakāya*), the Wisdom body (*jñānakāya*), the Enjoyment body and the Manifestation body. The implication behind the Dalai Lama's statement is that the bodies other than the Manifestation body precede the event of the Buddha's enlightenment but that the tantric practitioner can realize these bodies through practice. He then refers to the wheel-turnings model to differentiate levels of Buddhist doctrine.

> Likewise, when he teaches the different ways or paths, and the meditations proper to each one, the Buddha does not limit himself to the way of the thirty-seven aids of the Awakening, and especially not to the way of the nonexistence of the individual self. When the moment of the Greater Vehicle had come, the cycle of universal insubstantiality [emptiness?] acquired its breadth. . . . And so, once he had deepened and broadened his teachings on the Four Noble Truths, the Buddha turned the wheel of the intermediate Dharma, that of the Greater Vehicle, on the peak of the Vultures. He then pronounced the sutras of Transcendent Knowledge [*Perfection of Wisdom*]. In these sutras the Buddha minutely studies the noble truth of the cessation of suffering that he had taught with the other three truths at Benares. In the third cycle of his teachings, he taught a variety of sutras that, like the principal sutras explicit in Continuity Unexcelled [sic – *Uttara Tantra?*], such as the Sutra of the Potential of the Buddha [*Tathāgatagarbha sutra*], deal exclusively with the clear natural light of the mind.[15]

Reading between the lines of the 'three turnings' scheme here, the Dalai Lama presents the Lesser Vehicle as teaching the Four Noble Truths and the selflessness of the person. This makes some sense, since the sermon on the Four Noble Truths is called the Turning the Wheel of Dharma sermon and is presented as the Buddha's first sermon in the opening section of the Buddhist monastic code (*vinaya*). By the same token, the monastic code goes on to present the sermon on "the characteristics of selflessness" (i.e., the sermon teaching that none of the constituent parts of the person have the characteristics of a "self," nor are they "mine") as the second sermon delivered by the Buddha after his enlightenment. The Dalai Lama, in this instance refers to the "Lesser Vehicle" first turning of the wheel as the teaching of the "non-existence of the individual self" (presumably *pudgala-nairātmya*) in order to contrast it with the teachings of the Mahāyāna *Perfection of Wisdom* that teaches "universal insubstantiality" (presumably the "selflessness of all dharmas," *sarva dharma-nairātmya* or simply "emptiness").

The contrast the Dalai Lama appeals to here (i.e., Hīnayāna = selflessness of persons vs. Mahāyāna = selflessness of dharmas) is as old as it is odd. There are a number of early, ostensibly non-Mahāyāna canonical texts such as the *Dhammapada* that argue that all dharmas are selfless (*anatta*).[16] For our purposes, however, what is important is that a growing number of thinkers have come to believe that Mahāyāna is distinguished by teaching the selflessness of dharmas since the time of Vasubandhu (fourth century CE).[17] For his part, the Dalai Lama in this essay locates the distinction between the Hīnayāna selflessness of persons and the Mahāyāna selflessness of dharmas in the third of the Four Noble Truths – the truth of cessation which the Buddha attains during the "diamond-like *samādhi*" under the Bodhi tree. In other words, the truth of *cessation* is what makes them Buddhist; Mahāyāna or non-Mahāyāna reflect degrees of depth of understanding that cessation – with the highest being the third turning of the tantras,[18] characterized by teachings elaborating on the "clear natural light of the mind."

The passage might seem a bit jumbled if only read in the context of *The Essential Dalai Lama*. The distinction between Mahāyāna and the Lesser Vehicle appears to rest on a particular intersection between the cessation of suffering (the third Noble Truth), universal emptiness, the Buddha nature and finally the mind of clear light. But the essay in question does not explain the connection between these. It begins to make more sense when we turn to the larger body of lectures given at the Institute Karma Ling in Savoie, France in 1997 from which this chapter was excerpted. The key turns out to lie in his description of the Buddha bodies. Coming from the Dalai Lama, we should pay attention to what he says about the three bodies, since, as Mehrotra notes in his preface, the Dalai Lama is "a reincarnation of the compassionate Avalokiteshvara, the fourteenth incarnation in the line of Dalai Lamas." In fact, the technical term in Tibetan for what the Dalai Lama is is "*tulku*" (*sprul sku*), the standard Tibetan translation of *nirmāna-kāya* or manifestation body and while not all tulkus are understood to be incarnations of powerful bodhisattvas, the Dalai Lama is.

But the Dalai Lama is less interested in talking about himself as a *nirmāna-kāya* here than he is in discussing the highest body, the *dharma-kāya*. He describes the *dharma-kāya* (which the translator renders as the "absolute body of the Buddha") as follows:

> According to *Continuity Unexcelled*, a treatise of the Greater Vehicle,[19] the absolute body of the Buddha, which is maintained in a state of "thusness" without ever deviating from it – that immaculate dimension that never forsakes the real, and in which all conceptual constructions are altogether stilled – has received the name absolute body for his proper good.[20]

In other words, when the prototype of all bodhisattvas, Śākyamuni, sat under the Bodhi tree, he achieved a state of complete cessation of conceptualization in which the very distinction between subject and object did not arise. This singular mental state perfectly corresponds to the way that things actually are, viz. empty of conceptual constructions. This nature has, in fact, always been the case whether anyone realizes it or not, and potentially anyone could realize it. In attending to that reality, Śākyamuni conformed to it. As a result, he is Buddha fully realized. But for the Mahāyāna texts to which the Dalai Lama is referring, the *real* "Buddha" is primarily the eternal reality itself, not the human who comes to understand that reality. A bodhisattva becomes known as a Buddha by "realization" (both as understanding and as manifesting) of that reality. Anyone could realize it, but the fact of the matter is that very few are recognized to have a special claim to it.

Putting all this together, the Dalai Lama is saying that the Lesser Vehicle teaches that Śākyamuni was a mere man who became a Buddha through practice. The Mahāyāna of the Perfection of Wisdom literature teaches that the true nature of all things (or the ultimate truth that cannot be subsumed under any higher truth) is universal emptiness or suchness and that the latter is the *true* body of the Buddha to which Śākyamuni's practice was directed. In other words, for the Dalai Lama, the so-called Lesser Vehicle and the Greater Vehicle (and presumably the Tantra Vehicle as well) do not contradict one another. The Lesser Vehicle simply focuses on a set of practices that will lead to the realization of a reality while the latter describes the reality to which the practices will lead. Crucially, while the three and four bodies of the Buddha are somewhat later developments in Mahāyāna, the Dalai Lama ascribes the ideas constituting the essence of the Buddha body – emptiness, suchness, cessation of conceptuality, non-duality, etc. – to the vehicle of the Perfections epitomized by the *Perfection of Wisdom*. Second, while the *dharma-kāya* as emptiness is impersonal and ubiquitous, when spoken of as a "body" of a Buddha it becomes singular – and indeed it is not hard to find earlier Mahāyāna texts that refer to various Buddhas such as Amitabhā as *dharma-kāya* Buddhas.

I should point out that this rather cursory read of an admittedly small fragment of the Dalai Lama's impressively large oeuvre nowhere gives us systematic definition of Mahāyāna. It is rather through the reiteration of the themes of compassion, Buddha bodies, cessation, emptiness, mind and light as constitutive parts of the Mahāyāna distinction that we begin to develop a rather stable image of Mahāyāna and its distinction from non-Mahāyāna. Since I will be tracing many of the developments of Mahāyana back to the Perfection of Wisdom, it is worth noting that the latter makes a number of cameos in this writing – if only as references to the genre and not to a specific sutra. It also has a lot to say about the mind of clear light, with emptiness and light marking the highest attainments of the Mahāyāna (although it is far from clear that he is referring to the Perfection of Wisdom's articulation of it here). That said, there are also elements that are equally important for the Dalai Lama, namely his emphasis on the two kinds of selflessness, the Dharma Body and on bodhicitta as compassionate mind – features that I will argue are not in the earliest version of the Perfection of Wisdom.

It would not be hard to demonstrate that each of these elements (compassion, cessation, emptiness, the mind of clear light, etc.) have been a part of Tibetans' sense of the Mahāyāna distinction going all the way back to the time of Tri Songdetsan (756–797), the first Tibetan ruler to adopt Buddhism as the religion of the aristocracy – albeit not without substantial shifts in emphasis. For example, while almost all Tibetan savants would hold up compassion and *bodhicitta* as being crucially important to Mahāyāna, it is primarily the Dalai Lama's Gelukpa School, from the time of their founder Jay Tsongkhapa (1357–1419), that identifies *bodhicitta* as the *compassionate* mind.[21] The identification of *bodhicitta* with compassion (combined with wisdom) is a characteristic move of the Gelukpas. Earlier sources don't always associate it with compassion. They present *bodhicitta* as either the aspiration for enlightenment or more commonly as the mind that realizes emptiness (a realization which in turn may *result* in compassion).[22] For example the *Bodhicittavivarana* ascribed to Nāgārjuna (second – third century CE) states that, "Space (*ākāśa*), *bodhicitta* and enlightenment are without marks, without generation. They have no structure, they are beyond the path of words. Their mark . . . is non-duality."[23] Tantric texts give us two aspects of this *bodhicitta* insofar as it now represents the dual aspect of nirvana, bliss and emptiness. A different school of Tibetan Buddhism, the Nyingmapas, in their practice of the Great Perfection or *dzogchen* (following the *Hevajra Tantra*)[24] also use the word *bodhicitta* to refer to the drop of semen used in the tantric consecration (*abhiṣekha*) and the mind of orgasmic bliss that was devoid of both subject and object. Possibly contemporary with the *Hevajra*, Śāntideva's (eighth century) *Bodhicaryāvatāra*[25] bifurcates *bodhicitta*, albeit differently: "the mind having made the resolve for *bodhi* and the actual proceeding towards *bodhi*."[26] While classical Gelukpa authors emphasize *bodhicitta* as compassion, more contemporary Tibetan authors such as Khunu Rinpoche's (1894–1977) *Jeweled Lamp* split the two aspects of bodhicitta by mapping compassion and emptiness onto the Mādhyamika distinction between ultimate and conventional truths:

352. Meditate on the supreme conventional bodhicitta
By means of exchanging self for others and so on.
Meditate on the supreme ultimate bodhicitta
By means of the wisdom free from extremes and so on.[27]

The differences between Tibetan schools on the issue of *bodhicitta* tend to boil down to one of emphasis rather than doctrine *per se*. Certainly, no one is going to deny the importance of compassion. Yet, while one would not want to make a hard and fast rule out of this (since there is a lot of cross-pollination here), the Gelukpa sect tends to place the greatest emphasis on the emptiness (*qua* selflessness) of all phenomena, while other schools such as the Kagyupa with their *mahāmudrā* tend to emphasize the "sovereign all creating mind," (*kun byed rgyal po*) which turns out to be the self-aware manifestation of emptiness itself.

While much of what the 14th Dalai Lama discusses is in keeping with the Gelukpa tradition that he inherits, he stands apart from his predecessors in two important ways: his attitude toward science and human rights. In his 2002 essay on "Science and Spirituality"[28] he rather famously states,

> When there is a contradiction between the scientific account and the Buddhist scriptural description of the universe, we should accept what can be observed to be true. There is no need to be dogmatic or narrow-minded about it. This is not to disparage the Buddha's fundamental teachings. Reflecting on these, we can appreciate the vast profundity of the Dharma.[29]

Similarly, in other essays, he expresses a deep appreciation for human rights and the environment. In his 1989 Nobel Peace Prize Lecture, he connects human rights and environmental concern to the Buddhist project of mental cultivation.

> Peace can only last where human rights are respected, where the people are fed, and where individuals and nations are free. True peace, with oneself and with the world around us can only be achieved through the development of mental peace. The other phenomena mentioned above are similarly interrelated.

He goes on to claim that Tibetans are uniquely predisposed to respecting these human and environmental rights:

> Tibetans are always described by foreign visitors as being a happy, jovial people. This is part of our national character, formed by cultural and religious values that stress the importance of mental peace through the generation of love and kindness to all other living sentient beings, both human and animal.[30]

While, as pointed out above, compassion has long been a defining characteristic of Mahāyāna, the connection of meditations on loving kindness and compassion to human rights represents something of a shift for the Dalai Lama beginning in the 1980s.

Assessing the essence

The Dalai Lama's appeal to science and human rights should not be surprising. We shouldn't expect the Dalai Lama in these discourses to be *merely* or *simply* transmitting nuggets of wisdom from India's or even Tibet's hoary past. Yes, many of the terms and doctrines he discusses – compassion, emptiness and selflessness, not to mention the lectures on Nāgārjuna or the numerous Kālacakra tantric initiations he has performed across the globe – are, in a certain sense, quite traditional insofar as they do have a long genealogy in Tibetan Buddhism prior to its encounter with the West. And indeed, the Dalai Lama has been criticized on several fronts for the way he presents Tibet in general and Tibetan Buddhism in particular. Does this mean that he is distorting Tibetan Buddhism by somehow "modernizing" it? Donald Lopez has taken the Dalai Lama to task for presenting Tibetan Buddhism as a pre-modern form of human rights, democracy, environmentalism, scientific rationalism and non-violence,[30] a utopian Shangri-la for Western consumption. He also criticizes the Dalai Lama's Western followers for not only buying into this image, but for feeding it to the Dalai Lama in the first place.

Lopez is certainly correct that the image of Tibet that the Dalai Lama has been disseminating is far more monolithic than some in the Tibetan and Tibetan diaspora feel comfortable with. For instance, the Dalai Lama comes from the Gelukpa sect and as Lopez notes,[32] his renounciation of the worship of Dorje Shugden (a specifically Gelukpa deity who protects them from, among other things, Nyingmapa teachings) in 1979 as well as his teaching of *dzogchen* and *mahāmudrā* (traditionally Nyingmapa and Kagyupa teachings respectively) were seen by some as erasing of his Gelukpa School's exceptionalism at the hands of its leader. On the other hand, the Dalai Lama's insistence on the role of rationality and logic in his education initiatives in India has been seen by some Tibetans as the 'Gelupaization' of what should be a public school curriculum for all Tibetan children. Michael Lempert has documented that while the Dalai Lama's rhetoric of human rights and the concomitant value of rational persuasion versus corporal punishment plays well on the international stage, it does not fit so well with the traditional way of training monks.[33]

Lopez is correct to note that some of the tensions and contradictions that have arisen with the Dalai Lama's representation of Tibetan Buddhism both within and outside of the Tibetan community. But Lopez's mistake is to treat the Dalai Lama as a kind of free-floating auteur, naïvely choosing how he represents Tibet by adopting images from an equally naïve Western white audience. For Lopez, communication is a two-way Sausseurian sender and receiver model between the Dalai Lama and his either white Buddhist or Tibetan Buddhist audiences. Writing in the late 1990s Lopez might be forgiven for this, since it had been the explicit strategy of the Central Tibetan Administration after 1985 to send the Dalai Lama to the United States to garner political and public support in order to put pressure on China.[34] But if we take a longer view, the picture gets more complicated and gets to one of my main points in this book concerning Mahāyāna and the deployment of strategies of power.

Tibet as Buddhist: tracing the lines of power

The Dalai Lama was born in 1935 and reached the age of majority in 1950, only one year after Mao's land reforms and the shift from republican to communist rule in China. In 1959 he fled Tibet within months of having received his Geshe degree and set up a government in exile in Dharamsala, India on the model of earlier European governments in exile such as the French Vichy government at the end of World War II. From 1959 until 1988, the goal of the Dalai Lama and his Central Tibetan Administration was nothing short of return and full, independent nationhood for Tibet, and even after that the goal has remained autonomy and self-governance within China. As a result, we should look at all of the Dalai Lama's statements in exile as not only addressing a direct audience (a kind of 'vertical communication') ostensibly about religion, but also and simultaneously addressing an indirect audience (a kind of lateral communication)[35] with an argument for the legitimacy and self-sufficiency of an independent Tibetan polity. Thus, in his published talks to meditators and spiritual seekers throughout the world, the Dalai Lama is simultaneously addressing (or at least laying the foundation for a case to) the government of India, The People's Republic of China, and from the mid-1980s, the United Nations and the US Congress.

For instance, the Dalai Lama has from the very beginning of his exile represented the Tibet he seeks to reestablish as both inherently peaceful and uniformly Buddhist. While we, like Lopez, might harp on the contradictions in these representations, the fact of the matter is that they have always been just as strategic as they were didactic. Stephanie Roemer has pointed out that when the Dalai Lama first came to India in 1959, he met with Jawaharlal Nehru. Five years earlier, India had signed an agreement with China, and Nehru was reluctant to host the Tibetan exile community in fear of jeopardizing the agreement. Initially he referred to the Chinese military action against Tibet as "an internal affair." He did, however, recognize that many Indians understood Tibet to share a substantial heritage with India, namely "Buddhism". It was *as Buddhists* that Tibetans could claim legitimate ties to India and thereby a rationale for safe haven in India. Moreover, by 1959 Nehru's China policy was unpopular in India and so by taking on the Tibetan exile community he could mitigate the domestic opposition somewhat.[36] Hence, early on we should read the Dalai Lama's statements portraying Tibet as universally Buddhist as part of his effort to secure a place for them in India. By the same token, the Dalai Lama's statements concerning Tibetan non-violence would have resonated in 1959 not only with the example and the writings of Gandhi still in recent memory, but as a tacit reassurance to Nehru that Tibetans would not carry out extra-governmental attacks on China and disturb Sino-Indian relations. On the other hand, it was precisely Tibetan capacity for violence that proved useful in 1962 when the Sino-Indian war broke out and Tibetans were recruited for the elite Special Frontier Force on the border of India and China. Thus, when the Dalai Lama portrayed Tibet as uniformly Buddhist, peaceful, and democratic, it was to match *Indian* expectations of Buddhism, *satyagraha* (passive resistance) and democracy, *not* Euro-American expectations. By portraying Tibetans in this way, he saved not a few lives by ensuring that India would take in Tibetan refugees. It is true that even in the early 1960s the Dalai Lama was already employing the liberal discourse of regime performance and human rights to criticize China. While this rights discourse continues to rankle some in the exile community,[37] it was hardly a 'Western' discourse by the time the Dalai Lama began to use it.[38] That said, precedent is only half of the picture. The Dalai Lama was not only in dialogue with Nehru in 1959, but was also instrumental in getting three UN resolutions passed on Tibet (in 1959, 1961 and 1965). Since rights discourse was becoming part and parcel of the way the United Nations conducted itself, it should not be surprising that the Dalai Lama would adopt that idiom. I should add that if we keep in mind what was going on in China during the Great Leap Forward (1958 to 1961) and the Cultural Revolution (1966 until 1976) the human-rights case was pretty low hanging fruit in the 1960s and early 1970s.

While much more could be said about different aspects of the Dalai Lama's rhetoric, what I am particularly interested in are the ways which the Dalai Lama deploys the different elements of Mahāyāna Buddhism listed above in his construction not only of the validity of Tibet as a 'nation' but (until recently) of the legitimacy of the institution of the Dalai Lama at its head. In 1961, after experiencing Indian democracy for a few years, the Dalai Lama announced that the Tibetan people were to have a new constitution. By 1963, the newly minted Central Tibetan Administration produced a draft constitution – a document which would provide the template for negotiations with China for the next four decades. This document, along with the 1987 "Five-Point Plan" delivered to the US Congress, the 1988 Strassburg revision and the 1991 revised Charter of Tibetans-in-Exile, are fascinating for a number of reasons, but for our purposes there are a few points I would like to highlight. What is significant for our purposes is that the draft constitution replaces the earlier Tibetan government in exile (the Tibetan Welfare Association which had been run by Tibetan aristocratic families in exile) with the Central Tibetan Administration, a government whose structure closely mirrored the Qing dynasty Ganden-Phodrang system that had been in place in Tibet.

Beginning with the Fifth Dalai Lama (1617–1682), the Qing understood all temporal power over Central Tibet, Khams and Amdo to have been invested in the Dalai Lama by the Qianlong emperor.[39] The Chinese understanding was summed up in 1953 by Tsung-lien Shên and Shên-chi Liu, who had served as representatives of Republic of China to Lhasa from 1944 until its demise and relocation to Taiwan in 1949.

> Once the Dalai Lama with his superhuman claims is chosen, it is not difficult to set up something of a constitution for Tibet. As the incarnation of Bodhisattva (or *Chen-Re-Zi*, [i.e., Avalokiteśvara] the Compassionate) he is the religious head of Tibet. And since, thanks to his patron, the Chinese emperor, he has acquired the greatest part of Tibet as a sort of endowment, he is also the political head of Tibet. In him is thus summed up the authority in Tibet for both the church and the state.
>
> Tibet is a land dedicated to "the Law," as personified by the Dalai Lama. His possessions – the land and its people – are divided into two portions: first, the dominion of the church, and second, the dominion of the state. He

> assumes personal command of both. However, to assist him in governing, he has delegated his power over nonspiritual affairs to a government, named De-Pa-Zhung (Government of the Chief). On account of the Dalai Lama's dual role, such a government should represent equally both the religious and the secular communities of his domain, with precedence given to the former. In a land consecrated to Buddha, the secular community exists for the religious community and not vice versa. The state is contained within the church. For this reason, the chief of the administration should in principle always be a member of the holy order. He can be a layman only when the Dalai Lama is in personal charge of the government. During the absence of a Dalai Lama, such as the interim between his passing and the finding of a successor-incarnation as well as during the successor's years of minority, a regent should be elected from among the highest incarnation lamas of Tibet and invited to assume full responsibility of the government.[40]

The crucial difference with Tsung-lien Shên's description and the 1963 constitution is that despite the democratic overtones of the latter, the Dalai Lama is still explicitly stated to be the ultimate authority, whose power and legitimacy is subordinate to none. Chapter 5 Article 29 states, "The executive power of the State shall be vested in His Holiness the Dalai Lama on his attaining the age of eighteen and shall be exercised by him either directly or through officers subordinate to him in accordance with the provisions of this Constitution." And while the Tibet envisioned by the draft constitution would be a democracy insofar as its National Assembly would be elected, Article 35 states that, "All executive action of the Government of Tibet shall be expressed to be taken in the name of His Holiness the Dalai Lama." Article 29 outlines the areas of the Dalai Lama's prerogative:

His Holiness the Dalai Lama as the Head of the State shall:

(a) accredit or withdraw diplomatic representatives in foreign countries and receive foreign diplomatic representatives, and ratify international treaties with previous approval, in appropriate cases, of the National Assembly or the Standing Commission of the National Assembly;
(b) grant pardons, respite or remission of punishment or suspend, remit or commute the sentence of any person convicted of any offence;
(c) confer honours and patents of merit;
(d) promulgate laws and ordinances having the force and validity of laws;
(e) summon and prorogue the National Assembly;
(f) send messages to the National Assembly and address it whenever he, in his discretion, considers it necessary; and
(g) authorize the holding of a referendum in cases provided for by this Constitution.
(h) Nothing in this Article shall be deemed to alter or affect in any manner the power and authority of His Holiness the Dalai Lama as the Supreme Spiritual Head of the State.[41]

The Dalai Lama is empowered to appoint ministers to the Kashag or cabinet as well as to appoint a prime minister. The latter body is then to "aid and advise

His Holiness the Dalai Lama in the administration of the executive government of the State." While Article 29 states that the Dalai Lama is to "promulgate laws," Article 32 clarifies that the laws are to be first adopted by the elected National Assembly. However, the Dalai Lama has the power to dissolve the national assembly as long as an election is held within 40 days.

Emptiness and the analytic of power

While there are democratic elements within the Draft Constitution, the form of government would more accurately be described as a "constitutional monarchy" in which the monarch – in this case the Dalai Lama – occupies the political, juridical and more importantly, spiritual apex of the system. Even when the Central Tibetan Administration had abandoned the goal of independent statehood in 1988 with the Strassburg proposal, the language of the ultimate sovereignty of the Dalai Lama from the 1963 Draft Constitution is maintained intact in the 1991 Charter of the Tibetans-in-Exile (in Article 19). It is he alone who can call the assembly into session, adjourn it, or even disband it. While members of the National Assembly and other officials take care of many of the day-to-day issues of running a state and can act on certain things without the Dalai Lama's direct involvement, the Dalai Lama is the final appeal and all acts of government are "done in his name." He can formulate laws and he has ultimate veto power. He is the final judge and may pardon crimes. In short, the Dalai Lama is *sovereign* in the sense of being the one whose decisions determine law (i.e., its execution or suspension) but are not determined by it (or any higher authority, for that matter). His position, *vis-à-vis* the entire polity is one defining its very limits and in so doing defining the very nature of authority throughout the domain.

The Dalai Lama's juridical position is not just apical in the sense of being able to implement or suspend the legal system, but as a religious and legal construct he stands outside of legal time. The Dalai Lama is an "incarnation" or *tulku* of Chenrezig or Avalokiteśvara and has a legal status accordingly. While the fact of this incarnation means different things to different people, as far as the Constitution is concerned, it marks his unique position in the political system. As such, the Dalai Lama as Tenzin Gyatso is a temporary manifestation or tulku, while the Dalai Lama as Avalokiteśvara is not. Structurally, the office of the Dalai Lama in the Constitution corresponds more to Avalokiteśvara as the *dharma-kāya* or the "Primordial Buddha" ("*ādi-buddha*") that we find in texts like the *Kāraṇḍavyūha sūtra* than to the bodhisattva that he is normally associated with.

The unspoken relation between the Dalai Lama and Avalokiteśvara (i.e., that which makes the Dalai Lama the Dalai Lama) that grounds the political system laid out in the Constitution may sound remarkably similar to the 16th-century English juridical concept of the king's two bodies,[42] insofar as the sovereign's absolute doppelganger, i.e., the *dharma-kāya*, like the king's *body politic* transcends the ruler's temporal personality or body. The English king received his body politic from God and only it is his true body. The divine right of kings pertains to this God-granted body. The king then stands as its head just as Christ is head of the Church. The divine right of kings, as interpreted by 16th-century jurists such as Ploughden, is predicated upon the "Great Chain of Being," such as the one set out in the works of Pseudo-Dionysus and others, in which all beings stand in a hierarchy oriented toward God, who occupies the absolute pinnacle. God distributes or delegates authority first to the angels and then to kings who in turn delegate authority to ministers, dukes and marquises. The fabric of this pyramidal edifice is woven upon the disposition of obedience – of sons to fathers, wives to husbands, people to their lords, lords to kings, etc. By contrast, evil is defined by disobedience. If obedience finds its paradigmatic example in Christ, then disobedience is exemplified by Lucifer, who refused to recognize his place and whose reward is eternal damnation. So, while ordinary Tibetans may or may not necessarily see ultimacy in either the Dalai Lama or Avalokiteśvara, the Buddhist teachings and tantric initiations that he has been giving render emptiness and the dharma-body available to those audiences as the apex of the cosmos to ground the proposed political system. We can say, then, that the cosmology of emptiness and its explicitly sovereign emanations being taught in tantric Buddhism provide the presumably irrefutable ground upon which the construction of temporal and ecclesial authority rests in a fashion quite parallel to the way the Christian cosmic hierarchy provided the proper justification for medieval articulations of the ecclesial and regal hierarchies in relation to their subjects.

But ideologies like this don't just happen to happen. The English are not somehow naturally predisposed to believing their kings had a special sanction from God – as much as Charles I (who was beheaded in 1649) might have wished otherwise. There had to be both a mechanism and perceived need to inculcate the idea of the divine hierarchy and the dispositions toward its authority. While, theologically, the doctrine of the divine right of kings took centuries to evolve, it was only in the latter half of the 16th century that a mechanism for its dissemination was put into place. Thomas Cranmer, the Archbishop of Canterbury, felt the English monarchy needed the English Church to be recognized as having equal standing to Roman Catholicism, and so he initiated the twin apparatuses of state-issued *Homilies* and the *Book of Common Prayer* to disseminate both the idea and the proper Christian dispositions to monarchial authority. As David Wootton has pointed out, even by the middle of the 16th century, only a third of adult males were literate.[43] This meant that the primary media they received came from the pulpit, not from other treatises or even from the Bible itself. At the time, less than half of ministers were licensed to preach, which meant that the rest of ministers were required to read state-issued homilies. The first volume of 12 state-mandated sermons was issued in 1547 under Edward VI, with a second volume being issued under Elizabeth I in 1571.[44] The sermon that has been reproduced most often in modern anthologies ("An Homily against Disobedience and Wylful Rebellion") presents the Great Chain of Being as a political tool for inculcating obedience with all the subtlety of a sledgehammer. This is not too surprising, since it was appended to the second collection immediately after the Northern Rebellion in support of Mary Queen of Scots in 1569. But even in the 1547 volume of homilies, we find a similar message concerning the position of the sovereign in the divine order in the homily, "An Exhortation Concerning Good Order, and Obedience to Millers and Magistrates." The first collection of homilies was initiated by Thomas Cranmer, the Archbishop of Canterbury as early as 1542, and was approved by Edward VI for printing by the royal press in 1547. Edward's plan was for the royal press to place a copy of these homilies in every church in England, and that they should form the templates for all preaching throughout England. In his second injunction to the bishops of England he states that they

> should not at any time or place preach, or set forth unto the people, any doctrine contrary or repugnant to the effect and intent contained or set forth in the king's highness' homilies; neither yet should admit or give license to preach to any within their diocese, but to such as they should know, or at least assuredly trust, would do the same; and if at any time, by hearing or by report proved, they should perceive the contrary, they should then incontinent not only inhibit that person so offending, but also punish him, and revoke their license.[45]

The injunction to preach only what accords with these homilies is repeated by Elizabeth I in 1559 and by James I in 1622.[46]

We can say, then, that until the first few decades of the 17th century, the control of media and thereby the means to inculcate and structure dispositions to authority was still very much in the hands of court and king. As the 17th century moves on, of course, things begin to change. Literacy and especially private reading of the Bible increases as the impact of the Reformation reaches a crescendo in England with the Puritans. This allows for the possibility of multiple readings of the Bible in the justification of different types of government. The centrality of the Great Chain doctrine and the fundamentals of the Bible were beginning to be wrested from state control. It is not incidental that both Locke's *First Treatise on Government* and Thomas Paine's *On Common Sense* begin with a contrary reading of the Biblical account of creation and the first kings.

But concurrently, we also have the rise of the idea of 'science' with Francis Bacon's (1561–1626) *Novum Organum* (1620) and the rise of its officer, 'the scientist' slightly later with the burgeoning fortunes of Robert Boyle (1627–1691). While the role and authority of 'scientist' would not be fully established by Boyle until his published experiments in the 1650s and 1660s,[47] the idea that there was a cosmos that one could appeal to in order to ground one's political system that was different from the Biblical/liturgical order became the foundation for a new wave of political thinking. Thus Hobbes' *Leviathan* (1652) begins, not with a reference to a commonly accepted divine order, but with a chapter on the eye and how the eye functions. Religion comes in only much later in the book, and when it does he argues that what we have is not religion, but *interpretations* of religion. From the new vantage of scientific objectivity, Hobbes can see that the 'religion' that is employed in the political realm is only what is judged as such *by the sovereign*.

My point in all of this is that in the 17th century, in the very generation that began theorizing or re-theorizing the foundations of the nation-states that were to eventually leave no spot of earth unclaimed, both divine right theorists and the social contract theorists had to appeal to an order that they assumed to be true, real and most importantly *cosmic* in the sense of the *external* natural referent to the political system.

Returning to the Dalai Lama as *tulku*, he, like the early English king, is merely a temporal manifestation of a more real *saṃbhoga-kāya* of the god-like Avalokiteśvara. When the three or four bodies of the Buddha are taught in dharma discourses at meditation centers, the tacit assumption is that each of these bodies is a manifestation of the same dharma-body which is emptiness itself.[48] The result is a remarkable similarity, if not outcome, in the juridical treatment of property rights of the 16th-century king and some Tibetan *tulkus*. We see in Ploughden's reports, for instance, that the king is allowed to purchase real estate even though a minor, since his body politic is timeless.[49] By the same logic, Tibetan *tulkus* accumulate land and other wealth through religious donation. This wealth can never be redistributed through inheritance or estate tax because, legally, a *tulku* never dies.[50]

There is, however, an important difference. The body politic of the English king was granted by God (or the angels) while the Dalai Lama *is* in an ultimate sense, the entity he incarnates. While God only grants the *body politic* to one person at a time within a single domain (and could also withdraw it), in the Tibetan system there can be multiple manifestations of the same ultimate truth at any given time but no possibility of revocation. And indeed, while the Dalai Lama stands apart in many ways, there are many other *tulkus* in Tibet and the Tibetan diaspora, many of whom can claim to be manifestations of a bodhisattva.

Indeed, perhaps the greatest contrast with the European model of the body politic is precisely the fact that there can be multiple if not infinite manifestations of this *dharma-kāya*. So how does this work? Like other models of legitimation, the Mahāyāna model of legitimation begins with the absolute. As the ultimate truth (*paramārtha*), emptiness is the characterization of reality that can neither be superseded, sublated nor disproven. In classical Mahāyāna philosophy, it is that truth by which all subordinate truths are rendered possible. It is ultimate in its primordiality to the extent that it is the very condition of temporality itself. This truth is embodied, so to speak, in the *dharma-kāya*, which is both the personification of emptiness/truth itself but only as an impersonal personification. As the singular (or at least non-dual) font of all things, it occupies the apical and therefore sovereign position of transcendence, while at the very same time being the immanent condition that underlies everything.

It is, then, emptiness or the Dharma Body, as the ultimate source of font of authority that occupies the apical position parallel to God in the European political system. Now, many scholars of religion have argued "transcendence" to be a seminal feature of religion. What I am arguing is slightly different. Transcendence in the European context posits a binary: "transcendent/mundane" which maps onto "sacred/profane." What I hope to show in this and the following chapter is that the Mahāyāna apex, while transcendent, does not create a binary. It creates a vertex whose importance is not so much its difference from other points but its *relation* to them. The apex can only be thought of as an "apex" because of the points that are subordinate and aligned toward it. As such, the religio-political apex is more akin to the Aristotelian *telos* than to the Barthian 'God as *Ganz-Andere*' (wholly-other). Yet, just like the mathematical concept of the limit, while the limit itself (whether zero or infinity) remains constant, the use to which it is put depends on the larger equation into which it is inserted. In more anthropological terms, emptiness is a sign that can be recognized or misrecognized in a number of ways depending on one's ingrained dispositions.

In the Tibetan draft constitution, the executive position is functionally monarchial. Of course, the draft constitution is just a document and would be powerless if the description of power therein were not already recognized to be authoritative. Power is only power to the extent that it is *recognized*. But the recognition of sovereign power entails a reciprocal and tacit recognition of the body politic *as* a body politic. As Hobbes himself observed,

> A Multitude of men, are made One Person, when they are by one man . . . Represented [in the sovereign]. For it is the Unity of the Representer, not the Unity of the Represented, that maketh the Person One . . . And Unity, cannot otherwise be understood in Multitude.[51]

We could say, then, that the construction of the Dalai Lama as monarchial executive is not just (or even primarily) about the Dalai Lama's power. Rather, in identifying the executive as the absolute apex of the political system of "Tibet," the document constructs both a sense of the Tibetan people (as a unity) and from there Tibet as an independent nation.

Continuing this line of thought, this "Tibet" can only be said to be an independent nation if it is recognized to be such not only by its population but by its neighbors as well. This recognition will only be possible if its polity is recognized to be single and unified. The Central Tibetan Administration chose to position the Dalai Lama as the ultimate authority in the new polity largely because he (or his office) was *already recognized* by Tibetans and by some non-Tibetans to have precisely this kind of authority prior to exile.

But recognition is a fickle thing. As Webb Keane (1997) has amply demonstrated, once a sign is introduced into the public, it is no longer within the control of its author. Signs of authority and prestige can be recognized in the way their author hopes, or they can be misrecognized in a way that undermines or belittles the position of authority. At a coronation, the liturgically constructed person at the focal point of the rite can be recognized as a "king" or misrecognized as a "usurper." Recognition or misrecognition have very real consequences for the office-holder's subsequent attempts to lead subordinates or receive concessions from his or her foreign counterparts. The Dalai Lama's authority was hoped by the framers of the draft constitution to mark the apex of authority within the system. But the fact of the matter is that no other nation has officially recognized either Tibet as an independent nation or the Dalai Lama as a political sovereign.

The mode under which the status and nature of his sovereign position has been recognized has in fact proved to be unstable over time. In many ways, the attempt to represent the 14th Dalai Lama as absolute sovereign in the 20th century would not have been possible for Dalai Lamas in the 18th century. Indeed, from the time of the Fifth Dalai Lama (1617 to 1682) onward, i.e., precisely from the time period that produced the Dalai Lama's hegemony in the first place, that very hegemony was ostensibly predicated on the political suzerainty of the Qing Emperor.[52] However, given the distance between Lhasa and Beijing, it is not clear the extent to which the average Tibetan would have been aware of the suzereignty of the Qing. In any case, as Melvyn Goldstein points out, the Qing had by and large withdrawn from interfering in Tibetan affairs in the 19th century and the Dalai Lamas (or their regents) had been able to declare and prosecute war with a number of strategic interests without approval from Beijing.[53] During the life of the 13th Dalai Lama, the Qing fell and during the Republican Period the new China looked weak with its own internal divisions. In Tibet itself, by the time of the 14th Dalai Lama, the position could now be cast as both that of a full-fledged monarch as well as a religious leader. Despite the fact that the Chinese republican government attempted to reassert its authority over the selection of *tulkus* in 1936,[54] when the 14th Dalai Lama was brought to Lhasa on October 8, 1939 at age 4, he was greeted with a Tibetan band playing "God Save the King," which they had learned for the occasion from the British.[55] After his enthronement he then received heads of state, such as "representatives from the British government in India, the King of Nepal, the Maharajas of Sikkim and Bhutan and a Chinese representative named Wu Zongxin."[56] Contemporary American sources also seemed to recognize this monarchial status. The first Western popular source that I can find covering the Dalai Lama is *Life* magazine, which in 1945 ran their first photo spread on him, introducing Tibet to an American audience as a "theocracy," which it then has to define for the reader as a land ruled by priests. We find in the *Life* article little of the stardust or reverence that would mark American publications in the 1980s. The rather short article ends with the rather blunt observation: "But his future is uncertain. Most lamas die at 20, reportedly by poisoning."[57] In 1945, the Dalai Lama is just a boy in the middle of his education. The next story about him in *Life* comes in 1959, right after he flees to India. There, the Dalai Lama is referred to as Tibet's "Pope-like" leader. The article goes on to describe in more detail the nature of his position within Tibet.

> To the people of Tibet the Dalai Lama is both king and god. He is considered the direct reincarnation of a long line of saintly lamas who preceded him, and he is the final political authority over a national assembly called *Tsongdu* and a cabinet made up of five ministers called *Shapes*. . . . The men, beasts and lands of Tibet all belong to him.[58]

For Tibetans (and especially for the Khamba combatants who took on the Chinese army and were featured in the article), the office of Dalai Lama was a known quantity and did not have to be translated or defined. It did, however, for other heads of state and clearly in 1940 the term "king" was a serviceable enough form of recognition. For the American reading public, his occupation of the apex of political authority was signaled by the use of the word "king" while his position at the apex of religious authority was signaled by the word "god." The article attempts to reconcile these two positions to say that he is "Pope-like."

But if he was recognized as a king in the 1930s, this recognition has become more complicated as time moved on. Certainly, the politicians as well as citizens of India, the United Nations and European countries, not to mention the United States, have heard the Dalai Lama's pro-democratic, pro–human rights, pro-environmental agenda[59] in seeking an independent and sovereign Tibet – and heard it enough to award him the Nobel Peace Prize in 1989 – while still being deaf to the monarchial flavor of his proposed role in the constitution. In general, India, China and the United States at least, tended to be rather allergic to the idea of monarchy in the latter half of the 20th century – each having their own histories of jettisoning the British crown. And yet few in India or the US (apart from officials in the US State Department) have questioned the Dalai Lama's unique political authority to speak and make decisions for Tibetans. If the Tibetan government-in-exile now seeks autonomy within China, then it seeks it under the authority of a single figure: the Dalai Lama. And both the American public and their elected officials simply assume that he is the one to represent "Tibet" (in whatever form that might take).

While some of the Dalai Lama's ascribed political position may simply derive from political expediency, I suspect that a more poignant answer is that *the very idea* of the office of the Dalai Lama and the nature of its authority has been naturalized in a specific manner to the point that its political peculiarities are no longer *seen*. That the Dalai Lama is the ultimate, single and apical authority in relation to several entities ("Tibet," Tibetan Buddhism or occasionally "Buddhism" itself) has been normalized for Western audiences to the point of invisibility – but normalized as something quite different from a king. What is perhaps even more interesting is the fact that this shift in recognition has been orchestrated even among Americans after his exile.

Inculcating dispositions to authority: the *Kālacakra*

The Dalai Lama does not raise our anti-monarchial hackles because his authority (ironically even his executive authority) is construed to be "religious" and therefore not "political." If the Great Chain of Being was naturalized in Edwardian and Elizabethan England through the twin state instruments of the *Book of Common Prayer* and the *Homilies*, what was the mechanism by which "proper" recognition of the Dalai Lama was inculcated into non-Tibetan audiences? As discussed above, the Tibetans were allowed refugee status in 1959 by Nehru based at least partly on a claim of Buddhist identity. Eleven years later the Dalai Lama would be established enough in India to hold the first Indian Kālacakra initiation at Dharamsala in 1970. As they go, this one was rather small (according to the official website, attendance was around 30,000). In 1954 and 1956 he had performed similar initiations for crowds of around 100,000 in Lhasa. By 1974, however, he apparently hit his 100,000 mark again by performing the initiation at Bodhgāya, the place where Śākyamuni, the historical Buddha achieved enlightenment. The visuals of this performance would have been striking. Crowds this size for events in India are, of course, not unheard of. *Kumbha melās* tend to draw crowds in the tens of millions – although the *melā* crowds are not paying attention to a single figure on a single stage. According to scholars and attendees Ernst Haas and Gisela Minke,

> Buddhists from all the Himalayan countries and India descended into Bodhgaya. Exiled Tibetans joined Sikkimese, Bhutanesee, Nepalese, Ladakhis, people from the NEFA areas of India and pilgrims from Burma, Sri Lanka, Japan and the West. It is of great importance to every follower of Tibetan Buddhism to attend such a 'Wang' [*dbang* – *abhiṣekha*] at least once in his life-time.[60]

The crowd of initiates were then focused on a stage on which the Dalai Lama wore a five-paneled crown depicting five Buddhas and sat on a throne in front of a large Thanka depicting Kālacakra, an incarnation of Śākyamuni himself. Both the visuals as well as the liturgy would have conveyed (at least to the Tibetan speaking audience) the identification of the Dalai Lama as tantric guru with Kālacakra and by extension to Śākyamuni Buddha at the moment of his enlightenment under the Bodhi tree. Of course, even if the significance of Kālacakra had been missed, the connection of the Dalai Lama to the historical Buddha would have been apparent to anyone. The point is that here, while there might have been a range of degree or depth of recognition across the 100,000 initiates, the target audience of a ritual marking his religious authority had been expanded perhaps for the first time to include far more people than those who had traditionally acknowledged it.

At the time of this writing, the Dalai Lama has performed 35 such Kālacakra initiations in India, Mongolia, Europe and the US – always to crowds numbering in the thousands. If the Central Tibetan Administration's website is within the ballpark, the Dalai Lama has personally performed the Kālacakra initiation for around 1.8 million people since he left Tibet in 1959 and almost 16,000 in the US alone. I think we are warranted in looking at this initiation as an apparatus at least as compelling as the *Homilies* and the *Book of Common Prayer* in inculcating dispositions to a certain kind of ideological construction. These initiations, at least up until 2011, were apparatuses that reproduced in multiple venues for multiple audiences a particular, and specifically Mahāyāna idea of the sovereign subject so that it might be recognized in the *office* of the Dalai Lama, thereby effecting the tacit recognition of the concomitant sovereign object: "Tibet."

With so many who have received the initiation we have to assume that not all of these people would bring the same competencies to bear on correctly "reading" the ritual nor would each have been equally transformed by the experience. Tibetans, Mongolians, Ladakhians and Bhutanese, even without training, would have the necessary cultural competence or disposition to properly recognize the nature of the Dalai Lama's authority even if they undertook the initiation essentially as a blessing from the Dalai Lama. This would not necessarily be true for Japanese, Indians, Europeans or Americans. For those who merely attended the Kālacakra for its spectacle, the visuals identifying the Dalai Lama as sovereign (the throne, crown, *the Vajra*, a kind of ritual scepter, etc.) with Śākyamuni and Kālacakra would probably be sufficiently evident. At the very least, all participants would have to have been aware of the tantric vows, the first of which (not to disparage the guru) amounts to a vow of loyalty to the presiding guru, which in this case is the Dalai Lama himself.

But for many practitioners of Buddhism (both lay and monastic) the Kālacakra initiation would not have been a stand-alone event. Rather, it would have been the culmination of a series of trainings and/or initiations by other lamas. For these practitioners, the degree of competence to interpret the rite would be a function of the extent to which they had taken advantage of teachings offered elsewhere, either secret teachings from other gurus or public teachings found in publications or given in Tibetan Buddhist meditation centers scattered through the West. If we take the English-language volumes on the Kālacakra initiation written for American practitioners as an indication, we can see in the penumbra of practices and teachings surrounding the Kālacakra initiations a particular relationship between the doctrine of emptiness and the construction of authority of the guru that is remarkably similar to the construction of sovereignty in the Draft Constitution.

To take just one example, in an essay for Western practitioners Jhado Rinpoche gives English readers a short form of Kālacakra meditation to be done every day if they cannot do the full meditation. He begins the meditation by stating, "It is important to set your motivation for your practice. You need to develop the feeling that today you will follow Śākyamuni Buddha, Kālacakra, your teacher and the merit field." He then tells the practitioner to, "visualize Kālacakra in the nature of your teacher." In other words, one's teacher is the embodiment of all the regal authority of Kālacakra himself, sitting on the throne with his consort in the midst of the political mandala of his alliances with other deities. This authority, however, is not reified as an external master. Or if it is, the reification is not stable. The next move in the practice is to dissolve the guru Kālacakra into the crown of one's head and then to dissolve oneself into emptiness, the visualization here enacting the dissolution of emptiness both as a kind of personal death as well as a kind of cosmic *pralāya* or interstice between the cosmic destruction at the end of the cycle and the first creation of the new cycle. It is from this standpoint that emptiness ceases to be destructive and becomes the infinite potential of the moment prior to creation. The meditation resumes:

> The empty mind transforms itself into Kālacakra. This can be done elaborately or in a simple way . . .
>
> [The elaborate way:] Out of emptiness visualize an open-petalled lotus on top of a lion throne. On top of this are moon, sun, Rahu, and Kālāgni discs. On the Kālāgni disc is a dark blue HŪṂ, which transforms into a dark blue vajra with a small HŪṂ letter in its center. The vajra and HŪṂ

> transform into Kālacakra with either one face and two arms or four faces and twenty-four arms. This visualization purifies our ordinary rebirth, which has kept us in cyclic existence, and leaves the imprint in the future to attain a Buddha's Form Body. The dissolution of the merit field and subsequent meditation on emptiness purifies ordinary death. It leaves an imprint to attain a Buddha's Wisdom Body in the future. You should then meditate on the emptiness of this visualization.[61]

Geshe Drakpa Gelek, the Kālacakra teacher at Namgyal Monastery in Dharamsala, explains.

> Before this point in the sādhana the practitioner has cultivated the field of merit, imagining the entire field of the mandala with the principal deity, Kālacakra, and his consort, Viśvamāta, at the center. After the visualization of receiving the empowerments, but before generating oneself as Kālacakra, the practitioner imagines the entire mandala dissolving from the outside in and then into the principal deity at the center. Kālacakra then comes to the crown of the practitioner's head, melts, and dissolves into the practitioner's body, transforming his body fully into light. After merging completely together, the practitioner should feel that he has become one with the deity and his teacher and feel great joy. It is very important that the practitioner's mind becomes one with his root teacher who is inseparable from Kālacakra. Since this feeling can lead the practitioner into feeling some notion of solid existence, he should fall back into a meditation on emptiness at this point . . .
>
> Once he has reached the point of manifesting the most subtle mind, he then tries to remain fully focused on the notion of emptiness that he found earlier during analytical meditation. This is the actual practice of taking the Dharmakāya as a means to purify the ordinary death, and it depends on the capacity of the practitioner's mind. He should think that this very mind, the wisdom that realizes emptiness, which he uses for focusing on the emptiness, is in the form of the resultant state of Dharmakāya. The practitioner imagines strongly that this very wisdom that is now labeled as the Dharmakāya is actually the practitioner himself. He does this in order to develop the pride of thinking that the label of the Dharmakāya that has been applied to his subtle mind is himself. This is how he cultivates the divine pride of being in the state of Dharmakāya.[62]

In other words, the meditation begins with a meditation on a figure of ultimate authority, the Kālacakra/Śākyamuni Buddha. Kālacakra is then understood to be none other than one's guru. The guru dissolves, via a meditation on emptiness, into the practitioners themselves, who then dissolve into a primal emptiness. The latter emptiness in turn gives birth to the cosmos itself, ordered as Kālacakra's political mandala, which we can assume to be the political utopia of Shangri-la itself. Here, we have all the elements of political legitimation that we find in other religio-political systems: the proximate authority is a local stand-in for ultimate and absolute authority. There are, however, two crucial differences. First, the emptiness which is the lynchpin of the system is not merely asserted ritually, but has *elsewhere* been exhaustively studied and logically proven *to be* ultimate – i.e., among debate-monks in Geluk monasteries as well as by practitioners of this meditation everywhere. Second, the *dharma-kāya* may be the epitome of authority especially when instantiated in the Dalai Lama or another of the *tulkus*, but the nature of that authority is to be directly confirmed by practitioners here and now through meditation. Even if an individual neither meditates nor debates the doctrine of emptiness themselves, the fact that there are locally esteemed individuals who do lends weight to the authority of the Dalai Lama at the center of the mandala. Since meditation and initiations lie at the center of the construction of authority in Tibet, by disseminating these teachings and practices in the West by way of publications and meditation centers, Western practitioners are able to gain the cultural competencies necessary to properly recognize Tibetan authority.

The difference, of course, between Western practitioners and many Tibetan practitioners is the Western assumption that religion is a fundamentally separate sphere from politics. Thus, while American practitioners of Tibetan Buddhism might bow to the Dalai Lama, few of them think of him in the capacity of proposing legislation over, say, property taxes and tariffs in an independent Tibet. In some ways, the assumption that religion is the opposite of politics has worked to the advantage of the Tibetan exile government in the way that it has for Buddhists throughout the 20th century. Numerous studies have documented ways in which, under the gaze of repressive regimes, "religion" becomes a safe way to air political critiques precisely *because* its political import is misrecognized.[63] In the West, at least since the time of Locke's *Letter Concerning Toleration* (first published in 1689), religion could be thought of as a variety of "opinion," a largely private matter that is out of the jurisdiction of the magistrate. Its private nature, in turn, requires protection from the reach of the state.

"Freedom of religion" has been taken to be a hallmark of "modernity" not only in Euro-American circles, but also in places as culturally diverse as Egypt[64] and Japan.[65] If the 1963 Draft Constitution amalgamates the Dalai Lama's political sovereignty to his religious one, the two sides can be just as easily disjoined. The historical usefulness of emptiness as a political-theological category lies in precisely this ability to be just as easily joined to the political as to appear independent of it, and at least prior to the 20th century, the very authority of emptiness was partly a function of its perceived independence. Such was the case, as I will discuss in the next chapter, under Mongol and then Qing suzerainty.

But the past few decades have seen a disjoining of emptiness and the *dharma-kāya* from the political that is functionally quite different from that of the Qing dynasty and before. In a 2011 BBC interview, the Dalai Lama renounced all political responsibilities, and stated that his role would from then on be "purely religious." This was not the first time he had discussed the possibility but this time the move was officially ratified by the Tibetan Community in Exile. In many ways, this was a very shrewd move. The Dalai Lama was then 75 years old and aware that after his death the People's Republic of China would claim the right to name his next incarnation. As with the Panchen Lama, this incarnation could then be carefully groomed to be a mouthpiece for the Chinese state. By denying any political role for himself in this life, the Dalai Lama was essentially speaking for/as his own successor.

But there is more to it than this tactical issue. I see in this maneuver a specifically Buddhist shift. The 1963 Draft Constitution opens with an argument for Tibetan independence and the sovereignty of its executive based on the abysmal regime performance of the Mao government. After the Dalai Lama was awarded the Nobel Peace Prize in 1989, the Dalai Lama and the Central Tibetan Administration have increasingly been backing off from the language of Tibetan independence and moving more toward the language of "autonomy," for which, in particular, the practice of religion is respected. Concomitant with this shift is a move away from recognition of the Dalai Lama's political sovereignty. Partly this shift comes from the fact that China in 2011 is a very different China from that of 1963 or even 1993. In 1989 after the fall of the Berlin Wall it might have looked like China might undergo similar reforms with Deng Xiaoping. By 2011, however, China rose to a prominence that would have been hard to predict 20 years prior. Not that any state had ever recognized Tibet's independence, but with the rise of China's power, full independence was simply out of the question. However, in the 1970s and 1980s human rights took on a status and role that was in many ways quite new. According to Samuel Moyn, it was in this time period that the rights laid out in the 1948 Declaration of Human Rights began to be used as a measuring stick of political legitimacy that was understood to transcend the sovereign nation state itself.[66] Among those rights to be protected was, in Article 18, religion, and "freedom of religion" began to be one of the main concerns in the US State Department, Bureau of Democracy, Human Rights and Labor's *Country Reports on Human Rights Practices* that began to be issued annually in 1999. These reports single out China for its lack of respect of religion as a basic human right. In his Nobel Peace Prize acceptance speech, he connects discourse about human rights to the Buddhist doctrine of compassion and argues that it is a natural characteristic of the Tibetan people, but it is in the 1990s and early 2000s that the Dalai Lama begins more and more to talk of Tibetan's religion as that which must be respected and protected.

This maneuver, while in many ways quite grounded in an interpretation of Buddhism, marks a profound shift in tack. Earlier Dalai Lamas' authority would have been grounded in *both* the compassionate *bodhicitta* that had been defined by Tsongkhapa and others[67] as the *sine qua non* of Mahāyāna *and* the emptiness that lay at the ground of generation-stage yogas and the subsequent tantric pride of the cosmogonic sovereign embodied in the *tulku* (especially during ritual). In shifting his international appeal to human rights discourse, the 14th Dalai Lama is able to harness the pressure exerted by the US State Department on China, but only to the extent that he can represent his cause as a category protected under the Universal Declaration of Human Rights, namely the free *private* exercise of "religion." In declaring himself to be "a simple monk," in distancing himself from any political role and proclaiming his position to be "purely religious," he is able to place himself and "Tibetan Buddhism" into an internationally recognized and (somewhat) protected category. However, this move comes at a cost. In the particular regime of the Universal Declaration, to make Tibetan Buddhism visible as "religion" means to erase the previously universal, objective and transcendent features of sovereign emptiness. The erasure of the political renders it visible only as one among many culturally contingent "world religions." And this is precisely where we find it, shelved in the "Eastern Religions" section of Barnes & Noble. With the lives and livelihoods of so many exiles at stake, the loss is perhaps a small price to pay, but it does tend to occlude our vision of the political role of emptiness in earlier days.

Notes

1 Gach, (2009), p. 34.
2 Ibid., p. 191.
3 Landaw (2011), p. 75.
4 Bronkhorst (2013), p. 117. Apart from this point, Bronkhorst's book is remarkably good.
5 A 2010 Pew Research survey found that around 47% of Americans are aware that the Dalai Lama is Buddhist. I am sure that far fewer are aware that he has anything to do with Mahāyāna. See www.pewforum.org/2010/09/28/u-s-religious-knowledge-survey-who-knows-what-about-religion/#World. My thanks to Paul Harrison for pointing this out to me.
6 Many of them are transcriptions of lectures spoken in Tibetan and delivered to the audience by way of an interpreter.
7 Mehrotra (2006), pp. ix–x.
8 John Powers, personal communication, 4/25/2018.
9 Mehrotra, (2006), pp. 53–54. This essay was originally published in *Buddha Heart, Buddha Mind: Living the Four Noble Truths*, comprising a series of eight lectures given at the Institute Karma Ling in Savoie, France in 1997.
10 On this list (which includes the Four Noble Truths, the eightfold path along with a number of other such lists) see Gethin (1992).
11 He prefaces the above quote by noting that in Tibet not only do the followers of the *Prajñāpāramitā* denigrate the Hīnayānists and their practices, but that Tantric practitioners denigrate *Prajñāpāramitā* practitioners "especially where discipline is concerned."
12 Ibid.
13 Portions of this sutra were translated by Guṇabhadra sometime after he arrived in China in 435 CE. Cf. T. 478 and T. 479.
14 Mehrotra (2006), pp. 55–56.
15 Ibid.
16 *Dhammapada*, verse 279.
17 The earliest reference I have been able to find asserting the Hīnayāna/Mahāyāna distinction as having anything to do with selflessness of persons vs. dharmas is in a commentary on the *Diamond Sutra* ascribed to Vasubandhu. See T. 1511, pp. 788c29–789a2; T. 1513, p. 879c15–16. Older works mention the selflessness of dharmas, but merely as what the Buddha taught, not as anything peculiar to Mahāyāna. If Nāgārjuna was attempting to show that all dharmas were empty, then it may have been to demonstrate something that his audience already assumed to be the case.
18 Specifically a feature of the so-called "father tantras" such as the *Guhyasamāja* and the *Yamāntaka* cycle.
19 Something seems off about this translation. "*Continuity Unexcelled*" should translate *Anuttara Tantra*, which is the name of a class of Tantra, but not the name of a text. There is, however, a Mahāyāna treatise that does discuss the bodies of the Buddha which is called the [*Ratnagotravibhāga Mahāyāna-*] *Uttara Tantra*. It is probably the

latter to which the Dalai Lama is referring here since the *Uttara Tantra* tells us that the *dharma-kāya* is permanent due to its identity with non-conceptual nature of reality itself, a nature empty of the duality of subject and object.

20 Bstan-'dzin-rgya-mtsho Dalai Lama XIV (2000), p. 78

21 Tsong-kha-pa (2000), vol. 1, p. 18, "The *perfection of wisdom* is the mother of *both* Hīnayāna and Mahāyāna disciples, for it is spoken of as mother. Consequently do not distinguish Hīnayāna and Mahāyāna by the wisdom that knows emptiness but by the spirit of enlightenment and the greatly effective bodhisattva deeds."

22 Compare, for example, Apple (2015), p. 683. For other sources mentioning *bodhicitta* as emptiness, see Brassard, pp. 21–22.

23 Lindtner (1987), p. 199; *alakṣaṇam anutpādam asaṃsthitam avāṅmayam* | *ākāśaṃ bodhicittaṃ ca bodhir advayalakṣaṇā*||

24 See, e.g., Snellgrove (2010), p. 93.

25 Śāntideva is following the *Gaṇḍhavyūhasūtra* in this.

26 Brassard (2000), p. 41. On the two *bodhicittas* in Śāntideva, see Brassard (2000) *passim*, esp. pp. 41–46

27 Khunu Rinpoche (2012), p. 143.

28 Originally published as a chapter in *Advice on Dying* (2002).

29 Mehrotra, pp. 130–131.

30 Bstan-'dzin-rgya-mtsho Dalai Lama, X. I. V. (1989). "The 14th Dalai Lama's Nobel Lecture." Retrieved 9/8, 2017, from www.dalailama.com/messages/acceptance-speeches/nobel-peace-prize/nobel-peace-prize-nobel-lecture.

31 See Lopez (1998), chp. 7. The portrayal of Tibetan Buddhism as non-violent in particular is especially problematic in light of the fight that broke out in 1947 over the Dalai Lama's own regent, Reting. According to Van Schaik (2011), p. 5: "in 1947, Ngapo and his fellow ministers had called on the army to fight the monks of Sera monastery. This was the culmination of the power struggles that followed the death of the thirteenth Dalai Lama, and it almost turned into a civil war between the monastery and the government, ending with the shelling of Sera monastery and the murder of the previous regent, the abbot of Reting, who was accused of fomenting the rebellion."

32 Lopez, pp. 188ff.

33 "As the Dalai Lama recast Buddhism as a religion of reason comparable to empirical science, he struggled to incorporate other Enlightenment ideals, ideals of liberal-democratic provenance. This appropriation began during the early years of exile in the 1960s, but in the late 1980s the Geluk sect's institutions came under heightened scrutiny in ways that incited new forms of self-consciousness. The Tibetan government-in-exile settled upon a new, self-consciously "international" campaign focused on lobbying the US Congress and building grassroots support. For the first time the Dalai Lama was put forward to present the Tibet issue to the world, the signature proposal of the period being the Five Point Peace Plan. The plan included calls for increased autonomy in Tibet, environmental protections, religious freedom and above all human rights. The Dalai Lama became internationally renowned for making non-violence, peace and "universal compassion" Buddhism's essence, efforts that coincided with a political appeal: that the People's Republic of China (PRC) respect human rights in Tibet" Lempert (2012), p. 3.

34 Ibid., p. 131.

35 The classical study of lateral communication being Goffman (1981).

36 Roemer (2008), p. 64.

37 See Lempert (2012).

38 On the introduction of "rights" as a legitimating discourse in South Asia, see Rai (2004), chapter 3.

39 In practice, of course, it didn't always work out this way. As Melvyn Goldstein notes, from 1728 until 1751, the Qing shifted power from the seventh Dalai Lama to Pholane, who was then named king. The Dalai Lama resumed power after the assassination of Pholane's son. More to the point, however, Goldstein shows that (as of the time of his

writing in 1973), Dalai Lamas in fact ruled Tibet only 77% of the time between the Fifth Dalai Lama and 1973. This is because reincarnate lamas may only govern when they reach the age of majority (18 years). Until then, a regent (also a reincarnate lama) rules in their stead. It turns out that regents rule far more than the Dalai Lamas they serve. Nevertheless, it does not take too much imagination to see that the political system of Dalai Lamas and regents is held together by *the idea of* the Dalai Lama at its apex and not by the person occupying that position. See Goldstein (1973).

40 Shen (1953), pp. 101–102.
41 Central Tibetan Administration (1963).
42 See Kantorowicz, Ernst Hartwig (1957), especially chapters 1, 6 and 7.
43 See Wootton (2003), p. 27.
44 Lancashire (1997).
45 Cardwell (1839), pp. 23–24.
46 Lancashire (1997).
47 On the establishment of the idea of the scientist and its grounding in the moral and social concepts of gentlemen in 17th-century England, see Stephan Shapin, (1994).
48 On the Gelukpa teachings of the *svabhāvika-kaya* and the *dharma-kāya* and their relation to emptiness and the earlier *Perfection of Wisdom* traditions, see Makransky (1997), chapters 3 and 12.
49 Kantorowicz (1957), p. 7.
50 See Goldstein (1973).
51 Hobbes (1889), p. 80.
52 For two excellent accounts of this period, see Elverskog (2006), chapter 4 and Schwieger, chapters 4–6.
53 Goldstein (1991), p. 44.
54 Schwieger, 209.
55 Powers (1995), p. 168.
56 Ibid., p. 195.
57 *Life* (April 6, 1959), 35.
58 *Life*: 31.
59 While parts of this agenda were always there, the specific language of these issues becomes explicit only after the CTA backs off from complete independence and begins conscripting the help of NGOs dedicated to these issues. According to Lempert, "In what is reported to have been a series of high-level strategy sessions held by the CTA between 1985 and 1987, the exile government settled upon a strategy to make Tibet matter again, especially through securing support of the United States. A deliberately international campaign, it put the Dalai Lama forward as political emissary for the first time. . . . As part of this international campaign, the Dalai Lama-led government discursively conceded independence for autonomy and parceled out the Tibet question into smaller issues – human rights, religious freedom, environmental protection, women's rights – that were taken up by prominent NGO's like Amnesty International and Human Rights Watch" Lempert (2012), pp. 131–132.
60 Ernst Haas and Gisela Minke, "The Kalacakra Initiation" *The Tibet Journal* Vol. 1, No. 3/4 (Autumn 1976), pp. 29–31
61 Gelek (2009), p. 461.
62 Ibid., pp. 450–451.
63 See Jordt (2007) and McHale (2004).
64 See Agrama (2012)
65 John Breen and Mark Teeuwen (2010), 10.
66 Moyn (2012).
67 Of course, one of the reasons why Tibetan theorists took this position may well have to do with the fact that representations of the compassion of the ruler had always been a part of Tibetan royal culture even before Buddhism arrived. See Ramble (2006).

3

MAHĀYĀNA IN THE REPUBLIC, MAHĀYĀNA IN THE EMPIRE

Tracing "religion" from republican China to the early Qing Dynasty (1920s – 1723)

In the last chapter, I showed that, in the case of the Dalai Lama and the 20th-century construction of Tibetan Buddhism, some of the features of Mahāyāna that had been central to Tibetan polity – especially its doctrine of emptiness and the Dharma Body of the *tulku* – ceased to be available *as political* by the end of the century. But this rather profound shift in the optics of Buddhism is by no means confined to Tibet or Tibetan Buddhism. We see a similar shift occurring in China, Korea and Japan as well. The occultation of the political hues of Mahāyāna in each of the nations from which the West has inherited its understanding of Mahāyāna in the late 19th and 20th centuries has rendered emptiness available to us only as a private "religious" experience, a "philosophical" doctrine, a "scientific" truth or a kind of "therapy" (each of the terms in quotes having an interesting genealogy of its own in the late 19th and early 20th centuries). I am not arguing that any of these reclassifications are necessarily wrong, or even particularly "modern"[1] but rather that the configuration of the categories of "religion," "philosophy" and "science" that Mahāyāna now falls into, is itself the product of negotiations of power within the radical reconfigurations of nationhood across the globe in the late 19th and 20th centuries – reconfigurations that sought the political marginalization of religion. This chapter makes two claims. First is that the global privatization of religion that becomes ubiquitous in the 20th century is a function of the replacement of monarchies and empires by polities that were either outright republican or that shifted more powers from the singular sovereign to the governing assembly (the parliament, the congress, etc.). The rise of a new type of constitution – one that expressly located the origins of power in the people as opposed to Heaven, God or some other Ultimate – rendered increasingly obsolete (and therefore invisible) the role that religion had played formerly to structure and vouchsafe political obligations. The second claim is that, by contrast, when we look at the way that Mahāyāna was used in the Qing Dynasty (1644–1912; a dynasty encompassing Tibet, China and Mongolia) prior to the 20th century, we can see that Mahāyāna had been a crucial element in the Qing amalgamation of what had been distinct polities and ideologies. Indeed, it is not too hard to imagine that without the very idea of a "China," facilitated by this amalgamation, there would have been no "People" 國民全體 to whom Sun Yat-sen could grant "sovereignty" 主權 to in his 1912 *Provisional Constitution of the Republic of China.*

Religion vs. superstition in 20th-century East Asia

The shifts that we find in the categorization of the Dalai Lama's Buddhism occurred earlier for Buddhists in the eastern part of China, where we see the depoliticization of emptiness and the concomitant decoupling of Buddhism from the apparatus of state authorization begin much earlier. Needless to say, this decoupling reaches its zenith during the Cultural Revolution beginning in 1966. At that time, the Red Guards actively attacked Buddhist monasteries under the rationale that Buddhism, like Islam, Daoism and Christianity, was "superstition" (*mixin*) and an obstruction to the modernization of China. But the process of temple confiscation and the anti-religion rhetoric of the 1960s, although more complete, started long before the Cultural Revolution. Indeed, we find anti-religion campaigns off and on throughout the Republican Period. For Buddhists, the impact of these campaigns was felt primarily in terms of confiscation of temple lands and monastic property. In the 1920s this took two forms: the confiscation of temples to serve as army barracks and the repurposing of temples for public schools. The rhetoric of temple conversion for schools in particular pitted modern "knowledge" against religious "superstition" in a way that dovetailed with a new social mobility of village elites. According to Prasenjit Duara,

> In its zeal to eradicate superstition and establish a modern society, the Yuan administration sought to systematically dismantle the institutional foundations of popular religion. Its success in appropriating temples and temple property in the first phase was considerable. For instance, in Ding county, Zhili, the number of temples declined by 316, from 432 in 1900 to 116 in 1915. . . . This initial success was due largely to cooperation by the rural elite. The local elite saw new avenues of social mobility in the new schools and the formal positions of village government. Education had, of course, always been a route to advancement in imperial China and now it seemed to be more readily accessible to the village elite.[2]

In fact, however, the promised education was far less public than anticipated, because farming families usually could not spare children for schooling and so only wealthier villagers could take advantage. Nevertheless, it was the push to transform monasteries into secular schools during the Republican Period that made religion visible as science's "other" in a way that would have been concrete to villager and the urbanite alike. In the context of this juxtaposition, the performative utterances of Buddhism that had been used in a variety of social and political contexts were now visible only as a set of propositions to be measured against those of science for truth or falsity.

Of course, just because the anti-superstition rhetoric targeted Buddhist establishments and especially Buddhist monasticism does not mean that Buddhists simply abandoned Buddhism. There were, as Holmes Welch has documented, a group of revolutionaries during the Republican era who were not only steeped in the German, Russian and Chinese Marxist literature of the day, but were equally interested in Buddhist writings of mind-only "philosophy." Indeed, in the republican context "religion" (as "belief" 信教 or the newly coined *zongjiao*宗教) was a constitutionally protected category[3] but "superstition" (迷信 "false belief," its new opposite) was not. In the first three decades of the 20th century, Buddhists of all stripes (unlike their Christian counterparts)[4] had to make the case that Buddhism was a religion by showing that it was not superstition. For more revolutionary-minded monks, "Buddhist philosophy" and the social service of "redemptive societies" were the perfect vehicles within Buddhism to show that Buddhism was not contrary to science.

Taixu (1890–1947), a Chan (a.k.a. "Zen") monk, is perhaps the most famous of these revolutionary monks, but he was certainly not alone in this interest. Where Vietnamese revolutionaries in the 1920s and 1930s used the confines of lengthy prison sentences to teach Marxist ideology to other inmates,[5] some Chinese revolutionaries used their prison time to study mind-only philosophy. Holmes Welch reports that,

> Chang Ping-lin . . . was one of those arrested in the Su-pao case. He had already become immersed in the study of Buddhism, and while he was serving his three year sentence in Shanghai, he "devoted himself single-mindedly to the work of Maitreya and Vasubandhu." He expounded Buddhist scriptures to his fellow prisoner, Tsou Jung. "If you can understand these books," he told him, then you can spend their years in prison without any feeling of misery."[6]

But in the crucible of revolution, and in a setting where Buddhist "superstition" was pitted against "education," it would be precisely these reformers who would recast Buddhism as not only a newly coined term, "religion" (*zongjiao* 宗教)[7] but as "scientific" and "philosophy." But more to the point, this Buddhism was to be taught by coopting precisely the kind of educational reform that had threatened Buddhism in the first place. Taixu was one of the earliest of these educational reformers, and in 1912 sought to convert Jinshan monastery into a kind of Buddhist seminary. The movement never got off the ground, but Taixu would spend the rest of his life working toward such reform. For him, what might have, in earlier generations, been a practice or vocation is now a set of "doctrines" to be placed alongside the competing doctrines of other religions and science. In his English lectures he writes:

> For more than twenty years I have studied the Buddhist doctrines so that I think I may say to-day that I have come to fully realise the teaching of

> Buddha. That there exist many different schools of Buddhism, as well as other religious, philosophical and scientific beliefs does not discourage me, since after profound study of all these forms of thought, I have been able to grasp the real value of Buddhism, which, so far has been limited by certain prejudices and unable to spread throughout the world.[8]

His solution was, of course, a different kind of Buddhist pedagogy, one that actively promoted Buddhism as a set of doctrines by making *public* Buddhist texts that were previously proprietary.

> Buddhist texts, which hitherto were only studied by priests and hermits, are now in the hands of students, and chairs of Buddhism, [texts] which were only to be found in temples or monasteries are now organized by national and provincial authorities.[9]

Buddhist doctrine was to be transferred to public safekeeping in the new academic context of the school. The new Buddhism that was to be taught was not that which had been "limited by certain prejudices," but rather a Buddhism that would complete both the projects of science and philosophy. Taixu was optimistic the Buddhist doctrine could stand up to any and all competing doctrines.

> Science however, has never been able to perfectly understand the Universe and is always living on hypotheses. As can be shown, Buddhism is the only religion which does not contradict scientific truth, but rather confirms it, and on more than one subject can furnish a point of departure. In this way, the incomplete character of Science is overcome and its progress guaranteed. Therefore, we have to constitute a scientific Buddhism which will be the highest expression of belief of which the intellectual world is capable.[10]

For Taixu the culmination of Buddhism, and precisely the element that not only ran through all forms of Mahāyāna Buddhism but which surpassed both Western science and philosophy, was the doctrine that all things were nothing but Mind. According to Donald Pittman:

> Taixu came to claim that since no one school encompassed the entire canon and none was without a sound foundation in the Buddha's Dharma, practitioners would benefit from an authentic approach to enlightenment based on a broad study of scripture and tradition. Nevertheless, Xuming observes, while the reformer began to advocate forging a new religio-philosophical synthesis and was convinced that each school's perspectives were grounded in a "pure mind" (*jing xin*), he was always extremely appreciative of the idealistic philosophical perspectives that he discovered in the *Weishi* ["mind-only"] tradition. Thus, on the one hand, as Xuming asserts, it was most clearly in the terms of this tradition that Taixu "grasped the fundamental principles of Chinese Buddhism."[11]

In placing Mind at its center instead of deity, Buddhism was distinguished above other religions. In Taixu's eyes, Christianity's doctrines of God and the soul had failed in light of new scientific discoveries, and he hoped that Christians would turn to Buddhism as an alternative more in keeping with the findings of science. In his analysis of science, Taixu is mostly content to note that many of the discoveries of microbiology and astronomy appear to have been anticipated in Buddhist sutras. Taixu was also an avid reader of Western philosophy and again, he saw in Buddhism – and in particular mind-only writings – the culmination of a number of Western philosophical projects. After a summary of the trajectory of Western philosophy from the Greeks to his own age, he states:

> Today, many of the ancient theories are altogether discarded and replaced by entirely new principles, and yet, despite these changes, there is little real progress to be registered. In their search to discover the origin of the Universe these schools of thought resemble the Buddhists in their search for the Absolute Consciousness.[12]

Here we see Taixu's version of the Mahāyāna teaching of Mind recast as "philosophy" and its apical position juxtaposed with the Hegelian "absolute consciousness." Again, I am not arguing that Taixu was somehow wrong, or *misrepresenting* Buddhism. There is a certain reading under which the mind-only doctrine of mind *is* a kind of absolute consciousness. But when it is recast as "philosophy" (a preoccupation whose *Sitz in Leben* is the academic university) or as "science" (whose venue for Taixu would have been either in academia, a laboratory or a factory), Taixu's Buddhism can no longer be seen as staking out territory at the apex of the cosmos – i.e., territory formerly claimed for the emperor. It is now reduced to a "socially engaged Buddhism" (*renjian fojiao* 人間佛教) and affirms the state by simply taking on the same projects (i.e., education reform) as those spearheaded by the state.

The *Fin de Siècle* turning point

In many ways, Taixu's reforms are a legacy of the immediately preceding generation's efforts to reform the Qing Dynasty in its final days. Indeed, the Yogācāra philosophy and in particular its doctrine of mind-only played an important role both in educational reform and in the establishment of Buddhism as a "religion" even earlier among the Buddhist modernists at the very end of the Qing Dynasty/beginning of the Republican Period. But if Buddhism was becoming visible as something apart from empire and its authority, it is because the Qing emperorship as the center of gravity of the empire had been losing its centripetal force. The 1850s and 1860s saw the once invincible Qing Empire shaken by Muslim uprisings in Yunnan and even further degraded by the Christian Tai Ping Rebellion (1850–1864) that resulted in an estimated 20 million dead. In addition to internal conflicts and civil wars, the 19th century saw growing incursions by foreign powers: first the defeat at the hands of the British (the First Opium

War from 1839 to 1842, and the Second Opium War from 1856 to 1860) and then the French (1884 to 1885). Commodore Perry steaming into Japan's Edo Bay in July of 1853 and shooting his guns off, though not affecting China directly, was certainly a wake-up call to the dangers of Western technology as well. Intellectuals of the day were as keen to overthrow the Qing government as they were to resist the foreign imperialism of Europe and Japan. To the extent that Buddhism played a constitutive role in legitimating the consolidation of the Qing imperium, its stature becomes degraded with the degradation of the imperium it had legitimated. Of course, Buddhism did not completely go the way of the Qing because the legitimation of the emperor was never its only social and political function. Nevertheless, when Sun Yat-sen (1866–1925) proposes his *Provisional Constitution of the Republic of China* in 1912, its opening line states, "You shall know the truth, the truth will make you free."[13] Opening the first constitution of the Republic with a quote from the Gospel of John may in part be credited to the fact that Sun Yat-sen himself was a Christian and saw in Christianity the hope of a revolutionary spirit, but it also speaks to a radical shift that will have enduring implications for the ways that Buddhism can now be visible. For the previous 1,500 years at least in prior constitutions such as the Tang, Ming or Qing codes, sovereignty lay in the emperor, whose authority was a function of his unique cosmological position between heaven and earth. Officially sanctioned religion consisted of those cults that supported or reaffirmed the impero-cosmic ordering over which the emperor presided.

With the advent of the Republic, sovereignty now resided in the "people." Concomitant with this shift, we see that the religions (i.e., Buddhism, Daoism and Confucianism) that had traditionally anchored a singular political order with its single sovereign are now relegated to "beliefs/faiths" 信教 or "religions" 宗教, i.e., as either private opinion or as identity markers of the people to be protected under Articles 5 and 6 section 7 of the Provisional Constitution. As mentioned above, from an institutional point of view, Buddhism, Daoism and Confucianism were administratively part of the population and thus under the jurisdiction of the Department of the Interior. Christianity was dealt with by the Department of Education (since the way most Chinese encountered Christianity was through Christian schools) and through the Department of Foreign Affairs. Though there would be significant anti-Christian campaigns after the May Fourth movement of 1919, for Sun Yat-Sen the truths of Christianity could reasonably be held up as grounding the authority of the people and providing a contrast to the old regime.

We begin to see the decoupling of Buddhism from the Qing court in the late 19th century. Even as Buddhist intellectuals were becoming increasingly inured to the pull of the imperial court, the Qing court itself began to move toward different models of legitimacy. The crisis that would eventually render Buddhism visible as a "faith" dissociated from the state apparatus came to a head in 1898, when Kang Youwei (1858–1927) proposed to the young Guangxu emperor a series of reforms intended to modernize China and make it more competitive with foreign powers. These reforms, known as the "Hundred Days' Reform," were enacted almost immediately and they included a proposal that "all academies and temples in China, with the exception of those included in registers of state sacrifices, be turned into schools."[14] The schools were to embrace a 'modern' curriculum, meaning that instead of teaching Confucian classics and literature in preparation for the traditional Confucian examination, study was to focus instead on math and science. According to Vincent Goossaert, this was understood in the press as a religious reform:

> On three occasions in the following weeks, the editorial in the famous Shanghai daily *Shenbao* discussed the edict not as a piece of legislation aiming at facilitating the creation ex nihilo of a nationwide network of public schools but as the declaration of a religious reform, that is, a change in religious policy that would rid China of temple cults and their specialists: Buddhists, Taoists, and spirit mediums.[15]

In other words, what was originally worded as a call to the modernizing of education and the public appropriation of monastic property came to be understood by the public as Western reason's attack on Chinese religions and their "superstitions." Note here that "religion" was assumed to include not only Buddhism and Daoism, but other village spirit cults as well. Although the Hundred Days' Reforms were short-lived, this issue of temple confiscation proved to be a watershed moment marking a shift from religion in service of the empire to religion as "superstition" in China. From this perspective, Taixu's attempts to place Buddhist doctrine in schools should be seen as a response to the claim not 20 years earlier that Buddhism was superstition. As Goossaert documents it, Chinese perspectives on the temple reform proposals leading up to Kang's proposal differed significantly from perspectives after the fact. First of all, despite the fact that Kang really wanted to establish Confucianism as a state ideology on the model of the newly established "State Shintō" of Meiji Japan,[16] the reform itself simply wanted to convert any temple that was not officially registered as being in service of the government into a school. Goossaert notes that prior to 1900, the temple closures were understood to act on the distinction between temples that served the state and those that did not. Those temples that had imperial sanction were listed in the Sacrificial Registry (*sidian* 祀典). In addition to whatever Confucian sensibilities Kang had, the move to essentially purge non-registered temples may also have been a way to regain a bit of sovereign control lost during the Tai Ping rebellion. After the rebellion, the Qing Dynasty granted official status to increasing numbers of local temple cults – some Buddhist or Daoist, others not so easily categorized. As we will see below, while scholars of religion might worry about the boundaries between Daoism, Mahāyāna Buddhism and spirit cults in China, the recognition or lack of recognition of said boundary is largely a red herring when seen from the perspective of the exercise of power. While the Sacrificial Registry granted these cults a certain amount of protection against potential future purges, it was also a way for the Qing to coopt some of the legitimacy and perhaps even loyalty of all local temple cults.[17] As such, it was the collective weight and distribution of these cults, and not necessarily their denomination, that would prove crucial to the exercise of state power.

However, as the end of the Qing loomed closer, the tide appeared to be turning more toward constitutional rather than religious legitimation, and as early as 1875 the Qing began to slow the registration of local temple cults until about 1904 when it finally came to a stop.[18] The 20th century would witness spasmodic dismantling of these temples and their replacement by (or reoccupation) by public schools, police boxes, etc.[19] The network of officially recognized state registered temples was part of the apparatus by which the state extended its reach down to the district level. But with the fall of the entire imperial system at the birth of the Republic, the ideology that had been crucial to frame that sovereign authority as both cosmic and necessary was no longer seen as relevant. In the new Republic, as Rebecca Nedostup aptly observes, "the government no longer represented the cosmic order, but the apex of the social order – the "nanny" (*baomu*), in Sun Yat-sen's words, of the various components of society."[20]

There were multiple factors at play here. As Goosaert observes:

> A very explicit cause for the adoption of the antisuperstition discourse in many post-1900 texts was the Boxer Rebellion. The shock of the Boxer insurrection, and its dreadful consequences for China, pushed many observers into the camp of those willing to do away with village religion. Another, less explicit, motive was the religious organization of local society around temple cults, the "nexus of power" as Prasenjit Duara describes it: Temples were (and still are) places where symbolic power was vested on local leaders, where intra-and intervillage disputes were settled, and where local projects and resource management were negotiated. This organization was seen, not without reason, as the main obstacle to the building of a new vertically integrated society, in which the state is physically present in the villages and in which all villagers obey the state alone.[21]

The combination of the attempt to wrest power from local elites to create a new nation, along with a need to undermine the mechanisms of authorization for the old empire, turned unsanctioned cults into "superstition." It was against the charge of superstition that Chinese Buddhists, like their Japanese counterparts, began to argue that Buddhism was a "religion" (recently coined as "*zongjiao*"/Jap. "*shūkyō*") in part to distinguish themselves from the village cults with their seasonal festivals and processions, which could now be rendered "superstition". Censoring unsanctioned cults was nothing new; it was why the Sacrificial Registry was there in the first place. Censoring cults because they were "superstition," however, was something quite new insofar as the term now painted the offending cults as believing in something that simply does not exist.

The Qing imperium and the usefulness of Mahāyāna

The above picture of the framing or reframing of religion in the late 19th and 20th centuries resulting in its decoupling from the political arena stands in marked contrast to what had been the case earlier. If we hearken back to the Qing in its heyday, say to the time of the Qianlong Emperor (1711–1799), we find a very different picture of the place of Buddhism in the construction of imperial power within the empire. This picture, like power itself, is complicated. In general, scholars have tended to downplay the importance of Buddhism in the construction of state power in late imperial China. As Timothy Brook wryly observes of Sinologists, "Buddhism is not generally regarded as one of the elements constituting the socio-political structure of late-imperial China".[22] Brook goes on to show that part of this impression is a function of the genre of gazetteer writing in late imperial China. Magistrates who wrote gazetteer entries for their district were expected to denounce Buddhism and Daoism, even if they personally were patrons of the local Buddhist monastery. But if, as I am claiming, Mahāyāna Buddhism and its doctrines of emptiness and Mind were crucial to the structuring of sovereign authority, then how can I maintain this in light of the fact that Mahāyāna Buddhism was *never* held up as the "state religion" in late imperial China? The answer is that the set of expectations of what a "state-religion" would look like and how such a thing would wield power are more amenable to specific European contexts than to those of China. The salient religions of late imperial China were Confucianism, Daoism and Buddhism, but it would not be accurate to name any one of these as the state religion. By the same token, we should not expect any Chinese emperor to identify with one religion to the exclusion of all others. To do so would have limited his claim over a segment of the population. Rather, imperial power was wielded through an orchestrated economy or better yet, *ecosystem* of religions – and through the religions, their constituencies. And indeed, in the following chapter I will show how part of the usefulness of each of these three religions was their ability to bring other local cults into the imperial fold. Thus, Mahāyāna Buddhism was central to imperial power not as a stand-alone entity, but as a cluster of signs capable of being deployed in multiple registers. The Mahāyāna teachings of Mind and emptiness were deployed for both their polysemy as well as their polyvalency to engage and hopefully *oblige* multiple audiences simultaneously.

The Yonghegong Temple in Beijing and the political work of monuments

Probably the best place to begin to explore the polysemy and polyvalency of power and the role of Mahāyāna in the cultivation and maintenance of alliances in the Qing imperium would be with the imperial temples in Beijing where we find both imperial power and religion on display. There has been so much good work on these temples that there is really no need to discuss them exhaustively here.[23] I would, however, like to discuss a few features of the political use of these temples that I hope will illustrate a larger point about religion and power.

I begin with stelae inscribed in 1744 in which Emperor Qianlong (1711–1799) discusses the network of local cults and their subordination to the imperial center. The inscription begins with a rather academic discussion of the City God 城隍 temples:

> The emperor says: Mention of the "Walls and Moats" first appears in the Classic of Changes (*Yijing*). The usage of the terms in any detail discusses them as a sacrifice to the walls and moats of a city, one of the eight Imperial Thanksgiving sacrifices under King Yao.[24]

What follows is a first-person account of the emperor's scholarship in tracing the loss of the City Cult practice to Tang Dynasty histories and its revival in the Song. If the local cults mentioned above would have been patronized and run by local families, the shrines of the City God would have been administered by an (ostensibly Confucian) district magistrate. And just as the district magistrate had jurisdiction over the villages and hamlets within the district, so too the City God had jurisdiction over the local cults of those villages. During the Qing, the City God temples, in turn, were understood to be subordinate, and therefore bound to, the City God temple in Beijing. Here, Qianlong shows his erudition to garner the admiration (if not the support) of Confucian literati.

When he gets to the present day in the inscription, the emperor then tells us that not only are other provincial temples and their gods subordinate to the Beijing temple, but that all such City Gods receive their titles (and by extension their authority/jurisdiction) from the emperor.

> Today in the realm under Heaven, from the county, through department and prefecture, all the way to the province, at all administrative levels, no one has failed to found temples. The capital City God temple is especially looked upon as a standard by all under Heaven. None are its equal. City gods are often titled and given imperial rank according to the differential system of relations between directors and subordinates. As the gods prevent disaster and ward off evils, so the domain respects their merits.[25]

In the inscription at hand, the authority of each City God is a function of its title, indexing its relative position in the celestial hierarchy – a position indicated by the title granted by the emperor. The emperor in turn derives his authority directly from heaven and extends it through his military all the way to the borders.

> I have deferentially availed myself of the Grand Bestowal from Blue Heaven above, which extends to the entirety of the social and natural cosmos, to beyond the wilds. The various kingdoms and settlements of the western border are under our military control: they are called "nomadic

> kingdoms." Even those who have never heretofore had the protection of walls and moats have already arranged themselves in fortifications and started plowing. Raising walls that link up and extend, damming up a waterway that surrounds and entwines, they not only wall the cities as with golden teeth, they have moats full of rushes as well.[26]

The stelae ends with a discussion of those cults that were not officially recognized. Unlike his post–Boxer Rebellion counterpart, Qianlong displays benevolence by allowing the worship of these gods as well – so long as those provincial City Gods appeared at the Beijing City God temple.

> One oddity we did not change: the statues of the city gods from the provinces, which are lined up to the right and left of the side gate, each holding insignia of office. Although investigation showed that such an arrangement has no canonical reality, we do not think it was a mistake to let them stand there. Since the tableau resembles the coming and going of district magistrates, departmental and prefectural officials, as well as city governors who have come to the capital for audience, we left it standing and did not disturb it.[27]

The inscription presents the reader with something like a flowchart of power. The emperor receives his authority from a single source: heaven. He distributes this authority across the wide expanse of the Qing domain to its very limits through the distribution of titles to local gods and the sanctioning of their cults from the center. The emperor's role in the renovation and worship of the City god of Beijing then becomes the prototype of the extension of his power throughout the empire.

Here we find Qianlong asserting that the authority, prosperity and power of City God temples throughout the realm is hierarchically structured with rivulets of authority cascading down from the cult temple of Beijing at the summit and the Qianlong emperor at the apex of the summit. So, what do we call the ideology that animates this structure? If we consider that the magistrates who are most closely associated with the City God temples were Confucian degree holders, and that the titles granted these City Gods are more like Confucian titles than Daoist or Buddhist ones, then we might wish to call the Qing government "Confucian." And here we would not be wrong insofar as the Yonghegong Temple, which began as a personal chapel for the Yongzheng Emperor (1678–1735), was originally a temple used to house the tablets of the Qing imperial ancestors. Indeed, the name "Yonghe" is a reference to the Emperor Yongzheng, Qianlong's father. Confucian orthodoxy of the Qing was largely that of Zhu Xi (1130–1200) and the demonstration of filiality of the emperor toward his ancestors would have been crucial to his legitimacy among the Confucian literati managing the City God of his day. It is not surprising then that Qianlong has a long eulogy to his father inscribed in the palace.[28] This inscription, which appears in Chinese, Tibetan, Mongol and Manchu, eulogizes his father and as such renders at least the Chinese version as a "hymn on filial piety."[29] In this eulogy, he makes numerous references not only to his own father but to his grandfather and to the "tripod"[30] of their imperial reign (presumably a reference to the emperor forming a triad with heaven and earth in the *Xunzi* and the *Mean*).

In the first inscription discussed above, the Beijing City God occupies the apex of a system of City God temples (and by extension, their subordinate local cults). By Confucian logic, it occupies a position viz. subordinate temples, ministers and magistrates that the emperor occupies in relation to his domain. It was Dong Zhongshu (179–104 BCE), the inspiration behind the first imperial Confucian college in 124 BCE, who wrote, "He who rules the people is the basis 元 of the state. Issuing edicts and initiating undertakings, he is the pivot 樞機 of all living things. The pivot of all living things, he is the source/limit/peak 端 of honor and dishonor."[31] Notice here that in Dong's description of the sovereign, he employs three terms for a kind of apical limit, 元 and 端 both mean limit and origin, while 樞機 calls to mind the Daoist 太極 – great pivot, which was the celestial pole. Each of these assertions identifies the mundane sovereign with the singularity of the cosmos and its origin. Ironically (given the fact that 端 comes to mean "heresy" in later literature), it is the Zhou Dynasty idea of cosmic limit 端, not faith (信) that may come closest to what we mean by the word "religion." As Confucius warns, "To study other [cosmic] limits 異端, this is indeed injurious!" Dong's definition of the ruler as the "pivot" of all things would be repeated throughout Chinese history. Qianlong himself would no doubt have been aware of this discussion, since his grandfather Emperor Kangxi (1654–1722) references it under the heading of "king" in his *Kangxi Zidian*.[32]

There is no question that the Yonghegong inscription in which Qianlong shows his filiality to his father can and perhaps should be read in a Confucian register here. But we miss much of what is going on if we stop there. Indeed it is the *placing* of Confucianism within the larger religious economy of the temple that is important here. Religions occupy distinct spaces in the Yonghegong Temple, and stand in relations of domination or subordination through their spatial relations to other elements. But this spatialization is a coded spatialization. Kevin Greenwood has argued that the Yonghegong Temple was meant to be decoded through a particularly tantric Buddhist code as a three dimensional mandala.[33] Thus, the Chinese Qianlong inscription may be interpreted as Confucian, but this "Confucian" element is to be read as occupying a particular point on the periphery of a Buddhist mandala. In his masterful discussion of the social history of Tantra, Ronald Davidson has argued the term *maṇḍala* ("circle") was first a political term for the schematization of political alliances, with the sovereign in the center and orders of allies from his inner circle to more distant allies.[34] He argues that it is this political sense of one's "political circle" that is picked up "metaphorically" by tantric authors. Davidson's argument is, I think, brilliant and while no one quote can do justice to the complexity of the whole, I would like to consider the following paragraph from the standpoint of the Yonghegong Temple.

> Maṇḍalas are implicitly and explicitly articulations of a political horizon in which the central Buddha acts as the *Rājādirāja* [King of Kings] in relationship to the other figures of the maṇḍala. In their origin and

> evolution, religious maṇḍalas represent a Buddhist attempt to sanctify existing public life and recreate the meditator as the controlling personage in the disturbing world of Indic feudal practice. The other Buddhas and bodhisattvas live within or in proximity to his palace (*kūṭāgāra*). They assume their positions based on his will and through the agency of his bestowing coronation on them. They reflect his entourage in their own segmentary entourages, and then are ultimately dissolved into him, demonstrating their subordination to the veracity of his existence. At the borders of some maṇḍalas live the demons, snakes and other beings of marginal existence in the great charnel grounds. When a monk receives his coronation into the maṇḍala, therefore, he receives explicit authority to engage and manipulate phenomenal existence. His action presents the Buddhist institution placing an agent into the idiom and metaphor of public life, embodying the monastic institution's reactions while subverting its goals. Thus the maṇḍala represents a spiritual "state," a word that exhibits the paronomasia of both a mystical condition and a political reality in English as maṇḍala does in Sanskrit.[35]

In Davidson's argument, the political reality of medieval India was a kind of "*samānta*" or segmentary system in which a political actor forged alliances with local leaders (and, by extension, their allies) against a set of common enemies. Notice the way that the structure of authority in Davidson's description of the mandala meditations shows remarkable similarity to the structure of authority in Qianlong's inscription. In both, authority is bestowed on a central figure who then distributes it to lower and lower tiers of subordinates until it reaches the periphery of the domain. For Davidson, tantric authors have turned the political reality of "*samānta* feudalism" into a spiritual metaphor in which the meditator becomes the spiritual sovereign at the center of the spiritual mandala marking out the spiritual state. But how much of a metaphor is it when the principal meditator or mandala guru is the emperor and the mandala is a brick and mortar temple in the capital?

Davidson points out that the farther one moves outward from the center of the mandala, the more "foreign" the allies appear while nevertheless remaining a manifestation of the power of the center. Seen in this light, the placement of the emperor's filial relation to his grandfather at the periphery of the temple mandala demonstrates the ability of the emperor to manifest as a Confucian to his Confucian subordinates (as well as to his Confucian opposition) despite being a Manchu.

If the Yonghegong Temple were the only manifestation of mandala organization, all of the above might be an idle curiosity. However, Greenwood notes that when the Qing took over Beijing in 1644, they forcibly reorganized the entire city along a *maṇḍala*-like pattern with the Forbidden City being the innermost section surrounded by the Imperial City (of the central government and imperial family), the Inner City (for Manchus and Mongolian banners) and finally the Outer City, which is where Han Chinese were relocated.[36] For anyone living in a city that had been so abruptly and radically reorganized, the social memory alone would be enough for many viewers to have an intuitive sense of what they were looking at in temples like the Yonghegong Temple.

The organization of the Yonghegong Temple mirrors this city structure with the temple to Guandi and the Eastern (Confucian) Academy (representing the opposing poles of martial and civil power in classical Chinese thought)[37] on the outside marking the "Han" (majority Chinese) forms of power as outer allies to the inner "Buddhist" courts of the inner tantric mandala. Thus, if the first inscription depicts an ostensibly Confucian ordering of imperial power emanating from the capital City God and cascading across the empire to nourish even the most remote frontier shrine with imperial authority, then the placement of Qianlong's paean to his father in the outer court of the temple marks the subordination of Han discourse relative to the Tibetan Buddhist core of the inner mandala.

Encountering references to Confucian classics in the mouth of the emperor on the stela at the entrance to the temple also functions as a transition or segue to the Buddhist center. In the inscription, Qianlong doesn't just revere his father as an ancestor. In Qianlong's eulogy, Yongzheng is represented as both enlightened and as a manifestation of Śākyamuni Buddha. For the Tibetan and Mongol Buddhists at the temple (as well as for their brethren in the Tibetan realms and Mongol banners) this would have made Yongzheng not only the ancestor of the current Manchu emperor, but simultaneously the ancestor of Tibetan and Mongolian people as well. As Johan Elverskog has shown, Tibetan and Mongol histories get rewritten in the Qing to displace the origins of the Mongol people from Genghis Kahn onto Mahāsammata (the first king in the *Aggaññasutta* of the Buddhist *Dīgha Nikāya*) and Śākyamuni himself.[38] Under this reading, if Yongzheng is an imperial ancestor, he is a Buddhist one. As we will see, Qianlong's forays into the tantric Buddhism of Tibetans and Mongols is important to understand his relation not only to Tibetan and Mongol polities, but to Confucian ones as well.

Emperor Qianlong: the tantric initiate and the tantric state

When Qianlong erected the Yonghegong stela in 1744, its octagonal pavilion would have been near the entry to the original palace. In 1745, however, Qianlong ordered a renovation of the entire structure which included the addition Court II, which would have housed Tibetan and Mongolian monks studying and practicing Tantra and where the Qianlong emperor himself studied the Buddhist tantras that were to be practiced in the more interior parts of the Temple.

As Lessing documents, the tantric part of the temple contains shrines representing all of the major tantras of the day: the *Guhyasamājatantra*, *Hevajratantra*, *Kālacakratantra* and the *Cakrasamvaratantra*. There are also numerous shrines to Mahākāla ("Great Black One," the primary deity of the Mongolian Mukden temple)[39] and Yamāntaka (the wrathful manifestation of Mañjuśrī,[40] the "Ender of

Death"). Qing sources tell us that the Qianlong emperor himself studied Buddhist tantras and Gelukpa *lam rim* ("Stages of the Path") literature under the Mongolian Gelukpa monk Chankya Rolpai Dorje (1717–1786), and received initiation into the Luipa tradition of the *Cakrasamvaratantra* in 1745. While Qianlong's personal interest in tantric practice has been discussed at some length, there can be no denying that this initiation was seen as replicating (and thereby invoking) earlier famous tantric guru/royal client pairings in history. On the one hand, Chankya's choice of the Luipa *Cakrasamvaratantra* may well have been to reenact the fact that Luipa himself was to have initiated King Indrajāla of Oḍḍiyāna into the same tantra – Cankya's initiation thus replicating an older one. This is speculation. What is not speculation is the fact that the Qianlong emperor's initiation into the *Cakrasamvaratantra* was explicitly said to reenact Kublai Khan's initiation into the *Hevajratantra* by Pakpa, the nephew of Sakya Paṇḍita – making him a close relative of one of the most important figures of the Sakya lineage of Tibetan Buddhism. According to Chankya's disciple Thukwan Lobsang Chokyi Nyima (1737–1802):

Chankya declared to the Emperor,

> In the past, the Dharmaraja Leader of Beings, Phagpa conferred the *Hevajra* initiation on the Mongolian king Qubilai Sechen Khan in the water female ox year. I, likewise, conferred the *Cakrasamvara* initiation on the Great Emperor in the wood female ox year. Both of these years, though differing in element, were the same ox year.

To this, Thukwan boldly adds,

> I believe that in saying this, Chankya was [implicitly] asserting that he himself was the reincarnation of Phagpa Rinpoche. Indeed, Phagpa Rinpoche is listed in the Omniscient Panchen [Lama's] devotional verses [which chronicles] the succession of lives of the master lama [Chankya]. Moreover, Qubilai Sechen Khan was later listed among the Great Emperor's succession of lives. Undoubtedly, [the two] worked in the service of dharma in the manner of lama and patron over a garland of lifetimes.[41]

The Qianlong initiation reproduces, for Thukwan, another initiation that occurred at a pivotal moment in Chinese/Tibetan relations: the initiation of Kublai Khan (1215–1294) into the *Hevajra Tantra* by Pakpa (1235–1280). The latter initiation, in retrospect, turns out to be quite a big deal. In Tibet, this initiation would have included tantric vows that would have bound the two in an exclusive patron/priest relationship – a relationship that could then be mapped onto an *exclusive* bond between the polities that each represented. There is little reason to question whether Kublai actually received such an initiation or that it included a set of vows taken by Kublai to never denigrate his guru, Pakpa. Pakpa and his 'Khon family were enlisted into the Bureau of Buddhist and Tibetan Affairs (*Xuanzheng yuan* 宣政院),[42] and as Peter Schwieger has shown, we have evidence of the authority granted them by Kublai in the form of a decree concerning military garrisons, taxes and trade issued by Pakpa's half-brother Rinchen Gyeltsen. At the top, Gyeltsen issues the decree "by command of the Emperor" as his "imperial preceptor."[43] Yet, the initiation and obligations between Kublai and the Sakyas appear to have been advertised in Tibetan communities (in Tibetan language sources) and not in Chinese ones. For instance, the *Yar lung jo bo'i chos 'byung*, written in 1376, mentions Kublai receiving teachings from Pakpa.[44] Yet, as Shen Weirong has argued, the *Yuan shi* (compiled only nine years earlier in 1368) only mentions that a certain unnamed monk teaches Kublai Khan and his court the practice of the meditation in supreme bliss 大喜樂禪定 in addition to the practice of projecting one's life force into another (the 演揲兒法[45] or Tib. *phowa grong 'jug*) and the Fire of g*Tum mo*,[46] in which the meditator produces a kind of internal fire that rises up the mystical central channel in order to melt the "drops" in each of the *cakras*. It is thus highly probable that Kublai and his court were receiving some kind of instruction in the *Hevajra* and the Sakya "Path and Fruit" (*lam 'bras*) tradition that relies upon it.[47]

Indeed, the more likely pattern of the day was for Mongol lords to patronize many lamas from different sects. The exclusive obligations between Pakpa and Kublai Khan that would become the backbone of Chinese/Tibetan relations appear to have taken on their full political implications when they are invoked in the Qing. Qing sources had a way of rewriting the history of these lama/king encounters. Elverskog has documented how the story of the Altan Khan's granting of the title of "Dalai Lama" to Sönam Gyatso in 1577 and the latter recognizing the Altan Khan as the reincarnation of Kublai Khan (and himself as a reincarnation of Pakpa) was probably an retrospective invention of the Fifth Dalai Lama written while on his way to meet the Qing Shunzhi Emperor in 1652.[48] In fact, earlier histories of the Altan Khan showed him to patronize multiple Tibetan sects simultaneously, not just the Gelukpa. In rendering the exchange between the Altan Khan and the Dalai Lama to be exclusive, the Fifth Dalai Lama and the Shunzhi emperor could portray the relationship between the areas of Tibet controlled by the Dalai Lama and the Qing Emperor to be an exclusive patron/priest (*chö/yon*) relationship – one that notably excluded the Zunghars and the Khalkas as politically illegitimate – while also casting the new Qing Dynasty as the legitimate heir to the Yuan of Kublai.[49] According to Elverskog,

> The emperor's meeting with the Dalai Lama in many ways codified the ideal of "Buddhist rule," the "Lamaist-Caesaripapist" relationship that was to define the Buddhist Qing, since it confirmed the essential component of this vision: that indeed there was only one "priest" and one "patron." . . . The Qing engagement with the Gelukpa was thus aimed not only at bringing the Great Fifth into the Manchu orbit, but also at fostering a unifying religious discourse among the fractious Mongols. And the first evidence we have of this process of unification is from the 1652 meeting itself, in which the Dalai Lama was recognized as the supreme teacher of the Dharma during his audience with the Shunzhi emperor.[50]

Toward the end of his life, the Qianlong Emperor – after long battles on the Western frontier that included the complete annihilation of the Zunghar population[51] – makes what was perhaps the boldest attempt to assert not only the Qing Emperor's exclusive "one priest/one patron" relation to the Gelukpas, but to extend this authority to be able to name the incarnation of *all* reincarnate lamas.

In 1792, just seven years before he dies and almost 50 years after his first inscription, the Qianlong Emperor issues another inscription placed in the Yonghegong, referred to as *Qianlong's discourse on Lamas* 乾隆御笔喇嘛說, in which he explicitly states that he has used Tibetan Buddhism for political ends: "As the Yellow Church inside and outside (of China proper) is under the supreme rule of these two men, all the Mongol tribes bear allegiance to them. By patronizing the Yellow Church we maintain peace among the Mongols."[52] He then refers to Kublai naming Pakpa as "state preceptor" as the ostensive beginning of the relation between China and the Tibetans and Mongols. He acknowledges that during the Yuan (1271–1368) and Ming (1368–1644) Dynasties there were many such state preceptors at any given time. By contrast, he emphasizes that during the Qing, there is only one state preceptor, the Chankya Khutuku, who was installed as such by the Kangxi emperor (and whose future incarnation would be Qianlong's tantric guru). Just as his dynasty had bestowed this title upon the Chankya Khutuku, he states that, "The titles of *Dalai Lama* and *Paṇ-chen Erdeni* have only been conferred (by Our dynasty) in continuance of the precedents set by the Yuan and Ming dynasties."[53] This probably would have come as a bit of a surprise to many lamas in Tibet and Nepal who were apparently under the impression that they could choose their own reincarnations. The problem, as Qianlong argues, is that some reincarnate lamas or *khubilghans* among the Gurkhas were always chosen within the same clan – making the lamaship into more of a hereditary succession than he thought it should be. Qianlong then appeals to a Mahāyāna Buddhist ontology, saying, "But this is entirely against Our intentions, the more so because the Buddha was never born . . .; how could there be generations?" His solution was to create a golden urn into which the names of all eligible candidates were to be placed. Since the Qing Emperor is the one who grants titles, he would have then been the one to draw the name of the next incarnation out of the urn.

What is key for our purposes is the fact that he ends his assertion of absolute dominion over Tibetan and Mongol peoples and their reincarnate lamas by stating that his authority to do so comes not from the fact that he can (and did) annihilate any who questioned his authority, but from the fact that he had direct and personal knowledge of what he claims to be the Tibetan Buddhism. The main part of the inscription ends with the following justification:

> If one wishes to judge the merits of a thing, one must be familiar with it and understand the underlying principles. If I had not studied Tibetan scriptures, I should not be able to speak thus. When I started to learn the scriptures I was criticized ("by some Chinese", Ma. Translation) for being biased towards the Yellow Church).[54]

The tone of the 1792 inscription (which would play a prominent role in Chinese reassertion of jurisdiction over lama succession in 1936 and 1995) suggests that its intended audience was not Buddhist but Confucian, and the last statement attempts to justify why he spent so much time not only learning but *practicing* Buddhism. So why did he?

In the 1792 inscription, he presents his learning as merely so that he can know what he is talking about when making laws concerning the lamas. But we know that the Qianlong Emperor's knowledge of Tibetan Buddhism went far beyond solitary perusal of texts in the imperial library. By all accounts he not only studied, but practiced and meditated. Back in 1745 he had taken the *Cakrasamvara* initiation from Chankya. Qianlong may have placed himself under some pretty serious tantric obligations to the lama and his order, but the political payoff lay in replicating the relationships that occurred at the founding of the Yuan Dynasty. But again, representations can be recognized in the manner in which they were intended, or they can be *misrecognized* as the inverse. Whether a man is *recognized* as king or *misrecognized* as a usurper has *very* different power effects. While we might want to see Qianlong's reenactment of the Pakpa initiation to be "symbolic" – much like Barack Obama's swearing in on Lincoln's Bible sought to replicate one of the great presidencies of the past – Qianlong's reiteration here attempts to go far beyond the merely symbolic. The claim at least, is that Qianlong and Chankya *actually are* Kublai and Pakpa, that Qianlong in some sense *actually is* Mañjuśrī, and hence not only Yamāntaka, Mahākāla, Heruka, but Kublai Khan as well.[55]

Tantra, emptiness and the reincarnate emperor/lama, or why it's never too late to have a venerable past

But what it would even mean to say that Qianlong *really* is Kublai Khan. The institution of the *tulku* or reincarnate lama is so taken for granted today that it is difficult to see that it might have had to be justified through demonstrated practices represented for audiences for whom the doctrine was novel. By the time of Qianlong, I think it is fair to say that most Buddhists believed in reincarnation. But saying that Qianlong is the reincarnation of the Kublai Khan is a bit different from me saying that I am the reincarnation of Cleopatra. Mahāyāna Buddhism provides the theoretical backdrop for the statement that Qianlong *is* Kublai insofar as both of them are transformation bodies (Sanskrit *nirmāna-kāya*, Tibetan *tulku*, Mongolian *khutuku*) of bodhisattvas, yes, but also of the same *dharma-kāya*. The idea of the *tulku* had first appeared in Tibet not long before Pakpa was born. Peter Schwieger has pointed out that the first lama to be declared a reincarnation of another lama for the purposes of the transfer of abbotship was a contemporary of Pakpa, the tantric master and Kagyupa lama Karma Pakshi (1204/6–1283). It was Karma Pakshi who was declared to be the reincarnation of Düsum Khyenpa (1110–1193).[56] If Pakpa had understood himself to be a *tulku* capable of controlling his subsequent incarnations (which is what he is interpreted to have done) then he would have been in the very first generation of Tibetans to do so. Hence, in the 12th and 13th centuries when the idea of the *tulku* was a novelty, the meditation called "transfer of consciousness" that we hear was practiced in Kublai's court would have been crucial to the establishment of the very idea of controlled reincarnations[57] that would become the basis for the major institutional shifts in governance away from aristocratic families by the 15th century.[58]

Of course, merely claiming or getting someone else to declare you to be the transferred consciousness of a great person in a past life or of the *dharma-kāya* itself will only go so far even in a culture where reincarnation is largely taken for granted. Tantric ritual is a mechanism that frames the principal performer as the desired deity by invoking the deity and empowering the performer with relevant mantras. But even here the liturgy can be misrecognized as empty words angling for a self-serving prestige. In the end, the only thing that can concretize the claim to divine or reincarnated identity more than ritual and cultural representations is if the emperor is recognized to have had a personal direct experience of the consciousness that he is to instantiate. Theoretically, someone might question whether he in fact had the experience, but precisely because the experience is supposed to be "private" the claim will be a little difficult to controvert. The Qianlong emperor is therefore reported to have spent long hours not only practicing tantric ritual, but in studying the exoteric stages of the path (*lam rim* – a study that culminates in the meditation on emptiness) and in tantric meditations.[59] The latter presumably begins with meditation on the luminous mind, which then generates the central deity of the mandala.

What actually happened in the emperor's mind is politically less important than what is represented to have happened in his mind and its relationship to both the ecclesial hierarchy and the temporal one. It was in the Lama Hall constructed between 1745 and 1750 that the Qianlong Emperor took tantric initiation in 1745. According to Thukwan, the emperor came down from his throne and sat while Chankya sat on the throne and gave him initiation.[60] Presumably this would have happened in the Lama Hall. The centerpiece of the hall is a large statue of Tsongkhapa, the founder of the Gelukpa order of the Dalai Lama that Chankya belonged to. Tsongkhapa is also an incarnation of Mañjuśrī. The presiding lama would have sat on a throne immediately in front of Tsongkhapa – a move typical of Buddhist preaching venues, enabling the visual identification of the preacher with the founder with the king.[61]

At the heart of each of the tantras represented in the Yonghegong Temple is a teaching in which the initiate is to dissolve the various appearances of the world into some kind of non-conceptual, primordial mind *cum* cosmogonic font. For example, in the "Consecration" chapter of the *Hevajra Tantra*, we find that immediately after the disciple ingests a drop of the mingled fluids from the guru's sex with the yogini:

> From self-experiencing [or reflexive awareness *svasaṃvedanā*] comes this knowledge, which is free from ideas of self and other; like the sky it is pure and void, the essence supreme of non-existence and existence, a mingling of Wisdom and Means, a mingling of passion and absence of passion. It is

> the life of living things, it is the Unchanging One Supreme [or the highest syllable *paramākṣaraḥ*]; it is all pervading, abiding in all embodied things. It is the stuff the world is made of, and in it existence and non-existence have their origin. It is all other things that there are, the universal consciousness, the primeval man, *Iśvara, ātman, jva, sattva, kāla* and *pudgala*.[62]

Notice that the experience that arises from the tantric practice is one in which awareness becomes aware of itself as the very emptiness and (primordial) Mind that led to the origin of all things and which abides in the very heart of all things still. Indeed, as Robert Sharf has pointed out, one of the staples of the tantric tradition is to begin with a meditation on emptiness and to visualize Buddhist deities emerging from some kind of primal Mind. Pointing to one of the earlier tantras, the *Sarvatathāgatatattvasaṃgraha* (a.k.a the *Vajraśekharasūtra*), Sharf points to what was understood as a five-stage progression in Tang Dynasty tantras.

> In Chinese the five stages are known as *wuxiang chengshen guan* 五相成身觀, . . . and so on. These are not enumerated in the scripture itself, but are found in a number of associated ritual manuals. One of the more influential manuals was the *Jingangdingjing yujia shibahui zhigui* 金剛頂經瑜伽十八會指歸, attributed to Amoghavajra, which lists the stages as: (1), penetration of the original mind 通達本心; (2), cultivation of the bodhi-mind 修菩提心; (3), attainment of the vajra mind 成金剛心; (4), realization of the vajra-body 證金剛身; and (5), perfection of the buddha-body 佛身圓満 (T.869:18.284c22–23).[63]

In the *Vajraśekhara Sūtra*, Śākyamuni achieves enlightenment by first penetrating the original mind which is taught to be originally luminous. When the mind meditates on the mind, this is then said to be the cultivation of *bodhicitta*. From there, Śākyamuni must merely see that this mind is identical to that of all the Buddhas. Finally, once he meditates on his mind as the Buddha mind, he must merely meditate on the identity of his body with the body of a Buddha. Becoming a Buddha, in short, becomes a matter of meditating on one's mind (and then one's body and speech) as that of the Buddha. This idea of Mind as both the manifestation of emptiness and a manifestation of the Buddha is often represented in tantric material as a "mirror-mind." In the Yonghegong Temple, this mind is represented quite strikingly by the mirror hanging above the throne in the Lama Hall. According to Lessing's description:

> A globular mirror hangs in front of [the throne] from the ceiling. The lamas do not seem to regard it as the symbol of the sun, but as a representation of enlightenment (*bodhicitta*) or, more particularly, of the second category of the fivefold wisdom, the "mirror wisdom" (*ādarśa-jñāna-satya*, T. *me-long-gi lta-bui ye-śes*, Ch. *Ta-yüan-ching-chih* 大圓鏡智), the recognition of ultimate truth . . . The mirror is also recommended as a device to

> facilitate meditation. G. Tucci has pointed out its relation to *Vajrasattva*, whose statue is placed directly above it on the second floor of this hall.
>
> Besides this symbolic significance, the mirror has the magic function of discovering the otherwise invisible demons, who, when beholding their faces in it, flee in terror.[64]

The idea of the Buddha mind as a clear mirror is not just a trope in tantric forms of Buddhism, but in Chan (a.k.a "Zen") Buddhism as well. And indeed, the point of Sharf's article is to point out the genealogical relationships between Zen, tantric forms of Buddhism and what Yijing recognized as the "Buddhist Veda." Though, Qianlong himself did not engage Zen Buddhists directly, he probably didn't have to. His father, the Yongzheng emperor (1678–1735), both practiced and claimed a mastery of Zen.

Yongzheng emperor and the great Ming debate

Emperor Qianlong's rhetorical efforts focused primarily on laying claim to being heaven's pivot and demonstrations of filial piety toward his father, the Yongzheng emperor for the Confucians and toward being Mañjughoṣa for Tibetans and the Mongol banners. The energy and money he channeled into Tibetan and Mongolian representations of power and authority index the energy and money he devoted to military campaigns among Tibetans and Western Mongolians. If we find less concern with Tibetan Buddhism in the writings of the Yongzheng emperor, it may be because the latter was far more interested in withdrawing his military from the far provinces and consolidating his power closer to home.[65] More concerned with suppressing the remaining Ming loyalists in the East and South, we find the Yongzheng emperor devoting his attentions to Confucianism, Daoism and Chan (Zen) Buddhism. But like his son, he does this by, again, laying claim to the ideological apex of these religions and the networks they could claim: the mind of enlightenment. According to a gazetteer from Shuntian Prefecture dated 1886, the Yongzheng Emperor had a stela inscribed in 1726 in Bejing declaring the following:

> The Domainal Family has received the mandate of Heaven to rule. Of the many gods it gently enfolds there are none in the sacrificial canon that are not treated with seriousness and respect. How much more shall it be for those gods of the environs of the Imperial City, within the hub of the emperor's chariot? . . . Only when the gods have taken up our offerings and been thus infused with life do we have a sense of wisdom (*ge*). The way to feeling this sense of wisdom lies through integrity (*cheng*). With integrity one can enter into communication (*tong*). This communication allows us to know "rising and falling, the high and low" (that is, the relations between people and gods, the visible and invisible worlds) and the bestowing of luck upon the people. As such, it is sufficient to achieve the unhindered success of the yearly harvest, the happiness of the villages at

> work, and an increase of benefits day by day. There is nothing inappropriate about using this power to the fullest extent. I now wish, together with the people, to rely happily upon this power. Today the temple's appearance is new: the time is commemorated. Let those temple officials who have duties in this temple courtyard chant the words inscribed on this stone that they should learn how to fix their integrity within and show composure without. Let the ritual vessels be laid out precisely and the sweeping of the temple be pristine that the far-reaching aroma of sacrifice may be sweet in accordance with my thinking on the respectful performance of sacrifice to Heaven and Earth.[66]

Like the inscription of the Qianlong Emperor discussed above, the inscription here subordinates local city temples to the City God temple of the capital and connects wisdom with the cultivation of the virtues of integrity within and composure without. Yet, as Angela Zito points out in another article, unlike the Qianlong emperor, the Yongzheng emperor almost self-consciously does not position himself at the intersection of the cosmic and the social, military and cultic orders. He merely states that his family has received the mandate and then uses a number of devices to place himself along with the people.

> By speaking directly the emperor pervades the entire text, but doing so means that there will be no iconic reference to himself as the point of mediation between heaven and earth, as is usually the case. Can this form serve another purpose? Rounding out a picture of the cosmos as *ziran*, "self-so," is the orthodox king who rules by nonrule, an absence at its center. Indeed, the other direct reference to the imperial presence is made in a metaphor of absence: Especially important spirits are "within the hub of the emperor's chariot."[67]

The idea of ruling without ruling (e.g., the *wuwei* of the mythical Emperor Shun), of course, is just as Confucian as it is Daoist. Zito choses to translate *ziran* as "self-so" in order to avoid the more usual translation as "natural," since "The English word 'natural' immediately connotes an entire set of Western predispositions about the boundaries between the human and nonhuman, the biological and the artificial."[68] But if we look again at Yongzheng's appeal to the natural, we see a common strategy for legitimating any institution that exercises authority.[69]

We should not let the ostensive humility of the Yongzheng emperor fool us into thinking that he was naïve about how to wield ideology to consolidate his rule in an empire as ideologically pluralist as the early Qing Dynasty. After all, he had to embody sovereign legitimacy simultaneously to his fellow Manchus, to Tibetans and Mongols as well as to Confucian literati and Zen Buddhist monks throughout the land. We can see in the above inscription how he appeals to a Confucian understanding of the emperor as the pivot between heaven and earth at least insofar as he can claim the mandate of heaven. But this reading only scratches the surface. The inscription in question was executed in 1726, roughly

43 years after the Qing rule was fully established by the Kangxi Emperor, Yongzheng's father. At the fall of the Ming Dynasty, a Confucian literatus named Lu Liuliang wrote a treatise detailing reasons why the new Qing Dynasty was illegitimate.[70] In the late 1720s this argument was taken up by a Southern literati named Zeng Jing, who conspired along with a handful of other people to overthrow the Qing and reestablish the Ming. Even though the threat was probably small, the Yongzheng Emperor wrote a treatise on Confucian virtue in order to justify Qing rule to Confucian-educated gentry who might still harbor concerns about the legitimacy of the new dynasty. The treatise was entitled the *Dayi Juemilu* "Great Righteousness Resolving Confusion" which, according to Purdue, "The emperor required . . . to be distributed to every county school, and ordered punishments for education directors if their students had not read it."[71]

Two years later, he wrote a long treatise on Zen Buddhism entitled the *Imperial Anthology of [Zen] Discourses* (*Yuxuan yulu* 御選語錄) for the same audience of Confucian degree holders. This may sound counterintuitive, until we consider that since at least the Song Dynasty and probably much earlier, there were many Confucian scholars who were avid practitioners and patrons of Buddhism in general and of Chan Buddhism in particular.[72] His preface to the anthology gives us a sense of his understanding of the field of Buddhism and his relation to it.

> The Tathāgata's True Dharma-Eye Treasury is handed down outside the teaching [using words and letters]. The ultimate is the penetration of the three checkpoints to the principle 三關之理 which is the true explanation. One who has true speech, who does not have deluded speech, who does not have deceptive speech is the determination for the person of the way. Therefore, one must endeavor in one (of the checkpoints) and strive to get to the bottom of it. From the first to the third, step by step, all attachments will fall away. You won't be able to vacillate or dawdle as if your life was long. [Doing so, you] delude yourself and delude other people. I [朕 – *zhen*] have plumbed the depths of knowledge of these issues and do not regret that my words fall apart. [Just] follow this single finger toward the light of knowledge (*ming* 明).
>
> Now, when the learned person begins to ascend to the (first) checkpoint of liberation s/he first removes the suffering of karmic attachment and is enlightened [覺] with regard to mountains, rivers and the great earth. The ten directions of empty space are simultaneously completely dissipated 消殞. Not from (the lore of) great antiquity will s/he penetrate the hidden place of the tongue. [Rather], he knows he has attained the present seven foot long body that is nothing but earth, water, fire and wind. Its nature (*ziran*) is completely 徹底 pure 清淨 and is not hung up by even a single thread. This therefore is called the first step in penetrating the first (of the three checkpoints) in which past and future are broken.
>
> After he penetrates the first one 本參, he then knows mountains to be mountains, rivers to be rivers, the great earth to be the great earth and empty space of the ten directions to be empty space of the ten directions.

Earth, water, fire and wind 風 to be earth water fire and wind 屬. He then knows ignorance to be ignorance, *kleśas* to be *kleśas* and visibilia, sound, taste, touch and dharmas to be visibilia, sound, taste, touch and dharmas. All of these are originally distinguished and all are awakening (*bodhi*). There is not one thing that is not my body. There is not one thing that is my self. The objective world and knowledge interpenetrate. Form and emptiness do not obstruct one another. To seize great freedom always abide [in this] and never waver. This then is called penetrating the gate of seriousness. It is called the great death and the great rebirth . . .

After the penetration of the gate of seriousness, one's family home is the same as staying on the road 途. On the road, he does not abandon the family home. Bright face (Buddha) is in harmony. Dark face (Buddha) is in harmony. . . .

Therefore he is able to see the nature. At that moment there is no mind. Mind had already seen emptiness while not seeing nature. In this he appears like dry wood. The mind is equal to dead ashes. The ten thousand things arrive at the prior (state). The first emptiness has no counterpart. He is even able to endure death and sit until release, allowing the purity 精魂 from karma and consciousness, to say nothing of his attachment to the false extreme of annihilation.

Certainly the greatest change is like dancing flowers (before the eyes). It is said that cause and effect are entirely empty. He gives rein to rage 猖狂 but he does not return. How can it be that 豈 there is not one delusion in his mind? [Beings] as numerous as the sands of the Ganges are born and die but are not able to start 造 the karma of birth and death [nor?] cut off the roots of *bodhi*. Those beneath him see to obtain one that is (箇) clear and bright [*ling ling* 靈靈]. Then he is called a true person of no rank 無位真人. The forehead leaves and enters 出入? The eyebrows raise and the eyes blink. Hold erect the finger and lift the fist. Make a livelihood out of making one's consciousness divine (*shen*). Draw 張 the sun below to go beneath a single lamp. Jeweled fish eye is a bright pearl. Seek *candanam* 栴檀 (sandalwood?) in garbage/ordure earth. The bird wears a silver pill [噙著鐵丸].[73]

Yongzheng's introduction here is chock full of references to classical Zen and other Buddhist literature. These allusions allow the Yongzheng Emperor to not only establish his own erudition within Chan literature but also his own cultivation of it. By addressing the reader in first person, we get both a sense of immediacy as well the personality of its author. In so doing, he is establishing his own authority over Zen practitioners as someone who has direct and personal knowledge of Zen.

In the preface, Yongzheng mentions Mazu's (709–788) "Sun-faced Buddha/Moon-faced Buddha," and alludes to Qingyuan Weixin's (ninth century) "Mountains are mountains." The designation of "true person of no rank" was a signature expression of Linji (Jap. "Rinzai") himself,[74] while the practice of making one's mind a "no-mind" and making it like "dead ashes" or "dried wood" was the hallmark of the Caodong (Jap. "Sōtō") school from the time of Hongzhi and Qinglao.[75] The latter two teachings would have represented the two most prominent lineage distinctions of his day: the Caodong and Linji lineages that had become, respectively, the Sōtō and Rinzai lineages in Japan. Though these two schools would have significant disagreements in terms of practice, the thread that can be traced through both and into the Yongzheng emperor's discussion is the idea that the primordial mind of emptiness is the Buddha and yet is in some sense not other than the mind of the practitioner.

When Yongzheng refers to Linji's expression of "the true person of no rank," he is most likely referring to the version found in a version of the *Records of the Transmission of the Lamp* (*Chandeng lu*). The *Dongchan si* edition of this reads as follows:

> One day, Linji entered the [Dharma] Hall and said: "My fellow compatriots, within your lump of red flesh there is a true man with no rank, constantly entering and exiting the openings of your face. Any of you who haven't figured this out yet, look! At the time, a monk asked: "Who is the true man of no rank?" Linji got down off his meditation seat, grabbed the monk and said: "Speak! Speak!"
>
> The monk tried to say something. Linji let go of him, and said: "The true man with no rank – what a dried lump of shit!" He then returned to his quarters.[76]

Clearly, this story with its shocking nonsensical punchline and physical aggression was understood as a kōan and therefore something on which to meditate.[77] During the Song Dynasty the Linji lineage in China began to teach the meditation on the critical phrase (*huatou*) of such stories in order to produce doubt. According to Morten Schlütter, it is the capacity of doubt to collapse under its own weight that leads from the cultivation of doubt to the cessation of thought.[78] Although Yongzheng studiously avoids mentioning Dahui Zonggao (1089–1163) due to the latter's close ties to the literati,[79] the practice of meditating on a head phrase (or the explicit theorization of this practice) is usually traced to him. According to Schlütter:

> In a letter to an official, for example, Dahui wrote: "A monk asked Yunmen: 'What is the Buddha?' Yunmen answered: 'A piece of dried shit.' Just raise this word [in your mind], and when suddenly all your cleverness is exhausted, then that will be enlightenment." It seems that *kanhua* practice was supposed to bring the practitioner to a point where no thinking or conceptualizing of any kind is possible. But, to Dahui, a parallel function of concentrating on the *huatou* was that it focused a person's doubts. Doubts are detrimental to enlightenment, but the unenlightened mind will always have doubts. When one is immersed in *kanhua* practice, however, all doubts about other things should be forgotten in favor of (or concentrated in) the immense doubt generated by the *huatou*. According to Dahui, once doubt

is centered on the *huatou*, it will become like a huge, growing ball. Eventually, this ball of doubt will shatter, and all other doubts will disappear with it. This is the moment of enlightenment. Thus, Dahui wrote, "Great doubt will necessarily be followed by great enlightenment."[80]

While the story that Dahui meditated on most certainly does not go back to the time of Linji itself, the practice of cultivating doubt during kōan meditation – a practice that became the centerpiece of the Zen of Chinul (Korean master: 1158–1210) and of Hakuin (Japanese master: 1686–1768) – is primarily about taking doubt itself as the object of sustained meditation. When this is done, the practitioner's mind is meditating on mind itself in a kind of self-reflexive awareness. And just like visual consciousness cannot see itself, the mind is empty of mind to itself. Kōan meditation, then, is in keeping with the "perfected nature" of the Indian mind-only school and the subsequent "transformation of the basis" described by Asaṅga and Vasubandhu (third and fourth centuries). Yongzheng also mentions making the mind like dead wood. The "Silent Illumination" spread by Hongzhi similarly refers to a kind of cessation of thought, "becoming like dry wood" as Yongzheng states it. If we go back to Hongzhi's sermons, it appears that this practice was intended to produce a state of mental cessation homologous with the origins of the cosmos itself.

> Completely silently be at ease. In true thusness, separate yourself from all causes and conditions. Brightly luminous without defilements, you directly penetrate and are liberated. You have from the beginning been in this place; it is not something that is new to you today. *From the time before the vast eon when you dwelled in your old [original] home, everything is completely clear and unobscured and numinous and singularly bright.* But although this is the case, it is necessary that you act on it. When you act on it in this way, you must not give rise to the smallest strand of hair and not conceal a speck of dust. Cold and *like dry wood*, [you should practice] the great rest with broad and penetrating comprehension [*kuoche mingbai*]. If your rest and cessation is not complete and you wish to go to the realm [of the Buddha] and to leave birth and death, then [you should know] there is no such place. Just as you are, you must break through, understanding without the defilement of discursive thinking, and be pure without any worries.[81]

Indeed, it would certainly appear that the enlightenment sought by Zen Buddhists of all stripes was to attain a mental state understood to be both prior to (or underlying) thought as well as prior to (or underlying) the cosmos itself. In this structure, the ultimate source or cosmic font of all things is mind prior to thought (i.e., no-mind 無心).[82] The manifest cognitions of the cosmic panoply derive from this font and are subordinate to it in the sense of being its derivatives or progeny. The mind of no-mind, then, turns out to be the ultimate ancestor. (I shall return to this point in the following chapter.)

This assertion works in two ways. On the one hand, from the standpoint of mind-only doctrine, all perceptions are derivative of the universal mind. By the same token, we could also take this to be an assertion of the evolution of Zen itself. To the extent that Zen is said to be "the direct transmission of the mind of the Buddha apart from words and letters,"[83] the ultimate ancestor of all Zen lineages is precisely the "Mind of the Buddha," that Yongzheng says the heretics cannot penetrate. In penetrating the Buddha mind, it is not so much that one becomes a Buddha as one manifests the Buddha that one already is.

But we have been here before. In our discussion of the Qianlong emperor and the five stages of tantric practice from the Tang Dynasty, we noted that the first stage was to penetrate the original mind of the Buddha (referenced in the mirror hanging in the Lama Hall of the Yonghegong Temple), and from there to manifest the Buddha mind and the Buddha body. In short the description of the goals and the processes of Zen Buddhism and tantric Buddhism as understood in the court of an imperial father and son converge in the equation of mind with primordiality.

The Yongzheng emperor was not the first to present the essence of Mahāyāna Buddhism in this way. Indeed, the precedent trails backward both within Zen as well as within other schools of Buddhism in China. While modern practitioners and scholars of Zen see a watershed of Zen in the Song Dynasty in the writings of Dahui Zonggao and Hongzhi, the Yongzheng emperor appears to have been far more influenced by the slightly earlier 10th-century Zen master Yongming Yanshou, of whose *Records of the Source Mirror* [宗鏡 *zong jing*] he made an imperial abridged version.[84] Although Dahui Zonggao was not yet born, Yongming was aware of the subitist or "sudden enlightenment" rhetoric circulating among the Zen masters of his day, and yet he argues that Zen is perfectly concordant with the teachings of all the sutras and śāstras *insofar as the essential feature of both is the teaching of the mind.* Yongming states that his purpose in writing the work is

> to make evident the great purpose of the patriarchs and Buddhas and the correct implicit truth [*zong*] of Buddhist scriptures and treatises, I have condensed the profuse writings of Buddhism, seeking out only the essential teachings. By provisionally putting forth questions and answers, and citing extensively [from scriptures and treatises] to provide evidence, I advance that universal mind is the implicit truth [*zong*], revealing the myriad dharmas like a mirror [*jing*]. I have brought together here the profound doctrines formulated in times past, and selected and summarized what is contained throughout the entire corpus of writings in the "treasure storehouse" [i.e., canon of Buddhist scriptures]. All Buddhist writings are represented here.[85]

Welter translates *zong* here as "implicit truth" instead of the more common "ancestor," "ancestral lineage" or "school of thought,"[86] and there is certainly a sense in which he is correct. But I think we can retain the polyvalence of the term by translating it as "source" instead of "implicit truth" since Yongming uses the word to denote a kind of essential common factor of all Buddhist teachings.

Moreover, Yongming feels free to use both familial and imperial metaphors to describe mind as source; at one point he refers to this *zong* as "the deep abode of myriad good deeds, the profound origin of all wisdom, the precious ruler of all existence, or the primordial ancestor of the multitude of spiritual beings."[87] And for Yongming, it is the universal mind which is the common source of *all* Buddhist teachings, not just for Zen and its sometime rival, the Huayan school.[88] But key to his argument is the fact that this mind is, in fact, mindless. For him, it is this feature that connects Zen practice to the "mind-only" teachings of the *Laṅkāvatāra Sūtra.*

> Internally or externally, there is nothing to seek. Let your original nature reign free, but do not give reign to a "mind" [that exists over and above] nature. When a scripture [i.e., the *Laṅkāvatāra*] says: "All the various deliberations give rise to [notions of] physical bodies; I say they are accumulations of the mind [i.e., mind-only]," it refers to "mindless mind. 即無心之心.[89]

Elsewhere, he holds this same *zong* to be emptiness itself:

> If you are suddenly made to delve into the teaching of emptiness and experience its initial fruits, you will at once receive a prediction of future fame as a *tathāgata* . . . There is never a single dharma not tacitly joined to this implicit truth . . . [*zong*].[90]

The polyvalency between *zong* as ancestor/lineage and *zong* as source is particularly important for Yongming, since it is precisely the claim of Zen that it transmits the original mind of enlightenment and that Zen lineages are precisely lineages of this transmitted mind.

So how did the Yongzheng emperor's display of Zen erudition play out politically? According to Jiang Wu,[91] Yongzheng had studied and practiced Zen long before he became emperor. However, despite the fact that he studied and practiced Zen at the nearby Bailin monastery, when he did have a Zen enlightenment experience he did not have this experience confirmed by Jialing Xingyin, the Zen master at that monastery. On the contrary, although Jialing was eager to confirm the prince's experience, Yongzheng turned to the resident Mongolian Khutuku, Chankya Khutuku Ngag-dbang-blo-bzang-chos ldan (1642–1714) – the previous incarnation of the lama who would initiate his son, the Qianlong emperor, in 1745 – to confirm his Zen breakthrough. The latter, of course, only did so on the prince's third attempt, declaring that he had finally achieved "Great Freedom" (大自在). This is probably one of the first recorded cases in history of a Zen enlightenment being confirmed by a tantric master, and we are probably safe in assuming the choice was not arbitrary, since the emperor claimed authority over Zen as well as Tantric Buddhists.

The Yongzheng emperor composes the *Yuxuan yulu* as his pronouncement of a kind of Zen orthodoxy in 1733.[92] Prior to his intervention, there was no central authority to define Buddhist orthodoxy. Many Chinese emperors had outlawed sects in the past or had made lists of approved cults. And needless to say, not every Zen lineage saw eye to eye about what Zen was or should be. However, prior to the Yongzheng emperor, no other emperor had ventured to tell a religious group what its doctrines and practices ought to be. Why does he do so in 1733? Since many of the rebellious Ming loyalists considered themselves to be experts in Zen, if Yongzheng had merely claimed book knowledge of Zen his opponents would simply champion the opposing interpretation of Zen by claiming superior erudition to that of the emperor.[93] If he were to have any "street cred" at all, he would have to demonstrate that he had direct knowledge of the truths that his opponents had yet to discover. Thus, when the Yongzheng emperor intervened in one of the major Zen debates of his day,[94] or more to the point, when he wrote a treatise claiming his own enlightenment and defining the essence of Zen (by compiling an anthology of "the best of Zen" quotes) he threw down a gauntlet that had to be respected. He even invited any who disagreed to come to court and debate him.[95] At this the remaining Ming loyalists would have to either put up or shut up, since picking a fight with the Qing emperor in the late 17th century was not advisable. We should, therefore, pay some attention to what the Yongzheng emperor asserted to be Zen orthodoxy. Thus when he, in the preface quoted above, invites any perspective reader to follow his finger pointing at "illumination/wisdom" (*ming* 明), we might want to read this visual pun on the more common expression "the finger pointing at the moon" (*yue* 月) – a graphic pun that is clearly a veiled jab at Ming loyalists.

Now, I do not want to claim that all Mahāyānists throughout Chinese history thought of the primordial mind, or the mind of emptiness to be the one root and singular starting point of all Mahāyāna – although I have suggested that there were prominent authors who held to this position. Rather, what I have demonstrated here is that the Mahāyāna recognized by at least two emperors in the Qing Dynasty was not only closely associated with such a primordial mind but that the latter was deployed as part of a larger strategy to consolidate power across multiple constituencies with longstanding prior commitments to precisely these teachings. These two emperors were arguably the most powerful men in the world during their lifetimes. Mahāyāna was one of the reasons that they were.

Notes

1 Certainly therapeutic interpretations of Mahāyāna can be seen in medieval writers such as Bankei. See, Bankei (2000).
2 Duara (1991), p. 76.
3 Nedostup (2001), pp. 37–38 shows that the qualifier "within the scope of the law" was alternately proposed and rescinded in drafts of the constitution from 1912 to 1946 as a qualifier to the right to freedom of belief.
4 Ibid., p. 36, Nedostup argues that there were two reasons why Christians were treated differently. The first is that the term *zongjiao* was coined with Christianity as its prototype and so its status as a "religion" was not really in question. Second, Christianity, unlike Buddhism, Daoism and Islam, was under the jurisdiction of the Ministry of Education and Foreign Affairs, while Buddhism, Daoism and Islam were under the Office of Ritual and Censors in the Ministry of the Interior.

5 See McHale (2004), p. 133.
6 Welch (1967), p. 19.
7 See Goossaert (2006), p. 320.
8 Taixu (1928), p. 24.
9 Taixu (1928), pp. 24–25
10 Ibid., p. 27.
11 Pittman (2001), p. 86.
12 Taixu, p. 62.
13 Yat-Sen (1912), "你們必曉得真理, 真理必叫你們得以自由."
14 Goossaert (2006), p. 307.
15 Ibid.
16 Breen and Teeuwen (2010).
17 On the role of these local temple cults in the negotiation of center-periphery relations, see Zito (1987) and Duara (1988).
18 Goossaert (2006), p. 326.
19 Duara (1991).
20 Nedostup (2001), p. 85.
21 Goossaert (2006), pp. 327–328.
22 Brook (2005) p. 158.
23 I would like to mention in particular, Kevin Greenwood (2013) and his work on the Yonghegong Temple.
24 Zito (1996), p. 80.
25 Ibid.
26 Ibid., 81.
27 Ibid.
28 Lessing (1942), pp. 9–12.
29 Ibid., p. 13.
30 Ibid., p. 11.
31 De Bary et al. (1999), p. 298
32 Kanxi (1850).
33 Greenwood (2013).
34 Davidson (2002), chp. 4.
35 Davidson (2002), pp. 131–132.
36 Greenwood, p. 38.
37 Ibid., p. 49: *Wenzuo wuyou* 文左武右 ("civilian left, military right"). On this principle and its relation to gendered power, see Boretz (2011).
38 Elverskog (2006), p. 149.
39 See Grupper (1979).
40 Emperors have been identifying as bodhisattvas in China since the reign of Emperor Wu on the Liang (r. 502–549), and with Mañjuśr in particular since at least the time of Kublai Khan (r. 1260 to 1294) [see Farquhar, (1978); Janousch (1999)]. In identifying with Yamāntaka, the Qianlong emperor not only identifies with a particularly powerful form of Mañjuśr, but also identifies with all of the previous emperors who also identified with Mañjuśrī and his shrine on Mt. Wutai.
41 Illich (2006), pp. 491–492.
42 Weirong (2011), p. 542.
43 Schwieger (2015), p. 8.
44 Personal communication. Tenzin Ringpapontsang.
45 Weirong, 544.
46 Earlier in the *Yuan Shi*, the title "Treatise of Great Supreme Bliss" is said to be the Chinese translation of "*Xiebaizala*" Hevajra 歇白咱剌. See Weirong.
47 Weirong mentions both were strong in Mongol and Tangut circles during the 13th century.
48 Elverskog (2006), pp. 101–109, esp. 107.

49 When the *chöyon* relationship is invoked in terms of Pakpa and Kublai Khan, the "*yon*" is understood to be the Dalai Lama. However, as Schwieger points out, through much of the 17th century, when the *chöyon* relationship is invoked in official documents, the *yon* actually refers to the regent, not the Dalai Lama. See Schwieger (2015), p. 57.
50 Ibid., pp. 104–105
51 Perdue (2005), pp. 282–287.
52 Lessing, p. 59.
53 Lessing, p. 60.
54 Lessing, p. 61.
55 Ying Chua (2003), p. 46 refers to an inscription from 1246 that explicitly identifies Kublai Khan with Mañjuśrī. "That blessed bodhisattva, the Emperor Secen [the Wise Emperor, i.e., Kublai], possessed vast wisdom, about whom the prophesy was made that there would be someone named 'The Wise One from the vicinity of Mount Wutai [Mañjuṣrī],' who would become a great emperor." Also, see Farquhar (1978).
56 Schwieger, p. 18.
57 See Ibid., p. 12.
58 Ibid., p. 23.
59 Illich, p. 480.
60 This replicates Aśoka giving up his throne to a monk named Nigroda in the *Mahāvaṃsa.* See Walser (2009).
61 See for example the seated Buddha image in the *caityagṛhas* at Ellora.
62 Snellgrove, (2010) pp. 81-82; Sanskrit page 36. *Svasaṃvedyād bhaved jñānaṃ svaparavittivarjitaṃ*
Khasamaṃ virajaṃ śūnyaṃ bhāvābhāvātmakaṃ paraṃ
prajñōpāyavyatimiśraṃ rāgārāgavimiśritaṃ
sa eva prāṇināṃ prāṇaḥ sa eva paramākṣaraḥ
sarvavyāpī sa evāsau sarvadehavyavasthitaḥ
sa evāsau mahāprānaḥ sa evāsai jaganmayaḥ
bhāvābhāvau tadudbhūtau anyāni yāni tāni ca
sarvaṃ vijñānarūpaṃ ca puruṣaḥ purāṇa īśvaro
ātma jīvaṃ ca sattvaṃ ca kālaḥ pudgala eva ca
sarvabhāvasvabhāvo 'sau māyārūpī ca saṃsthitaḥ.
63 Sharf (2017), p. 97, note 16.
64 Lessing, pp. 65–66.
65 Perdue, pp. 240–255. He was not always able to accommodate this interest, as affairs in Lhasa and among the Zunghars kept drawing his military into campaigns (some of them disastrous) on the Tibetan plateau. Also, see Purdue, Appendix.
66 Zito (1996), pp. 78–79.
67 Zito (1987), p. 346.
68 Ibid., p. 338
69 As Mary Douglas observed long ago: "It is assumed that most established institutions, if challenged, are able to rest their claims to legitimacy on their fit with the nature of the universe. A convention is institutionalized when, in reply to the question, "Why do you do it like this?" although the first answer may be framed in terms of mutual convenience, in response to further questioning the final answer refers to the way the planets are fixed in the sky or the way that plants or humans or animals naturally behave" Douglas (1986), pp. 46–47.
70 See De Bary et al. (2010) vol 2, pp. 18–25. Much of Lu's argument involved a racial element insofar as, according to him, the Qing were barbarians and the civilized should never bow down to barbarians.
71 Perdue, p. 471.
72 Schlütter (2008), pp. 26–30; Brook (2005), ch. 8; and Brook (1993).
73 X. 1319, p. 523c8–524a20; for a discussion see Wu (2008), chapter 6.
74 See Welter (2008), pp. 87–90.

75 Schlütler, p. 132.
76 Welter (2008), pp. 135–136.
77 Welter shows, however, the ways that the story morphed from a simple sermon to include these violent elements over time. See Welter, chapter 5.
78 Schlütter, p. 109.
79 Wu (2008), pp. 174, 258.
80 Schlütter, pp. 108–109.
81 Schlütter, p. 152.
82 Robert Sharf discusses a number of early Zen sources that hold up some version of no-mind as the goal. See Sharf (2014), pp. 945ff.
83 See, e.g., Pine (1989) pp. 2–3.
84 Yongzheng (2003), vol 2.
85 Welter (2011), p. 240.
86 In modern Mandarin, the term still conveys an interesting range of meanings that combine a sense of origin, ancestry and political power. For example, *zong* itself still means ancestor or clan or school or purpose, 宗 *zongjiao* 宗教 means religion, *zhengzong* 正宗 – authentic, *zongmiao* 宗廟 ancestral temple, *zongshe* 宗社 the state or country, *zongshi* 宗室 imperial and *zongzhuquan* 宗主權 suzerainty.
87 See Welter (2011), p. 234: 眾哲之玄源。一字之寶王。群靈之元祖.
88 On this school, see Williams (2009), chapter 6.
89 Welter (2011), p. 252.
90 Ibid., p. 239.
91 Wu (2008), pp. 166–168.
92 Ibid., p. 177.
93 Ibid., pp. 181–182.
94 On this debate, see Wu, chapter 6.
95 Wu, p. 180.

4

THE IMAGE OF EMPTINESS ACROSS THE LANDSCAPE OF POWER (CHINA: 11TH CENTURY BCE – 15TH CENTURY CE)

As important as the ideas of emptiness or the cosmic mind were for the statecraft and "internal colonialism" of the Yongzheng and Qianlong emperors, there is a certain danger in focusing only on the sovereign. I do not want to give the impression that the doctrine of emptiness or mind is *really* about politics, and not about personal enlightenment, sorcery, exorcism, etc. On the contrary, emptiness can only be a political force when it is *already* forceful in all these other domains. We have already seen this with the authority of the Dalai Lama. The political authority of the Dalai Lama will only be fully appreciated in a new cultural context if there are some who have direct and personal knowledge of his cosmic significance. There is nothing like private experience cultivated in meditation to vouch for public authority. In this chapter, I will explore ways in which the structures and images of authority and obligation found in local populations are coopted by royal courts through the use of specific images in ritual and meditation to turn the focus of local obedience from local polities to the imperial center. In other words, to truly understand how empires become powerful, we have to begin to look at the imperial center from the perspective of the populations that will ultimately grant it power. I will show that the image of emptiness was central to court strategies to coopt sets of obligations already at play in local populations from as early as the Shang Dynasty (second millennium BCE), i.e., long before Buddhism ever arrived in China. Indeed, one of the central theses of this chapter is to show that images can have the social and political effects that they do if and only if they are *not* exclusive to any one religion. When Chinese began to embrace Buddhist discussions of emptiness, it was because they could recognize it as being similar in structure and function to something that they already had. I then show that this image of emptiness continued to be part of court strategies well into the Ming even before (as we saw in the last chapter) it became part of the strategies of Yongzheng and Qianlong in the Qing.

Before I get into the historical materials, I would first like to take a brief theoretical detour into the nature of power. Contrary to the Marxian position of *The German Ideology* in which "the ideas of the ruling class are in every epoch the ruling ideas,"[1] i.e., in which the ruling class manufactures ideology and then feeds it to the masses, what I am arguing here is that for any ideology to be considered "ruling" it must *already be authoritative* among those who are to be ruled. Much ink has been spilled on issues of the reach of the state and center-periphery relations. But, if we examine some of the ways that ideological power works, the center-periphery dichotomy turns out to be a red herring. Ruling ideologies cannot really be created; they are at best coopted. But since governance is hardly the exclusive domain of the imperial capital (as every monastery, village council or PTA president knows), we should be sensitive to the fact that cooption goes in both directions. This is possible because power is exerted, manipulated, coopted or delegated through the currency of *images* of power.

Power has to be transacted or at least displayed through such images precisely because it is itself imageless. Unlike concepts like "chair" or "nail" that quickly bring to mind a prototypical token of the class, the words "power" or "authority" do not conjure to mind any particular image. Power is an abstract concept despite the fact that its effects can be devastatingly and brutally concrete. Yet to wield it, it is necessary to render it readily understandable in some way. As Lakoff and Johnson point out, many of our abstract concepts begin life as metaphors grounded in "image-schemas" of more concrete phenomena. In other words, while we do not have a mental picture of something abstract like frustration, if I say she is "spinning her wheels," the mental image of a car being stuck in the snow or mud structures our experience of the frustration being talked about. They point out that while we have a number of different image schemas to choose from to describe abstract concepts, our experience of the abstraction retains the structure of the image scheme we use to represent it. They call this the "invariance principle."

> In the examples we have just considered, the image-schemas characterizing the source domains (containers, paths) are mapped onto the target domains (categories, linear scales). This observation leads to the following hypothesis, called "The Invariance Principle": Metaphorical mappings preserve the cognitive topology (that is, the image-schema structure) of the source domain, in a way consistent with the inherent structure of the target domain.[2]

In ancient China, there are three image-schemas that become metaphors of power in imperial ideologies: the patriarchal ancestor, the celestial pole and the soil. Each of these three become metaphors for authority as arising from a single point of origin and each would become both the site and the stake of struggles between Confucianism, Daoism and Buddhism. The occasional antagonism between the latter three,[3] then, derives more from the fact that their constituent groups were vying with one another for exclusive claim to the same image rather than their being necessarily incommensurate and incompatible doctrines.

In the following, I will be arguing that each of these three image-schemas were central and structured discourses of power in pre-modern China and that each converged with the image of emptiness as an important component of the semiotics of power and authority throughout Chinese history. The semiotics of emptiness and its signification of authority are not exactly straightforward and will require some explanation. We all know what emptiness is. I walk to where I parked the car and to my horror find the parking space empty. Similarly, I assume that we all have at least a passing acquaintance with our relatives and ancestors and with the pole star in the sky or soil from the ground. These are items that are simply among the *realia* that populate our lives. But when used in discourses of power in China, they have to be treated as what Stuart Hall has dubbed "coded signs."

For Hall, a coded sign is another way of talking about Pierce's "iconic sign." An icon represents the signified by having some of its features. For Hall, even video footage of a dog will be a coded sign insofar as the image has only some of the features of the real dog (i.e., "it can bark but it can't bite").[4] As such, even such a "naturalistic" representation as video of a dog is still interpreted within certain discursive codes.

> Iconic signs are therefore coded signs too – even if the codes here work differently from those of other signs. There is no degree zero in language. Naturalism and 'realism' – the apparent fidelity of the representation to the thing or concept represented – is the result, the effect of a certain specific articulation of language on the 'real'. It is the result of a discursive practice.[5]

Thus, even things that we consider to be 'naturally there' are in fact always already embedded in discourse. It is only the degree of hegemony of the discourse that renders the discursive coding of the object invisible. If I show a video of a man taking his dog for a walk, we might understand it to be a perfectly natural situation that needs no extra information to interpret it. But this is precisely because we live in a cultural context in which pet ownership is taken for granted. Feral dogs don't need humans to take them around the block to pee. For Hall, the producers and distributers of the video have "encoded" the image to be interpreted through a hegemonic code that interprets the man as the dog's owner. The image only attains full sense if the viewer understands pet ownership.

Once the image has been produced and disseminated, the producer is no longer in control of the way it is decoded. Hall argues that there are analytically three types of decoding. Most signs are decoded according to the way they were encoded precisely because the code is hegemonic. This is the dominant-hegemonic position.

> The definition of a hegemonic viewpoint is (a) that it defines within its terms the mental horizon, the universe, of possible meanings, of a whole sector of relations in a society or culture; and (b) that it carries with it the stamp of legitimacy – it appears coterminous with what is 'natural', 'inevitable', 'taken for granted' about the social order.[6]

Thus, if I say "the tank is empty" or "the pole star is in that direction" the discourses about pole stars and empty gas tanks are so hegemonic that their referents appear to simply be "objective" and the code used to decode them invisible. When we come up with a metaphor, we are extending the code into new territory. The listener knows how to decode it, but the coding is to some extent more visible. This is what Hall calls "negotiated decoding."

> Decoding within the negotiated version contains a mixture of adaptive and oppositional elements: it acknowledges the legitimacy of the hegemonic definition to make the grand significations (abstract), while, at a more restricted, situational, (situated) level, it makes its own ground rules – it operates with exceptions to the rule. It accords the privileged position to the dominant definitions of events while reserving the right to make a more negotiated application to 'local conditions', to its own more corporate positions. This negotiated version of the dominant ideology is thus shot through with contradictions, though these are only on certain occasions brought to full visibility. Negotiated codes operate through what we might call particular or situated logics: and these logics are sustained by their differential and unequal relation to the discourses and logics of power.[7]

A simple example of this can be found in political discourses in which the lord of the kingdom would have been a known figure that was 'naturally' available. Everybody knew what a king was. The term "lord" is initially used metaphorically to talk about the sovereignty of God. But when we get Christians calling out, "Lord!" as a name of a deity, the coding has become hegemonic and "Lord" now simply names one of the entities that populates the natural world for that community. Of course, and this is key, what starts out as "metaphorical" or a "negotiated decoding" can become the dominant or hegemonic code.[8] When this happens, the code becomes once again invisible and the sign no longer visible as metaphorical: it is now a thing in its own right.

The ancestor image

I think it is fair to say that the coding of father, mother and child became hegemonic (which is not to say homogeneous) quite early on in human history. Probably one of the earliest recorded negotiated decoding of familial relations for political purposes in China can be found in the records of the Shang Dynasty (ca. 1600–1046 BCE). In the Shang Dynasty (if not before), the kings would inaugurate sacrifices for their dead relatives, thereby rendering them "ancestors" *zu* 祖, who would then be established in the court of the high god, Di 帝, where they could entertain (*bin* 賓) him.[9] The cult of the ancestors was a crucial element in the construction of power in the Shang capital, and yet this early model of imperial authority is derived from what we have to assume was a common and presumably ubiquitous experience of authority: having parents and having to obey them. In other words, obedience in the context of families is a kind of raw material that is already out there – the Shang cult just had to mine it and forge it into something recognizably authoritative and yet at the same time no longer recognizable as *common* parental authority. Conversely, if obedience to relatives were not already ubiquitous, there would be no reason to ritualize it.

The Shang take the image of obedience to one's parents and denature it through a liturgy and cult to render the Shang 'ancestors' a category separate from everyone else's mere dead relatives. One could not become an ancestor merely by dying; sacrifices were necessary to set them up in Di's court. Hence only the king would have seven generations of ancestors established in heaven and therefore only he could have significant influence on Di himself. As Michael Puett observes, it is not that the Shang assumed the cosmos to be hierarchical; rather, "instead of representing a bureaucratic mentality, the ritual involved an attempt to create hierarchy. Hierarchy was not an assumption; it was the goal."[10]

Shang bone oracles show that in the chain of ancestors the more recently deceased an ancestor, the more likely it would be to haunt the living and need to be appeased by sacrifices. Conversely, the more remote the ancestor, the more powerful but also the more abstract he or she would be represented. To some extent, this follows the logic of patriarchy. If the parent has authority over the child, then the grandparent has authority over the parent and the child *ad infinitum*. The more remote the ancestor, the more theoretically authoritative they become. But since authority indexes temporal remoteness from the present, an increase in authority runs in tandem with a fading of familial memory of the ancestor's personality. As a result, if we are to posit a maximal authority in this lineage, then it would correspond to the point of maximal abstraction.[11] And this is pretty much what we find with Di. He does not receive sacrifices himself during the Shang and was considered too remote to deal with directly. The Shang would appeal to their immediate ancestors to entertain other ancestors to entertain Di in order to influence him.[12]

The image of emptiness: Di, space and the celestial pole

As an image of both the absolute limit of authority and impersonal abstraction, it should not come as a surprise to find the image of emptiness used to represent ultimate ancestry/authority. We find emptiness becoming a coded icon for the power and authority of Di himself. As David Pankenier has argued,[13] it is likely that the god Di was understood to either be or to occupy the celestial pole. As Pankenier notes, the main buildings of the Shang ritual center at Yinxu were oriented on an axis that runs between 5 and 12 degrees east of true north-south.[14] He argues that, due to axial precession, sometime around 2775 BCE the star Thuban would have occupied the exact celestial pole and would have been the pole star (our pole star, Polaris, would have been a long way off). By the beginning of the Shang Dynasty, the true celestial north would have been almost exactly in the middle of Thuban and Kochab – making the true celestial pole the black, *empty* space in between the two. Pankenier argues that the original glyph found on Shang bone oracles for the character Di traces out the visible stars surrounding the celestial pole with intersecting lines between the stars marking the empty pole itself. While this spot was an empty blackness, it was encoded through the larger discourse about kingship, ancestry and the heavens to be read in the context of absoluteness. But over the course of the Shang, Di as the emptiness of the celestial pole became the hegemonic coding; Di *naturally* ruled his court and emptiness simply *was* the pivot of the cosmos.

> Perhaps it is not too farfetched to imagine this shape subsequently being adopted to symbolize the supreme numinous power resident at that strangely empty spot in the sky. The gradual obsolescence of the polar location so identified by the time of Shang ascendency in the mid- to late second millennium BC could also have produced the easterly offset of structures at this epoch, given the margin of error such a method likely entailed.[15]

Sarah Allen in a subsequent article[16] has argued for a different genesis of the Shang character for Di and presents an argument that Di should simply be interpreted as the pole star itself – without ever identifying what that pole star would be. On the one hand, given the orientation of Shang architecture toward Kochab that Pankenier discusses, she might be right for the Shang. But identification of the celestial pivot with any particular star would have become increasingly difficult in the Zhou because as Pankenier notes, "Unlike Thuban, however, Kochab never approached closer than 6.5° to the pole, and by the mid-1st millennium, during Confucius' time, the pole was withdrawing from the vicinity of Kochab."[17] He points out that when Confucius refers to the "North Star" as the pivot of authority, he uses the character *chen* (辰 i.e., an asterism) instead of the more usual *xing* 星 for star.

Allen might be correct that the early Shang and perhaps even the early Zhou Dynasty (i.e., the Western Zhou: 1046 until 771 BCE) understood Di to be a pole *star*. But for our purposes, the relevant question is whether Di represented authority because he was a star or whether he represented authority because of his position *vis-à-vis* the rest of the revolving cosmos. There are lots of stars, but few that can even be charitably interpreted to have the cosmos revolve around them. As the Zhou Dynasty continued and Kochab moved progressively farther from the celestial pole, this interpretive charity would start to feel some strain. So it is certainly possible that the equation of the *dao* with emptiness that we begin to see in early Daoist texts may have something to do with the precession of the axis and the fact that the point in space that seemed to control everything (without appearing to do anything) was manifestly empty.

In the way that the ultimate ancestor codes ultimate authority in the form of a temporal limit, Di as celestial pole becomes a coded image of authority read here as a spatial limit – both as zenith but also as a center to any possible periphery. As Confucius famously pointed out,

> Lunyu 2:1, The Master said: To conduct government by virtue may be compared to the Northern Asterism 北辰: it occupies its place, while the myriad stars revolve around it.[18]

The ideal of rule, both in Daoist and Confucian circles, is a kind of effortless (*wuwei*) rule in which the ruler does nothing and all things fall into place of their own accord. The ideal exemplar of this kind of rule is the legendary Shun, who merely sat in his house and, like celestial north itself, faced south.

The system of ancestral sacrifice carried over into the Western Zhou Dynasty with a few minor adjustments, namely that Heaven (Tian) could now remove its mandate from an existing ancestral line and replace it with another if that lineage was considered morally corrupt. The second change is that the earlier entity that marked spatial ultimacy, Di, now becomes the first ancestor of the Zhou,[19] thereby joining what had been two separate lines of thought in the Shang.

The role of ancestry and the display of filial perfection in one's familial relations would become crucial to court politics insofar as the Western Zhou established its control over the empire through enfeoffment of family members. Enfeoffment was both empowerment and subordination as it involved both the granting of earth and the erasure of independent ancestry. According to Von Glahn:

> Later histories record that most benefices were awarded to men bearing the royal surname, Ji. By subsuming most ruling lineages into the royal clan, the Zhou perhaps sought to obliterate the ancestry of formerly independent noble lineages, yoking their fortunes even more tightly to those of the royal house. The protocols of investiture also included an important rite wherein the vassal received a clod of earth taken from the Soil Altar (*She*) of the royal capital, which then was placed at the Soil Altar of the vassal's own capital. The tangible joining of king and vassal through the Soil Altars, whose role in Zhou ritual life paralleled that of the ancestral temples, no doubt reinforced the vassal's awareness of the derivative nature of his own sovereign powers.[20]

By Confucius' time during the first half of the Zhou Dynasty, an elaborate system of sacrifices to ancestors and mourning procedures had been established in court circles – one's grade within the bureaucratic hierarchy being indexed by the number of generations of ancestor to which one *was allowed to* make sacrifices. No one who was not an officer of the court would be permitted to offer sacrifices to ancestors until the Song Dynasty (960–1279 CE). Furthermore, only the eldest son could sacrifice to the ancestors and then only to the first sons among the ancestors at the ancestral shrine. When a younger brother founded a collateral line, he would then be treated as the primal ancestor (*shizu* 始祖 or *xianzu* 先祖 or *zong* 宗) of the new line. The descendants in this new line would not be allowed to worship the ancestor of the dominant line. These restrictions created an institution within court culture of aristocratic "decent lines" *zong* 宗 from a singular primal ancestor and a hierarchy of ancestors marking the dominance and subordination of one lineage over another. We have seen this character before; *zong* was both the source but also the lineage and the ultimate Mind/emptiness in Yongming Yanshou's *Records of the Source Mirror* [*zong jing*]. It is also the term that would form half of the term *zongjiao* 宗教 or "religion" in the 19th century. In the Han Dynasty (206 BCE – 220 CE), *zong* would become important in organizing the hierarchy of aristocratic circles. According to the *Liji*, a "Great Lineage" consisted of a line of eldest sons worshiping their father if he was an eldest son going back a hundred generations.[21] A "Lesser Lineage" consisted of subsequent sons going back a maximum of five generations. The *Comprehensive Discussion at the White Tiger Hall* (白虎通 composed during the reign of the Han Emperor Zhang – r. 75–88 CE)[22] adds that:

> *Zong* 宗, what is it? Reverence to the ancestor (*zong* 宗) means to value 主 the first ancestor (*shizu* 先祖), and what is honored is the (first) person of the lineage 宗人 . . . . How can the wise be certain there is such an ancestor? When there is peace and harmony for a long time. The great lineage should lead the small lineage. The small lineage should lead the group of younger brothers.[23]

The singularity and unilinearity were important, among other things, for the continued integrity of the fief, since property was under the control of the lineage head and could not be divided among brothers.[24] The fact that the enfeoffed clans took on the surname of the ruling dynasty coupled with the regulation that they worship the soil given to them by the king marked their land as well as their ancestors as belonging to a collateral lineage tracing back to the singular imperial center. But more importantly, the fact that social and political hierarchy and one's position within it was indexed by the number of generations of ancestors that the family head *was allowed to* sacrifice to, supreme authority would have been indexed by the ability to sacrifice to the ultimate ancestor going back the most number of generations.

For the early Zhou, then, when they took over both the political and the ritual system from the Shang, they enacted a negotiated decoding of Di himself and coded him as the ultimate Zhou ancestor. Again, the status of being emperor was grounded in the fact that only the emperor could make sacrifices directly to Di. But since the icons of authority (ancestry, the empty celestial pole, etc.) themselves were not exclusive property of the court, these very images could also be coopted and denatured from their court context to decode either parallel or competing claims to authority elsewhere. As the Zhou began its slow decline beginning in the eighth century BCE, regional powers began to look for ways to coopt this system into their own regimes. Thus, we find both the ancestral and spatial metaphors of the power of Di coopted in the Warring States period *Daodejing*.

> Thirty spokes converge on a single hub, but it is in the space where there is nothing that the usefulness of the wheel lies.[25]

Here, instead of Di, we have the mysterious "Dao" occupying the position of the celestial pole – an empty space that, though, still controls and orients all that moves very much like Di. It is precisely this image of emptiness as the still pivot point or fulcrum leveraging all things that we found in Shang Di. Furthermore, the *dao* as emptiness is also presented as the ultimate ancestor – usurping even Di.

> The Dao is empty 沖.
> It may be used without ever being exhausted.
> Fathomless, it seems to be the ancestor (*zong*) of all things.
> . . . Whose child it is I do not know.
> It seems to have existed before Di.[26]

At a time when there was a weakening center and rising regional power centers, a text offering access to a foundational point surpassing the ancestry of the Zhou would have been a *desideratum*. The *Daodejing* was there to fill the need. Again, in a cultural context in which the ability to worship the founding ancestor was limited and therefore a marker of status, being known as the worshiper of the ultimate ancestor could be ultimately authenticating. Early *dao* enthusiasts were apparently eager to bring the term *dao* into the project of a negotiated decoding of Di and emptiness in order to subordinate the latter two to an increasingly naturalized *dao*. That the *dao* that it offered up was understood to be political is borne out by the fact that other texts explicitly instruct the king to meditate on it to consolidate his rule. In what may be a slightly later text, the *Source of the Dao*, found among the Mawangdui manuscripts (interred in a tomb of a marquis sometime between 206 BCE and 9 BCE), we find an exhortation to the king to meditate on the *dao* as a pivotal and primal emptiness in order to consolidate his rule.

> I
>
> From the beginning when there was constantly nothing 恒無之初
> It has been deeply merged with Vast Emptiness 大虛.
> Empty and merged as one [虛同爲一]. Constantly One and nothing more.
> . . .
>
> III
>
> Therefore, only Sages are able to discern it in the Formless
> And hear it in the Soundless.
> After knowing the reality of its emptiness, 知虛之實
> They [alt. "the ruler" 后] can become totally empty 后能大虛,
> And then be absorbed in the purest essence of Heaven-and Earth . . .
>
> IV
>
> If sage kings make use of this,
> All-under-Heaven will acquiesce.
> Devoid of likes and dislikes,
> If the one above makes use of this, [the ones below will respond,]
> And the people will not be confused and deluded.

If the one above (i.e., the ruler) is empty, the ones below (i.e., the ruled) will be tranquil,
and the Way will actualize the right course.[27]

Eventually the Zhou fell completely and with the rise of the Qin Dynasty in 221 BCE, a new imperium began. The question was, how to begin a new dynasty when one's own ancestry was clearly not imperial? The answer was to establish a new name with Heaven and to receive its mandate and then to sacrifice to earth in order to establish a new claim to earth. The first Qin emperor, Shihuang Di, did this by devising a new set of rituals: the *feng* 封 and *shan* 禪 rituals. These rituals would be part of the inaugural rituals for new dynasties for the next 1,200 years. A number of details of these rituals are lacking, but according to the post-Han work, the *Baihutong* (*Virtuous Discussions of the White Tiger Hall*), the emperor was to perform the *feng* (enfeoffment?) sacrifice on Mount Tai where he would declare his new dynastic name and receive the mandate of Heaven and record the new name on a rock. He would then go to base of the lower Mount Liangfu to perform the *shan* sacrifice to earth for her great generosity.[28]

Throughout Chinese history, whenever we see the imperial center get weak, we see the rise of regional and sometimes rural powers who end up appropriating the court rhetoric for their own purposes. Once imperial control of regional centers began to loosen after a series of rebellions in the latter Han Dynasty, local powers began to claim autonomy in the same terms or terms superior to that of the emperor. And when they did so, they employed formerly imperial metaphors that mimicked the court itself. One need merely to look at the Han Dynasty Celestial Masters led by Zhang Daoling to see court metaphors decoded for new institutional contexts.[29] But in addition to bringing Han court hierarchies to non-government communities, the Celestial Masters also disseminated the notions of cosmic and cosmogonic ultimacy that we find in early Daoist texts outside of court circles.

As the Celestial Masters spread (or *were spread* through forcible relocation and enfeoffment after their defeat by Cao Cao in 215 CE) they brought with them cosmogonic texts such as the *Register of [the Heavenly King] of Primordial Beginning.*[30] In doing so, they naturalized what was becoming the hegemonic reading of the political *cum* cosmic ultimate as emptiness. Hence, we find in the latter text a version of a cosmogonic myth that would continue to be invoked even in the Ming Dynasty (1368–1644 CE).

> Anciently, when the two deportments (*yi* 儀) were not yet distinguished, it was a dark watery expanse, a vast concealment that had not yet attained form. Heaven and earth, sun and moon were not yet complete. Their form was like a baby bird 雞子. After (this state of) primal nondifferentiation *hundun*, the mysterious yellow, was Pangu the true person, the semen of heaven and earth who designates himself as the Heavenly King of Primordial Beginning 元始天王. He wanders in this and primordial ocean and aligns the four *kalpa*. Heaven's shape is like a great umbrella. Above it

> there is nothing holding it up. Below it has no root. Heaven and earth are outside. A distant connection is without limit 遼屬無端. Dark, dark, it is great emptiness 玄玄太空.[31]

This text which is attributed to Ge Hong (283–343 CE) probably dates from the Six Dynasties period (ca. 220–589 CE) but provides an important point of departure for later cosmogonies. For our purposes what is important is that the cosmic beginning is described as lying in emptiness, which is personified as the primordial sovereign Pangu.

In another short cosmogonic text assigned to the same period, the *Scripture on the Creation of the World, by the Most High Lord Lao,*[32] we find Pangu replaced with a deified Laozi, the putative author of the *Daodejing*. This text begins with the assertion that, "In the beginning, Lord Lao followed Empty space and then descended as the Master of the Great Beginning."[33] *The Scripture of the Marvelous Beginning,*[34] a fifth-century text begins with the assertion,

> The Great High Lord Lao said, "The Dao came out of the formless, the nameless, the soundless, the colorless, the tasteless. Indifferent as to whether it had emptiness or non-existence for an ancestor, spontaneously it arose with the *qi* of pure subtle dark origin for its beginning. Its work was without apex."[35]

Throughout these periods, the cosmic starting point was not merely the stuff of myth, it was the object of meditation. Early Daoist texts have the practitioner meditate on the *dao* as emptiness or as the "primal breath" *yuanqi* 元氣. Even in the Yuan Dynasty (1271–1368 CE), we find meditation discussed in Daoist texts such as *The Lingbao Treatise on Returning to Emptiness,*[36] and in texts on internal alchemy (*neidan*) especially from the Southern school, whose goal is to return to primal emptiness.[37] But if the idea of finding a Daoist text promulgating a "return to emptiness" strikes the reader as merely the Daoist appropriation of a Mahāyāna idea, then we need merely to look at the *Treasure Store Treatise*[38] that has been studied exhaustively by Robert Sharf. The text is interlaced throughout with allusions to and reworkings of the *Daodejing*. Its third chapter is particularly important to the case I am making here. It is titled, "The Empty Mystery of the Point of Genesis" 本際虛玄. It begins,

> The point of genesis is the unobstructed nirvana-nature of all living beings. How is it, then, that the deluded mind and its various attendant perversions suddenly come into being? It is merely due to the confusions of a single instant of thought. Moreover, this thought itself arises from the One, and the One arises from nonthinking [不思議]. Nonthinking is itself without origin. Therefore, the scripture says: "The Way initially begets One." The one is the unconditioned. "One begets two." Two is the deluded mind, since in knowing One, there is the division into two. Two begets the *yin* and the *yang*, and the *yin* and *yang* are movement and stillness. With *yang* there is

clarity and with yin turbidity. Thus the clear pneuma constitutes the interior space [內虛] of the mind, and the turbid pneuma congeals without as form, creating the two dharmas of mind and form.[39]

This passage, as Sharf points out, clearly reworks *Daodejing* chapter 42 to talk about cosmic origins in a way that can be read in both "Buddhist" and "Daoist" registers. While 不思議 usually translates "unthinkable" (*acintya*), the contrast with the *nian* 念 that it is supposed to precede inclines me to agree with Sharp's translation of "nonthinking" and to suggest that the author had something more like non-cognition (in Sanskrit, this would be *acitta*) in mind.[40] As such, the text seems to be reading an ostensibly Daoist cosmogony through an ontology that, as we will see, is fundamental to the *Perfection of Wisdom in 8,000 Lines*. Under this reading, the origin of all things lies in the mind prior to cognition. It is with cognition and distinguishing that we have the condition for the possibility of either *yin* and *yang* or mind and form. We could get hung up on whether this or the *Returning to Emptiness* is "Buddhist" or "Daoist," but we would have to remember that that both the question and consternation are far more ours than theirs. Discussions of emptiness in either tradition are meaningful and powerful in part because it is recognized across traditions as having something to do with authority. What was important for the authors (and most likely the audiences) of both texts was simply the image of cosmic origin and how to appropriate it to authorize human institutions.

To some extent, the attempt at coopting existing icons of imperial authority is as old as the Buddhist communities in China themselves. There is some indication that the first translators of Buddhism into Chinese understood the political implications of meditation in general and of meditation on emptiness in particular. The first translator of Indic texts into Chinese, An Shigao (d. ca. 180 CE), was an Iranian who translated the first group of Buddhist texts into Chinese at the end of the Han Dynasty. To do so, he had to make up translation terms to represent Indic sounds. It was probably An Shigao who chose to represent the Prakrit sound *dhyān* (Pali – *jhāna*, Skt. *dhyāna*) with the Chinese character that today we pronounce as "*chan*" 禪 (although it is perhaps best known through its Japanese pronunciation, "Zen"). What I find interesting is that, if we consult works on Han Dynasty phonology, there were a number of other characters that could have represented the same "*chan*" sound better.[41] The character that he did choose is an odd choice. First of all, it was not pronounced "*chan*," but as we have seen, "*shan*," which had been the word for the inaugural sacrifice at the founding of all dynasties since the Qin. The pronunciation "*shan*" was phonetically farther from "*dhyāna*" than a number of other possible choices available to An Shigao. Indeed, this *shan* was a rare term in the Qin and Han Dynasties. Most readers in the Han Dynasty and afterward would have been familiar with it *only* from references to the imperial *Fang* and *Shan* sacrifices. The fact that An Shigao chose *shan*, may well indicate that, he, his expatriate audience as well as his budding Chinese audiences understood Buddhist meditation to be something relevant to sovereignty and the founding of empires – a practice that would have been particularly poignant as the Han Dynasty was beginning to fall apart.

It was in the early Tang Dynasty (618–907 CE) that Buddhists who were engaged in this *chan/shan* meditation began to appropriate the old aristocratic terminology of the *zong*. By the Tang, the aristocracy themselves had stopped thinking of themselves as organized along the lines of *zong* and no longer sacrificed to primal ancestors – only the emperor or empress could do so. It was first the Tiantai school and quickly thereafter the budding Zen school that took up the term *zong* to describe the transmission of the abbacy from one monk to his disciples.[42] Initially, this would have been understood as a kind of negotiated decoding or a metaphor, but as we have seen, by the time of Yongming Yanshou in the 10th century the *zong* of Buddhism had become a naturalized thing – as had emptiness itself (now usually rendered *kong* 空 instead of *xu* 虛). The rhetoric was that just as emperorship passed from the emperor to his eldest son in a chain going all the way back to the founding ancestor, so too the Buddhist abbotship was constituted by the direct transmission of the mind of the original founder, the Buddha, all the way to the present abbot. As a *zong*, the Zen lineage (and Tiantai and Huayen would follow suit in claiming their own lineages) was a kind of parallel state in its structure of authority. "Lineage" or *zong* in Zen relied on prior knowledge of the *zong* of the emperor for its sense and yet denied the connection even as it appropriates it.[43]

Beyond merely connecting the abbot to the ultimate authority of the Buddha, the idea of lineage became a way of affiliating monasteries across geography. But if Zen monks such as Faru (d. 689) and Shenhui (684–758 CE)[44] appropriated the language of *zong* from the imperial court to ingratiate themselves with members of that court, then with the decline of the Tang after the An Lushan Rebellion (755–763 CE), the rising regional powers in the South were free to appropriate the same image to themselves by sponsoring and becoming the primary benefactors to Zen monks during the Five Dynasty and Ten Kingdoms period (ca. 907–979 CE).[45]

It should be clear from the above discussion that coded icons such as emptiness are by their very nature subject to appropriation and counter-appropriation, encoding and negotiated re-encoding. To be effectively decoded *as authoritative* they must already be hegemonic, but to be hegemonic they must to some extent have already become common property and thus susceptible to further negotiation. We have seen the icon of emptiness jockeying back and forth from the pole star to Di to the *dao* to nirvana. Instead of seeing these "religions" as bearers of mutually exclusive doctrines like emptiness or the *dao*, we are better off seeing icons of authority and the struggle by different constituencies to lay claim to them. Early courts were attempting to coopt the authority of ancestry from society at large and join it to the icon of empty space to render it (or denature it) as ultimate. Early Daoists coopted the icon of Di, empty space and the founding ancestor to ground their model of authority for rising regional powers toward the end of the Zhou. When Buddhists came to China, they were already using emptiness as an icon of ultimacy and were able to rather quickly decode the emptiness of Daoist and Confucian discourse as their own emptiness. In return, courts from the early Han onward begin to coopt the *dao* or Buddhist icons of emptiness or the bodhisattva to decode the authority of their own emperors. That the idea of the cosmic zenith or apex remained a potent image of authority is confirmed by the fact that even in the Ming and Qing law codes, if an ordinary person worships High Heaven or the Dipper, they will receive 80 blows from a heavy bamboo stick.[46]

As if all this is not complicated enough we must also take into account the fact that coopting Buddhist, Confucian or Daoist icons of authority would never be sufficient if the majority of the Chinese population did not recognize any of these religions as authoritative to begin with. In order for courts to truly gain control over the entire population[47] the courts would either have to promulgate one or all of the three religions in rural areas and then claim authority over each of the religions or would have to get the three religions to coopt local icons of authority on their own and then coopt their authority.

The image of the earth and control of the cults

If images of apical emptiness that were already in play were deployed to garner recognition of court authority, then images of earth refracted through "earth altars" and their eventual subordination to the City Gods that were discussed at length in Qianlong's 1744 inscription were part of a longstanding strategy by Chinese courts to conscript local cults (and thereby their followers) into the empire. Indeed, so crucial were the images of the "earth altar" to the imperial project, that the *Tang Code*, defines of "rebellion" against the state (a capital crime) as: "Plotting rebellion means to plot to endanger the Altars of Soil and Grain [*she chi* 社稷, that is, the ruler and the state which he rules]."[48] This law along with the reference to the destruction of the *she* altar will be repeated as the very first of the "Ten Abominations" requiring the death penalty in the Ming[49] and the Qing Codes.[50]

These soil altars have a long history as part of the imperial machinery. Edouard Chavannes traced the soil altars back to the Han Dynasty although it may have been slightly earlier. Apparently, quite early on, there were altars of the soil established in the various administrative districts. Sima Qian records an episode in which the Duke of Zhou offers to "give" 封 Confucius soil altars of 700 cantons.[51] The term *feng* here does just mean to give, but more properly means to enfeoff, to give a very practical dominion over. In other words, land was governed by the god of the soil, who was worshipped at the soil altar. But it was the king who could grant dominion over land and its inhabitants, and he did so by giving the soil altar and presumably its god to the person he wishes to enfeoff. In the Han the soil altars in various districts had a corresponding rectangular soil altar in the capital. This altar would have had five visible sides, each painted with a different color, and when princes were enfeoffed, they would receive soil of a particular color from the emperor's altar to establish their own altar in their assigned districts.[52]

> At the time of the Han the great god of the soil, that is to say, that which was placed in the imperial palace, had a rectangular altar which measured 50 feet side by side; Each of the four faces was made of earth having the

> color corresponding to one of the directions of space, green for the east, red for the south, white for the west, black for the north; At the top of the altar the earth was yellow. For the lord the altar of the god of the regional soil was 25 feet long; it was entirely made of earth of a single color, namely the color corresponding to the direction of the space in which the fief lay. The reason for employing lands of five colors for the altar of the great god of the regional soil is found in the rites by which the investiture was carried out.[53]

Much like the "taking of salt" ritual in Mughal India,[54] the gift of soil as a ritual of enfeoffment was as simple as it was powerful. With the regional soil altar being a partial representation (one color and half the size) of the five-colored altar in the imperial palace, the regional soil altar becomes a coded icon for the derivative authority of the lord. As such, the cult of the soil god was the interface between imperial and local rule. Local populations organized themselves to worship the soil god at his altar in the fall and spring, and the king would assert control (through donations and periodic legislations) over the altars of each district under his control. In turn, dominion over the ceded district and its altar would fall under patrilineal succession (*zong*), with father passing the fief in its entirety to his eldest son. Hence, we should not read these soil altars as some kind of indigenous worship of fertility or harvest deities. Rather, as Chavannes points out, these altars were ordered to be built in districts.[55]

Kenneth Dean has argued that, over time, many of these altars (known later as altars of the soil and the five grains *sheji citan* 社稷祠壇) either fell into disuse[56] or were repurposed for local cults to tutelary deities. Distinctions became blurred. Indeed, over the course of Chinese history there has been a kind of tug of war over control of local shrines. In the Tang, Song and Ming Dynasties, new emperors would periodically mandate that official shrines to the soil and the five grains or some other local divinities be built in each district as a token of spreading court orthodoxy. But during the Song we see local shrines begin to change in particular ways. According to James McDermott, during the Song, what had begun sometimes as a simple gravesite began to be enclosed by small shrines or chapels. Furthermore, many of these local shrines were administered by some attendant for whom the shrine was their sole responsibility. Finally, the local shrines began increasingly to have named tutelary deities – usually historical figures who either founded the settlement or who protected it in some significant way. In so doing, many of these shrines came to be known as shrines to the primal ancestor or early ancestor of a village or family.[57]

But the transformation of these shrines, even when they moved out of the orbit of official control nevertheless appear to have been responding to larger cultural trends in China. For example, we cannot look at the transformation of these shrines into ancestor shrines apart from the trends in Song Dynasty Confucianism. It is in the Song that the movement usually called in Western scholarship "Neo-Confucianism" gets under way. Beginning with Zhou Dunyi (1017–1073 CE) and Zhang Zai (1020–1077 CE), we get a number of reforms within Confucian thinking which produce (or revive) a Confucian version of apical cosmic emptiness. Thus, in the first chapter of his *Correcting Youthful Ignorance*, we find:

> The Supreme Vacuity (*taixu*) has no physical form. It is the original substance of material-force. Its integration and disintegration are but objectifications caused by change. Human nature at its source is absolutely tranquil and unaffected by externality. When it is affected by contact with the external world, consciousness and knowledge emerge. Only those who fully develop their nature can unify the state of formlessness and unaffectedness, and the state of objectification and affectedness . . .
>
> When it is understood that Vacuity, Emptiness, is nothing but material-force, [知虛空即氣] then something and nothing, the hidden and the manifest, spirit and external transformation, and human nature and destiny, are all one and not a duality. He who apprehends integration and disintegration, appearance and disappearance, form and absence of form, and can trace them to their source, penetrates the secret of change. [能推本所從來 ， 則深於易者也].[58]

Examples of cosmic apical monogenesis among early Neo-Confucian scholars can be multiplied.[59] What is important for our purposes is that, at least in the case of Zhang Zai, the articulation of a kind of (singular) primal emptiness lies at the foundation both of the cosmic order and of human nature. His attempt appears to be very much in keeping with both the Daoist and Buddhist versions of emptiness, despite an (at least from our perspective) awkward attempt to put some daylight between his version of emptiness and that of the Daoists and the Buddhists.[60]

While bringing a monogenetic cosmogony into Confucianism, Zhang Zai and Cheng Yi (1033–1107 CE) were both interested in reviving lineage sacrifices, and it is at least worth asking the question as to whether these two moves were related. When lineage sacrifices were practiced in the Zhou Dynasty, they were only conducted by lords who had received fiefs. By the Song, the system of ranks prevalent in the Zhou was long gone and there was no obvious way to apply the Zhou ritual manuals to the new social order. Furthermore, the *zong* system of passing on domains was also gone and had been replaced by the family as the primary unit. In families, unlike *zong* lineages, when the father dies, the property is divided equally among children, given that lineages no longer existed (at least outside of Buddhist monasteries) and that there were no enfeoffed lords to perform these rites anyway. Patricia Ebrey has argued that Song Neo-Confucians addressed the problem by mapping the new bureaucratic ranks onto the family ranks of the Zhou.[61] Zhang Zai was among a group of 11th-century scholars who worked hard to bring the *zong* system back.

> When the system of differentiated descent lines is not practiced, people do not know the organization of the lines or the places that they came from. Very few people in ancient times were ignorant of their places of origin, After the system of differentiated descent lines decayed, later generations

> still honored genealogical writing, so that some of the spirit persisted. Now that genealogical writing has also decayed people do not know where they come from; there are no hundred year families (*jia*) . . . Moreover, without the establishment of the system of differentiated descent lines, the court can have no hereditary officials, for instance, a minister can rise up in a day from a poor and humble position. If he does not set up a *zong* system, once he dies his agnates (*zi*) will scatter and his house (*jia*) will not continue . . . If in this way, they cannot preserve their houses, how can they preserve the state?[62]

The reconstitution of the *zong* system was also taken up by Zhang Zai's nephew, Cheng Yi. Cheng Yi essentially democratizes the *zong* system, urging that all families work out their genealogies and while continuing to perform rites for ancestors up to the great grandfather in their household shrines, sacrifices to the primal ancestor should be performed at the winter solstice and to the ancestors between the first and the great grandfather in the spring at a "family altar." Ebrey argues that, while Zhu Xi (1130–1200 CE) would become far more influential in late imperial China than the Cheng brothers, on this matter (Zhu thought it presumptuous that ordinary families would perform *zong* sacrifices), Zhu was largely ignored.[63]

Ironically, as McDermott has observed, the growing popularity of Neo-Confucian family rituals and increasing interest in establishing family altars to primal ancestors led to a proliferation of Buddhism in many areas. In the Song, Yuan and Ming Dynasties, worship of the primal ancestors would not necessarily have been restricted to blood decedents of the primal ancestor. In fact, even when shrines were built to house ancestral tablets of prominent families, Buddhist or Daoist priests were often hired to recite sutras for the ancestors – as they assumed that hiring someone to perform these ritual obligations was more reliable than dedicating the eldest son to these tasks.[64] As a result, many of these ancestor shrines or earth shrines were managed by a Buddhist or Daoist incumbent and only by the late Ming were these shrines repurposed into lineage shrines.

Exorcism and the state: when possession is nine-tenths

In the government's eyes, these temples were ostensibly Confucian and connected to filial piety and the worship of ancestors – even if, as Patricia Ebrey has argued, Confucian rituals had to be radically reworked to fit the non-court context of the Song Dynasty and beyond. Once established, however, many of these shrines were repurposed (or reinterpreted)[65] by local communities into shrines for the worship of any locally popular (usually, but not always a martial) deity.[66] In some cases the term *she* altar merged with other local cults[67] (sometimes called a *shemiao*) while in some villages the *she* remained independent of the *miao* temple.[68] From the perspective of the government, the more autonomous the cult, the more likely it was to be considered a kind of demon worship. Thus there are numerous calls to reinstitute the *she* altar sacrifices as a corrective to "licentious cults."

Indeed, to some extent Confucianism and to an even greater extent Daoism and Buddhism became important not only for their apical cosmologies that gave a cosmic framing for the pinnacle of imperial power, but because each developed technologies to draw in other errant cults to align themselves with the same pinnacle in the manner that we saw with the Qianlong inscription. For Daoism and Buddhism the primary mechanism for this was exorcism. Exorcism was part of the imperial effort in the Song and Ming Dynasties to integrate local cults into the "religions" controlled by the imperial center. Probably the earliest of the Daoist exorcism texts to achieve large-scale popularity were the rites of the celestial heart. These were a series of rites utilizing talismans to the sun, the moon and the stars that were thought to derive, "from the northernmost extremity of the celestial realm."[69] As Edward Davis has documented for the Song Dynasty, the eighth Song emperor, Emperor Huizong used Daoism and especially its newly refurbished "thunder" exorcism rituals (of "sublimation" *liandu* 鍊度) to bring a range of local deities and temples into what would become an extensive network of temples from local rural areas stretching all the way up the capital in Kaifeng, where Huizong himself laid claim to the title "Sovereign of the Grand Empyrean" 太霄帝君 at the suggestion of the Daoist master, Lin Lingsu (1076–1120). Lin is generally credited with, among other things, the introduction into the Daoist canon of a new revelation of the Shenxiao 神霄 or Divine Empyrean, whose deities transcend and preside over the highest of the traditional Daoist heavens of the Lingbao. There were many reasons to want to ritually subordinate these local cults.[70] For one, as Mark Muelenbeld has pointed out, since the foci of many of these local cults were martial deities it should come as no surprise that some of these shrines were set up either by army units in the Yuan Dynasty or were places where local militias practiced their drills and worshipped the tutelary marital deity within. By subordinating the local war god to a "general" god residing elsewhere, the assumption was that the local devotees of the god would be equally subordinate to the human counterpart higher up the command.[71] As Sovereign of the Grand Empyrean, Huizong was told by Lin that he was the eldest son of Shang Di (again, following the logic of patriarchy) who resides at the nadir of the southern celestial pole in the center of the eight cardinal directions.[72] Once this pyramidal or apical structure of the divine Daoist hierarchy was officially adopted by Huizong, Daoism became politically quite useful in absorbing local cults into the imperial system. From the top down, we see this in Huizong's 1111 edict, in which he

> called for the abolition of approximately thirteen hundred 'Spirit altars' (*shenci*) in Kaifeng. This so-called abolition, however, actually entailed the removal of the spirits of those altars – or, rather images – into Buddhist monasteries, Daoist abbeys, and community temples (*ben miao*). Images of Zhenwu, for instance, were moved into Daoist abbeys while images of earth-spirits (*tudi shen*) were transferred to City God temples (*chenghuang miao*). Here we find not so much suppression as integration of cults and spirits into a hierarchy of temples and gods.[73]

If the emperor, in reference to the new Daoist liturgy, was the manifestation of the apical god in the Grand Empyrian, then local gods were brought to subordination by the military prowess of the thunder gods – a group of marital spirits. The structure brought about by these exorcism rituals (a structure popularized by Ming novels such as the *Canonization of the Gods*),[74] then, subordinated/subjugated local deities to the thunder deities who were subordinates to the Eastern Peak, who in turn was subordinate to the Grand Empyrean/the emperor.

Religion in the service of taxation

By the later Jin and Yuan Dynasties these local cults had taken on both intra-village and extra-village authority, such that the government gave responsibility of tax collection to these cults. But it was in the Ming that the hierarchy of temples that we see in the Qianlong inscription takes on its mature form. According to Meulenbeld, it was the first Ming emperor, Hongwu, who in 1368 hosts all of the gods in the empire and then ranks the nine temples of the capital according to their hierarchical position in Daoist exorcism rituals. Around 1360 Emperor Hongwu meets with a celestial master named Zhang Zhengchang, a master of the thunder rituals. In 1370, he institutes a type of new altars for his domain, the Altar for Baleful Spirits (*litan*) 厲壇:

> It derives its powers from a comprehensive absorption of the masses of autonomous spirits at the local level (territorial cult) into the sacrificial liturgies that are presided over by the City god and the gods above him, from Eastern Peak to Dark Emperor and Jade Emperor. The new emperor reforms his City Gods vis a vis the Eastern Peak, and the City Gods are made to relate institutionally to the autonomous spirits of local communities by establishing the Altar for Baleful Spirits.[75]

The intention of this new altar was to be a refuge for orphaned spirits with no one to take care of them (e.g., the war dead, those who had died a violent death, etc.). These altars would then be under the authority of the tutelary deity of the area where the *litan* was found. Shortly thereafter, Hongwu "[d]ivests these [tutelary] gods of their locally specific epithets and imposes the universalizing Daoist format of addressing them as divine officials assigned to localities."[76] In other words, the local gods are no longer addressed by name, but are to be addressed simply as "the City God of such and such a place". It was at the *litan* that communal sacrifices were to take place several times a year and the emperor ordered one to be built for every 100 households along with drinking pavilions where government mandates could be read out as part of its *lijia* 里甲 system. But it is notable here that what was essentially a cadastral move was implemented in tandem with the establishment of shrines.

> The government first decreed the establishment of pavilions for wine drinking ceremonies in which government drafted documents would be

> proclaimed. A unified ritual order known as the *lishe xiangli* 里社鄉厲 system was decreed in Hongwu 8 (1376) whereby each *li* 里 subcanton was to have a *sheji* altar of the soil and of the grain, and a *litan* 厲壇 (altar to the unrequited dead). In Hongwu 13 and 14 (1380–1381), the court decreed that the population should be divided into *li* 里 (subcantons) and *jia* 甲 (groupings of ten families within a subcanton). Almost simultaneously, the court issued the tax registration system known as the *huangce* 黃冊 (Yellow Registers).[77]

I think that we can safely assume that villages already had a hierarchy of families and so the selection of which local leaders would become "headmen" (*jiashou* 甲首) for the purposes of tax collection was not arbitrary but based on existing local precedent. But here again, we see what was once a marker of authority granted from the center to more distant lords is now precisely a relatively autonomous structure of power that the central administration seeks to appropriate as part of the state apparatus. By all accounts, Hongwu's reforms lapsed completely by the 16th century and the advent of the Single Whip Tax that would become the economic impetus facilitating the rise of European powers.[78] But the power of these liturgical forms to create and maintain networks into and across rural areas persisted.

> [T]he *lijia* 里甲 system of the early Ming had disintegrated while the *she* 社 that had been officially founded in the administrative subcantons or *tu* 圖 levels continued to provide an organizing framework for local social and cultural self-organization. The *she* began to mutate from a government shrine into a fundamental building block of the local temple system. This process of mutation can be seen in the process of the founding of new villages or the branching off of new villages from earlier ones. As the population expanded, new settlements were formed. These new settlements sought to found branch *she* altars as the symbolic basis of their new territory, but many, for one reason or another, were not able to do so.[79]

Despite the fact that government attempts to subordinate and control local temples had mixed and temporary results, what is important is that the government recognized shrines as potentially important interfaces between local polities and imperial policies and understood Confucianism, Daoism and Buddhism with their respective cosmologies to be the proper tools to align (or conscript) these cults into the imperial order. Here, the government interest in regulating and, more importantly *incorporating* local temples and temple networks into state administration in many ways anticipates the "Temple Registry System" in Tokugawa Japan that coopted Zen "root and branch" networks to enable accurate cadastral mapping and control of rural populations.[80]

Buddhist exorcism and the heart of Mahāyāna

But for all his Daoist predilections, Huizong does not just incorporate local shrines into Daoist abbeys, but into Buddhist monasteries as well. As Davis shows, Song Dynasty Buddhists were also performing their own version of exorcism known generally as the "Rite of the Three Altars" *santanfa*. From what can be discerned from Song sources, these practitioners (who may or may not have been attached to monasteries) would cause infecting spirits to enter into either a mirror or a local boy, with whom the practitioner would negotiate the release of the possessed. This procedure stands in marked contrast to the practice of local mediums who would themselves be possessed directly by the malignant spirit. Some rites would involve children to become possessed by sets of three, five, six or 10 divinities of the mandala, who would then do battle with the infecting spirit. The fivefold division of the mandala (with the primary Buddha and consort occupying the center and subordinate Buddhas in the four cardinal directions) is standard for Buddhist mandala texts and was well known in the Tang ("five divisions" was a common epithet for tantric Buddhism in the Tang). Within the tantric texts translated in the Tang, the imperial significance of this fivefold configuration brought from India would not have been lost on its Chinese audience, since it is precisely the imperial ordering that we find in the *Liji*[81] and in the five-colored imperial *She* altar.

It is unclear to what extent the liturgy was standardized in the Song and it may well be that such exorcisms were not directly based on one textual precedent. Davis, however, does indicate that their practice has at least two textual reference points if not texts. First of all, practitioners of the *Rite of the Three Altars* were known to also practice something called the *Diamond Samādhi*[82] – presumably named after the *Diamond Sutra of the Perfection of Wisdom*, since it seems unlikely that rural exorcists would have read Xuanzang's translations of *abhidharma*[83] texts discussing the "diamond" *samādhi* (*vajropama samādhi*). Second, the idea of the spirit entering another person appears to be loosely tied to a number of what Davis calls tantric *āveśa* ("entering") texts "generally reflective of the practices of a number of Esoteric Buddhist masters at the courts of the emperors Xuanzong and Taizong."[84]

> All in all, the *āveśa* rituals seem to have been not too distant from the most popular kind of séance performed by the Tang-dynasty spirit medium for officials and members of the aristocracy. In these séances the spirit-medium summoned a divinity either into himself or into some other localized place. Then he either answered himself, or communicated the divinity's responses to, specific questions posed by the supplicant about "good and evil fortune," "matters past, present, and future," or "things yet to come." What has changed in the *āveśa* rites is the fact that the spirit-medium's trance was officiated by a Tantric master and resulted from the power conferred on the master by his own identification with a Buddhist deity.[85]

Davis culls his summary of what the Song esoteric Buddhists may have been practicing from a collection of six, mostly Tang Dynasty, tantric texts.[86] What is curious about these exorcism texts is that half of them ground their ontology in either a doctrine of universal emptiness or an original mind.[87] This is in keeping with other, perhaps better-known Tang Dynasty tantric translations, such as the *Mahāvairocana Sūtra* and the *Sarvatathāgatatattvasaṃgraha.*

Conclusion

As much as we might like to assume that the three teachings of Daoism, Buddhism and Confucianism were mutually exclusive (and there is no question that the rhetoric between them could get acerbic from time to time),[88] what was more important to the imperial center was the fact that each of them promulgated the kind of hierarchical and apical structure or schema of authority that I discussed in the previous chapter. What I would like to highlight here is that in addition to preempting attempts to trump the ideological source of authority by describing the ultimate in a way that it cannot be superseded, the apical nature of these religions also serve to absorb (or, better yet "align" 經) local nexuses of a similar structure. If we find the emperor cast as the pinnacle of the cosmos in these three religions, then it is not (or, well, not *primarily*) to massage his ego. A pinnacle cannot be understood to be a pinnacle apart from the points subordinate to it. By the same token, these very subordinate points become aligned with one another through the act of subordination to the peak. On the other hand, it is precisely the fact that local cults had the same apical structures as the imperial court that allowed the possibility for them *not* to recognize the imperial center but to recognize their own hierarchy as ultimate. At worst such a group could become revolutionary and seek to establish its own state, or more commonly to serve as a kind of buffer to the reach of the state.[89] Either way, with the fall of the Qing Dynasty in 1911, the entire edifice of imbricated hierarchies that had been defined by the office of the emperor through the totalizing grammar of the three teachings was forever broken – replaced by a rather more flattened and fractured cosmos with Sun Yat-sen as its caretaker. But the shift in cosmogonic *cum* political assumptions was to have far-reaching repercussions in the very ability of the state to engage structures of authority in local populations. As Prasenjit Duara has argued:

> I argue that not only local power structures but the imperial state itself had relied significantly on the cultural nexus to establish their authority among the rural communities of North China through at least the end of the 19th century. The fateful efforts of the 20th-century state to penetrate rural society through means outside the cultural nexus and to destroy parts of it would ultimately undermine this state itself.[90]

But if Mahāyāna articulations of emptiness were used as a metaphor for ultimacy in imperial China, then it was because it was already being used in this capacity in Confucianism and Daoism before Mahāyāna arrived. One might even venture to say that the reason why Mahāyāna forms of Buddhism were so emphasized in China and not, say, in Sri Lanka, was precisely because this metaphor of power was already to some extent established.

But this raises the question: Did emptiness and mind-only serve the same function in India where they originated? And if so, what structures of power were they part of before they were transplanted to Tibet or China? Robert Sharf supplies us with a clue. In a recent paper he points out that the meditation on mind that forms the centerpiece in many Zen lineages (epitomized in Mazu's slogan that "This mind is the Buddha") actually dovetails nicely with a number of tantric meditations that we find in Tang Dynasty translations of tantras such as the *Sarvatathāgatatattvasaṃgraha* (a.k.a. *Vajraśekharasūtra*) that present enlightenment and indeed Buddhahood as something innate to the practitioner. Though he does not make claims about Mahāyāna more broadly, it wouldn't be too far of a stretch to say that the claim Sharf makes that the intersection between Zen and Tantra lies in innate Buddha nature could be made equally for the primordial mind that features prominently in both.

For our purposes, what is telling about Sharf's treatment of this material is the fact that he shows that the cohort of monks and practitioners utilizing the new tantric translations in the Tang court identify this form of Buddhism as a "Buddhist Veda."

> Yixing 一行 (683–727), a student of both Śubhakarasiṃha and Vajrabodhi, noted the similarities between the new Buddhist practices coming from the West, notably the *homa* or fire ritual, and non-Buddhist traditions of Vedic sacrifice. In his influential commentary to the Mahāvairocana-abhisaṃbodhi-sūtra, Yixing explains that Śākyamuni understood the allure of these popular rites, and so he intentionally appropriated them and imbued them with Buddhist meanings. Yixing refers to the result as "Buddhist Veda" (*fo weituo* 佛韋陀) – outwardly it has the form of Brahmanical sacrifice but inwardly the teachings are those of orthodox Mahāyāna.[91]

In a footnote, Sharf translates from Yixing's chapter on the "mundane and supramundane Homa" (*humo* 護摩, fire ritual) in the *Dapiluzhe'na chengfo jingshu* (大毘盧遮那成佛經疏):

> The Buddha himself taught the very foundation of the Vedas, and in that way manifested the correct principles and method of the true Homa. This is the 'Buddha Veda.'[92]

So, what do we do with this Buddhist Veda? From our 21st-century vantage point, the Vedas are the principal religious texts of Hinduism. A "Buddhist Veda" should be something of a contradiction in terms, like a "Mormon Koran." Was it an invention of a mere infelicitous slip of the brush on the part of Yijing or does it tell us something about the social configuration and context of these teachings in India? It is to these questions that we shall now turn.

Notes

1 Marx and Engels (2004), p. 64.
2 Lakoff (1992), p. 13.
3 See for example, Raz (2014).
4 Hall (1993), p. 95.
5 Ibid.
6 Hall, p. 102.
7 Ibid.
8 Benjamin Bergen has argued that newly coined metaphors of action are more likely to engage the motor cortex when they are heard than well-worn hegemonic metaphors. See, Bergen, (2012), chapter 9.
9 The following discussion is based on Puett (2002), pp. 48ff.
10 Puett, p. 52
11 Von Glahn (2004), p. 24. "The recent dead appear to have retained many of their personal attributes and temperament, but with the passage of time and erasure of memory the ancestors were gradually reduced to the abstractions of rank and title. Depersonalization became congruent with authority: the distant ancestors exercised greater power than the recently deceased, and the supreme deity Di was shorn of any personal qualities whatsoever. Therefore the mortuary ritual of the Shang eschewed veneration of exemplary, "heroic" individuals; instead it concentrated on securing the place of each individual in the eternal hierarchical order of the lineage."
12 Puett, p. 49 and note 50.
13 Pankenier (2004).
14 Ibid., p. 226.
15 Pankenier, p. 234.
16 Allan (2007).
17 Pankenier, p. 228.
18 Pankenier's translation, p. 211.
19 In the ode, "Birth of the People" *Shengmin* in the *Book of Odes*, Jiang Yuan performs two sacrifices to end her barrenness and Di impregnates her when she steps in his toe print. See Ward (2008), p. 163.
20 Von Glahn, p. 28.
21 Ebrey (1991), p. 29.
22 Chan (2012), pp. 9–10.
23 白虎通, *juan* 8, section 3, "宗族" paragraph 1. http://ctext.org/bai-hu-tong/zong-zu.
24 "In ancient times, descent lines were the core of kinship groups . . . The *tsung* system was suited to the Chou aristocratic system in which the family patrimony was an indivisible office or appanage, rather than private property that could be freely bought, sold, or mortgaged. Brothers were differentiated according to age, with the eldest son responsible for preserving the ancestral rites and the patrimony that supported them." Ebrey, p. 56.
25 Pankenier, p. 220.
26 De Bary et al. (1999), p. 81.
27 De Bary et al. (1999, pp. 253–255. *Mawangdui Boshu* (1980), p. 87. Of course, this discussion of emptiness is not confined to Daoist texts. Xunzi gives us the following: "How do people know the Way (*dao*)? I say: with the heart (*xin* = 'mind'). How does the heart know the Way? I say: it is through emptiness, singlemindedness and stillness (虛壹而靜) . . . As for those who have not yet grasped the Way but are seeking the Way, I say to them: emptiness, single-mindedness, and stillness – make these your principles. If one who would search for the Way achieves emptiness, then he may enter upon it. . . . For such a one, none of the myriad things takes form and is not seen. None is seen and not judged. None is judged and loses its proper position. He sits in his chamber yet sees all within the four seas. He dwells in today yet judges what is long ago and far away in time. He comprehensively observes the myriad things and knows their true dispositions. He

inspects and examines order and disorder and discerns their measures. He sets straight Heaven and Earth, and arranges and makes useful the myriad things. He institutes great order, and the whole world is encompassed therein" *Xunzi* (2014), pp. 228–229. It should go without saying that emptiness, singularity and stillness were each understood to be characteristics both of the celestial pole and Di as well as the emperor who (as pointed out above, the same author) casts as the pinnacle of heaven and earth.

28 Lai (2007).

29 For a good overview of the early Celestial Masters movement, see Bokenkamp (1997) pp. 29–78.

30 *Yuanshi Shangzhen zhongxian ji* 元始上真眾仙記, DZ 166 [www.kanripo.org/text/KR5a0167]; Schipper and Verellen (2004), vol. 1, pp. 107–108.

31 DZ 166, p. 2a. 昔二儀未分溟津鴻濛未有成形天地日月未具狀如雞子混沌玄黄已有盤古眞人天地之精自號元始天王遊乎其中溟涬經四劫天形如巨蓋上無所係下無所根天地之外遼屬無端玄玄太空.

32 *Taishang Laojun Kaitian jing*, 太上老君開天經 DZ 1437. See Schipper, pp. 108–109.

33 太初之時老君從虛空而下爲太初之師口吐 . . . DZ 1437, p. 1b. [www.kanripo.org/text/KR5h0006]

34 *Taishang Miaoshi jing* 太上妙始經, DZ 658; Schipper, p. 123.

35 太上老君曰道出於無形無名無聲無色無味淡然以虛無爲宗自然爲生以清微玄元之氣爲本有無極之功 . . . DZ 658, p. 1a. [www.kanripo.org/text/KR5c0039]

36 *Lingbao guikong jue* 靈寶歸空訣, DZ 568 [www.kanripo.org/text/KR5b0273]; Schipper, p. 792.

37 See, Pregadio and Lowell (2000), p. 482.

38 T. 1857 寶藏論.

39 Sharf (2002), pp. 238–239.

40 Indeed, this whole section bears a number of thematic resemblances to the *Awakening of Faith in Mahāyāna*. See Hakeda (1967), pp. 32–38.

41 See, Schuessler; (2009), pp. 255–256.

嬋 *dźan* attractive, feminine, to be attached to
戰? *tśan* to wage war
燀 *tshan* to make a fire
樿 *tśan* white wood
幝 *tśhan* to be damaged
繟 *tśhan* loose, gentle
闡 *tśhan* explain, clarify
嘽 *tśan/than* to slow or exhaust; to pant or snort
單 *dźan* or tan One, single, singular
墠 *dźan* to smooth a hard spot made level for sacrifices
撣 *dźan* to grasp; to be discreet, to be prudent, to be cautious; to refrain from, to abstain from, to use moderation in
禪 *shàn the inaugural sacrifice or "to meditate."*

42 For an excellent study of the adoption of *zong* in Zen, see Jorgensen (1987).

43 On this use of language and reference, see Bourdieu (1991).

44 On these two, see McRae (1986), pp. 2–10; 43, Jorgenson, pp. 101ff. and Welter (2006), chp. 2.

45 See Welter, pp. 32–33; Benjamin Brose (2015).

46 See Jiang (2005), p. 112; Staunton (1810), p. 174.

47 Something that, by the way, has never occurred – but nevertheless was seen as a desideratum.

48 Johnson (1979), p. 63.

49 Jiang (2005), p. 18.

50 Staunton (1810), p. 3.

51 Chavannes (1910), p. 440, note 5. 昭王將以書社地七百里封孔子.

52 Chavannes, p. 453 notes: "Sima Qian has preserved the original text of the commission for the investiture of three sons of Emperor Wu, all of whom were named kings on 12 June 117 BC; For the first, who received the fief of Ts'i, the commission begins with these words: 'Now in the sixth year [yuan cheou], the fourth month, the yi-ssu

day, the emperor charges yu che ta (Tchang) T'ang to confer in the ancestral temple the title of King of Ts'i to the son whose personal name is Hong, and he addresses to him these words: Oh! My young son Hong, receive this god from the green soil. I, continuing the conduct of my grandfather and my deceased father, and taking into account the examples of antiquity, I institute for you a royal house, and give you a fief in the eastern territory.'"

53 Ibid., pp. 451–452.
54 Eaton (1993), pp. 162–164.
55 He also mentions a command by Emperor Gaozu of the Han to institute them in each canton in 207 BCE. See Chavannes p. 441, note 5.
56 See Dean (1998), pp. 19–75. Timothy Brook gives an excellent account of the perception of abandoned stelae in the late Ming. See Brook (2005), chapter 2.
57 McDermott (2013), p. 57.
58 De Bary et al. (1999), p. 685.
59 For example, see Zhou Dunyi's essay on the Supreme Ultimate or Cheng Yi's essay on the single principle.
60 He claims that because the Buddhists do not understand that emptiness and things are mutually conditioned [sic], they assert that all things are illusions. See De Bary et al. (1999), p. 686.
61 Ebrey (1991), p. 37.
62 Ibid., pp. 37–38.
63 Ibid., p. 39.
64 Dean (1998), p. 24; McDermott (2013), pp. 89–90.
65 Dean, p. 25.
66 Ibid. "[T]he underlying factor in these changes was the uncertainty of the economic status of the direct descent line over time. As the numbers of those involved in ancestral worship grew, the pressures (both economic and administrative) on the eldest member of the direct descent line could become unbearable, especially if his line was in decline. By opening up worship of a common early pioneer ancestor, as well as branch ancestors who had made particular contributions, the way was clear for descent groups to overcome the limitations of the direct descent line, and expand into a more flexible "lineage" organizations. Buddhist chapels and monastic landholdings were reappropriated. Many of these increasingly powerful descent groups/lineages sponsored the canonization of the local gods worshipped in their communities. The temples dedicated to these gods often merged with or absorbed altars to the soil and grain."
67 Dean, p. 26.
68 Ibid., p. 41.
69 Boltz (1987), p. 34.
70 Davis (2001), chapter 2.
71 Meulenbeld (2015), pp. 115ff.
72 Davis, pp. 36–37.
73 Davis, p. 63.
74 This is the central thesis of Meulenbeld (2015).
75 Meulenbeld p. 138.
76 Ibid., pp. 138–139.
77 Dean, p. 33.
78 See Flynn and Giráldez (1995).
79 Dean, p. 45.
80 See Williams (2005).
81 Meulenbeld pp. 78–79.
82 Davis, p. 121.
83 *Abhidharma* texts are systematic treatises on Buddhist doctrine. See Walser (2015).
84 Ibid., p. 123.
85 Ibid., pp. 124–125.

86 See Ibid., p. 280, note 27. The texts are T. 867, 895, 896, 1202, 1217, 1229, and 1277.

87 Davis reconstructs his *āveśa* rites from T. 867, T. 895 (and its 10th-century translation, T. 896), T. 1202, T. 1217, T. 1229 and T. 1277. Of these, T. 895 and 896 (both translations of the *Subāhuparipṛcchā*) contain several discussions of emptiness and an original mind. T. 1202 also has a discussion of knowing one's original mind.

88 Raz (2014).

89 For examples of this kind of thing, see Shue (1988) and Mueggler (2001).

90 Duara (1988), p. 5.

91 Sharf (2017), pp. 85–86.

92 Ibid., p. 86, note 2; T.1796, 39, 780b13–15: 今佛自說韋陀原本。而於其中更顯正理眞護摩法。此佛韋陀.

5

BUDDHA VEDA

An Indian genealogy of emptiness (20th century – sixth century CE)

Sharf argues that the central features of Tang Dynasty tantra and Zen were labeled by at least one Tang Dynasty observer as coming from "Buddhist Veda." He then argues that we should understand the Mahāyāna trajectory of these trends in India as a "Brahmanization of Buddhism."

> As Indian Buddhists appropriated ritual elements from surrounding Brahmanical culture – a process that seems to have accelerated in the seventh and eighth centuries – the gap between Buddhist and non-Buddhist forms of worship narrowed. This phenomenon may well have contributed to the eventual disappearance of Buddhism in the land of its birth.[1]

Indeed, it is fairly common among academics to speak of things like the "Brahmanization of Buddhism," or the "amalgamation of Buddhism to Brahmanism," as if the resulting hybrid Mahāyāna were a kind of religious mule, the offspring of a Brahmanical horse and a Buddhist donkey. The assumption here is that the default or natural state of each religion is marked by incompatible or incommensurate doctrines. According to conventional academic wisdom, Brahmanism teaches that there is a permanent soul. Buddhism teaches that there is no soul. Brahmanism teaches that the highest reality is *brahman*, which may be meditated upon or in some cases worshiped. Buddhism teaches that the highest reality is either nirvana or emptiness, either of which may be meditated upon but neither of which may be worshipped. But as I have pointed out in the introduction: distinctions are something that people *make*. People either distinguish thing A from thing B, or they don't. There is no *natural* distinction between Buddhism and Brahmanism independent of the observer any more than, as we saw in the last chapter, there was a natural distinction between Buddhism and Daoism in China. More to the point, the discussion in the last chapter has pointed out that doctrines can and do mark out sectarian distinctions – but deceptively so. We saw that the coded image of emptiness rose to the surface as a marker of Mahāyāna Buddhist distinction in China because it was *already* being used as a metaphor for authority within Daoism and Confucianism and in the imperial cult more generally. In other words, an image whose coding is ubiquitous or hegemonic (to use Hall's term) can become recognized as proprietary to a specific cult only through a process by which its ubiquity is misrecognized as exclusive. The image can become a distinguishing doctrine of a religion only if it has already achieved a sufficient level of saturation within the culture at large (i.e., outside the cult). One can imagine that the early Jesus movement would have made little headway with their contention that Jesus was the Son of God if the phrase "Son of God" hadn't been printed on the Roman coins of Caesar Augustus used in Palestine in the decades before Jesus' birth.

Thus, in dealing with the Buddhist Veda, we have to deal with a number of issues at once: the "religions" of Buddhism and Brahmanism (whether they were recognized as distinct or not distinct) and the doctrines of emptiness and *brahman* (whether they were recognized as being incommensurate or not; whether they were understood as proprietary to either of the religions). The last chapter showed that emptiness (whether Buddhist, Daoist or Confucian) was used as a coded image of authority. In tracing the uses of emptiness and Mind I have not confined myself to Mahāyāna or even Buddhist accounts any more than one would confine the genealogy of a person to only the male ancestors. For any group to survive, exogamy will be as important as lineal descent and primogeniture. As an image, emptiness was available for a range of negotiated decodings between coherent traditions. It was fungible and could thus be used within multiple coherent traditions like Zen or Kagyu *mahāmudrā* to legitimate power precisely because it was not exclusive to any one tradition. The present chapter will argue that exactly the same state of affairs obtains in India. Emptiness and or/the primordial mind function as coded images for sovereign authority just as in Tibet and China. Just like the above two places we find these images coding authority within coherent traditions and absorbing local traditions as part of waves of state formation.

Emptiness and power in Orissa: from Mahima Dharma Sampradāya to Jagannātha of Puri

The place to begin, then, will be with contemporary Orissa. There, especially in the Dhenkanal and Koraput districts, we find the Mahima Dharma Saṃpradāya as a sect of monastic, non-Brahmin, vegetarian, saffron-clad, matted-haired yogis founded in the mid-19th century by Mahima Gosain, considered to be the incarnation of Mahima Alekh. The ascetics of the sect (and its two sub-sects: the bark-clad Balkaldharis and the waistcloth-wearing Kaupindharis) are involved in the usual *sannyāsi* activities of teaching, preaching, healing, performing fire sacrifices and worshiping and meditating on God. God, for them is *alekh* (unwritten) and *śūnya* (empty).[2] But how do we situate this emptiness? Due to a legal dispute between the two sects over ritual rites at the founder's *samādhi* at

Joranda beginning in 1936, the Mahima Dharma was determined by the courts to be part of the "Hindu Dharma."[3] The classification as a sect of "Hinduism" was aided, no doubt, by the publication in the previous year of the *Satya Mahima Dharmara Itihasa* by Bishwanath Baba (a member of the Balkadhari sect), who sought to inscribe the history of the Mahima Dharmis within the larger history of "Hinduism" using *itihāsa* ("epic") and *purāṇic* genre conventions. Ishita Banerjee-Dube has argued that this *Itihāsa* became an important document in the legal proceedings that ultimately determined the identity of the sect and that the Kaupindharis (who wrote their own *Itihāsa* in 1958) were far less sanguine about ascribing to Hindu identity.[4]

Given that Mahima Dharmis themselves debated how to categorize the sect, how are we to know where to place them? On the one hand, the yogis of this sect look very much like other yogis such as the Daśanāmis, with their long matted hair and saffron attire. On the other hand, however, they are marked in other ways by the absence of features that mark other Hindu sects. Their god is "empty" and not explicitly identified with any Hindu deity, and the founder's *samādhi* (here meaning "tomb") at Joranda Gaḍi has no images whatsoever. While the founder is said in Bishwanath's *Itihāsa* to have been a Brahmin himself, the yogis of this sect are non-Brahmin. In fact, the sanyāsis of this sect will accept food from neither Brahmins nor Kṣatriyas (nor for that matter Caṇḍalas) but regularly accept cooked rice from the many scheduled castes and tribals of Orissa.

Yet, as we saw in China, it is precisely the ambiguities and ambivalences swirling around emptiness that render the yogis useful for the extension of power into tribal areas. Their success in the particular social context of Orissa may in fact lie in the ambiguity itself as a strategy of what Bourdieu calls "censorship" or "misrecognition," insofar as the Mahima yogis are assertively non-Brahmin and yet by being vegetarian and doing fire sacrifices they play a Brahmanic role. In other words, while they have the marks of Brahmanic authority, those who patronize a Mahima Dharmi make a display of *not* patronizing a Brahmin ascetic.

Politically, the Mahima Dharmi yogis are important for non-Brahmin/non-Kṣatriya land-holding castes as holy men who make themselves available to receive donations. "By sponsoring the holy men, rituals as well as the places of worship, worldly patrons gain religious benefits and the moral reconfirmation of being a good ruler."[5] By the same token, the Mahima Dharma has made inroads in tribal areas of Southern Orissa again by being willing to receive donations from castes that Brahmin ascetics might refuse. Lidia Guzy has argued that the Mahima Dharma sects are compelling to tribal groups precisely because their version of God is emptiness. In context, the emptiness both invokes local tribal goddess cults while simultaneously denying them – a fact that ultimately allows them to absorb those cults.

> The ascetic religion rejects the dominant Brahmin tradition on the one hand; on the other hand it reproduces its dominant ritual features. On the one hand ascetics of Mahima Dharma religion (*saṃpradāya*) carry out ritual functions similar to Brahmin priests and, while doing it, deny the existence of local Goddesses. On the other hand they continue to perform

> the ritual functions of former local non Brahmin priests who are especially responsible for the ritual worship of local goddesses. The differences between local forms of Goddesses worship and belief consist in Mahima Dharma asceticism in a) the rejection of blood sacrifices in ritual worship and b) in the negation of the existence of the Goddess within the ascetic theology. Instead of the Goddess, Mahima Dharma ascetics venerate the concept of *sunya* – the void – and the God Alekha – the absolute and the unwritten. The theology and ritual practice of the void substitutes *and integrates* the theology of the Goddess.[6]

How does meditation on emptiness integrate the goddess cults? Through the equation of emptiness with power (*śākti*):

> The strict celibacy of the ascetics transforms them into representatives of *shakti*, the traditional concept of the power of the Goddess. The idea of the disciplined and thus sacred body in the Mahima Dharma doctrine integrates the theology of the Goddess which shows itself in the concept of *shakti* and in the concentration on the body of a ritual specialist as a crucial matrix of the divine. In their disciplined bodies ascetics incorporate the divine strength and at the same time they become the vegetarian and controlled priests of the God Alekha. As such, ascetics carry in their bodies the old power of the Goddess and the new supremacy of the God Alekh.[7]

While adherents of the Mahima Dharma are relatively few, the idea of God being identified with emptiness is hardly uncommon in Eastern India. In addition to the fact that "empty" is one of the epithets of Viṣṇu in the popular *Viṣṇu Sahasranāma* (*śloka* 79), the Dharma Thakur cult of Western Bengal worships Dharmarāj (a.k.a Brahmā), who is likewise described in the Bengali *Śūnya Purāṇ* as being empty (*śūnya*) and spotless (*nirañjana*).[8] We also find the ultimate described as empty in the Assamese poem *Mahāśūnya* by Dharmeṣvari Devi Baruani (1892–1960).[9] The term "emptiness" in each of these contexts displays little or no awareness of a Buddhist provenance for the term "emptiness," nor is emptiness in any of these examples held up as proprietary to the particular tradition. As in the Chinese examples, emptiness is simply an image coded as the ultimate.

The particular theology of the Orissan Mahima Dharmis is a legacy of the Orissan *santha* or *pañcaśākhā* tradition of the 16th century[10] that has been the focus of a recent work by Tandra Patnaik.[11] The Orissan tradition goes back to five *santhas* or saints, each of whom professed affiliation to the Vaiṣṇava tradition of Caitānya (1486–1534), with whom they were contemporary. Now, scholars might assume, given the historical Caitānya's allergy to all things Buddhist, that the Vaiṣṇava affiliation of the five *santhas* would preclude them from anything that might have looked like Buddhism. But this just isn't the case. The *santhas* understand Caitānya himself to be an incarnation of both the Buddha and Lord Jagannāth.[12]

The focus of the five *santhas* is the worship of Lord Jagannāth in the temple of Puri: a god who manifests as a wooden post with eyes and a mouth painted on it, whom they likewise understand to be Buddha and Kṛṣṇā. What is important for our purposes is the fact that each of these 15th-century saints refers to Lord Jagannāth as the "Empty Person" (*Śūnyapuruṣa*). For example, Bālarama Dasa (b. 1472) writes:

> He has no form, no outline,
> He is *Śūnyapuruṣa*
> He is the Brahman and the *Śūnya*.
> How can He have any name?[13]

So, why would a group of 15th-century Orissan saints praise a deity who takes the form of a wooden post as being the manifestation of emptiness? Just as we saw in the contemporaneous Ming Dynasty, emptiness is being used here both as fungible image of ultimacy and as one component in the internal colonialism of late medieval Orissa. The five *santhas* were written during the heyday of the worship of the three gods of Puri. It was in 1230 that King Anaṅgamabhīma dedicated his entire kingdom to Puruṣottama Jagannātha of Pūri (thereby making transgressions against him transgressions against God)[14] and in 1568 the Jagannāth temple would be sacked by Afghan armies.[15] But in between these dates, we find the Jagannāth cult in full bloom with its main deity identified as Kṛṣṇā accompanied by his brother Bālarama and Subhadrā or Lakṣmī.

As of 2011, the population of "scheduled tribes" in Orissa amounted to around 23%.[16] In the past, the percentage of the population who would have been functionally "tribal" (in the pre-modern context meaning something like "people on the outskirts of taxation and conscription") would have been much higher. As Kermann Kulke has pointed out,[17] there were nuclear settlements leading to small kingdoms in Orissa as early as the fifth century. But these kingdoms – many of which were ruled by *rājās* who were themselves tribal or formerly tribal chiefs – were not self-sufficient. Their very existence required cooperation with the surrounding tribes in trade and defense.[18] Kulke has illustrated how temples became a key component of the integration of these kingdoms into the surrounding tribal polity. Essentially, what Kulke shows is the way that kings presented their solidarity with the tribes they governed by first making lavish displays of worshiping those deities and then building temples to them. In the construction of the temple, a temple town would be created to house the carpenters, artisans and the Brahmins. These new villages could then be built using textual or *śāstric* ideals of town planning along cosmic lines. All of this enabled what Kulke calls "vertical legitimacy," i.e., the legitimacy of the local *rājā vis-à-vis* his subject population. However, kings also needed a kind of "horizontal legitimacy" that would be recognized by other kings across India; hence in the creation of new temples to house local deities, the local deities were assimilated to pan-regional "Hindu" gods.

However, assimilation never meant replacement. As Kulke points out, tribal groups in Orissa still worship their local deities in the form of wooden posts. As a wooden post himself, then, Lord Jagannāth of Puri was to be recognized as a local post-bearing deity and yet simultaneously *misrecognized* as being the lord of all such deities (and hence, contrary to appearances, *not* a tribal deity himself). Jagannāth could thus be lord of all deities in the realm *and* the proprietary deity of the Gājapati king and the priests of the Puri temple *and* the apical deity of the *Pañcarātra tantras*[19] *and* possibly of "Buddhism" as well (if this were still a functional category for those who worshipped the Buddha back then). In other words the temple image had to orchestrate a dual signification (and dual forgetting) simultaneously: it had to signify the local deity as the trans-local one in such a way that access to that deity could now be restricted to a single place and that audiences with the deity are now favors to be bestowed by the king.[20]

But how to effect this delicate set of recognitions and misrecognitions? By stating that the god is really empty or a formless Brahman, the Empty Lord allows for the interpretation that he can manifest in any form (an idea that was already fundamental to *Pañcarātra tantra* although the term "emptiness" wasn't used in that regard). This enabled worshippers to see past the form of the post toward a transregional (and *śāstric*) formless Brahman/emptiness while still accepting a post as a legitimate form of the Lord.[21] Hence we find Acyutananda Dasa (b. ca. 1502), author of the *Śūnya Saṃhitā*, emphasizing the fact that, although he appears in a form, his form is formless:

> It has no shape, no colour,
> It is invisible and without a name.
> This Brahman is called Śūnya Brahman.[22]

In a poem entitled *Śūnya Śūnya Boḷi*, he writes:

> There is nothing but only *śūnya* and *śūnya*, as if it is endless.
> There is no mark or sign so that it can be recognised. How
> shall I explain it? With what illustration? For no description can fit it.[23]

In the end, each of these *santhas* is steeped in the Vaiṣṇavite and Kṛiṣṇaite theology of the *Mahābhārata* and *Bhagavad Gīta*, and while they identified Buddha with Viṣṇu, institutionally they would have considered themselves more a part of the budding network of Hindu monasteries (*maṭhs*) than any network of Buddhist monasteries (i.e., *vihāras*). Thus when they invoke emptiness as the ultimate, it was not understood to necessarily be Buddhist. For example, Balarāma Dāsa has Kṛṣṇā say:

> "*Mahāśūnya* is my abode, how can speech reach me. In fact, no name can be ascribed to me since I am the formless Brahman."[24]

Then again, as early as the 14th century, we find the Vaiṣṇavite *Nīlādri Mahodayam*, give Buddha a more central place in the Jagganāth cult:

> My salutation to Buddha
> who is manifested in the form of
> the wooden Brahman – Jagannātha.[25]

As Patnaik notes, it was not just Vaiṣṇavites who saw Lord Jagannāth as a manifestation of the Buddha. The *Jñānasiddhi* ascribed to Indrabhūti offers the following praise of Jagannātha:

> My salutations to you, oh, Jagannatha, the object of worship
> of all wise people. You are as expansive as the sky, identical
> with Buddha and source of all power.[26]

Here as well as in the *Prajñopāya Viniścaya* of Anaṅgavajra – both texts of what would become the Mahāmudrā ("Great Seal") tradition of the Kagyupas in Tibet, we find Buddha identified with another divinity referred to as Jagannātha.

Buddhism and Brahmanism in Maitrīpa (ca. 1010–1097 CE)

From the above examples (and they can be multiplied) we are dealing with a situation similar to what we saw in China with Daoism and Confucianism. The Orissan Lord Jagannāth appears to have embodied contemporaneous versions of what we would call Buddhism and Hinduism in much the same way as the Lord of the Three in One embodies Buddhism, Daoism and Confucianism in contemporary Fujian.[27] Modern scholars may want to associate emptiness exclusively with Mahāyāna Buddhism, but if we were to take a trip into the way-back machine we would find that emptiness is better described as a partially detachable image that shuttled between traditions (Buddhist/non-Buddhist, Brahmanical/non-Brahmanical and tribal) to function as its apex – with or without accentuating an air of "otherness." All of this raises a number of questions. If we cannot assume that Buddhism was simply Brahmanism's "other," then what did the relationship between Buddhism and Brahmanism look like, and to what extent can we say that Brahmanism was particularly associated with Mahāyāna Buddhism in India? To address these questions, I would like to follow a bit further the Mahāmudrā thread mentioned above by discussing another Mahāmudrā author, Maitrīpa or Maitrīgupta, the teacher of Marpa the Translator and a foundational figure in the Kagyu school's formulation (or reformulation) of the practice of *mahāmudrā* and author of the *Tattvaratnāvalī*. According to Ulrich Kragh, "Maitrīpa was one of the key figures in the eleventh-century process of merging the Tāntrika subculture with the culture of the Common Mahāyāna."[28]

The *Tattvaratnāvalī* is especially useful for our purposes because it gives us an Indian survey of the doctrinal (*siddhānta*) landscape representing at least one author's perception of the fault lines of tradition. The metaphor Maitrīpa himself uses is that of a staircase (*sopāna*) going from the lowest and most basic Buddhist teachings to its most lofty attainments. The main outlines of its ascent will be familiar from the presentation of the Dalai Lama discussed in Chapter 2. Maitrīpa[29] begins by dividing Buddhism into three vehicles: the lowest being the disciples' vehicle (*śrāvaka-yāna*), followed by the independent buddha's vehicle (*pratyekabuddha-yāna*) and topped by the Greater Vehicle (*mahāyāna*). He also provides us a parallel classification according to four positions ("*sthita*": the Vaibhāṣika, Sautrāntika, Yogācāra and Mādhyamaka). These two groupings map onto one another with the Vaibhāṣikas (whom he divides into "Western" [Gandharan?] and "Kashmiri") being placed in either the "disciple" or "independent buddha" categories and the Sautrāntika, Yogācāra and Mādhyamika being three different possibilities within Mahāyāna. In addition, he divides Mahāyāna itself into two: the way of the perfections (*pāramitā*) and the way of the mantras (i.e., Tantra). The way of the perfections encompasses the Sautrāntika, Yogācāra and Mādhyamaka while the way of the mantras is comprised only of Yogācāra and Mādhyamika. Finally, he divides Yogācāra into those who argue consciousness has forms or aspects (*sākāra*) and those who do not (*nirākāra*), while Mādhyamika splits into those who argue the world is non-dual like an illusion and those who argue that everything is without any objective support whatsoever.[30] Writing in the 11th century, the basics of this staircase would become standard fare for the next millennium in Tibetan discussions of Buddhist doctrine.

However, when we get into some of the smaller details of Maitrīpa's discussion we find some things that are not so standard. Like the 14th Dalai Lama, he points out that non-Mahāyānists also meditate on emptiness, although this meditation only occurs among the greater disciples.

> The greater [practitioners of the disciples' vehicle] agree to the existence of external objects and establish selflessness of the body. They meditate on emptiness of the person while recognizing the four noble truths [*catur-āryyasatya [sic]-parijñāne pudgalasya śūnyatā-darśanaṃ dhyānam*]. In those [four noble truths], suffering has the nature of the five aggregates and is to be known, its arising is differentiation and is to be eliminated, its cessation is insight and is to be experienced. Their path has the defect (*mala*) of concentration that superimposes the state of Sadā Śiva for emptiness [*mārgaḥ śūnyatāyāḥ sadāśivarūpatā 'dhyāropo dhyāna-mala*].[31]

The greater disciples' emptiness meditation is the practice of cessation within the Four Noble Truths. Fair enough. Where Maitrīpa's criticism gets interesting is when he explains the shortcomings of non-Mahāyānists.

According to him, the meditation on emptiness attained through the practice of the Noble Eightfold Path leads these Buddhists to see the emptiness of cessation as an embodiment of Śiva himself (as Sadā Śiva). By the same token, those of the independent buddha vehicle (*pratyekabuddhas*) who meditate on emptiness see the person as:

> empty, inconceivable and devoid of characteristics. The teacher is self-arisen and his knowledge comes from calm (samartha) and insight (vipaśyanā) meditation. There, vipaśyanā is the cessation of the sense faculties and samartha of the body, speech and mind are the nonapprehension of the person. This is their meditation (*dhyāna*), (but) here the defect of this concentration is that it is a meditation on the state of bliss of the mind in which

> the faculties do not exist and is a meditation that abides in the state of sleep without dreams (*suṣupta*). In this, we enter the thought of Bhāskara.[32]

Here again, Maitrīpa has this second group of Buddhists meditating on emptiness by ceasing all cognitive activity and attaining the state of "sleep without dreams" that was the hallmark of "the thought of Bhāskara."

When we get to the Mahāyāna proper, he presents the Sautrāntika Mahāyānists as essentially followers of Dharmakīrti (ca. seventh century), who argue that cognition has "aspects" (*sākāra*). What he means by this is that what we perceive is not the objective world per se, but mere *representations* or "aspects" of it by the mind. We can then meaningfully distinguish the representations of the world (which are multiple) from the mind itself (which is itself not represented and thus "thoughtless"). Maitrīpa then gives us a rather rare glimpse of how these Sautrāntika Dharmakīrtians might practice meditation.

> When practicing by awakening to the thoughtlessness of thought, wherever it goes or stays, I don't see thought . . .[33]
>
> The defect of their *samādhi* is the same as (the greater disciples' vehicle). [The Dharmakīrtian] approach is to course in the five perfections, the essential nature of which is the perfection of wisdom that is free from objectification of the three spheres [of giving] and dedicate [the merit] to the welfare of sentient beings without regard to a fruition for oneself.[34]

Moving on to Yogācārins, he divides them into those who hold that consciousness has aspects (*ākāra*) and those who do not (*nirākāra-vādin*). For those who do, the defect in their meditation is that

> in the Samādhi in which they understand consciousness to be permanent and ultimately real (*paramārthasat*), they enter into the ideas in the same camp (*saṃsthita*) as the *vedāntins* from that of the Blessed One. They want the world to be a form of transformation indistinguishable from Brahman in the form of their own mind which is ultimately true and permanent.[35]

The second type of Yogācārin is those who believe that consciousness does not have aspects or that the representations of consciousness are not real. The fault of this position, according to Maitrīpa, is that for *nirākārins* all consciousness is self-awareness (*svasaṃvedana*).

> In this, there is the fault [*prasaṅga*] of following Vedāntic thought, and dwelling in the ideas of Bhāskara. That is to say, one understands Brahman as limitless in luminosity, continual, and permanent, entirely free of mental and physical parts [*nāma-rūpa*, "name and form"] and of the error of fabrication.[36]

Maitrīpa likes the Mādhyamikas best and he puts them at the pinnacle of his doctrinal scheme right under the "mantra vehicle" – which he won't discuss for reasons of secrecy. He says they are the best because they posit neither "existence" (*sat*) nor "non-existence" (*asat*), nor both, nor neither. To those Mādhyamikas who hold that everything is an illusion-like non-duality, he attributes the fault of "conceptual adherence to nihilism" – even if he also says that theirs is the "fulfillment of the six perfections." Above even the "illusionists" (*māyāvādin*) are the Mādhyamikas, who hold that there is no objective or subjective support for anything.

> Those who profess the unsupportedness of all phenomena [*sarva dharma apratiṣṭha-vādin*].
> The wise know the reality of things
> In terms of "All this is unsupported";
> Then also the mind that thinks about it,
> They do not know by mind.
> . . . Any understanding that is effortless
> May be termed "beyond thought";
> Non-thought while thinking about it.
> Does not function as "beyond thought."
>
> What does this come to? Their meditation is the experience of the real nature of the unsuperimposed-upon object, by virtue of not engaging in conceptual adherence. The defect of their meditation is the view of the nullity of all objects, making them like a piece of dead meat. Their approach is fulfilling the six perfections in the absence of superimposition.[37]

Note here that, while post–14th-century Tibetans would almost universally divide Mādhyamika into *svātāntrika* (those who think that Mādhyamikas have an "independent thesis" following the sixth-century Bhāviveka) and *prāsaṅgika* (those who think that the Mādhyamikas should only draw out unwanted "consequences" from others' theses, following the seventh-century Candrakīrti) camps, it should be remembered that Candrakīrti was still an obscure figure in the 11th century and would not be resurrected until the time of Jayānanda and Patsab Nayimdrak in the 12th century.[38] Maitrīpa's Mādhyamika is probably more akin to that of Śāntarakṣita and Bhāviveka (about whom, see below). For our purposes there are two aspects to Maitrīpa's discussion that are particularly interesting. The first is the fact that while he gives us a fairly standard doctrinal hierarchy from the disciples' vehicle right on up to the Mādhyamikas, emptiness characterizes all rungs of the Buddhist ladder. The difference between the levels of Buddhism lies in how that emptiness is understood. Disciples understand emptiness to mean the selflessness of the person. Sautrāntikas understand emptiness to be that the apparently objective world is nothing but representations of a mind that is itself unrepresented. Meditation on emptiness for them is meditating on the fact that through all the representations the mind cannot be found. Yogācārins are quite similar to the Sautrāntikas in the sense that they understand objective sense impressions to be either "aspects" of mind or mind's self-awareness. In either case, mind is emptiness. Finally, with the Mādhyamikas, the highest realization is that there is no objective support for cognition out there, a realization in which no attention is paid to the mind that knows it or to the fact that the realization occurs at all. In other words, all three forms of Mahāyāna emptinesses involve a recognition of the ubiquity of mind and an awareness that the ubiquitous mind is, at bottom, *unthought*.

The second point that is interesting about Maitṛpa's treatment of Buddhism's rise here is that while he gives us the standard gradations of the three vehicles, he does ***not*** (as Śāntarakṣita, Tibetan *sgrub mtha* and some Chinese *panjiao* doxographical works do) relegate Brahmanical schools to the lowest rungs of the doctrinal latter. From the stage of the greater disciples onward, he presents the goal of the stage and then warns the reader of ways that each stage might veer off into a parallel attainment current among vedāntins. Thus the greater disciple's meditation on emptiness might lead to the perception of the "Eternal Śiva": the *pratyekabuddha* stopping of the sense faculties comes close to the vedāntic practice of making the mind like "sleep without dreams," and the *nirākārin* Yogācārins might veer into the vedāntic camp of Bhāskara by taking their own self-awareness to be "Brahman as limitless in luminosity, continual, and permanent, entirely free of mental and physical parts . . . [etc.]." Vedānta here is not presented as *beneath* Buddhism but running *alongside it*.

Maitrīpa's Buddhism is therefore *not* the polar opposite of Brahmanism. He makes no mention of the ātman/anātman distinction as distinguishing between the two. Yet, clearly Maitrīpa wants to put some daylight between the teaching of the "Blessed One" and something else. But what exactly is the scope of this "something else"? It is doubtful that he had any sense of a unified "Hinduism" in the 11th century. Maitrīpa identifies the danger twice as those who tout the vedānta (*vedāntavādin*) and the "ideas of Bhāskara." Now, Tatz, following Hajime Nakamura,[39] assumes this Bhāskara to be the pre–10th-century[40] promulgator of *bhedābheda* ("difference and non-difference") *vedānta* and the latter expresses some surprise that he would reference Bhāskara and not mention Śaṅkara, who presumably would have been better known by the 11th century. I think, however, that the fact that Maitrīpa says that the danger of the disciple's meditation on emptiness is that they might project "Sadā Śiva" onto emptiness suggests that the Bhāskara he is referring to is the 11th-century Kaśmiri author of the commentary on the *Śiva Sūtras*, who would have been a contemporary of Maitrīpa.[41] This is, of course, speculation, and if the Bhāskara he is referring to is the author of the *Brahmāsūtra Bhāṣya* attributed to this name, then the fact that Śaṅkara is not mentioned is also interesting since the vedāntin Bhāskara was one of the first to criticize Śaṅkara as being crypto-Buddhist due to the latter's advocating that everything was illusion[42] – precisely the form of Mādhyamika that Maitrīpa likes best.

If Maitrīpa attempts to denigrate some meditations on emptiness as lower, it is because his opponents were already engaged in those meditations. In other words, in India (like we saw in China) meditation on emptiness was not understood to be *exclusive* property of Buddhists. It held pride of place among Buddhists precisely because it was a prize that everyone (ok, *almost* everyone) was after. The term *śūnya* appears in numerous texts of later Kaśmīri Śaivism, such as Utpāladeva's *Pratyabhijñāhṛdaya43* and *Vijñānabhairava*[44] or Bhāskara's *Śiva Sūtras*[45] as a kind of proximate enlightenment similar to the *pralāyam* or period in between cosmic destruction and cosmic creation. In none of these works is there any indication that the ideal of emptiness they discuss is a Buddhist idea.

Indeed, if we look at much of this medieval material, there appear to be many different ways to ascribe sectarian identity – and many of these do not align with our own. For example, when Kṣemarāja (10th–11th century) comments on the Buddhist's understanding of the term *śūnya*, he lumps the Mādhyamikas together with the vedāntins as adhering to original Non-being taught in the *Taittirīya Upaniṣad*.

> The Brahmavādins . . . who consider non-being (*abhāva*) as the fundamental principle on the ground (of the Upaniṣadic [i.e., Taittirīya U.] dictum) that 'all this was originally non-being', accept the position of the void, and are (thus) landed in it. The Mādhyamikas are also in the same position.[46]

Kṣemarāja is saying here that where the vedāntins (Brahmavādins) go wrong is in the way they read and interpret the Upaniṣads. He then includes the Mādhyamikas in the same category such that we are left to wonder whether he assumes the Mādhyamikas see themselves as interpreting the *Taittirīya Upaniṣad* as well. Sadānanda's 15th-century *Vedāntasāra* is even more explicit in making Mādhyamikas a school of Vedic interpretation. It divides Buddhists into two groups. The first consists of those who hold that the soul is consciousness itself, again based on the *Taittirīya Upaniṣad*.

> A Bauddha says that understanding is the Soul, because the Veda declares that "the other, the inner Soul, consists of knowledge"; and because, in the absence of an agent, there is no power in the instrument and because one is conscious that "It is I that act," or "it is I that experience."[47]

The second group consists of those who understand all things to be *śūnya* due to their misreading of the *Nāsadīyasukta* of the *Ṛg Veda*.

> Another Bauddha says that nihility is the Soul, because the Veda declares that "This (universe) previously was simply non-existent," [Ṛg Veda X.129] &c., and because in profound sleep everything ceases to exist; and because one, on arising from a deep sleep, has a conviction which has for its object the recollection of his own non-existence – (thus), "During that deep sleep, I was not."[48]

Now, it might be objected here that Kṣemarāja and Sadānanda present Buddhism here as a variety of Vedic interpretation because Buddhism had already died out and hence there were no Buddhists around to point out that Buddhism was in fact a separate religion from the Vedic tradition. However, given the fact that the Jesuit Roberto De Nobili finds Buddhist Brahmins not far from

Vijayanagar at the beginning of the 17th century, the assumption of Buddhism's demise in the 13th and 15th centuries is probably premature.[49] Furthermore, given the fact that the Buddhists that De Nobili finds among the Tamils are Brahmins who wear the sacred thread, I am inclined to think that Kṣemarāja and Sadānanda were probably characterizing Buddhists that they knew. I would also like to suggest that the type of Buddhist Brahmin encountered by De Nobili in the 17th century, by Sadānanda in the 15th, by Kṣemarāja in the 13th, for that matter, or by Bāṇa in the eighth, would have been a relatively familiar figure within Buddhist communities going all the way back possibly to the time of the Buddha himself.

So, if some like Maitrīpa assume Mahāyāna to have achieved the very perfection of non-objectifying reality that the "Bhāskara vedāntins" outside the Buddhist fold *also* aspire to, then there were others who saw Mahāyāna and especially the Mādhyamika Mahāyānists to simply be an incorrect branch of vedic interpretation. Finally, there also appear to be some, such as the author of the fourth–sixth-century *Viṣṇudharmapurāṇa* who understood Mahāyāna as something distinct from both Buddhism and Brahmanism.[50]

Bhāviveka's sixth-century Mahāyāna

So how would earlier generations categorize Mahāyāna? Next, I suggest we turn to the sixth-century Mādhyamika author, Bhāviveka, whose work becomes a kind of template for many subsequent Mahāyāna doxographies, especially in Tibet. While I have discussed at length elsewhere what I think the practice of Mahāyāna would have looked like in early Buddhist monasteries in India,[51] with Bhāviveka we get an interesting perspective both on what he understood Mahāyāna to be as well as some insight into his understanding of what others thought about it – good and bad. In particular, his *Mādhyamakahṛdayakārikā*, written sometime between 500 and 570 CE, contains a lengthy argument about the status of Mahāyāna and its boundaries. His arguments, recently translated and discussed by David Malcolm Eckel,[52] present us with a glimpse of the debates as to where different stakeholders might have drawn the lines between Mahāyāna and non-Mahāyāna as well as between Mahāyāna and Brahmanism.

While Maitrīpa in the 11th century takes it for granted the Mahāyāna is the pinnacle of Buddhism, in the sixth century the question of whether or not Mahāyāna is even Buddhist was apparently something that still had to be justified. Bhāviveka addresses the issue of Mahāyāna's Buddhist credentials in the chapter entitled, "Analysis of Reality according to the *śrāvakas*." *Śrāvaka* or "disciple" was the common term used by Mahāyānists for non-Mahāyāna Buddhists. The opponent's understanding is that Mahāyāna stands outside of the boundary demarcating Buddhism or "what the Buddha has taught" because: it constitutes a separate "way" or path (verses 4.1–6); it is taught in different scriptures than those of the *Tripiṭaka* and its goal (*mārgānta*) and teachings are different; like the Vedāntic view (4.7), it teaches a different set of doctrines, like the Nāstika[53] or the Lokāyata (4.8ab); and finally, it is not Buddhist, because there are 18 schools of Buddhism and Mahāyāna is not one of them (4.8cd). Verses 9–14 of that chapter constitute what Eckel terms "Miscellaneous Objections," insofar as they are not really organized by a particular theme.[54]

In Bhāviveka's discussion we see that there must have been a readership that needed to be convinced that Mahāyāna *was* Buddhism. Contrary to these claims, Bhāviveka argues that Mahāyāna is the very heart of Buddhism since it pertains directly to the Buddha and his realization. I take the fact that Bhāviveka had to make this case to be an indication that there were those (perhaps even some who adopted the word "Mahāyāna" for themselves) who understood Mahāyāna to be taught in separate sutras, to follow doctrines that were not sanctioned by any of the "traditional" 18 sects and possibly to be more akin to Vedic schools than Buddhist ones.

The opponent's first objection is that Mahāyāna teaches a different path. The opponent argues at 4.2 that all 18 schools of Buddhism accept that "[t]he word 'Buddha' refers to the moment of cognition that follows the diamond-like concentration (*vajropamasamādhi*)."[55] Buddhahood is thus synonymous with "non-conceptual cognition," (*nirvikalpa jñāna*) and cannot be identified with some kind of ethereal body such as the Mahāyānist doctrine of the *dharma-kāya*. The opponent argues that Mahāyāna is different from the path taught in Buddhist sects, because it identifies *bodhi* with five aspects: "an eternal body, thusness (*tathatā*) as a mere dharma, the understanding of conditions, the understanding of no-arising and omniscience."[56] (Notice that emptiness does not appear in this list.) By contrast, the opponent argues in verse 4.3, that the Buddha's path is none other than the Noble Eightfold Path just like the path of all Buddhists. The opponent goes on to argue that Mahāyāna is a different teaching from that of the disciples because it over-negates; denying the existence of self in anything, it negates the possibility of cause and effect like a form of nihilism.[57]

Bhāviveka's response is, in effect, to argue that the "distinction" between Mahāyāna and the other Buddhist vehicles is not so much a *separation* from other vehicles as it is that which *distinguishes* (i.e., elevates) the Buddha *above* his disciples. In other words, for Bhāviveka, the Mahāyāna is synonymous with the Buddha vehicle that is already understood by his opponents. As such, the Mahāyāna path is in no way separate from the Noble Eightfold Path of his followers; it is merely a more excellent implementation of it.[58] Bhāviveka's method is to start with his opponent's thesis and to show key Mahāyāna points are already implied in the central position of the opponent. Thus, returning to the initial claim of his interlocutor that identifies the Buddha with non-constructed awareness (*nirvikalpa jñāna*), Bhāviveka begins his response in verse 4.16:

> [We] think that the Teacher's cognition is non-conceptual, because his cognition apprehends no self, just as it has the no-self of persons as its object.

and 4.18

> Since there is no object of cognition, awakening is understood as the no-arising of cognition with regard to this [no-object], because this [no-arising] is consistent with the reality (*tattva*) of the object.[59]

The opponent appeals here to the doctrine that the Buddha's awakening amounts to the state of non-conceptual awareness. Bhāviveka agrees and argues that the Buddha's cognition is this way because reality itself is, in fact, devoid of realia to cognize. Since there is nothing that has an identity (*svabhāva*) to be cognized, the cognition eschewing all identifications will necessarily be an accurate representation of that state of affairs.[60] This is simultaneously an understanding of selflessness, but not as a proposition (i.e., "The self does not exist"). In the absence of any conceptualization, the self is among those things not conceived.

The opponent had initially identified Buddhahood with non-conceptual awareness and then argued that the Buddha achieved this through the Noble Eightfold Path (vs. 4.3), usually understood as, "right vision, right thought, right speech, right action, right livelihood, right effort, right mindfulness and right concentration." The opponent, however, did not explain how or why the Eightfold Path would lead to non-conceptual awareness. Bhāviveka connects the two in a way that will be crucial to the central concerns of this book.

> 4.20–21 Someone who practices the path that begins with right vision has no vision, no thought, no speech, no action, no livelihood, no effort, no mindfulness, and no concentration . . .

and thus

> When [the opponents] say that awakening is achieved by the eightfold path, they prove something that has already been accepted.[61]

The opponent then argues that while it may be reasonable to practice the Noble Eightfold Path this way, such a practice contradicts the Mahāyāna tradition that Bhāviveka is defending. Bhāviveka then quotes from three Mahāyāna texts (the *Ārya Sarvadharmāpravṛttinirdeśasūtra*, *The Perfection of Wisdom* and the *Akṣayamatinirdeśasūtra*) to demonstrate that "right view" is understood by Mahāyāna texts to be, in fact, "no view."

Even though it appears as his second citation, his use of the *Perfection of Wisdom* is interesting here. He states: "Likewise, in *The Perfection of Wisdom* it says: 'One should practice the right view based on isolation, non-attachment, and cessation with the approach of no-apprehension.' "[62] I have been unable to locate this passage in any existing text of the *Perfection of Wisdom* corpus, so it could either be from an edition that is now lost or may simply be Bhāviveka's paraphrase. Whatever the case may be, Bhāviveka chose to interpret the "right view" of the Noble Eightfold Path as a "no seeing" based on the approach of no-apprehension, which in turn is equated with cessation, isolation and non-attachment.

His choice of passage from the *Perfection of Wisdom* is not tangential. As we shall see in the following chapters, not only would it be accurate to say that no-apprehension is the "approach" of the first chapter of the *Perfection of Wisdom*, its version of "right view" could also be accurately summarized as a "not-seeing" (here the relevant phrase is *na sam-anu + √paś*). Moreover, since the tradition of virtually every generation of Buddhism inflected by Tibetan schools reads the

Perfection of Wisdom in 8,000 Lines through the lens of the *Abhisamayālaṃkāra*, it is important to note that the first chapter of the *Perfection* was understood in the *Abhisamayālaṃkāra* as epitomizing "omniscience of all aspects" (*sarva-ākāra-jñātā*), the awareness that is exclusive to the Buddha and bodhisattvas not so much by virtue of having different content, but by a deeper penetration into the same Buddhist truths.[63] In the same manner, when Bhāviveka returns to the question of whether Mahāyāna sutras should be considered to belong to the *Tripiṭaka*, he invokes the approach of non-apprehension as both epitomizing the Mahāyāna as well as characterizing the Buddha's awareness "in the other vehicle." Non-apprehension, thus becomes a kind of cipher for revealing the Mahāyāna to constitute the very heart of the *Tripiṭaka* - only at a deeper level.

> [The Opponent:] [A]ccording to us, the three baskets (*tripiṭaka*) cause one to obtain [the three jewels], but the Mahāyāna does not. Since we do not accept that it is the Buddha's teaching, this [argument that Mahāyāna causes one to obtain the three jewels] suffers the fault of not being accepted by both parties.
>
> Reply: Undefiled ignorance (*akliṣṭāvidyā*) is removed by a single moment of a Self-Existent One's correct knowledge, which understands all dharmas. Someone who has practiced no-apprehension is free [from undefiled ignorance]. This was taught by the Buddha in the other vehicle, so it is not the case that this point is not accepted by both parties.[64]

Earlier, the opponent had objected that Mahāyānists denied the enlightenment of arhats and even insulted them. Yet Mahāyānists were hardly innovative in contrasting the arhat, an enlightened person who is nevertheless not as perfect as the Buddha, to the Buddha. Certainly by Bhāviveka's time the Sarvāstivādins (and probably others as well) understood the difference between the enlightenment of the arhat and the enlightenment of the Buddha to lie in the fact that an arhat could be ignorant of minor things (the names of plants, etc.) while a Buddha was not ignorant of anything because he understands all dharmas.[65] The ignorance of an arhat is stated to be an "undefiled ignorance" (*akliṣṭāvidyā*), an ignorance which is contrasted with the Buddha's omniscience (*sarvajñā*). Bhāviveka here equates the non-apprehension with the Buddha's practice, which produces the understanding which destroys even the undefiled ignorance of the arhat. He then points out that the non-apprehension that epitomizes the Mahāyāna is also found in the other vehicle and hence cannot be said to be outside either the *Tripiṭaka* or for that reason outside the traditional Buddhist sects.

The commentary goes on to argue that Mahāyāna is none other than the canonical teachings to the extent that it removes defilements. It is distinguished[66] above those teachings, however, insofar as it uses the approach of no-apprehension – the approach special to the Buddha himself.

> The teachings of the Mahāyāna, such as the truths of suffering, arising, cessation, and the path, the faculties (*indriya*), the strengths (*bala*),

> the limbs of awakening (*bodhyaṅga*) . . . [etc.] are taught word for word in the Vinaya, sūtras and Abhidharma. [The teachings of the Mahāyāna] are the same in the way they use these practices to remove defilements. They are distinctive in that only the Blessed One uses the Mahāyāna approach of no-apprehension to remove the obstacles to knowledge. Therefore, because the truths taught in the Vinaya and so forth are fully explained in the Mahāyāna, the Sutras and so forth are consistent with the Mahāyāna. Since the Mahāyāna is included implicitly in the Sūtras and so forth, the opponent's reason is not accepted.[67]

At this point, I would like to make a few observations. Bhāviveka is aware that others understood Mahāyāna texts and doctrines to fall outside the pale of Buddhism. Bhāviveka's rejoinder is somewhat unexpected. Modern scholarly predilections and the genealogy of Mahāyāna we have been tracing so far would expect him to argue that the word emptiness (*śūnyatā*) found in Mahāyāna texts can also be found in the *Tripiṭaka*, and therefore Mahāyāna is Buddhist. He does not do this – at least for the first 35 verses.[68] For Bhāviveka, emptiness (*śūnyatā*) does not appear to be the primary marker of Mahāyāna. Indeed, he holds up non-apprehension (*anupalabha*) as the epitome of Mahāyāna – ***not*** emptiness or even the "selflessness of dharmas" (*dharma-nairātmya*),[69] which is not mentioned at all. If anything, emptiness for Bhāviveka is the epistemic result of non-apprehension. Here, it should be pointed out that Bhāviveka does not have to argue that non-apprehension can be found in the *Tripiṭaka*; he assumes his opponent is already aware of this. It is only after verse 36, which forms a kind of coda to the issue of the Noble Eightfold Path discussed earlier, that the doctrine of "emptiness" comes up as a specifically Mahāyāna doctrine,[70] as Bhāviveka rehearses Nāgārjuna's arguments about the Four Noble Truths. But even in this discussion, the term "emptiness" is not held up as the banner of Mahāyāna so much as the "non-seeing," which amounts to "right view" of the path.

> 4.54 [We] think that liberation is the complete no-vision [*sarvathā adarśana*] of the four noble truths, so the example is impossible and the reason is unaccepted.
>
> The position of the Mahāyāna stated here is that liberation is the complete no-vision of the four noble truths. The no-vision of these truths is beyond the reach of the Śrāvakas and others who see nothing but dharmas. . . . The reason, "[because the Mahāyāna] teaches a different path is also unaccepted. Why? (verse 55) This very same path, beginning with right vision, is taught in the Mahāyāna, so the reason is unaccepted.
>
> From a relative point of view (*saṃvṛtyā*) one should practice the eightfold path literally, but when one understands reality (*tattva*) one should practice it as no-vision and so forth. So a distinctive practice is taught in the Mahāyāna, but not a different path [*des na theg pa chen po 'dir bsgom pa bye brag tu bstan pa yin gyi yang lam gzhan ni ma yin pas*]. Therefore, the reason, "because [the Mahāyāna] teaches a different path," is unaccepted.[71]

Thus, in arguing that Mahāyāna is actually included in the *Tripiṭaka*, Bhāviveka appeals to the term "no-apprehension" (*an-upa√labh*) and the "unseen" (*adṛṣṭa*) as common ground for Mahāyāna within the *Tripiṭaka.*

While he would wallow in obscurity for another six centuries, whatever disagreements Candrakīrti may have had with Bhāviveka, he took the idea of "non-perception" even further than Bhāviveka. Candrakīrti argues rather famously that both mind and mental concomitants cease for the Buddha and hence the Buddha apprehends nothing.[72] Though Candrakīrti does not use this term himself, one could say that his Buddha is "mindless" or *acitta* - an idea that we will see also occupies a prominent place in the first chapter of the *Perfection of Wisdom in 8,000 Lines.*

Thus, despite the alleged differences between Candrakīrti and Bhāviveka that would become so important for later Tibetan Buddhism, both of them are operating within what can only be described as slightly different, though equally robust, readings of the first chapter of the *Perfection of Wisdom in 8,000 Lines.* In all of this we don't really see Mahāyānists arguing for Mahāyāna to be a separate sectarian position or a separate Buddhist identity but rather that it was a *distinguished* Buddhist identity. Nevertheless, Bhāviveka's argument also makes it clear that some did see a marked difference between Mahāyāna and the forms of Buddhism they were aware of. Hence, at least by the sixth century, the question of whether or not Mahāyāna was "Buddhism" was contested by the very people involved. Where some saw a borderline, others saw a distinction.

Bhāviveka, Mahāyāna and Yogācāra

So what about Yogācāra? Throughout each of the previous chapters, I have referred to the ultimate as either "emptiness" or some kind of primordial Mind and have hinted that for many Mahāyānists throughout history, there would not have been an appreciable difference between the two. But in India, we have two schools that did not always get along: the Mādhyamika and the Yogācāra or "mind-only" school. Were there in India two Mahāyānas corresponding to the doctrine of emptiness and mind-only or only one? To what extent could the doctrine of mind-only also seen to be encompassed by the teachings of the *Perfection of Wisdom*?

Clearly, Bhāviveka knew he had to make the case that there was only one - which means that there were those who needed to be convinced. To make his case, Bhāviveka presents both Yogācāra and Mādhyamika philosophies as, at least in part,[73] grounded in a certain reading of the same core pericope of the *Perfection of Wisdom.* At the end of the Yogācāra opponent's presentation of mind-only philosophy, the opponent rounds out the argument by saying, "This approach to the Perfection of Wisdom is [the means] to attain omniscience, and the one that concentrates on the negation of arising and cessation is not."[74] In a footnote to this verse Eckel notes:

> In verse 5.7, the Yogācāras make an exclusive claim for the validity of their own position. A comparable claim can be found in verses 27–29 of Dignāga's *Prajñāpāramitāpiṇḍārtha* ["Epitome of the Perfection of Wisdom"]: "The teaching in the Perfection of Wisdom is based on three [identities]:

> imagined, dependent, and absolute. The words 'do not exist' rule out everything that is imagined. Examples such as illusion (*māyā*) teach dependent [identity]. The fourfold purification teaches absolute [identity]. The Buddha has no other teaching in the Perfection of Wisdom." Verse 5.7 clearly shows that Bhāviveka thought the dispute between Yogācāra and Madhyamika was provoked by the Yogācāra interpretation of the Perfection of Wisdom.[75]

In the commentary on this verse, Bhāviveka's Yogācāra opponent grounds his doctrine in an interpretation of four verses from the *Prajñāpāramitā*:

1 "When he thus by means of these dharmas softens the dharmas, fulfills, and clarifies, and perfects them, then [he realizes that] there is no self and nothing that belongs to the self"
2 Mind is no mind
3 No-mind is inconceivable
4 Thus material form is a cognitive sign (*nimitta*), and everything up to awakening is a cognitive sign.[76]

These four statements are cited as evidence of, respectively: 1) the storehouse consciousness, 2) the absence of subject and object, 3) the fact of mind-only and 4) the doctrine of the imagined nature of things – four items that are seminal doctrines for Yogācāra philosophy. Now, the first three of these quotes appear in the *Perfection of Wisdom in 25,000 Lines*, which may be where Bhāviveka found them, but the second appears in the latter text as a reiteration of a passage from the *Perfection of Wisdom in 8,000 Lines*. When the phrase, "the no-mind is inconceivable" appears in the *Perfection of Wisdom in 25,000 Lines* (as well as in the *Perfection of Wisdom in 100,000 Lines*), we can read it as one of a series of adaptations of the phrase "this mind is no-mind" from the beginning of the *Perfection of Wisdom in 8,000 Lines*. Thus we have in the *Perfection of Wisdom in 8,000 Lines*:

> Thus the student should also not consider himself to have *bodhicitta*. What is the reason? Because this mind is no-mind.[77]

This passage appears in a greatly expanded version in the *Perfection of Wisdom in 25,000 Lines*,[78] and from there the phrase "this mind is no-mind" gets reworked in at least two other contexts in that text. Hence we find:

> Because this mind is depending on no-mind, the unthinkable, I do not consider myself to be wise.[79]

and then finally the passage that Bhāviveka is quoting (which also appears in the *Perfection of Wisdom in 100,000 Lines*):

> Thus Śakra Lord of the devas said to the Elder Subhūti: How is it reverend Subhūti that the ripening mind is not brought into contact with the

> bodhicitta? How is it that the mind of awakening is not brought into contact with the ripening mind? And how is it that the bodhicitta is not perceived nor found in the ripening mind. How is it that the developing mind is not perceived nor found in bodhicitta? Subhūti said, "Kauśika, the ripening mind is no-mind (or thoughtless, *acitta*). Bodhicitta is no-mind and indeed does not ripen in the mental state (*cittatā*) of mindlessness (*acittatā*). Thus, indeed, that which is no mind is unthinkable. That which is unthinkable, that no-mind ripens in the mental state of mindlessness. This, Kauśika, is the perfection of wisdom of the bodhisattva Mahāsattvas.[80]

In short, Bhāviveka here has his Yogācāra opponents tracing at least two of their seminal doctrines (the absence of subject and object [= *abhūta-parikalpa*] and the doctrine that everything is mind-only) to passages in *Perfection of Wisdom* literature that can be traced to the first chapter of the *Perfection of Wisdom in 8,000 Lines*. Moreover, it seems likely that Bhāviveka is representing an actual exegesis that was being discussed in Yogācāra circles in his day and not merely presenting a strawman argument, since he never comes back to any of these passages to explain how the Yogācārins misinterpreted these passages.

Bhāviveka, Mahāyāna and Brahmanism

Bhāviveka emphasizes the common ground between his own position and that of his opponents, an "inclusivistic" move that Wilhelm Halbfass[81] says characterizes much of Indian doxographic literature more generally. His twin moves of appealing to "no-apprehension" and seeing which is no-seeing and his appeal to the common ground of Mādhyamika and Yogacāra within the statement that "the mind is mindless" both hearken back to the first few paragraphs of the *Perfection of Wisdom in 8,000 Lines* where those two doctrines are brought together.

But what about the claim that Mahāyāna is not Buddhist at all but rather Brahmanical, or "*vedānta*"?[82] The very question seems to assume that there is some kind of divide between Buddhism and Brahmanism, such that Mahāyāna belongs more to the latter than the former. This objection of Mahāyāna being Brahmanical is not unheard of. In the *Chusanzang jiji*, there is a story of a certain Zhu Shixing who obtains a copy of what is probably the *Perfection of Wisdom in 25,000 Lines* from Khotan. The local monks are all said to be Chinese *śramanas* or mendicants of the "Hīnayāna." They order the king to burn the book because it is a "Brahmin book."[83] By the same token, when a school called "Vedānta" does arise (presumably after Bhāviveka) we find the charge going in the other direction: Śaṅkara in particular was accused by Bhāskara and Vijñānabhikṣu as being a crypto-Buddhist[84] and the propinquity between Mahāyāna and Vedānta even in earlier generations of the latter has been well documented by Richard King in his work on the Mahāyāna context of the *Gauḍapādakārikā*.[85]

But what exactly did Bhāviveka and his contemporaries understand to be the difference between Buddhism and Brahmanism? We might assume Buddhists to be those who adhere to Buddhist sutras while "vedāntins" rely on Brahmanical scriptures like the Vedas and the Upaniṣads in the same way that Muslims revere the Koran while the Mormons use the *Book of the Mormon*. But a simple mapping of sectarian identity onto books is not exactly true to the literary world of early historical India. Granted, the opponent has argued that Mahāyāna does not appear in the sutras and so some textual affiliation is assumed here. Buddhists *are* assumed to read the Buddhist sutras, but to say that they are therefore expected to eschew other textual traditions as a condition for their status as Buddhist is not quite right either.

The commentary on 4.7 makes it clear that the opponent thinks Mahāyāna is "like Vedānta" insofar as Mahāyānists follow the *same* teachings and practices as those designated as *vedānta*. Specifically, the opponent objects that *vedānta* texts[86] say "that one [removes] impurities and attains liberation by bathing at pilgrimage places on rivers such as the Ganges, by fasting, and by reciting mantras in three ways . . ." and likewise "The adherents of the Mahāyāna also bathe in the four rivers . . . drink from them, and, while standing in them, initiate and repeat *dhāraṇīs* and mantras to remove impurities and increase merit."[87] The emphasis here seems to be on the practices and teachings of a tradition rather than any specific textual corpus. Nowhere do we get the sense that Buddhists shouldn't be paying attention to a set of texts, but rather that they should adhere to practices and goals that may or may not be found in any number of places.

Hence, in responding to the objection that Mahāyāna is closer to vedānta, we find Bhāviveka to be just as inclusive toward this "*vedānta*" as he was toward the Śrāvakayāna or the Yogācāra – meaning that he includes them *with a twist*. And again, he never exactly says that the *vedāntin* is wrong. That he does not flatly denounce *vedānta* – supposedly Buddhism's other – has stirred up not a little controversy in our era. Bhāviveka responds to the objection that Mahāyāna is really Brahmanism (*vedānta*) by saying, "Everything that is well spoken (*sūkta*) in the Vedānta is taught by the Buddha." The commentary explains this by stating, "The [parts of the] Vedas that are well spoken and do not contradict the teaching of the Buddha should be accepted, and those that are not well spoken should not be accepted."[88] Bhāviveka leaves open (as most Buddhist texts do) the possibility that truth can be found in Vedic texts just as much as anywhere else. The text is less important than the ability of the practitioner to recognize what is true and what is not in texts. Indeed, we don't find the charge that Buddhists deny the Vedas until at least the eighth century – some 200 years after Bhāviveka. The *Laws of Manu* (2.11) states that all of dharma has its roots in the Vedas and the derivative law treatises (*smṛti*). Furthermore, if any "twice-born disparages these two by relying on the science of logic, he ought to be ostracized by good people as an infidel [*nāstika*] and a denigrator of the Veda."[89] Manu himself does not identify who might be wielding this logic. Medhatīthi (eighth–10th century?) does identify the challenge as coming from the treatises of the Buddhists and Cārvākas,[90] but it isn't clear whether his objection to them is due to their use of a wholly different set of scriptures or simply because they were known as pugnacious logicians. In any case, it does not appear that anyone understood the difference between Buddhism and Vedānta to boil down to a difference in scripture (or at least that this was not a very widespread assumption) until Vijñānabhikṣu and Madhusūdana Sarasvatī in the 16th century. Andrew Nicholson has argued that it is likely that their doxographic stance arose in response to increasing salience of the Koran in the rising Mughal Dynasty.[91]

However, as much Bhāviveka's response to the vedāntin may be read as "inclusivistic," he was not exactly the type to sit down and sing "*kumbaya*" with just any Brahmanical partisan. Despite Xuanzang's assertion that, "on the outside, [Bhāviveka] showed himself to be a follower of Sāṃkhya,"[92] he shows no affinities to that particular school. Nevertheless, in his eighth chapter devoted exclusively to arguing with a vedāntin he does suggest that the Mahāyānist might find agreement among some readers of Brahmanical texts on the nature of the soul (*ātman*) and *brahman*. As to the former, Bhāviveka acknowledges (as Nāgārjuna himself did) that the Buddha taught both soul and non-soul and merely argues that non-arising (*ajāta*) is the nature of the soul. While Bhāviveka might have anticipated that some would balk at this idea, the *vedānta* chapter seems to assume that some vedāntins may actually already agree with the Mahāyāna position on the nature (or lack thereof) of the soul. Qvarnström's translation of verse 94 and 95 renders the tone of the argument.

> 94. It [the soul] is expressible by virtue of the imposition of conceptual constructions (*kalpanāsamāropa*), but it is inexpressible (*avācya*) in reality (*tattvataḥ*), and furthermore because it is in every respect inexpressible (*avāvyatva*), it is said to be unmanifest (*nirañjana*).
>
> 95. Obviously, if such a Self . . . is accepted even by you, [then] that . . . is infallible (*nirdoṣa*) and completely proper (*upapattika*) because of the extensive conceptual correspondence with regard to name, etc.[93]

While much has been made of the Buddhist so-called denial of the Brahmanical soul,[94] the fact of the matter is that upaniṣadic texts show quite a bit of variation as to what that *ātman* actually is. Certainly, Śaṅkara's assertion that the *ātman* is "being, consciousness and Bliss" (*sat cit ānanda*) was not around at the time of Bhāviveka and articulations of the *ātman* among some Yajurvedin schools come far closer to what Buddhists claim to adhere to. Thus, the articulation of *Bṛhadāraṇyaka Upaniṣad* that rather famously equates *ātman* with *brahman*[95] thereby renders the *ātman* devoid of qualities (*nirguṇa*)[96] and not something that can be spoken of (it is said to be "neither this nor that" *neti neti*).[97] The *Śvetāśvatara Upaniṣad* tells us that the "one god" who is the inner self (*sarva bhūta antar ātmā*) of all things[98] is "without parts, without activity, tranquil, without blemish, the highest bridge to immortality like a fire with its fuel burnt,[99] blemishless" (*nirañjana*). The last two qualifications in particular would have been something Bhāviveka would agree with since he himself states that the soul is *nirañjana* and the extinguished fire is a common reference to the enlightened state of a Tathāgata (the common epithet for a Buddha) in Buddhist sutras such as the *Aggivaccagottasutta* of the *Majjhima Nikāya*.

If the *vedāntin* finds in the Mahāyāna argument certain points that he or she already knows from the *Yajurveda Upaniṣads*, does that mean that Bhāviveka is acknowledging that Mahāyāna is Vedānta? Not exactly. In verse 8.86 he accounts for the, apparently undeniable similarities between Brahmanical teachings and Mahāyāna by stating that it is the outsiders ("*tīrthikas*") who out of their burning desire have claimed the Buddhist teachings their own. The commentary is quite explicit that those who claim that these teachings are in the vedānta are guilty of the fault of mixing what are in fact mutually contradictory things (although he never says exactly wherein they contradict).[100]

It is highly questionable whether Bhāviveka's contemporaries would have conflated all things Brahmanical with the doctrine of the eternal *ātman*.[101] To wit, Brahmanical texts aren't just interested in *ātman*, they also have a lot to say about the doctrine of *brahman*. Bhāviveka equates the Mahāyāna Dharma Body of the Buddha with *brahman*. The following translation is from Gokhale with select portions of the commentary translated in brackets.

> (279) Being invisible either to the physical or the divine eye, this (*Dharmakāya*) is difficult to perceive either by conceptual or non-conceptual knowledge. (280): It is outside the ken of dialecticians, just as the Heaven is outside that of the sinners, or a state of concord is outside that of the passionate ones, or the sun is outside that of those, who are born blind. (281): It is neither existent, nor non-existent, nor both existent and non-existent, nor different from both of the above, nor anything else. It is neither subtle, nor gross, nor alone, nor far, nor near. (282): Nothing and in no way is anything born from, or manifested by it. There is none here, who either endures or perishes. (283): This is the great Brahman, which cannot be grasped by the (god) Brahmā [or Viṣṇu or Maheśvara and others, whose views are rooted in self-complex. 'Brahman', which means both "the Lord of the living beings" (Prajāpati), as well as "the state of having gone beyond suffering" (*nirvāṇa*), is to be understood here only in the latter sense, i.e. *nirvaṇa*, which these gods are not in a position to perceive, because perception is not possible by means of a knowledge which is contingent (*sālambana*)]. (284) (It is this) which the learned seers (*sūrayaḥ*), like Ārya Avalokiteśvara, Ārya Maitreya and others adore by the method of non-adoration (*anupāsanayoga*). [Many seers, too, like Ārya Avalokiteśvara, Ārya Maitreya, Samantabhadra and Mañjuśrī-kumārabhūta, etc. who being endowed with the Perfections (*Pāramitās*), have obtained mastery over the ten *Bhūmis*, and who being purified by abstract (*nirālambana*) meditations, are well versed in the non-substantiality of all things, worship it (i.e., the Brahma) through non-worshipping, inasmuch as salutations, recitations of hymns and meditations are just illusory manifestations of the unsubstantial body, speech and mind.][102]

This passage has produced some anxiety among scholars, with some eager to defend Bhāviveka's "Buddhist" credentials,[103] while others pointing out that there really wasn't much difference between the Mahāyāna doctrine of the Dharma Body and the doctrine of Brahman anyway.[104] Like the Greek *archē*, the Brahmanical *brahman* was the ultimate source or origin of all things as well as their governing principle (identical to the *ātman* in some readings). It was not only the source of all potential magical power but formed the ritual basis of legitimate political authority as well. This *brahman* was the subject of *brahmodyas*, or court philosophical debates about first things. The purpose of these debates was to determine whose understanding of the origin was more primordial or more fundamental. The priest whose understanding was determined to transcend the others would then take on a legitimating function *vis-à-vis* the dynasty, either as the court sacrificial priest (*ṛtvij*) or as *purohita*. Yogis, as those with direct experience of this origin, were especially suited to take on this legitimating function.

For this reason, as I am sure Bhāviveka was well aware, *brahman* was not a static doctrine to be refuted but rather the very stakes of the religious agon itself. To claim that it didn't exist would be tantamount to not playing the game. And, in fact, I am not aware of any Buddhist text, *ever*, that denies the existence of *brahman*. In any case, Bhāviveka's strategy, like every other Buddhist, was not to *deny* the game but rather to *win* it. Thus, when Bhāviveka declares the *dharma-kāya/brahman* to be "neither existent, nor non-existent, nor both existent and non-existent, nor different from both the above, nor anything else," he is asserting the Buddhist understanding of the ultimate to transcend the alternatives of being and non-being, and to go beyond even passages such as *Ṛg Veda* X.129, that declare "the One" to be before existence and non-existence (*sat* and *asat*). Bhāviveka's tactic here is again similar to that of Nāgārjuna, who in his *Ratnāvalī* tells the king, "Ask the Sāṃkhyas, the followers of Kaṇaḍa, Nirgranthas, and the worldly proponents of a person and aggregates, whether they propound what passes beyond 'is' and 'is not.' "[105] What Nāgārjuna assumes here is that the Sāmkhyas, etc. somehow fall short of "passing beyond" (*vyati√kram*) 'is' and 'is not," and that finding those who pass furthest beyond would be relevant to the king. I will return to this point in the concluding chapter.

For Bhāviveka, then, how does the Mahāyāna *dharma-kāya* surpass its competitors? In his answer, we hear distant echoes of the *Perfection of Wisdom* and its approach of non-apprehension and no-seeing. Although he does not use *anupa√labh* here, he does say that the *dharma-kāya* cannot be "grasped" (*na gṛhyate*) by even the highest of the gods and that it cannot be seen by either the physical eye or by the divine eye. Even Bhāviveka's statement that the sages "adore it by the method of non-adoration (*anupāsana-yoga*)"[106] may be meant to echo the "not seeing" (*na samanu√paś*) of the *Perfection of Wisdom* insofar as *anupāsana* can mean to "sit near" or "to worship" as Gokhale has it or as in Monier-Williams, simply "to regard or consider as." In short, the approach of no-apprehension and no-seeing that is the centerpiece of the *Perfection of Wisdom* is also the method to attain the most profound comprehension of that which surpasses and transcends all else, namely the *dharma-kāya/brahman*.

Bhāviveka is thus quite willing to dispense with doctrines that do not pertain to the legitimation of sovereignty while maintaining that the basic parameters concerning the ultimate as articulated in the Vedic texts are accomplished more fully by Mahāyāna. Does this make his Mahāyāna a form of Brahmanism? If it does, then it makes Buddhism itself a form of Brahmanism, since he has already shown that what is most salient in the Mahāyāna to be the irreducible core of the Buddhist doctrine of the enlightenment of the Buddha. But whether Mahāyāna is or is not a form of Brahmanism is precisely the *wrong* question. The very debate that Bhāviveka joins here shows that some people assumed the two to be separate while for Bhāviveka Mahāyāna is distinguished *above* its competitors but is not necessarily distinct *from* them. I will be arguing that the same dynamic that motivates Bhāviveka's response was very much at work in the composition of the *Perfection of Wisdom in 8,000 Lines.*

Preliminary conclusion

At this point the journey backward from my local Barnes & Noble has reached something in the range of what we might call an "origin" of Mahāyāna Buddhism. In this retrospective a few themes keep recurring. On the one hand, we have heard a lot about emptiness and the cessation of thought. The 14th Dalai Lama teaches that emptiness is the "selflessness of all dharmas" that one realizes in the state of cessation (the *vajra*-like *samādhi*) that is the third noble truth. The mark of Mahāyāna, on the other hand, is the presence of *bodhicitta* – the compassionate mind. Others have understood *bodhicitta* as the mind that abides in emptiness. For many tantrics, the mind at the pinnacle of tantric practice is identical to the ontological emptiness/luminosity of the cosmos itself. Throughout these chapters we have seen repeatedly that the mind that does not cognize entities amounts to the creative font of all things (whether seen as illusions or not) and as a manifestation of emptiness itself. With Bhāviveka in the sixth century, we find him making the case that the cessation of cognition (i.e., non-apprehension) marks the culmination of that for which both Buddhists and vedāntins aspire – and as such it is distinguished as the Mahāyāna. However, to make his case, he essentially argues that his Buddhist opponents have misread the *Perfection of Wisdom in 8,000 Lines*. Given that Bhāviveka grounds his case for Mādhyamika and Yogācāra in terminology from the first chapter of the *Perfection of Wisdom in 8,000 Lines*, we can reasonably say that the latter text marks a point on the horizon that grounded the authoritative distinction between Mahāyāna and other forms of Buddhism. Again, this is not to say that the *Perfection of Wisdom* marks the historical starting point Mahāyāna, but rather the threshold of what is visible as Mahāyāna from the perspective of at least the sixth century. To proceed any further, however, we will have to shift our vantage point to the forces that formed and informed the compilation of the *Perfection of Wisdom* itself. It is to the composition of the latter that I now turn.

Notes

1 Sharf (2017), p. 85.
2 Guzy (2005), p. 2.
3 Banerjee-Dube (2015), p. 623.
4 Ibid., pp. 624–625.
5 Guzy, p. 3.
6 Guzy p. 4.
7 Guzy, p. 5.
8 Korom (2004), p. 856.
9 Choudhury (1997), pp. 229–230.
10 Subhakanta Behera (1997), p. 2096.
11 Patnaik (2005). My thanks to Aniket De for drawing my attention to this source.
12 Ibid., p. 92.
13 Ibid., p. 117.
14 Kulke (1993), pp. 35–36.
15 Ibid., 36.
16 Mohanty (2014), p. 9.
17 I am summarizing the argument of Kulke (1980).
18 Kulke (1993), pp. 4–5.
19 Kulke (1993), pp. 24–26.
20 Ibid., pp. 55–56.
21 Of course, as a coded image, Jagannāth as a post was not always coded as emptiness. Sometime after 1568, Jagannāth and his relation to the eight rural goddesses (each of whom is also represented by wooden posts) comes to be referred to as the central post of a tent and the goddesses as the eight wooden pegs of the tent. See Kulke (1980), p. 31.
22 Patnaik, p. 117.
23 Ibid., p. 116.
24 Ibid., p. 117.
25 Patnaik, fronticepiece.
26 Ibid., p. 113.
27 See Dean (1998).
28 Kragh (2015), p. 71.
29 See Mark Tatz (1990).
30 See Tatz, pp. 494–495; Sanskrit from Shastri (1927), pp. 14–22.
31 Adapted from Tatz. p. 496.
32 Shastri, p. 16.
33 Ibid., p. 17; *cittam niscitya bodhena abhyāsaṃ kurute yadā tadā cittam na pasyāmi kva gataṃ kva sthitaṃ bhavet.*
34 Adapted from Tatz, p. 498.
35 *Paramārtha-sannitya-sākāra-vijñāna-samādhau bhagavataḥ saṃsthita-vedāntavādi-matānupraveśaḥ. Sa hi paramārtha-sannityaṃ svacind-rūpa-brahmābhinna-pariṇāmarūpaṃ jagadicchati.*
36 Adapted from Tatz, p. 500.
37 Ibid., p. 501.
38 See Vose (2009).
39 Nakamura, vol. 1 (1983), pp. 260–263.
40 Dasgupta (1940), vol. 3, p. 1.
41 See Dyczkowski (1992).
42 Dasgupta, Ibid.
43 Singh (1998), pp. 37, 54–55; 60, 62, 64, 66, 81.
44 Singh (2003), Verses 39 and 58.
45 Dyczkowski (1992), pp. 31–32.

46 Singh (1998), p. 66.
47 Ballantyne (1898), p. 38; Dhole (1888), p. 37.
48 Ballantyne, ibid.; Dhole, p. 38. Although not attributed to a Buddhist, similar objections by those who wish to read this Vedic passage as asserting universal emptiness can also be found in Śaṅkara's *Bṛhadāraṇyakopaniṣadbhāṣya*, section I.2.1.
49 See R. De Nobili (1972), pp. 29, 34–35. Elverskog (2010) gives other examples.
50 Hazra (1963), p. 149.
51 See Walser (2005), esp. pp. 110–115.
52 Eckel (2009).
53 Note, "*nāstika*" does not mean someone who denies the Vedas here. That definition would have to wait for Vijñānabhikṣu (See Nicholson, 2010). Presumably, *nāstika* is used here in the sense that we find in the Pali Canon as those who deny the afterlife and the efficacy of offering (*huta*) and sacrifice (*yañña*).
54 Eckel sums up these objections on pp. 126–127.
55 Ibid., p. 105.
56 Ibid., p. 106.
57 Ibid., p. 112.
58 Though Bhāviveka does not appear to have been aware of it (see ibid., p. 111: "and not even the word "Mahāyāna" is mentioned in the Sūtrāntas, Abhidharma and Vinaya"), there was a tradition among the Dharmaguptakas identifying the Mahāyāna with the Noble Eightfold Path. See Walser (2007), p. 240. White (2009), p. 74 has discussed a passage in the Mahābhārata that bears remarkable similarities to the *Jānussoṇisūtra* in which we find the term "Mahāyāna" in the Chinese.
59 Eckel, pp. 132–133.
60 Ibid., p. 134.
61 Ibid., pp. 135–136.
62 Ibid., p. 137; *mi dmigs pa'i tshul gyis – *anupalabha-nayena.*
63 See Obermiller (1999), pp. 57–58; Conze (1954), pp. 13–16.
64 Eckel, p. 146.
65 See, Jaini (1992).
66 The Tibetan *khad par*, just as the term *viśeṣa* that it translates, has much of the same range as the English word "distinct" which can mean "separate" and "specific" as well as "special" or "distinguished."
67 Eckel, p. 147.
68 It may even be that this section was interpolated by a later author. See Ruegg (1990) and Vose (2009), pp. 24–27.
69 He is aware of *dharma-nairātmya*, but apparently not as that which distinguishes Mahāyāna from *śrāvakayāna*.
70 Emptiness is mentioned quite a few times earlier in the chapter, but not as a special or unique doctrine of Mahāyāna. It is, if anything, presented as a synonym for selflessness.
71 Eckel, p. 198.
72 See Vose, pp. 112ff.
73 Obviously the *Daśabhūmikasūtra* also plays a big role here as well.
74 Eckel, pp. 224–225.
75 Ibid., pp. 224–225.
76 Ibid., p. 225.
77 Vaidya (1960), p. 3.
78 Dutt (1934), p. 121.
79 Dutt, p. 85.
80 Kimura (1986), p. 4.
81 Halbfass (1988).

82 Eckel, 4.7. From context, it appears that Bhāviveka uses the term *vedānta* to refer to what we might call "Brahmanism" as represented in the Upaniṣads and *Gṛhyasūtras*, rather than to a particular philosophical school, such as the later "Advaita Vedānta," the Śaṅkaraite form of which will not come about for a few more centuries.
83 T. 2145, p. 97a18-b12; Walser (2005), p. 57.
84 *Pracchannabauddha*. See note 40 above and Nicholson (2010), p. 189.
85 See King (1995).
86 Prior to the formal school of Vedānta, it is difficult to say exactly to whom the term *vedānta* refers.
87 Eckel, pp. 111–112.
88 Eckel, pp. 199–200.
89 Olivelle (2004), p. 23.
90 Jha (1932), p. 72.
91 Nicholson (2010), chp. 10.
92 Beal has, "Externally he was a disciple of Kapila (Sāṅkhya), but inwardly he was fully possessed of the learning of Nāgārjuna" (Beal (1968), vol. 2, p. 223); T. 2087, p. 930c28, "外示僧佉之服 内弘龍猛之學." Though there is not much evidence to support it, one wonders if 佉 was a copyist mistake for 法. Thus, instead of contrasting the idea that Bhāviveka was externally "a Sāṃkhya" 僧佉 with his internal Mādhyamika sensibilities, perhaps Xuanzang was contrasting his external obedience to the "*saṅgha-dharma*" 僧法 (i.e., the *vinaya*?) with his Mādhyamika learning. I prefer Beal's reading for the reason that I find it difficult to imagine why Xuanzang of all people would have thought it remarkable for a Mādhyamika to be a good monk. Nevertheless, the latter reading is also possible.
93 Qvarnström 95.
94 This alleged denial is problematic on a number of fronts. See Walser (2018).
95 See *Bṛhadāraṇyaka Upaniṣad* I.4.10.
96 See Śaṅkara's commentary on *Bṛhadaraṇyakopaniṣad* II.3.6.
97 See Ibid. II.3.6.
98 Śvet. 2.11.
99 Śvet. 2.19.
100 Qvarnström 133, note 35.
101 Also, see Walser (2018) for relations between Buddhism and Brahmanism generally.
102 Gokhale (1962), p. 274.
103 Qvarnström (1989), pp. 101ff.
104 Gokhale (1962).
105 Hopkins (1998), p. 102.
106 This term "*upāsana*" in the context of Brahmanical practice is quite a bit more complicated than the translation "adoration." For a good discussion of this practice both historically and among contemporary Brahmins, see Dubois (2014).

PART II

The genealogy of the *Perfection of Wisdom*

6

WHAT DID THE TEXT OF THE *PERFECTION OF WISDOM* LOOK LIKE?

The *Perfection of Wisdom in 8,000 Lines* is a well-known early Mahāyāna sutra and is best known to Western audiences through the 1958 translation of Edward Conze. However, as numerous scholars have shown, the version of the text that Conze translates is not the original version. The text has been messed with considerably, so any attempt to discuss the authorship or motivating concerns of the text using Conze's translation will be misleading. This chapter will attempt to establish what the earliest version of the text was so that in subsequent chapters we can delve into the factors that gave rise to it.

The versions

The oldest extant version (or small portion of a version, really) of the *Perfection of Wisdom* is one partial Gāndhārī manuscript in Kharoṣṭhī script discovered near the Pakistan-Afghanistan border whose C_{14} dates register it somewhere in the neighborhood of 47–147 CE.[1] The next earliest Sanskrit manuscript is a partial Kuṣāna manuscript in Brahmi script dating from around the third century CE.[2] Apart from these two[3] manuscripts of the *Perfection of Wisdom in 8,000 Lines*, the remaining six Sanskrit manuscripts were edited into what is now the standard edition of the text by Rajendralal Mitra in 1888. Concerning this edition, P.L. Vaidya writes:

> This edition was based on six Mss. five of which were obtained by different scholars from Nepal and one was a Bengali transcript of a Nepalese original. The oldest dated Ms, bears the date 1061 A.D.; one of the Cambridge Mss. is held by Rajendralal Mitra to bear the date of 1020 A.D., while Bendall thinks its date to be A.D. 1155 or 1255. Two more Mss. used by Rajendralal Mitra are copies prepared in Nalanda or its neighbourhood in the reigns of Govinda and Rāma of the Pāla dynasty of Bengal-Bihar. No new Mss. of this work have come to light, though copies are often prepared in Nepal.[4]

Vaidya goes on to note that, although the earliest of these full manuscripts dates only from the 11th century, the text agrees for the most part with the *Āloka* commentary by Haribhadra, composed in the eighth/ninth century. The Tibetan translation by Śākyasena, Jñānasiddhi and Dharmatāśīla dates from the early ninth century[5] and so corresponds quite closely to the Sanskrit edition.

Apart from the two early partial texts, then, the earliest complete versions of the *Perfection of Wisdom* are preserved in Chinese. There are seven Chinese translations ranging from the second to the 10th century, as follows:

T. 224, translated by Lokakṣema in 179 CE.

T. 225, the *Da Mingdu Jing*. The translator of the first chapter of this work is unknown, but Jan Nattier argues[6] that the interlinear commentary running throughout the chapter was most likely penned by someone in the community of Kang Senghui in the third century.[7] The remainder of the chapters are clearly by a different translator who can safely be identified as Zhi Qian (early third century). Since the translator of the first chapter is unknown, I will refer to this text by its title and not by its translator.

T. 226, translated by Zhu Fonian and Dharmapriya during the late Eastern Jin Dynasty (fl. 365 – fourth century).[8]

T. 227 translated by Kumārajīva in 408 CE.

T. 220 (I) translated by Xuanzang ca. 660 CE.

T. 220 (II) translated by Xuanzang.

T. 228 translated by Dānapāla in 985 CE.

Seishi Karashima, who recently made an edition based on Lokakṣema's translation, argues that these translations correspond to at least four different versions of the text:

1) Lokakṣema, the *Da Mingdu Jing*, Zhu Fonian and the *Split Manuscript*
2) Kumārajīva and Xuanzang II
3) Xuanzang I
4) the Sanskrit manuscripts, Dānapāla's Chinese translation and the Tibetan translation.[9]

Yoke Meei Choong groups the versions into three groups (she includes both Xuanzang translations in the same group as Kumārajīva). She also observes, astutely I think, that the versions from Kumārajīva onward have been influenced by the *Perfection of Wisdom in 25,000 Lines*.[10]

The quest for the ur-sūtra

In 1943 Kun Kajiyoshi argued that the first chapter of the *Perfection of Wisdom in 8,000 Lines* was the original kernel and that subsequent chapters were all added later.[11] In response, in 1953, Hikata Ryushō argues that the original text must have comprised the first two chapters, noting that the second chapter ends with an "entrusting part," which is missing in the first. He further argues that even if this entrusting section had been moved from the end of the first chapter, the first chapter could have never stood alone.[12] Chapter 2, in turn, appears to belong to a larger unit extending through the middle of Lokakṣema's 11th chapter (= the end of the 13th chapter of the Sanskrit), since "the Sūtra has made one round of accounts of the more important doctrines . . . and at the end of that portion we have: 'When the Buddha told this discourse, 500 bhikṣus and 30 bhikṣuṇīs obtained Arhatship, 60 upāsakas and 30 upāsikās attained to Srotāpanna (*sic*), 30 bodhisattvas obtained Anutpattika-dharma-kṣānti . . . and all [the bodhisattvas?] could receive Vyākaraṇa to become Buddha in the Bhadrakalpa.' "[13] After this, the sutra begins a second round of discussing many of the same topics that were discussed in 2–11.5. This second iteration may have ended in the middle of Lokakṣema's 25th chapter (= midway through the 28th chapter of the Sanskrit) where the sutra was entrusted to Ānanda.

The second half of that chapter in the translations of Kumārajīva and Xuanzang as well as in the Sanskrit and Tibetan editions moves into a discussion of seeing Akṣobhya Buddha followed by an exhortation for Buddhists to be as dedicated as Gandhahastin in Akṣobhya's Pure Land. Hikata notes that in the fifth division of Xuanzang's translation and in Kumārajīva's translation there is a concluding sentence that is missing from other versions. After the Akṣobhya chapters there is a chapter entitled *Anugama*, and then the whole text ends with the story of Sadāprarūdita. Hikata follows most other scholars in considering the Akṣobhya and Sadāprarudita chapters to be later insertions, although he argues for a close relationship between the Akṣobhya chapters (especially chapter 26) of the *Perfection of Wisdom in 8,000 Lines* and the *Akṣobhya-buddha-kṣetra-sūtra*.[14]

This exchange sparked a number of subsequent studies looking for the original ur-sūtra. A decade after Hikata's study, Lewis Lancaster analyzed the *Perfection of Wisdom in 8,000 Lines* in his 1968 dissertation. Through a close comparison of all Chinese versions with the Sanskrit, he argued that a comparison of the Chinese versions can neither confirm nor deny the evolution of the chapters of the *Perfection of Wisdom in 8,000 Lines* since all the chapters are present in the Lokakṣema's 179 CE translation. Lancaster argued that, while there are accretions as the text develops over time, these tend to proceed on a sentence-by-sentence (not chapter-by-chapter) basis. What we see over time is the introduction or highlighting of certain technical terms and that these additions occur across the chapters. Lancaster states that, as a result of these dynamics,

> The 'ur' text which Conze describes is beyond the reach of the Chinese translations. The early text which has been part of the documentation for this study is part of a tradition in which the sutra had already assumed the basic format preserved in the Sanskrit, and no chapters are left out completely.[15]

Lancaster is correct that a simple appeal to the Chinese translations cannot *prove* that one chapter is necessarily older than any other. In fact, it is difficult to imagine any kind of textual evidence that could prove beyond a doubt the priority of part to another. But our inability to prove order of composition does not mean that such an order does not exist. There is no getting around the fact that the structural breaks and inconsistencies certainly suggest an order of composition or accretion that existed prior to its first translation into Chinese. Chapters 1 and 2 are thematically self-sufficient, while most of the other chapters refer in some way back to the teachings expounded in the first two chapters. The chapters extolling the merit of the *Perfection of Wisdom* and the benefits of reciting it have the first two chapters as their *raison d'être*, just as the chapters urging bodhisattvas not to fall into the goal of the arhat reject that goal on the basis of its failure to comprehend the teachings of the first two chapters.

Taking seriously Lancaster's suggestion that changes were introduced on a sentence by sentence basis, Lambert Schmithausen was the next scholar to take up the challenge of the pre-Lokakṣema form of the *Perfection of Wisdom* in a brilliant 1977 article entitled, "Textgeschichtliche Beobachtungen zum 1. Kapitel der *Aṣṭasāhasrikā Prajñāpāramitā*" ("Text-historical Observations on the 1st Chapter of the *Aṣṭasāhasrikā Prajñāpāramitā*").[16] As Schmithausen's observations and conclusions will provide a foundation for the arguments of subsequent chapters, much of the remainder of this chapter will be devoted to an exposition and evaluation of his argument.

By comparing the Sanskrit texts with the earliest sources, Schmithausen comes to an important conclusion: while it has been long known that the *Perfection of Wisdom in 25,000 Lines, 100,000 Lines*, etc. contain chunks of text lifted verbatim from the *Perfection of Wisdom in 8,000 Lines*, Schmithausen points out that the Sanskrit of the 25,000- and 100,000-line versions[17] is often closer to the earliest Chinese translations than to the extant Sanskrit edition of the 8,000-line version.

Comparing the Sanskrit versions against the earliest tier of Chinese translations enables Schmithausen to identify which words or phrases go all the way back to Lokakṣema's time and which do not. Furthermore, by establishing a sense of what the original Indic version of Lokakṣema's text might have been, we are able to spot mistranslations and/or interlinear commentary inserted by the translator. After establishing what the earliest Chinese translators' version might have been, he looks for grammatical and textual inconsistencies, interruptions and repetitions to determine which portions were interpolated or moved from one place to another.

Schmithausen's article focuses only on the first chapter of the *Perfection of Wisdom*, since he like most other scholars considers it to contain the ur-sūtra. While there are many insights in his article, perhaps the most important is that there is a section of the first chapter discussing the non-perception and non-apprehension of the bodhisattva that is repeated several times throughout the first chapter, forming almost a doctrinal coda. On this basis, he argues that the first iteration of the doctrine forms the original ur-sūtra.

Finally, the most recent and perhaps the most thorough study of the *Perfection of Wisdom* to date is the 2012 dissertation of Matthew Orsborn (aka. Shi Huifeng) from the University of Hong Kong. Orsborn examines the thematic structure of the *Perfection of Wisdom*, using Lokakṣema's translation as his basis and amending it where necessary with other versions. Using this approach, he makes a convincing case that despite what some have taken to be an arbitrary assemblage of themes, the received *Perfection of Wisdom* is actually a highly structured text, with repeating and recursive chiastic structures throughout. He shows that the first two chapters (what he calls the "prologue") consist of a sequence of themes leading up to a discussion of the *Mahāyāna*, the *Mahāsattva* and the *Mahāsaṃnāda* (Great Armor), after which the themes leading up to that point are revisited but in reverse order. He shows the same pattern to obtain in the last chapter and again (given the similarity between the first and the last chapters) in the complete *Perfection of Wisdom* as a whole. In laying out in exacting detail the structure of the whole, Orsborn not only makes a strong argument that the complete text in all of its chapters can be read as a coherent whole, but that the chiastic structures draw a number of thematic arrows for us, pointing to certain themes as being, quite literally, *central* to the whole project. In the prologue, the structure points to the discussion with Purṇa Maitrāyaṇīputra about the Mahāyāna that neither comes from anywhere nor goes anywhere (*nopaiti*) and the mahāsattva who is unattached to anything. This finds its parallel in the concluding story (*avadāna*) of Sadāprarudita, which centers on the sermon of Dharmodgata about the Tathāgata who, due to "thusness" neither comes nor goes (is neither *gata* nor *āgata*). Finally, both the prologue and the conclusion of the text frame the chapter on "thusness" as being thematically central. Thus, he finds the chiastic structure of the whole text to be recursive in the prologue and conclusion and in each place to mark the theme of Mahāyāna and the Tathāgata to neither come nor go due to the nature of thusness itself.

In many ways, Orsborn's study moves us in a different direction from the previously mentioned attempts to find the ur-sūtra. Instead of looking for inconsistencies indicative of an interpolation or accretion, he invites us to look at the 179 CE translation as representing a well thought out whole with a unified message. Furthermore, his study shies away from earlier attempts to identify an ur-sūtra within one portion of the whole. However, toward the end of his book, he does speculate on the implications of the chiastic structure for the ur-sūtra, offering a number of possibilities. He personally feels the first two chapters may have been the ur-sūtra, but acknowledges that as long as one takes the integrity of the chiastic structure as an indication of original unity, one might equally argue that the first and the last chapters were the ur-sūtra or that the whole 37 chapters were the ur-sūtra since this is where we find the structure.

Orsborn's argument cannot simply be dismissed and I will have a number of opportunities to return to his observations. Nevertheless, in keeping with the genealogical orientation of the current study, I would like to return to the question of the ur-sūtra. And here, I think there are some good reasons *not* to take structural integrity as an index of unity of composition. The most obvious is that the structural integrity that Orsborn demonstrates could just as easily be attributed to the genius of the redactor as to the insight of the author (with no guarantee that author and redactor are the same person). I think there are equally compelling structural reasons to suspect that the themes Orsborn finds at the center of his chiasms were attempts to domesticate the themes of the ur-sūtra and render it more palatable to the larger Buddhist community. For that reason, I would like to return to Schmithausen's study and then work my way back to assess the significance of Orsborn's conclusions in Chapter 8 and in the conclusion.

The core pericope

Schmithausen's basic premise, similar to that of Kajiyoshi, is that the *Perfection of Wisdom* began as a short sutra of just a few pages, similar to what we find in the larger collections of the *Aṅguttara* or *Saṃyutta Nikāyas*. It is in these pages, even more than the themes identified in Orsborn's chiasms, that we find not only the introduction of hard thematic elements that historically come to stand metonymically for the *Perfection of Wisdom* as a whole, but also the original kernel of the sutra forming a kind of initial utterance beginning the dialog that forms the rest of the *Perfection of Wisdom* tradition. As Orsborn himself points out,

> From Hikata's tables . . . and Conze's chart . . . we see clearly the expanded structural format: The very first chapter of the smaller text is distributed throughout twenty or more chapters in the medium text. The second and third chapters of the smaller text are also spread through several chapters of the medium text. After this, the rest of the chapters, from four to twenty-eight of the smaller text, are all basically in a one-to-one relationship. Then, the medium sūtras have some twenty chapters of new material, unseen in the small texts. Finally, the last three chapters, namely the Sadāprarudita avadāna and Parīndanā, are basically equivalent in all the texts where they appear.[18]

While, as we will see later on, the Sadāprarudita chapter will also be important historically, it is in the first few pages identified by Schmithausen as the ur-sūtra that we find two of the main elements that have been discussed in the preceding chapters as elements of Mahāyāna. For this reason, it will be worth our while to determine as best we can its provenance and social context.

For the purposes of discussion, I include below a translation of this kernel from Lokakṣema. I do this ***not*** because I believe he had the "original" in front of him, but because I believe his version was relatively close to what the original must have been. Indeed, I will argue that Lokakṣema's translation reflects a tradition that may in some ways be even older than that represented in the chronologically older *Split Manuscript*. In my translation, I have kept the section divisions from Schmithausen and given each section a title for ease of reference in the discussion that follows. The page numbers in brackets are from

Karashima's 2011 edition. An analysis of each section in light of other versions will follow.

Kernel of the *Perfection of Wisdom in 8,000 Lines* in Lokakṣema's translation

A Introduction

[39] The Buddha was staying at Rājagṛha on Vulture's Peak. There was a great saṅgha of innumerable monks, disciples headed by Śāriputra, [40] Subhūti, and so forth. Great bodhisattvas without number – Maitreya bodhisattva, Manjuśrī bodhisattva and so forth. On the full moon day of the *prātimokṣa* recitation.

B The Buddha's Charge

The Buddha told Subhūti: "Today [there] is a great gathering of bodhisattvas. For the sake[19] of the bodhisattvas, explain the perfection of wisdom. The bodhisattvas should accomplish this learning."

C The Legitimation Section

Śāriputra thought in his mind: "Now, he has commanded Subhūti to teach the Perfection of Wisdom for the bodhisattvas. Is it by his own power that he teaches, or does he teach by the Buddha's magical power?" Subhūti knew what Śāriputra's mind had thought and said to Śāriputra: "Whatever dharmas the disciples of the Buddha teach, [41] and the dharma they accomplish, they are all supported by the Buddha's power. Why? They are realized in the dharma that the Buddha taught. Following the dharma, they teach one another and they mature one another.[20] They never dispute with one another about the dharma. Why? When they preach the dharma, they are satisfied if there is no one who does not feel joy. Good men and good women will, then, train [in it]."

D The Non-Apprehension Section

Subhūti said to the Buddha: The Buddha ordered me to teach the Perfection of Wisdom for the bodhisattvas so that the bodhisattvas will accordingly train in and accomplish it. The Buddha ordered me to discuss the bodhisattva. [If a bodhisattva has [that] name then there will be attachment to it. Is 'bodhisattva' an existing name or a non-existing name?] Among what dharmas is the designation "bodhisattva"? I don't see that there is a dharma 'bodhisattva' at all. Neither name nor dharma of the bodhisattva exists at all, nor do I see a bodhisattva **[42]** nor do I see his state. Where is the bodhisattva to whom I should teach the perfection of wisdom? When this explanation of the perfection of wisdom has been made, the bodhisattva who hears this [yet], whose mind is not depressed, is not afraid, is not timid, is not confused, is not fearful, then, that bodhisattva should consider this (his) training. Should consider this (his) dwelling, should consider this (his) training.

E The Mindlessness Section

Having entered therein, his mind should not think itself to be a bodhisattva. What is the reason? [His] existing mind is mindless. [43]

Śāriputra said to Subhūti: "How is this existing mind mindless?"

Subhūti replied: "The mind neither exists, nor does not exist, nor can it be grasped nor can it be found."

Śāriputra told Subhūti: "How then does the mind neither exist, nor not exist, [how] can it be ungraspable, how can it be unfindable? Like this it neither exists nor does not exist, and there is no existence of an existent mind nor non-existence of a non-existent mind."

Subhūti replied: "Indeed, there is no existence of an existent mind nor non-existence of a non-existent mind."

Śāriputra said: "Excellent, Subhūti! You were taught[21] by the Buddha! Having been taught by the Buddha, [44] you have discussed the empty body wisdom. [Your] empty body wisdom is said [by the Buddha] to be foremost."

F The Irreversibility Section

Therefore, the bodhisattva afterwards achieves irreversibility and is raised to [that] title. To the end, he will never again lose the perfection of wisdom. [It is thus that the bodhisattva abides in the perfection of wisdom.]

G The Propagation Section

Like this, those desiring to train in the arhat dharma, should listen to the perfection of wisdom, should train in it, should retain it, should protect it. Those desiring to train in the *pratyekabuddha* [independently awakened ones'] dharma should listen to the perfection of wisdom, should train in it, should retain it, should protect it. Those desiring to train in the bodhisattva dharma should listen to the perfection of wisdom, should train in it, should retain it, should protect it. What is the reason? The perfection of wisdom dharma is deep. The bodhisattva accordingly should train thus. [45]

Although this translation represents a very early edition of the text (preceded chronologically so far only by the *Split Manuscript*), I believe that neither it nor the *Split Manuscript* represents the earliest version. The remainder of this chapter will delve into the philological issues surrounding this section to try to determine what a more original version might have looked like.

The ending

One of the important issues raised by Orsborn's work is the question of what would constitute evidence for the ur-sūtra. Scholars from Kajiyoshi to Schmithausen have used traditional text-critical methods to determine both the ur-sūtra and textual accretion. Orsborn makes the simple observation that: a) every version of the sutra that we have appears to have multiple chapters and b) if we take structural integrity to be our standard, then we have to assume a much bigger ur-sūtra – possibly encompassing all 30 chapters of the current translation by Lokakṣema. On this, let me be clear: though I will take a stand on the ur-sūtra, there are no smoking guns here. Orsborn could be right. That said, I do think an argument can be made to support Kajiyoshi and Schmithausen's contention that the ur-sūtra comprised the above translated section. Schmithausen's assertion rests on section G, the Propagation Section, being the concluding section of the sutra – something about which he himself was a bit ambivalent.[22] If, however, if we delve deeper into the textual history of this section, I believe that his hypothesis turns out to be on solid ground. While the Sanskrit text of the *Perfection of Wisdom in 8,000 Lines* has something to the effect that the *Perfection of Wisdom* "should be listened to (*śrotavyā*), taken up (*udgrahītavyā*), retained (*dhārayitavyā*), recited (*vācayitavyā*), studied/mastered (*paryavāptavyā*) and spread among others (*pravartayitavyā*)," the Sanskrit of the Dutt and Gilgit editions of the *Perfection of Wisdom in 25,000 Lines* and the *Perfection of Wisdom on 100,000 Lines* contain only the first four verbs here, omitting *pravartayitavyā*.[23]

On the other hand, the *Split Manuscript*, which tends to abbreviate anyway, only has the first of these: "*śodava*."[24] Looking at the earliest Chinese translations (Lokakṣema, the *Da Mingdu Jing* and the translations of Zhu Fonian and Kumārajīva) it would appear that these early versions had only three verbs, none of which is *śrotavyā*." For example, Lokakṣema has "當學, 當持, 當守." *Dang* here conveys the sense of the future participial ending of the Sanskrit -*tavyā* for each term, but while 當學 is an acceptable translation for *udgrahītavyā*, 欲學 was used a sentence earlier to translate *śikṣitukāmena*. This may not be so much of a problem, since the roots √*śikṣ* and *ud*√*grah* both mean to learn. Further, Lokakṣema may have wanted to use 學 again for *ud*√*grah* since the character visually depicts the "handling" of knowledge implicit in the verb √*grah*. The second 當持 poses no problem as a translation for *dhārayitavyā*, since 持 later becomes the standard translation for verbs having √*dhṛ* as a root. The last 當守 however makes this rather uncertain again, since 守 also means "To guard; to protect. To observe; to keep, as observances; to attend to. To hold onto; to maintain."[25] Each of these definitions could work well for *dhārayitavyā* but not particularly well for *paryavāptavyā*, "to study." Nevertheless, if we take 持 to translate √*dhṛ*, we are left to choose whether 守 translates *paryavāptavyā* or *pravartayitavyā*. Given this choice, 守 comes closer to the verb √*āp* of *paryavāptavyā* – "to obtain, gain, take possession of" than to the sense of dissemination of *pravartayitavyā*.

This suggests that the original that Lokakṣema contained only the three verbs *udgrahītavyā*, *dhārayitavyā* and *paryavāptavyā*, in that order. While the *Da*

Mingdu Jing's translation 擇取奉持 won't help us much, Kumārajīva's translation 受持讀誦 confirms our suspicion, since 讀誦 carries the sense of chanting a text, i.e., which, though not a standard translation, would have been the fifth-century equivalent of what we think of as "studying."

Now, we find a corresponding phrase in the Pali Canon in at least three places: in the *Āṭānāṭiyasutta*[26] of the *Dīgha Nikāya*, in the *Dhammacetiyasutta*[27] of the *Majjhima Nikāya* and in the *Tāyanagātha*[28] of the *Saṃyutta Nikāya*. In all three cases, the formula serves as a concluding sentence to the sutra. For example, the *Dhammacetiyasutta* ends with the following:

> Then soon after he had left, the Blessed One addressed the bhikkhus thus: Bhikkhus, before rising from his seat and departing, this King Pasendadi uttered monuments to the Dhamma [i.e., *dhammacetiya*, the title of the sutra]. ***Learn [uggaṇhatha = Skt. udgṛhṇīta] the monuments to the Dhamma, bhikkhus; master [pariyāpuṇātha = Skt. paryavāpnuta] the monuments to the Dhamma; remember [dhāretha = Skt. dharata] the monuments to the Dhamma.*** The monuments to the Dhamma are beneficial, bhikkhus, and they belong to the fundamentals of the holy life.
>
> That is what the Blessed One said. The bhikkhus were satisfied and delighted in the Blessed One's words.[29]

If we adjust the future participial sense of the passage in Lokakṣema's *Perfection of Wisdom* to match the imperative mode of the *Dhammacetiyasutta* passage, the two passages would be virtually identical. One then needs merely to substitute the title of the sutra, "*prajñāpāramitā*," for the title of the Pali sutra, "*dhammacetiya*." In light of these other instances where the phrase is used, I think we can conclude that it was meant to be a concluding element in the *Perfection of Wisdom*. It would also appear, then, that the call of this text to reproduce itself – a feature that has been lauded as uniquely Mahāyānist in the wake of Gregory Schopen's article on the "Cult of the Book" – was in fact borrowed from earlier canonical texts and not as uniquely Mahāyānist as one might wish.

Subhūti's non-apprehension

If the above section G was the original ending of the sutra, then the original teaching of that sutra was neither the Mahāyāna of the first chapter, nor the *tathatā* (reality) or the Tathāgata (the one who has gone to tathatā, i.e., the Buddha) which Orborn had identified as central themes of the remaining chiasma, nor the "emptiness" which becomes thematic in certain Mādhyamika readings. There are only two themes in the ur-sūtra if we take G as the conclusion: Subhūti's non-perception and his discussion of the mindless mind. So, what exactly did these two sections intend? Starting with the discussion of Subhūti's non-perception, we notice that this paragraph has undergone a few changes before it took its final form in the current Sanskrit manuscript. For ease of reference, I shall give Conze's translation of this passage below:

Conze's Translation	***Lokakṣema's Translation***
Thereupon the Venerable Subhuti, by the Buddha's might, said to the Lord: The Lord has said, 'Make it clear now, Subhuti, to the Bodhisattvas, the great beings, starting from perfect wisdom, how the Bodhisattvas, the great beings go forth into perfect wisdom!'	Subhūti said to the Buddha: The Buddha told me to teach the Perfection of Wisdom for the sake of the bodhisattvas so that the bodhisattvas will accordingly train in and accomplish it. The Buddha ordered me to preach to the bodhisattvas.
When one speaks of a 'Bodhisattva,' what dharma does that word 'Bodhisattva' denote? *I do not, O Lord, see that dharma 'Bodhisattva' nor a dharma called 'perfect wisdom'. Since I neither find, nor apprehend, nor see a bodhisattva nor a dharma 'Bodhisattva,' or a 'perfect wisdom,' what Bodhisattva shall I instruct and admonish in perfect wisdom?*	If bodhisattva is a name then there will be attachment to it. [Is bodhisattva an existing name or a non-existing name?] Among what dharmas is the designation "bodhisattva"? *I don't see an existing dharma bodhisattva at all.* [Neither name nor dharma of the bodhisattva exists at all], *nor do I see a bodhisattva [42] nor do I see his state. Where is the bodhisattva to whom I should teach the perfection of wisdom?*
And yet, O Lord, if, when this is pointed out, a Bodhisattva's heart does not become cowed, nor stolid, does not despair nor despond, if he does not turn away or become dejected, does not tremble, is not frightened or terrified, it is just this Bodhisattva, this great being who should be instructed in perfect wisdom. It is precisely this that should be recognized as the perfect wisdom of that Bodhisattva, as his instruction in perfect wisdom. When he thus stands firm, that is his instruction and admonition.[30]	When this explanation of the perfection of wisdom has been made, the bodhisattva who hears this [yet], whose mind is not depressed, is not afraid, is not timid, is not confused, is not fearful, then, that bodhisattva should consider this (his) training. Should consider this (his) dwelling, should consider this (his) training.

The italicized portion is attested in all of the early sources with some important variations. In particular, Lokakṣema and Zhu Fonian's versions of the paragraph omit Subhūti's statement that he "cannot *find* a Perfection of Wisdom" [i.e., they simply say he cannot *see* it]. Beyond this Lokakṣema tells us, "Bodhisattva is a name causing attachment. Is bodhisattva an existing name or a non-existing name?" and then three sentences later, "neither name nor dharma of the bodhisattva exists at all." In comparison, the Sanskrit and the *Split Manuscript* has only one slightly different sentence mentioning the relationship between a word and a dharma. The Sanskrit, for example, has Subhūti ask, "'Bodhisattva, bodhisattva.' When one speaks of a 'Bodhisattva,' what dharma does that word (*adhivacanaṃ*) 'Bodhisattva' denote?" Although there is still much work to do on the *Split Manuscript* and parts of this sentence are not clear to me, it does appear to have a sentence similar to the Sanskrit.[31]

Lokakṣema's extra sentences (bracketed and in italics) appear to be arguing that the "person" has only a nominal existence. The problem is that these sentences appear in no other manuscript, even that of Zhu Fonian,[32] who for the most part appears to have had a copy of Lokakṣema's translation in front of him. The most likely explanation for at least the first of these extra sentences from Lokakṣema's translation is that they are explanatory asides (or interlinear notes) of the translator himself that became incorporated into the text.[33] The fact that Zhu Fonian omits them suggests that he recognized them as such and omitted them from his translation. They also show that Lokakṣema interpreted this passage at least partly through the lens of canonical discussions of nominalism.

Schmithausen finds another insertion at the point where Subhūti claims to see neither "bodhisattva nor bodhisattva dharma." According to Schmithausen,

> the differentiating phrase: *bodhisattvaṃ vā bodhisattvadharmaṃ vā* (that is: not only is a substantial person 'bodhisattva' not evident, but neither are nameable dharmas like 'Bodhisattva' evident in the sense of the dharma analysis of the Hīnayāna schools). These words also occur only in the late versions, whereas in the [*Larger Perfection of Wisdom* texts] just as in T. 224, 225, 226, and 227 one only finds "bodhisattvam."[34]

We need to be careful here. In the Sanskrit, we find three sentences:

'Bodhisattva,' when one speaks of a 'Bodhisattva,' what dharma does that word 'Bodhisattva' denote?	bodhisattvo bodhisattva iti yad idaṃ bhagavann ucyate, katamasy-aitad bhagavan dharmasy-ādhivacanaṃ yad uta bodhisattva iti?
I do not, O Lord, see that dharma 'Bodhisattva' nor a dharma called 'perfect wisdom'.	nāhaṃ bhagavaṃs taṃ dharmaṃ **samanupaśyāmi** yad uta bodhisattva iti/tam apy ahaṃ bhagavan dharmaṃ na **samanupaśyāmi** yad uta prajñāpāramitā- nāma /

*Since I neither **find**, nor **apprehend**, nor see a bodhisattva nor a dharma 'Bodhisattva,' or a 'perfect wisdom,' what Bodhisattva shall I instruct and admonish in perfect wisdom?*	so 'haṃ bhagavan bodhisattvaṃ vā bodhisattva-dharmaṃ vā **avindan anupalabhamāno 'samanupaśyan**, prajñāpāramitāmapy-avindan anupalabhamāno 'samanupaśyan katamaṃ bodhisattvaṃ katamasyāṃ prajñāpāramitāyām-avavadiṣyāmi anuśāsiṣyāmi?

The first sentence is present in all versions, although in simplified form: "i.e, "of which dharma is there the word 'bodhisattva'?". The next sentence in which Subhūti sees neither the bodhisattva nor the bodhisattva's dharma is also present in all versions, minus the above mentioned phrase "nor a dharma called perfection of wisdom." Schmithausen's comment only applies to the third sentence, which Lokakṣema and Zhu Fonian render as saying that Subhūti can neither *see* the bodhisattva {full stop} nor can he *find* the bodhisattva {full stop}. From this, we can say that the distinction between the word "bodhisattva" and the bodhisattva dharma does exist in Lokakṣema's version, although it appears to have migrated to the third sentence from the second sometime after Lokakṣema. Though quite a few characters are missing in this section of the *Split Manuscript*, it does not deviate from Lokakṣema too much with the exception of line I-13 that inserts a kind of interpretive paraphrase: "I am the unperceiving bodhisattva and that perfection is the perfection of wisdom" (*[s]o ahaṃ aṇualahamaṇa bosisatvo sa ca paramida prañaparamida*).[35]

Schmithausen argues that the point of this paragraph assumes the *abhidharma* distinction between two kinds of existents: those entities that exist only as names for a collection of components (*prajñaptisat* or collective entities such as "forest" or "army") and those entities that exist ultimately, namely dharmas. In the classical formulation, the "self" exists only as a name designating a fluctuating collection of dharmas (the five aggregates) that *are* real. Since there are really only two types of existents in this scheme, to say that the bodhisattva exists as neither a name nor as a dharma is to say that *the bodhisattva simply doesn't exist*. Schmithausen reads the earliest iteration of this passage in Lokakṣema as little more than a traditional "Hīnayāna" argument that the self is merely a name or simply that there are aggregates but no dharma corresponding to the word "bodhisattva." The problem with this reading is that this portion of the sutra as it stands does not read as a sutra on selflessness in any straightforward manner. Now, as Orsborn has observed, we do find two stories[36] about Subhūti in the *Mahāvibhāṣa* in which his touted abilities in the meditative state called the *araṇavihāra* or the state of "non-dispute" (about which I will have a few things to say in Chapter 9) are connected to the teaching of selflessness. At one point, someone simply asks Subhūti who he is. The story in the *Mahāvibhāṣa* continues:

> The Venerable Subhūti, due to abiding in non-dispute for a considerable time and cultivating the practice of not self, was silent and unable

> to answer "I am Subhūti". Having been asked a second and third time, he finally answered: "This is what is conventionally designated as 'Subhūti'."[37]

Note that while Subhūti's awkward hesitation may seem similar to his inability to find a bodhisattva in the *Perfection of Wisdom*, the two are quite different. The *Mahāvibhāṣa* story is explicit, telling us four times that the reason why Subhūti hesitates is because he has been cultivating the practice of not-self 修無我行. Nowhere in our ur-sūtra is selflessness mentioned. Nowhere is there any indication of a denial of the usual themes of a sutra on selflessness, i.e., self (*ātman*), sentient being (*sattva*), person (*pudgala*) or existent (*bhāva*). To read Subhūti's inability to see or find a bodhisattva as a statement of selflessness is, I think, a bit of wishful thinking.

After the statements concerning Subhūti not perceiving the bodhisattva there is a passage telling us about the one who has received this kind of instruction – in essence, that the instructed bodhisattva is neither afraid nor depressed. Again, if we take sutras from the *Tripiṭaka* as our standard, there are quite a few sutras that discuss selflessness, but all of them end with the listener being (if anything) overjoyed at the teaching. Never do we find the teaching of selflessness depicted as something potentially scary.

Of crucial importance here is the fact that the subject of the sentence in all versions is not the bodhisattva, but the bodhisattva's *mind*. In Vaidya's Sanskrit edition, we find the following verbs describing the mind of the bodhisattva who has been instructed according to Subhūti's teaching. It is: *na avalīyate, na saṃlīyate, na viṣīdati, na viṣādam āpadyate, nāsya viprṣṭhībhavati mānasam, na bhagnaprṣṭhībhavati, nottrasyati, na samtrasyati, na saṃtrāsam āpadyate, etc.* This is quite a long list, certainly longer than we find in earlier manuscripts. The first two are basically synonyms meaning something like "not daunted or discouraged."[38]

The remaining terms also appear to be groups of synonyms. *Viṣīdati* ("is despondent") and *viṣādam āpadyate* ("falls into despondency") are virtual synonyms as are *viprṣṭhībhavati mānasam* ("broken mind") and *bhagnaprṣṭhībhavati* ("becomes broken backed," which Böhtlingk-Roth also define as "*gegenüberstehend*").[39] Finally, *nottrasyati, na saṃtrasyati* and *na saṃtrāsam āpadyate* are again repetitions with no real new information. Looking at earlier versions, the biggest difference we find is that instead of Vaidya's, "if when so taught and instructed, the mind of the bodhisattva is not (etc.)" both the Dutt and Gilgit versions of the *Perfection of Wisdom in 25,000 Lines* have "not seeing [*asamanupaśyan*], (he) is does not become afraid, does not tremble, (etc.)"[40] while Konow's fragment C of the *Perfection of Wisdom in 18,000 Lines* has, "*having heard* (*śrūtvā*) the profound perfection of wisdom that is being taught, he does not . . ." (*te ca punar imāṃ gaṃbhīrāṃ prajñāpāramitāṃ śrutvā bhāṣyamāṇāṃ . . .*). [41] This "having heard," while implicit in Vaidya's Sanskrit, is represented in Lokakṣema's translation as well as in the *Da Mingdu Jing*.

The long list of verbs denoting fear has been expanded through repetition, but all the variations and repetitions tend to be clusters of synonyms of three verbs – two of which are verbs of stasis and one a verb of motion: √*lī* – to lie down, to cower; √*sad* – to sit down, to despair; and √*tras* – to tremble, to be afraid. For their part, the earliest Chinese translations have only five of these verbs. Lokakṣema and Zhu

Fonian have: 不懈 (Lokakṣema has 懈怠) = not negligent, 不恐 not afraid, 不怯 not nervous, 不難 not in difficulty and 不畏 not afraid. The *Da Mingdu Jing* has eight: 不移 does not shift/move, 不捨 does not tremble, 不驚 does not shake, 不怛 is not anxious, 不以恐受 does not feel afraid, 不疲 is not worn down, 不息 *buxī* does not rest (perhaps a mistake for *buxī* 不惜 – "without lament" possibly translating *vipratisārī bhavati mānasam*, which we find substituted in Dutt's manuscript for the more common *viprṣṭhībhavati mānasam*),[42] 不惡難 without trouble and distress. For the most part, these lists appear to reflect the later Sanskrit versions, with the exception that Lokakṣema and Zhu Fonian have the item "negligence" (不懈 and 不懈怠, respectively), which has no equivalent in the Sanskrit. Kumārajīva also omits this and has 不驚 does not tremble, 不怖 is not afraid, 不沒 does not sink and 不退 does not flee. In all, it appears that the early Chinese versions knew a series of synonyms of √*tras* and √*lī*, which is more or less confirmed by the *Split Manuscript*, which has three of these verbs represented: *ṇa oliati* (= *avalīyate*), *ṇa viparapriṭhibhavati* (*viprṣṭhībhavati mānasam*) and *ṇa saṃtraso avajati* (*saṃtrāsam āpadyate*).[43] These three will be important to the analysis in the next chapter.

The Mindlessness section and its relation to the Irreversibility section

If Subhūti's non-perception of the bodhisattva is the first theme of the sutra, the dialogue between Śāriputra and Subhūti concerning the mindless mind both constitutes the second theme and serves as the narrative climax of our ur–*Perfection of Wisdom*. Even taking the Sanskrit edition at face value, the passage is of interest because it may well constitute one of the first discussions of the word *bodhicitta*, of which we have heard so much. It is also the earliest source to discuss the "mindless mind" (*cittaṃ acittaṃ*) that we have seen has been a theme in different Mahāyāna manifestations throughout Asia. That said, as the punchline of the ur-sūtra, the text of the paragraph that has been transmitted to us is more than a little frustrating. Since it appears to have undergone far more revision than the previous paragraph, it will thus require careful analysis. Conze translates the Sanskrit of this section as follows:

> *[Mindlessness Section]*
>
> Moreover, when a Bodhisattva courses in perfect wisdom and develops it, he should so train himself that he does not pride himself on that thought of enlightenment [with which he has begun his career]. That thought is no thought, since in its essential original nature thought is transparently luminous.
>
> *Sariputra:* That thought which is no thought, is that something which is?
>
> *Subhūti:* Does there exist, or can one apprehend in this state of absence of thought either a there is nor a there is not?

Sariputra: No, not that.
Subhūti: Was it then a suitable question when the Venerable Sariputra asked whether that thought which is no thought is something which is?
Sariputra: What then is this state of absence of thought?
Subhūti: It is without modification or discrimination.
Sariputra: Well do you expound this, Subhūti, you whom the Lord has declared to be the foremost of those who dwell in Peace.

[Irreversibility Section]

And for that reason [i.e., because he does not pride himself on that thought of enlightenment] should a bodhisattva be considered as incapable of turning away from full enlightenment, and as one who will never cease from taking perfection of wisdom to heart.[44]

Through a close examination of the manuscripts and taking careful note of grammatical inconsistencies, Schmithausen argues that the entire Mindlessness section, along with its dialogue concerning the ontological status of the mind, was an interpolation from a section that occurs later in the chapter. While it is omitted from the *Ratnaguṇasaṃcāyagāthā* entirely, Schmithausen argues that it was probably transplanted from the discussion of the Mahāyāna and the Mahāsattva that comes later (Schmithausen's section J, which for Orsborn the center of the first prologue chiasmus).[45] His reasoning is twofold. First, the discussion of mind here in Sanskrit ends with the phrase *tenāpi bodhicittena na manyeta* ("he does not pride himself on that *bodhicitta*"). Schmithausen argues that the *tena* here must refer to some previously mentioned *bodhicitta*.[46] Left on its own, the *bodhicitta* drops in as something of a non-sequitur which helps explain Conze's awkward use of bracketed verbiage here ("that he does not pride himself on that thought of enlightenment [*with which he has begun his career*]"). On this basis, Schmithausen argues that the entire Mindlessness section that follows is an interpolation from a more natural spot later in the chapter.

The second textual infelicity that he points to would demarcate the end of that interpolation. A few sentences down, Śāriputra states that Subhūti has been declared by the Buddha to be foremost in the practice of a concentration called the *araṇavihāra*. The text then says, "*And for that reason* . . . should a bodhisattva be considered as incapable of turning away from full enlightenment." Schmithausen argues that *Subhūti's* achievement of the *araṇavihāra* can in no way be the cause of *some other bodhisattva's* achievement of irreversibility.[47] The "therefore" is thus out of place here. If, however, we remove this entire section, the "for that reason" (*atas*) would refer to the bodhisattva's mind that is not afraid at the end of the non-apprehension section.

But is there a way to make this section make sense without assuming it was simply inserted? On the one hand, we might hope that if it had been inserted, the person responsible would have done a better job smoothing out the text. But more importantly, there is considerable evidence to suggest that the current problematic wording was not original and was likely a result of errors introduced into the text at some point after its composition. These errors will turn out to be important.

The place to start, then, is to figure out what would have made sense here and then work our way back to how the text got to its current form. Interpretive charity requires us to assume that the original had to make sense, at least to its author. So if the original wasn't the local equivalent of the Sanskrit "*tenāpi bodhicittena*" then what was it? Among early witnesses to this passage there are three variants of this sentence to be sorted out. The *Da Mingdu Jing* appears to have had something like the current *bodhicittena*, but Kumārajīva apparently had either *bodhisattvacittena* or *bodhisattvena cittena*,[48] and Lokakṣema and Zhu Fonian had something else entirely. The question is whether these are three random variations or whether we can make sense of them in order to posit a progression and thus a chronological sequence of versions leading up to the current *bodhicittena*.

Let's begin with phrase that gave Schmithausen so much trouble: "*punaraparaṁ bhagavan bodhisattvena mahāsattvena prajñāpāramitāyāṁ caratā prajñāpāramitāyāṁ bhāvayatā evaṁ śikṣitavyaṁ yathā asau śikṣyamāṇas-tenāpi bodhicittena na manyeta.*" The first part of the sentence is fairly straightforward: "Moreover, Lord, the bodhisattva mahāsattva who practices in the perfection of wisdom and meditates on the perfection of wisdom should train such that while he is training. . . ." It is the remaining part of the sentence beginning with *tenāpi* (its punchline, if you will) that gives us difficulty. I would like to argue that the mystery of the errant *bodhicitta* begins to unravel once we decide how to render the verb *manyeta*. Conze, following the Tibetan,[49] renders the verb as "to take pride in." While that is certainly an acceptable translation, none of the early Chinese translators understood the *manyeta* to have anything to do with "pride." It looks like Lokakṣema understood this sentence to indicate that the bodhisattva shouldn't think or recognize (念) "this is a bodhisattva." Indeed, the verb √*man* is consistently represented by *nian* not only in Lokakṣema's translation, but in the *Da Mingdu Jing*, Zhu Fonian and Kumārajīva as well. Only Xuanzang translates the verb as 執著, which in any case would be "is not attached to" (*anabhiniviśyate* or *asakta*), not "to have pride in."

Manyeta is third-person optative of √*man* "to think," "consider" or "conceptualize" but whether it is used as middle voice or passive voice is determined by whether the agent is in the nominative or the instrumental. The Sanskrit as we currently have it (remember, all Sanskrit manuscripts of this text are quite late), has to be read as middle voice, since the agent of the thinking would then have to be in the nominative, "that trainee/the one who is learning" (*asau śikṣyamānas*). The sentence would then read: "One should train such that while training he does not conceptualize/is not conceptualized even by means of that *bodhicitta*," which doesn't make much sense. Alternately, we could read the *tenāpi bodhicittena* as a predicative instrumental[50] and render it as, "That trainee should not think of him/herself *as* the *bodhicitta*" – which makes even less sense. On the other hand, if we take the sentence to be a *passive* optative construction, then the instrumental *tenāpi bodhicittena* becomes the agent and "that one who is learning" (*asau śikṣyamāṇa*) would have to be an oddly placed predicate nominative *viz.* "the *bodhicitta* does not consider itself to be the trainee." (The more usual construction would be *tena bodhicittena asau śikṣyamāno manyeta* – with the predicate nominative coming right before the verb.)[51] Even without the testimony of the early Chinese translations, none of the above ways of rendering the sentence are plausible since, as Schmithausen points out, each of these interpretations would require a prior *bodhicitta* for the *tena* to refer to. Additionally, while it may be grammatically correct to talk about a bodhisattva "thinking with the *bodhicitta*" or "being *bodhicitta*," such constructions are "ungrammatical" within the Buddhist sociolect. One can "attain" or "give rise to" the *bodhicitta*, but one cannot think something with one's *bodhicitta*, nor can one be *bodhicitta*.

But, if the majority of our early translations don't have the problematic "*tena* . . . *bodhicittena*" that we find in all Sanskrit manuscripts, then where did it come from? Schmithausen suspects haplography (i.e., an "eye-skip") although he is ambivalent as to whether the original had been *bodhisattvacittena* which was subsequently changed to *bodhicitta* or vice versa.

> A reading that would say . . . *tenāpi bodhisattvacittena would thus also not be without difficulties, although it would certainly be smoother than the tenāpi bodhicittena of the received Sanskrit text. It is certainly conceivable that bodhicitta in the sense of its later terminological development could have taken the place of the unidiomatic *bodhisattvacitta. But the reading of *tenāpi bodhisattvacittena (or the corresponding Chinese translation initiated by T. 224 and adopted by other translators) could at least with equal justification in its turn be understood as a retroactive attempt to eliminate the incoherence given by the original wording tenāpi bodhicittena. – The latter certainly is the case for the peculiar rendering of our sentence through the later translation T. 228, which reads: ". . . and when that Bodhisattva practices in that way, he must not let the thought (citta) arise: 'I practice thus.'[52]

Among the early Chinese translations, only the *Da Mingdu Jing* and one of Xuanzang's translations have *bodhicitta* here,[53] and since Schmithausen's publication the reading of Lokakṣema, Zhu Fonian and Kumārajīva is confirmed by the recently discovered *Split Manuscript*. Although the relevant passage is missing the very end of the line,[54] it is clear that it could not have read "*bodhicittena*," since it reads "*bosisat[v]*." While only the bottom part of the *-v* is visible (hence there is no indication of the vowel attached to it), the *sa* of the *satva* is clearly legible and cannot be mistaken for a *ci*. Nevertheless, we can't completely dismiss the *bodhicitta* entirely, since the first chapter of the *Da Mingdu Jing* was probably translated by either Kang Sengui or someone of his school,[55] probably only a couple of decades after Lokakṣema's translation presumably using a manuscript that did have *bodhicitta*.

Both Lokakṣema and Zhu Fonian have sentences made up of two clauses. The subject of the first clause in Lokakṣema has the bodhisattva as the one who is, "to be recognized as studying it, should be regarded as dwelling in it, and should be considered as studying it."[56] Similarly, Zhu Fonian has something like, "the Bodhisattva Mahāsattva's perfection of wisdom should produce this learning that is learned." Both translations are awkward, but if their manuscripts had *śikṣati*, "he learns," (like we find in the *Split Manuscript*), then could render this clause as "he learns what is to be learned by the bodhisattva." The *Split Manuscript* has a clear punctuation mark at this point in the sentence, marking the remainder of the sentence as a separate clause. If we punctuate the Chinese translations accordingly, we have:

Lokakṣema: 菩薩當念作是學當念作是住當念作是學，入中心不當念是菩薩. (T. 224, p. 425c25)
Zhu Fonian: 菩薩摩訶薩行般若波羅蜜當作是學學，其心不當自念我是菩薩 (T. 226, p. 508c16).[57]

If we look at the second clause, we are back to the problematic *tenāpi bodhicittena na manyeta*. If it is punctuated as a clause we should expect it to have both subject and a predicate. Both Lokakṣema and Zhu Fonian appear to have "mind" as the agent of the verb "thinking" (there is no reason not to assume it is *manyeta* here) and the phrase "this is a bodhisattva" or "I am a bodhisattva" as the predicate of what is thought. If "*citta*" is the agent of the verb and "bodhisattva" is the predicate, then whether we take *maneyta* as passive or middle voice determines whether we assume the original that Lokakṣema (and Zhu Fonian) were looking at had an instrumental or nominative. Since the predicate of the sentence could be either a predicate nominative or predicative instrumental, the word bodhisattva could have been either instrumental or nominative without affecting the meaning (or for that matter the translation into Chinese). But the original form of *citta* here would be different depending on whether the predicate had been a passive- or middle-voice construction. If the sentence had been a passive construction, it would have looked like *bodhisattvaś/ena* ***cittena*** *na manyeta* (or Gāndhārī: *bosisatvo/eṇa* ***citeṇa*** *na mañea*): "[His] mind should not think itself to be a bodhisattva." A middle-voice construction would switch *citta* from instrumental to nominative (i.e., *cittena* to *cittaṃ*), thus: "*bodhisattvaś (or bodhisattvena)* ***cittaṃ*** *na manyeta* (= Gāndhārī: *bosisatvo/eṇa* ***cito*** *na mañea*).

Unfortunately, this is precisely where the *Split Manuscript* is not so helpful. The case ending of bodhisattva is cut off and although it appears that the line ends with the *(t)v-* we can neither rule out the possibility of a connected downward stroke (making it "*tvo*") nor can we rule out the possibility of an additional *-ṇa* (making *-tveṇa* a possibility as well).[58] The next line is intriguing. The first few letters of the entire right-hand side of the manuscript are either worn or broken off. Falk and Karashima discern a *kisa hedu*, but with a bit of imagination it is possible to make out a "*ta*" immediately preceding it. However, if we overlay a grid onto the whole manuscript and look to the most complete lines (1–28 and 1–30) and assume a fairly stable right-hand margin, we can guess that there were between five and six syllables missing from the beginning of lines 1–18 (Falk and Karashima have four missing syllables here, which I think is too few). If either *bosisatvo* or *bosisatveṇa* had been complete at the end of lines 1–17, there still would have been no earthly way to fit the equivalent of the Sanskrit *citena na manyeta| ta . . .* (i.e., "*citeṇa na mañea*[59] · *ta*") before the *kisa*, since that would be nine characters if we include the punctuation. Even *cito na mañea· ta* (eight characters) would have been too much of a squeeze. However, unless the *Split Manuscript* has something quite different from all other exemplars (which seems unlikely to me), then we are left to assume that the scribe did manage to somehow squeeze it all in. In that case, we may want to consider the possibility that the scribe might have omitted the punctuation mark before the *ta*, since his punctuation marks are often quite prominent and can take up the space of a proper letter. This would make the missing portion amount to seven characters, which is possible. It is certainly not unheard of for a scribe to omit a punctuation mark.[60] If that were the case here, it is in fact conceivable that the manuscript had *cito na mañea* not *citeṇa na mañea*.

If we can take the *Split Manuscript* to indicate that the earliest manuscripts had "mind" in the nominative declension and not instrumental, then, returning to Lokakṣema and Zhu's translations, I think it was more likely that they read *manyeta* or *mañea* as middle voice than as passive. While Lokakṣema's sentence could have had *citta* as either nominative or instrumental, his successor Zhu Fonian, who in most other cases copies directly from Lokakṣema, appears to have made an explicit decision to clarify his predecessor here. Zhu Fonian amends Lokakṣema's translation by prefixing the reflexive particle 自 *si* to the verb and inserting a subject, 我 *wo* – presumably to render the "should consider" (*manyeta*) as middle voice: "His mind should not think of itself, "I am a bodhisattva." Now this may, as one anonymous reviewer objected, be a case of "over-interpreting early Chinese translations," since Zhu Fonian often "makes Lokaṣema's version more explicit." He does indeed, but Zhu happened to make Lokakṣema's translation more explicit by rendering it explicitly middle voice-*ish* (since we are talking about Chinese) instead of passive. When he amends Lokakṣema's 當念 to 當自念, he uses a construction that Lokakṣema himself uses later to render another attested middle-voice declension (in this case future middle voice) of √*man* – *maṃsyante*.[61] While neither Zhu's emendation nor the number of spaces in the *Split Manuscript* are conclusive in themselves, if we combine the two with the fact that *citeṇa* is really unlikely in the *Split Manuscript*, then it looks increasingly likely that both the *Split Manuscript* and the manuscripts of Lokakṣema and Zhu Fonian had the local equivalent of the Sanskrit "*bodhisattvena cittaṃ na manyeta*" – "the mind (nom.) should not think of itself (optative, middle-voice) as a bodhisattva (predicative instrumental)." I would like to suggest, then, that *bodhisattvena cittaṃ na manyeta* constitutes the original reading of this passage. In Chapter 9, I will show how *bodhisattvena cittaṃ na manyeta* becomes *bodhicittena na maneyta* through a series of steps. But if the term *bodhicitta* was somehow derived from this passage (and I will argue that it was), then the original purport of the term *bodhicitta* when it does appear in the *Da Mingdu Jing* would have been the mind that does not cognize or apprehend anything (the *acitta citta*) not the mind of compassion.

Given that the *Split Manuscript* clearly does not have *bodhicitta*, the weight of the evidence points to the *bodhicitta* being the haplograph. If this is correct, and I think that it is, then we should at least be open to the possibility that one of the most monumental terms in Mahāyāna Buddhism was essentially the result of a typo. As someone who is tragically prone to typos, this gives me some hope. But for our present purposes, the above evidence suggests that early communities using this text understood this sentence to be a statement that the bodhisattva should not be having a notion of "bodhisattva" – a reading which develops rather seamlessly from the theme of Subhūti's "not seeing" the bodhisattva from the previous section. Thus, the reading we find in Lokakṣema, the *Split Manuscript*, Zhu Fonian, Kumārajīva and Xuanzang's second version gives us no reason to suspect an interpolation since the discussion seems to be a logical continuation of what precedes it.

The message of the original *Perfection of Wisdom*

Having determined the extent of the original *Perfection of Wisdom in 8,000 Lines* was (i.e., when there were far fewer than 8,000 lines), I would like to outline briefly what we should understand its message to be (the message along with all of its implications is a much larger issue and will be the topic of the next two chapters). The most straightforward reading of this passage is that it touts a state of mind in which no conceptual identifications are to be made. It is a state of "non-perception" or "non-grasping," which is referred to as being "mindless" or "thoughtless" (*acitta*). Whether this section ever circulated as an independent treatise or not, there are two things about this section that I find particularly interesting. The first is that these two themes, probably more than any other part of the larger sutra (with the exception of the discussion of the Dharma Body in the last chapter), become recurring themes in different forms of later Mahāyāna traditions. The second thing that I find interesting about this section is what it is *not* about – or at least what it is not obviously about. Despite Nāgārjuna's treatment of *Perfection of Wisdom*[62] in his *Mūlamadhyamakakārikā*, the word "emptiness" is nowhere present in this section. Nor does the opening section mention "omniscience" (*sarvajñā*), which Haribhadra takes as the theme of this chapter. Nor do we find any mention of "Mahāyāna," selflessness (*anātman*) or suchness (*tathatā*) in this section – each themes that Orsborn identifies as being central to the *Perfection of Wisdom*.

Now, I think that Orsborn is absolutely correct that the entire first chapter of the *Perfection of Wisdom* displays a kind of chiastic structure, although I would structure that chiasm a bit differently. Following Schmithausen, I see the first chapter as a series of iterations of certain phrases. The main structural elements of the ur-sūtra are Subhūti's non-perception followed by a statement to the effect that one whose mind is not afraid of that is to be known as being established in perfection of wisdom. Schmithausen points out that this structure is reiterated several times in the first chapter (he labels these iterations H, J, KI, KII, KIII and KIV). He thus finds six iterations, but if we look for the fear formula, I think that there is at least one more. If we take these iterations as our basis for structuring the chapter, then it looks like each iteration takes up the theme of

Subhūti's non-perception and recasts it in the mold of a specific Buddhist doctrine. So, for example, section H rewrites Subhūti's non-apprehension to be the non-apprehension of "titles" (*nāmadheya*). Section KIII rewrites the Subhūti's non-apprehension to be about selflessness. As Schmithausen points out, this is the most elaborated and modified of the iterations of the first passage. For ease of reference, I shall reproduce it here:

> I do not see that dharma which the word 'Bodhisattva' denotes . . . 'Buddha', 'Bodhisattva', 'perfect wisdom' all these are mere words. And what they denote is something uncreated. It is as with the self. Although we speak of a 'self', yet absolutely the self is something uncreated. Since therefore all dharmas are without own being, what is that form, etc., which cannot be seized, and which is something uncreated? Thus the fact that all dharmas are without own-being [*svabhāva*], what is that form, etc. which cannot be seized, and which is something uncreated? Thus the fact that all dharmas are without own-being is that same as the fact that they are uncreated. But the non-creation of all dharmas differs from those dharmas [themselves]. How shall I instruct and admonish a non-creation in a perfect wisdom which is also a non-creation. And yet, one cannot apprehend as other than uncreated all the dharmas be they those which constitute a Buddha, or a Bodhisattva, or him who marches to enlightenment. If a Bodhisattva, when this is being taught, is not afraid, then one should know that 'this Bodhisattva, this great being, courses in perfect wisdom, develops it, investigates it and meditates on it.'[63]

This section ends with two sentences stating that the bodhisattva who is not afraid of this teaching really practices the perfection of wisdom. Schmithausen points out that that the first sentence referring to the bodhisattva's lack of fear is a copy of the same sentence at the end of the Non-Apprehension section, while the phrase, "then one should know that this Bodhisattva . . . courses in perfect wisdom" hearkens back to a version of the Non-Retrogression section that appears in the *Ratnaguṇasaṃcāyagāthā* (Rgs. I, 5d).

What I find interesting about this iteration, as with each of them, is that it takes the original wording of the opening section and modifies it so that it looks like Subhūti is really talking about, in this case, selflessness. The same can be said about the other iterations. Schmithausen's section J describes the Mahāyāna which neither comes nor goes anywhere and the donning of the great armor. This section ends with the phrase, "if a bodhisattva hears this and is not afraid," then he is to be known as one who is armed with the great armor. In every case, the non-perception is brought up in order to connect it to an already accepted Buddhist doctrine. Clearly, the doctrine of *anātman* or selflessness was well established in certain circles prior to the *Perfection of Wisdom*. The above section merely connects Subhūti's non-perception to the doctrine of selflessness. By the same token, as I have argued elsewhere,[64] the term "Mahāyāna" was already a term used to describe Buddhism and the Noble Eightfold Path.

Here, the *Perfection of Wisdom* makes the case that Subhūti's non-apprehension of even the Mahāyāna is the *real* Mahāyāna. Indeed, one can make the same case for "emptiness" (*śūnyatā*), which makes its first appearance at the beginning of the second chapter, and for "suchness" (*tathatā*), which Orsborn identifies as the center of the complete smaller *Perfection of Wisdom*. Both emptiness and suchness were already well-established terms in the canon, and yet, as the discussion of Bhāviveka in the previous chapter shows, the Mahāyāna-inflected "emptiness" never really loses its sense of non-perception and non-conceptualization. What the *Perfection of Wisdom* does then is to inflect each of these already familiar terms through juxtaposition with non-apprehension and mindlessness. As such, we cannot claim, as Schmithausen would have it, that the ur-sūtra was simply a "Hīnayānist" teaching of selflessness. Though I will make a more lengthy argument to this effect in the following chapter: if it had been recognizable as a sermon on selflessness, there would not have been a need to rewrite it to connect it with selflessness in section KIII. On the contrary, the remainder of the first chapter inflects and recasts the canonical doctrines in light of non-apprehension and mindlessness of the first section so that the canonical doctrine of emptiness, suchness or selflessness are not quite the same doctrines anymore.

I think that at least some of these iterations were made by different authors since, for example, the ur-sūtra (section G) recommends arhats, *pratyekabuddhas* and bodhisattvas all train in this teaching, while section J right before the reiteration of the Mindlessness section tells us that the concentration of the bodhisattvas is "not held in common by the *śrāvakas* [Lokakṣema has arhat 阿羅漢 here] and *pratyekabuddhas*."[65] By the same token, among the earliest Chinese translations, we find the term "Mahāsattva" confined largely to section J, which again suggests different authorship. It suggests, but does not prove, and we need to be careful not to put too much weight on different authorship. Nevertheless, what is important for our purposes is the fact that someone thought that connecting the doctrine of the ur-sūtra to already accepted Buddhist doctrines *was work that needed to be done* to convince constituencies that needed to be convinced. In other words, I believe that what we are looking at in the expanded first chapter is a negotiated text representing a compromise position of more than one constituency.

Mahāyāna

Clearly, early *Perfection of Wisdom* enthusiasts added on to this original kernel as it grew to 8,000, 10,000, 18,000, 25,000 and 100,000 lines, and it is in the textual accretions that we learn how its early communities understood its teaching. Later on in the first chapter (after the reiteration of the Mindlessness section), we are treated to a discussion of Mahāyāna.

> Pūrṇa, the son of Maitrāyaṇī said to the Buddha, "What is the reason for saying that bodhisattvas are *mahā-samnāha-samnāddha* (armed with the great armor) and are mahāyāna-saṃprasthita (set out on the Mahayana)?" . . .

> Subhuti said to the Buddha, "For what reason does one set out in the Mahāyāna? What is the Mahāyāna?" . . . The Buddha said to Subhūti, "[To say] 'Mahāyāna, Mahāyāna' is not correct. It cannot be delimited." [428a] Subhuti asked the Buddha, "I wish to know where the *yāna* comes from. From the triple world [lit: places] it goes forth. It spontaneously abides in omniscience and nothing comes forth from it. Nothing will come forth in the future. Why, Deva of Devas?"
>
> The Buddha said, "If there are the two dharmas of that which actually arises and that which will arise in the future, then both cannot be apprehended. If dharmas are not apprehended then from what dharma do they come forth?" Subhuti said to the Buddha, "The Mahāyāna is unsurpassed and without equal among the heavenly beings and among the beings below heaven. This *yāna* is equal to the sky. As the sky covers countless people, so the Mahāyāna covers countless *asaṃkhyeyas* of beings. This is why it is called the Mahāyāna. And one cannot see when the Mahāyāna comes, or when it goes, or see its dwelling place. Nor can its center or edges be seen. Nor can it be seen or heard in this [discourse]. It cannot be seen anywhere and it cannot be seen in the triple world. Deva of Devas, this is why it has the name Mahāyāna." . . .
>
> Pūrṇa the son of Maitrāyaṇī said to the Buddha, "The Buddha has had the Venerable Subhuti explain the *prajñāpāramitā*; [has he done so] to the point of explaining the Mahāyāna as an object/a thing?"[66]

Clearly, whoever added this section to the original core wanted to stake out the non-apprehension teaching of the original sutra as constituting the very heart of Mahāyāna itself. But the character Pūrṇa here does not appear to quite be on board. He appears to be fine with the idea of not conceptualizing things, but not necessarily with making non-perception into something called Mahāyāna. Taking this to its logical conclusion, Maitrāyaṇī's question that ends the segment suggests that if Subhūti does not take the perfection of wisdom to be a thing, then he should not take Mahāyāna to be a thing either. Hence, Mahāyāna as the practice of non-apprehension is epitomized in the non-apprehension or conceptualization of even Mahāyāna itself. On the one hand, all of this assumes that the reader is already familiar with the word "Mahāyāna," and that the author of this section seeks only to get the reader to recognize the sutra's claim on the title. On the other hand, it appears that some (represented here by Pūrṇa Maitrāyaṇīputra) were reluctant to take the original sutra in this direction – although at least in the final redaction, the opposition is represented as acquiescing.

Bodhisattvas

I think that while the *Perfection of Wisdom* may be responsible for the term (though probably *not* the idea of) "*bodhicitta*," it is safe to assume that the terms "Mahāyāna," "emptiness" and "bodhisattva" were already established *before* the writing of the earliest section of the *Perfection of Wisdom*. The text comes to be seen by later

Mahāyānists as an important source of Mahāyāna, but that does not mean we should see it as the historical starting point of Mahāyāna. The text was clearly written to arrogate each of these terms (Mahāyāna, emptiness, etc.) for its own teachings. Since I have written about the non-Mahāyāna use of the word "Mahāyāna" elsewhere,[67] I think it will be useful here to discuss the place of this text within the development of the idea of the bodhisattva. The text assumes that there is a class of contemporary, living persons (i.e., persons in the sutra's imagined audience) called "bodhisattvas." Much has been written about the evolution of the idea of the bodhisattva.[68] Suffice it to say that the idea begins (and persists) as a designation of the Buddha prior to his enlightenment (or prior to the life in which he becomes enlightened). The term shows up periodically in the Pali Canon, where it is most prominently connected to the genre of Jātaka or past-life tales of the Buddha.

Indeed, it is at least arguable[69] that the term *bodhisattva-piṭaka* or *Bodhisattva-piṭaka sutra* was a precursor to the term "Mahāyāna sutra." In his excellent survey of the bodhisattva doctrine in the *Ratnakūṭa* corpus (which seems to me to be representative of the range of early Mahāyāna texts), Ulrich Pagel points out that by the second or third century, there had already been considerable development in the bodhisattva theme. Pagel discerns three phases of the development of the bodhisattva doctrine.[70]

The first, representing what is found in the very earliest Chinese translations, presents us with a rather loose collection of good qualities and moral and spiritual excellences that largely accentuate the ethics and religious practices that were already the stock and trade of canonical Buddhism. Furthermore,

> Mahāyāna practices such as the perfections or skillful means are relegated to the background and figure only sporadically. In fact, none of these early *Ratnakūṭa* translations proposes any formal scheme for the bodhisattva training that is particularly different from the Buddhist training we find in canonical texts. The practices are cited either on an individual basis or otherwise are loosely drawn together in tetrads.[71]

The primary exemplars of this early category among the *Ratnakūṭa* texts are the *Rāṣṭrapālaparipṛcchā*, the *Ugraparipṛcchā*, the *Ratnarāśī*, *Upāliparipṛcchā* and portions of the *Kāśyapaparivarta*.

The next phase described by Pagel consists of texts that roll out a highly structured architecture of the bodhisattva path along a 10-stage (*daśabhūmi*) schema that either makes a nod to the inclusion of the six or 10 perfections (e.g., the *Svapnanirdeśa* and *Akṣayamatiparipṛcchā*) or else includes them as an integral part of the stage process (the *Bodhisattvapiṭaka*). Pagel's third and final phase consists in texts that elaborate or adapt the earlier path structure to suit some doctrinal innovation, such as we find in the *Śrīmaladevīsiṃhanādasūtra*, which adapts the 10-stages scheme to suit its innovation in *tathāgatagarbha* theory.

Since the *Perfection of Wisdom in 8,000 Lines* seems to be completely unaware of the 10-stages scheme, I think we can only assume that it had not yet been devised. In fact, since the core sutra presents its perfection of wisdom as vital to the path of the arhat, I think that we can assume its authors initially understood its teaching on non-conceptualization *not* to mark out a different path, but to epitomize the path that everyone already subscribed to. This, of course, changes in later strata even within the first chapter so that we get the passage later in the first chapter[72] saying that the *samādhi* of non-grasping is *not* held in common with the *śrāvakas* or *pratyekabuddhas*. Thus, whatever kind of ecumenism obtained when and where the core sutra was written, it was replaced rather early with the idea that there were two methods leading to two goals – certainly before Lokakṣema translates his version.

What's missing?

Having looked at more developed versions of Mahāyāna in other times and places, it is remarkable what is missing from the opening section of the *Perfection of Wisdom*. I have argued above that the term *bodhicitta* probably began with haplography.[73] Now one might object that even if there were an eye-skip, the term *bodhicitta* was inserted because it was already well known. I am not convinced. Certainly the idea of giving rise to the inspiration to attain liberation or to help others attain liberation is quite old and probably older than this text. But most early Mahāyāna texts simply discuss this in terms of "giving rise to the thought" 發意[74] or to the "first thought."[75] The term *bodhicitta* itself is very rare. Nāgārjuna (if we assume that he did not write the *Bodhicittavivaraṇa*) seems to be unfamiliar with the term,[76] and I cannot be certain that it predates the *Da Mingdu Jing*,[77] suggesting that the term was coined sometime after the second or third century. Nor is there any hint of the 10 stages of the *Daśabhūmika Sūtra*. The only stages of a path mentioned are the attainments of irreversibility and unexcelled complete enlightenment. There is no discussion of compassion, the bodhisattva's delay in attaining enlightenment or skill in means (*upāya*).[78] The only hint that a bodhisattva might work toward others' enlightenment is the mention of Subhūti's skill in the *araṇavihāra* – an attribute that is well established in canonical texts. Furthermore – at least in the original sutra – it is assumed that the perfection of wisdom (*a la* section G) is for everybody: *śrāvakas*, *pratyekabuddhas*, arhats *and* bodhisattvas. There is no sense in this part of the chapter that the *Perfection of Wisdom* constitutes a separate teaching from what the *arhats*, *pratyekabuddhas* or *śravakas* should learn.

The doctrine of dependent origination (so central to the *Daśabhūmika*'s discussion of emptiness, and from there to Nāgārjuna's articulations of emptiness) is also missing. As mentioned above, the original sutra did not even mention the emptiness of all things. The phrase, "form is empty" is only mentioned once later on in the first chapter – and then only as one of the "signs" (*nimitta*) that the bodhisattva should *not* meditate on.[79] Presumably, meditation on all dharmas as being empty was understood as something that other, competing Buddhist communities were already doing. If anything, the first chapter appears to be far more interested in connecting its "*samādhi* of non-perception" to "signlessness" than to "emptiness." Given that the sutra appears to be unaware of many of the features of Mahāyāna as a developed and independent institution and path, I think it is fair to say that, while it was not the earliest Mahāyāna sutra, it was among a coterie or suite of earliest Mahāyāna sutras. As such it marks the threshold between developed Mahāyāna and whatever immediately preceded it. It is to the latter that I now turn.

Notes

1 Falk (2011a), p. 20.
2 See Sander (2000).
3 There are a number of small fragments discovered at Turfan, Qizil and Tunhuang. These are discussed by Karashima (2011) at their corresponding place. Since none of these correspond to the first chapter, I will not be discussing them.
4 Vaidya (1960), p. ix.
5 See Verboom (1998), p. 4, note 20.
6 See, Nattier (2008b [2010]).
7 For a discussion of his dates, see Ibid., p. 149.
8 See Nattier (2008a), p. 97.
9 Karashima (2011), p. xii.
10 Choong (2006), pp. 5–6.
11 Hikata (1953), pp. XXXIX–XXXX.
12 "[T]his chapter does introduce something new – a doctrine thereto unheard of, almost paradoxical, which is presented in the form of a summary without any detailed discussion to accompany it. This part, if taken independently, is surely liable to be misleading for uninitiated people, and therefore, not good enough to stand alone as an early Prajñāpāramitā-sūtra, for any early PPS, complete in itself, would no doubt have been expected to be in a more desirable form: it would have contained a detailed and elaborate account of its teachings, and by excluding every possibility of misunderstanding, it would have aimed at a more successful propagation of the first object and purport of the sūtra" Hikata (1953), p. XXXX (sic).
13 Ibid., p. XXXXI.
14 Ibid., XXXXIV.
15 Lancaster (1968), p. 317.
16 Arie Verboom (1998) certainly also deserves a note here, as he has in some ways considerably expanded on Schmithausen's work, although it should be noted that his aim was not to reconstruct the ur-text of the first chapter, but to establish what the chapter would have been for Kumārajīva. Regardless, his study is absolutely invaluable for anyone wishing to study the *Perfection of Wisdom* corpus.
17 For a full discussion of these sources see Verboom, p. 5:

"**PañcaD.** *Pañcaviṃśati Sāhasrikā Prajñāpāramitā* e.d N. Dutt based on four Nepalese mss that are dated 18th and 19th century.
PañcaG. *Pañcaviṃśati Sāhasrikā Prajñāpāramitā* a photographical facsimilie-edition of a 'Gilgit-ms' by Lokesh Chandra. The ms can be dated possibly as early as the beginning of the sixth century, and probably not later than the end of the seventh century.
Śata. *Śata Sāhasrikā Prajñāpāramitā*, ed. P. Ghosha [manuscript date unknown].
RGS. *Ratnaguṇasaṃcayagāthāḥ*, ed. A. Yuyama (1976). According to Yuyama the best available ms is dated 1174 CE."

18 Orsborn (2012), p. 55.
19 Taking Karashima's emendation of 用 for the Taishō edition's 因. See Karashima (2011), p. 2, note 8.
20 Following Karashima here (2011), p. 3 note 12.
21 Karashima amends T. 224, 426a3 學 with 舉, "chosen," which corresponds more closely with other manuscripts as well as the Sanskrit *nirdiṣṭo nirdiśasi*. Karashima, p. 6, note 32.

22 Schmithausen (1977), p. 56.
23 Ghoṣa (1902), vol. II, fascicle 3, p. 227.
24 Śodava is Gāndhārī for the Sanskrit śrotavya. Falk and Karashima (2012), p. 38.
25 Mathews (1943), p. 825.
26 D.N. 3.206.
27 M.N. 2.125.
28 S.N. 1.50.
29 Bodhi (1995), p. 733.
30 Conze (1958), pp. 1–2.
31 Though I should probably avoid saying anything definitive about the *Split Manuscript* before all the experts have had their say, as far as I can tell, Falk and Karashima's rendering of this sentence seems right – the main difference between it and the Sanskrit is that it has only one "*bosisatva*" and it lacks "*yad uta*" "which one speaks of." Instead it has "*kadaṃasa edo dhaṃmasa adivayaṇo bosisatvo di,*" "the designation bodhisattva belongs to which dharma?"
32 Cp. T. 226, p. 508c7.
33 Again, if we could get a better handle on the lacunae and obscured syllables in the *Split Manuscript* we might be able to settle hypotheses like this one way or another.
34 Schmithausen (1977), pp. 45–46.
35 Falk and Karashima (2012), p. 32.
36 The two stories are at T. 1545, p. 899a26-b3. Note that T. 1545 was translated by Xuanzang in the seventh century and we cannot be sure that the story that he finds in his version of the *Mahāvibhāṣa* existed at the time of the composition of the *Perfection of Wisdom*.
37 Orsborn (2012), p. 146.
38 Tony Duff (2000) writes the following in his entry on *mi 'gong*: "According to [ULS] this term was revised during the skad gsar bcad language revisions and meant, when written in new signs mi zhum. [LGK] gives more information: it means mi zhum and mi skrag pa, i.e., not timid, not scared (of things). In fact, these are the negatives of the verb 'gong ba q.v. for further meanings." Though *saṃ√lī* means "to cling to" in Monier-Williams dictionary, we find *sallīna* in Rhys-David's Pali-English Dictionary, meaning "sluggish, cowering" [s.v], which corresponds nicely with Tibetan *mi thum*.
39 Böhtlingk, vol. 5 (1868), p. 175.
40 Dutt p. 115.12–14.
41 Konow (1942), fol. 209.
42 See Dutt (1934), pp. 115, 154, 245, 254.
43 Falk and Karashima (2012), p. 34.
44 Conze (1958), p. 2.
45 Orsborn (2012), p. 158. Orsborn thinks that the Mindlessness section here is an anomaly.
46 Schmithausen (1977), pp. 47–51.
47 Ibid., p. 54.
48 T. 227, 537b13–14 菩薩行般若波羅蜜時，應如是學, 不念是菩薩心.
49 The Tibetan has "*rlom sems su mi bgyid pa.*"
50 See Edgerton (1985), vol. 1, §7.38, p. 45.
51 See Whitney (1879), p. 81, §268.
52 Schmithausen, p. 48.
53 *Da Mingdu Jing*: T. 225, p. 478c20: 如受此者不當念: 是我知道意; Xuanzang I: T. 220, p. 763c17: . . . 應如是學謂不執著大*菩提心*.
54 Falk and Karashima (2012), p. 34.
55 Nattier (2008a), p. 137. See also, Nattier (2008b). The *Da Mingdu Jing* (T. 225, p. 478c20) has: 如受此者 不當念 是我知道意. As Nakamura points out, 道意 is a common translation of *bodhicitta* in the translations of the *Pañcaviṃśatisāhasrikā Prajñāpāramitā* by Mokṣala and Dharmarakṣa [see, Verboom (1998), p. 222. Similarly, Xuanzang's first translation has (T. 220 p. 763c17) 謂不執著大菩提心. Cp. his second translation: (T. 220, p. 866a 9–10) 謂不執著是菩薩心.

56 Karashima (2011), p. 4, n. 22.

57 Note, this is precisely where we find punctuation in the *Split Manuscript*, which reads: *+++++gava ° bosisatveṇa mahasatveṇa evaṃ śi<kṣi>tavo yaṃ ca śikṣati teṇa yeva °teṇa yeva bosisa(t)v·* ++++ (1–17/1–18). Notice the repetition of "*teṇa yeva*" before and after the punctuation. It seems that this might have been a mistaken duplication, which might explain why the first of them is very faint (erased?).

58 It is unclear as to whether there could have been an – *e* at this point in the manuscript.

59 I am assuming it probably had *mañea* here, since all of the Sanskrit manuscripts have *manyeta*. For the purposes of determining the declension of *citta* here, however, it doesn't matter what the form of √*man* was since, apart from *maṃñadi* (Skt. *manyate*), all other third-person forms of √*man* in Gāndhārī have three akṣaras; e.g. third-person sing. *mañati, maṇati, meñati*, opt. sg. third *mañea*, abs. *mañati*. See Baums and Glass A Dictionary of Gāndhārī.

60 See Salomon and Glass (2008), p. 98.

61 Cp. T. 224, p. 441c2 and T. 226, p. 523a26; Karashima (2011), p. 170; Vaidya (1960), p. 92.

62 Even if one assumes the verses of praise of the introduction not to be a reference to the *Perfection of Wisdom in 18,000 Lines* (see Walser, 2005, p. 170 and notes 53, 54 and 55 of the fifth chapter), the whole discussion about "going" in the famous second chapter (the *Gatāgata Parīkṣa*), should probably be read as a philosophical footnote to the Mahāyāna or "suchness" or, more importantly the "Tathāgata" each of which is said in the *Perfection of Wisdom* to neither come nor go.

63 Conze (1958), pp. 10–11.

64 Walser (2009).

65 Vaidya p. 20: *yadapi tad bhagavan bodhicittaṁ sarvajñatā cittam anāsravaṁ cittam asamaṁ cittaṁ asamasamaṁ cittam asādhāraṇaṁ sarva-śrāvaka-pratyekabuddhaiḥ*. Cp. T. 224, p. 427b23ff; T. 225, p. 480c11ff.; T. 226, p. 510b15ff.

66 Fronsdal (2014), pp. 31–32.

67 See Walser (2009).

68 Most notably, Dayal (1975) and Anālayo (2010).

69 Pagel devotes a sizable portion of his book to this problem. It appears that the term *Bodhisattva-piṭaka* (like the term *Ratnakūṭa* itself) sometimes refers to a collection of genre of texts and sometimes appears to be the name of a specific text. Pagel argues that it probably first appears (in the *Drumakinnararājasutra* and *Ksāyapaparivarta*) as a collective noun and only later does it become the title of specific works such as the eponymous *Bodhisattvapiṭaka sūtra* (T. 310.12) and the *Pūrṇa(Maitrāyaṇīputra) paripṛcchā* (T. 310.17). See Pagel (1995), p. 26.

70 See Pagel (1995) chapter 3, passim.

71 Pagel, p. 101.

72 Vaidya (1960), pp. 7.10–13; T. 224, p. 426c18–21.

73 Though I think the haplography began in this text, I cannot rule out that it happened in some other text. For instance, in *Mañjuśrī's Inquiry to the Bodhisattvas*, we have the possibility that the arousing of *bodhicitta* came from a haplography of the phrase, "the bodhisattva's production of the thought as the anuttarasamyaksambodhi-citta," i.e., the phrase 菩薩發意為阿耨多羅三耶三菩提心 at T. 458, p. 440b26–27 getting shortened to 菩薩發意為*菩提心* – the bodhisattva gives rise to the thought which is *bodhicitta*.

74 E.g., T. 458, p. 435b22.

75 See Schlosser (2016), pp. 110–111; *paḍhama-c[i]tupa[de] = prathamācittotpāda*.

76 First pointed out by Robinson (1978), p. 63.

77 See Lancaster (1968), pp. 77–92.

78 Again, each of these is discussed by Lancaster.

79 See Karashima (2011), pp. 12ff.

7

MAHĀYĀNA SŪTRA AS PALIMPSEST

Discerning traces of the *Tripiṭaka*

Beyond "origin" as mere advent

In the introduction to this book, I argued that the problem of the origins of Mahāyāna essentially devolves into two separate problems. The first is a genealogy of the genre itself, a classification that I argue often involves retroactive classification of prototypical works. The second problem is the genealogy of the works that would eventually become prototypical in this manner. Chapters 2 through 5 argue that much of what is understood to be Mahāyāna in Asia points back to the doctrines of the first chapter of the *Perfection of Wisdom*. In the last chapter, I laid out what I see as the textual history of the *Perfection of Wisdom* itself based on Schmithausen's claim that the first few pages of the first chapter constituted the original core of the sutra.

But does the trail stop here? Doesn't the textual history of the *Perfection of Wisdom* discussed in the last chapter merely give support to the contention that the early Mahāyāna materials we possess have already undergone a long process of accretion? If we can identify precursors to our extant manuscripts, then don't we have to assume that there were precursors to those precursors which have left no trace, texts or sermons that either occurred "off camera"[1] or for a variety of reasons have not been preserved in the historical record? Under such a scenario, wouldn't we have to assume that the earliest phase of the *Perfection of Wisdom* is simply out of reach?

There is no question that the *Perfection of Wisdom* did indeed undergo significant accretion and no, we don't have the earliest manuscript of it. But this fact does not really make it stand out from any other ancient text, Buddhist or Biblical. The fact that our *manuscripts and translations* are fairly late does not mean that we cannot make reasonable (if fallibilist) inferences about the history of the text's composition based on those manuscripts. Paul Harrison says that our earliest manuscripts draw on "older traditions, both textual and ritual," and that he prefers "to think of most of the extant translations of this period as works of the *early middle* period of the movement and to regard the early period as more or less out of reach."[2] On the one hand, Harrison wants to infer that our early Mahāyāna texts are based on even earlier texts and rituals – which is fair enough. It is the latter assertion, however, that I would like to investigate in this chapter: namely, the hypothesis that those earlier texts and rituals are in fact "out of reach."

To infer that there must be an inspiring text or ritual is *pari passu* to infer something *about* that text or ritual – even if we don't have it. Parsimony dictates that we do not populate our mental universe with any more texts or rituals than we have specific evidence for. In other words, we cannot talk about texts or rituals or sermons that are no longer extant *in general*, and expect that *absence* to carry any historiographic weight. For example, if I write a witty and slightly off-color limerick on a piece of palm parchment and then quickly wash the ink off and then write a pious Buddhist sutra as soon as the parchment dries, we may agree that the limerick was *chronologically prior* to the sutra, but not that it is the *precursor* of the sutra. For an absent text, ritual or sermon to be a precursor to a text, the latter must retain some kind of trace of the earlier composition – whether by way of allusion, reference, quotation or parody. Short of that, we are not warranted to say the prior text is a "precursor" at all, nor can it in any meaningful way be claimed to be a factor in the text's genealogy.

But when we look for a precursor, what are we really looking for? An earlier version of the "same" text? At what point in the accretion does the text *become* the *Perfection of Wisdom in 8,000 Lines*? When the Non-Apprehension section was authored? When the first addition was tacked on after the propagation section to defend the Mindlessness section? In each of these scenarios we find ourselves once again faced with the retroactive force of history. As far as drafts go, even if we could locate earlier drafts of the core sutra, I am not sure they would necessarily tell us more than the versions we have any more than if someone hacked into earlier discarded versions of this book that those versions would reveal much about its "original intent."

Even assuming that we have isolated the earliest textual moments of the *Perfection of Wisdom*, we are left with a sense that the question of its origins has not been fully answered. Here I would merely like to point out that questions of origin and genealogy are not merely about chronology; they are also about *rationale*. It is not enough to conclude that the core of this sutra was composed by, say, a certain Mahādeva on an otherwise lazy Saturday morning, the 23rd of March in 54 CE at the Guhyavihāra next to Maṭ. In searching for the origin, we want to know *why* it was written. What was it in response to? In short, we want to know the life-world into which this text was composed, in order to know the background assumptions against which we should read it. It is pretty clear *what* the text denotes (i.e., Subhūti does not see or apprehend the bodhisattva and his mind is a no-mind), but not so clear *why* someone wrote this or what *significance* we should see in it. While textual analysis and philology are adequate to establish the former, we require a more expanded view of textuality to arrive at the latter.

Heteroglossia and textual rationale

To get at the origin *cum* rationale of the text, I would like to suggest that we look at the beginning of the *Perfection of Wisdom* not as a static fragment of manuscript, but rather as a rejoinder in an ongoing discussion – a snippet of a conversation into which we are eavesdropping. And here, I would like to point out the obvious: writers are also readers. Since part of the "meaning" of a text is how it positions itself against previous positions staked out by other authors, we can find the traces of what our authors were reading in what they write.

This idea that not only utterances but entire works can be understood to be in dialogue with earlier works comes, of course, from Bakhtin. "Heteroglossia" (currently enjoying a happy afterlife as "intertextuality") is his term for the situation in which the meaning of an utterance is not confined to the semantic and lexical meaning but is partially a function of the degree to which the audience recognizes the iterated nature of what is being said. We don't just hear words and interpret grammar when we communicate, we also recognize them as iterations of speech patterns we have encountered elsewhere. These are the turns of phrase, or ideas from distant or non-specific others upon which the utterance draws. Here, Bakhtin points to the obvious fact that in our speech, the words that we use are not our own. In "The Problem of Speech Genres," he writes,

> Our speech . . . is filled with others' words, varying degrees of otherness or varying degrees of 'our-ownness,' varying degrees of awareness and detachment. These words of others carry with them their own expression, their own evaluative tone, which we assimilate, rework, and re-accentuate.[3]

In Bakhtin's examples, we find two different modes of iteration: that of the producer and that of the audience. The producer of the utterance manipulates snippets of speech from any number of sources and weaves these together to produce a meaningful new whole. In producing the new utterance the producer can either accentuate or obscure the iterated nature of what is said. But either way something of the original source of the author's words remains in the present text as a kind of palimpsest. Some palimpsests boldly announce themselves while others blend in, and some texts even preserve signs of attempted erasure of the iterated source. In the following, I will attempt to show that the opening section of the *Perfection of Wisdom* contains a number of speech patterns adopted or adapted from a rather small suite of texts and as such it should be seen as engaging in and taking up a position within the set of concerns being debated within the suite.

While some iterated utterances, such as quotations, are copies of the original supplied with a new framing, other iterated utterances or speech patterns, such as allusions or parodies are not. Either way, in any iterated utterance, difference is introduced by the mere fact that the iterated utterance is also reframed and reaccented to produce either a new interpretation of the source text or, retroactively, a commentary on it. And here it should be noted that quotation does not require the audience to necessarily be aware of the source text, while allusion does.

There is thus a kind of twofold process going on in linguistic reception. On the one hand, the reader must exercise a unidirectional, teleological awareness of the sequence of lexemes or phonemes making up the utterance as well as the succession of boundaries laid down by series of changes in speaker. On the other hand, lexical items, phrases, motifs, tropes, etc. call to mind earlier instances of the same. In short, the mind is constantly identifying, connecting and comparing iterations. Such comparisons can be made against what one has previously read in a single text, or against anything one has read or heard elsewhere. Though the historian or scholar may make these connections explicit, making these connections is simply part of the way the brain interprets cultural works, or as T.S. Eliot puts it, it is "a principle of æsthetic, not merely historical, criticism."[4]

Texts exist, therefore, in at least three dimensions, marked by the sequence of reception on the one hand and the two directions of comparison (retroactively or intertexutally within the same text, and laterally or intertextually to other texts/utterances) on the other. Yet, when I say the audience "compares" texts, the result of this comparison is not always a simple judgment of sameness or difference. More commonly, when an intertext is cued for the audience, the intertext is understood to be the presupposition of the text – with the significance of the intertext inflecting the referring text.

So how do we identify intertexts in texts? What signs cue the perceiver to start comparing texts? Michael Riffaterre, like Bakhtin, begins with the fact that the iterations we recognize are structures, but that, "Like all structures, these are actualized in the form of variants. Such variants in a text must necessarily be verbal shapes, that is, words considered at one or more of three levels: phonetic, lexical, and syntactic."[5] According to Riffaterre:

> One of the basic components of a text's literariness . . . is that the text is not simply a sequence of words organized as syntagms but a sequence of presuppositions. In literary writing every lexical element is the tip of an iceberg, of a lexical complex whose whole semantic system is compressed within the one word that presupposes it. To put it otherwise: the literary text is a sequence of embeddings with each significant word summarizing the syntagm situated elsewhere.[6]

How do we know that a text is signaling to the reader that there is an iceberg to be recognized by a particular word or phrase? For Riffaterre, reference to another's speech or writing becomes significant (becomes allusion) when the full sense of the utterance is missing without reference to that utterance.

> The ability to connect or collocate texts does not, however, result from merely superficial similarities of wording or topic; two or more literary passages are collocable and comparable as text and intertext only if they are variants

> of the same structure. Intertextual connection takes place when the reader's attention is triggered by the clues mentioned above, by intratextual anomalies – obscure wordings, phrasings that the context alone will not suffice to explain – in short, ungrammaticalities within the idiolectic norm (though not necessarily ungrammaticalities vis-à-vis the sociolect) which are traces left by the absent intertext, signs of an in-completeness to be completed elsewhere. These, in turn, are enough to set in train an intertextual reading, even if the intertext is not yet known or has been lost with the tradition it reflected. [7]

For the reader, then, the intertext retains a presence in the text to the extent that the text itself cannot be understood or would be understood with a socially inappropriate value without the connotations provided by the intertext.

Intertextuality and adaptation in Buddhist literature

But if intertextuality forms a crucial element in the reception of a text, it also becomes a key feature in the composition of texts. Given the importance of memorization in Buddhism across the board, the relevant "verbal shapes" that would be recognizable to early audiences would be the sets of clichés or stock phrases around which Buddhist sutras weave their narratives. These clichés are usually short, patterned utterances such as doctrinal lists (e.g. the *Four Noble Truths*, the *twelve links of dependent-origination*, etc.) or simply turns of phrase that appear so often that they immediately cue a certain genre, setting or suite of texts (e.g., "Thus have I heard at one time . . .").[8] While the clichés' original purpose may have been to aid oral memorization, they would for that reason also have become a key concern or factor in the composition of new texts – which by the first century CE cannot simply be assumed to have been a strictly oral affair. As such, many of these clichés form a kind of doctrinal alphabet from which the poetry of the sutras was composed. They can be so used precisely because they can be recognized as iterated, iterable and therefore (for any would-be sutra composer) *fungible* elements. But to recognize iteration is simultaneously to key[9] the other texts and contexts in which a given phrase occurs – the range of other texts thus keyed will of course be a function of the accumulated cultural, or more specifically *bibliographic*, capital of the listener.

When we turn from the practice of internalizing and interpreting sutras to that of composing them, we should again note that composers of texts are invariably also consumers of other texts. Thus, when sutra authors introduce a cliché into a text, it – like any borrowed speech – displays various degrees of reaccentuation, various degrees of "own-ness" or "otherness" deployed as a strategic means to facilitate the recognition or misrecognition of the contexts of its prior iterations. As such, the iteration of clichés constitutes a recognizable genre feature of Buddhist texts in the sense that the particular cliché will necessarily be interpreted against the horizon of the other instances evoked.

Note that the way that genre functions here is quite different from the issue of genre classification that is the concern of the critic. When we are talking about clichés keying generic horizons, we are not saying that every text invoking the Four Noble Truths would have been recognized to belong to the "the Four Noble Truths" genre. The four truths, in fact, appear often in sutras where they are not the main teaching, e.g., in sutras discussing the gradual path to awakening such as the *Sāmaññaphalasutta* or in sutras cataloguing the range of Buddhist teachings, such as the *Saṅgītisutta*. Rather, as John Frow points out, "texts . . . do not belong to genres but are rather uses of them; they refer not to a genre but to a field or economy of genres and their complexity derives from the complexity of that relation."[10]

The extensive use of clichés in Buddhist literature means that we should not make a hard and fast distinction between adaptation and allusion, but simply note the relationship between particular configurations of bibliographic capital and the retroactive readings and evaluations made possible by the recognizably iterated nature of these clichés. In the remainder of this chapter, I will examine the ur-sūtra of the *Perfection of Wisdom* as an adaptation of earlier Buddhist sutras. In keeping with the twofold nature of the origins of works described above, I will attempt to both identify the suite of source texts the *Perfection of Wisdom* is adapting as well as to discuss the significance communicated by adapting those texts in this manner.

One final note: in investigating possible intertexts for the *Perfection of Wisdom* among Pali texts and Āgama translations, I am assuming that the *Sūtra Piṭaka* texts I discuss predate the *Perfection of Wisdom*. While actually dating the composition of any text in the *Sūtra Piṭaka* is extremely tricky business, my methodology here does not commit me to any of these texts being older than first century CE. While it is possible that some of them may in fact be younger than that, I will let my arguments for textual allusion in the *Perfection of Wisdom* itself be evidence for composition prior to that text.

The Non-Apprehension section and its intertexts

As discussed in the last chapter, the "punchline" of the introduction to the *Perfection of Wisdom* occurs in the Non-Apprehension and Mindlessness sections. While the term "emptiness" is not used in either section, the beginning of its second chapter refers to the teaching in this section as an "emptiness samādhi." If, then, we want to think of the roots of a specifically Mahāyāna form of emptiness or mind, then it would make most sense to turn to these paragraphs in order to place their statements within the larger discussions that were going on. Edward Conze has given us a more or less workable translation of the *Perfection of Wisdom*, but when the English-speaking reader reaches the Non-Apprehension section, they are greeted with the following:

> The Lord has said, "Make it clear now, Subhuti, to the Bodhisattvas, the great beings, starting from perfect wisdom, how the Bodhisattvas, the great beings go forth into perfect wisdom!' When one speaks of a 'Bodhisattva,'

> what dharma does that word 'Bodhisattva' denote? I do not, O Lord, see that dharma 'Bodhisattva,' nor a dharma called 'perfect wisdom.' Since I neither find, nor apprehend, nor see a dharma 'Bodhisattva', nor a 'perfect wisdom' what Bodhisattva shall I instruct and admonish in what perfect wisdom? And yet, O Lord, if, when this is pointed out, a Bodhisattva's heart does not become cowed, nor stolid, does not despair (etc.) . . . it is just this Bodhisattva this great being who should be instructed in perfect wisdom. It is precisely this that should be recognized as the perfect wisdom of that Bodhisattva, as his instruction in perfect wisdom.[11]

To one not steeped in the appropriate idiolect or socialect, this passage might be read as almost comedic: The Buddha asks Subhūti to preach to the bodhisattvas. The latter looks this way and that, with a bewildered expression and tells the Buddha that he doesn't see anyone. He then shifts gears, stands up tall and says that anyone who is told of this temporary blindness and is not afraid should be known as being instructed in perfection of wisdom. The not-seeing and its connected lack of fear are then said to *be* the perfection of wisdom itself. In short, even a straightforward and grammatically accurate translation such as Conze's reads like so much nonsense.

Sermon on selflessness?

So what set of intertexts must we read it against in order for it to *make* sense? To figure this out, we have to try on different possibilities to see which ones fit. Taking up first the proposition that the ur-sūtra should be read as a teaching on selflessness, I would like to examine some of Schmithausen's claims in more detail. Schmithausen finds especially significant the fact that early versions of the non-apprehension section omit Subhūti's non-apprehension of the perfection of wisdom. For him, this omission has important implications for both our doctrinal interpretation as well as the textual history of the passage.

> [I]n the oldest version of fragment D the impossibility of the Bodhisattvas to proclaim [the Perfection of Wisdom] only would only be based on the indeterminability, i.e., the non-existence of a Bodhisattva. This is also asserted from the traditional standpoint of the Hīnayana-dogmatic: insofar, namely, as a Bodhisattva as person (*pudgala*), as substantial self (*ātman*) or as "whole" is inexistent. Insofar as the [*Perfection of Wisdom*], originally included at least the original version of section D, its wording is little more than the insight into the hīnayānist "essencelessness of the person" (*pudgalanairātmya*). With time, however, the text became expanded in such a way that the Perfection of Wisdom henceforth explicitly incorporates the insight into the Mahāyānist '(further) essencelessness (substancelessness) of the factors of existence' (*dharmanairātmya*), into which the indeterminability of the Perfection of Wisdom itself – as a rather prominent spiritual Dharma – became added, etc.[12]

Thus, Schmithausen takes the earliest kernel of the Non-Apprehension section to center on the thesis that the bodhisattva is not perceived (*na sam-anu√paś*) – a teaching that he argues is tantamount to the standard "hīnayānist"[13] Buddhist doctrine of the "essencelessness" or selflessness of the person (*pudgala-nairātmya*). Schmithausen then claims that the text develops in the direction of the latter-day Mahāyāna doctrine of the selflessness of all dharmas (*dharma-nairātmya*) when it includes "perfection of wisdom" among the things that Subhūti cannot find. This interpretation would certainly be in keeping both with later strands of Mahāyāna interpretation (such as we saw with the Dalai Lama) that hold emptiness to be a deeper interpretation of the general Buddhist teaching of selflessness as well as with later portions of the first chapter that we discussed in the previous chapter. In short, Schmithausen portrays the textual history of this section as a short, relatively innocent non-Mahāyāna text that gets transmogrified into a Mahāyāna text over time by applying selflessness to dharmas.

Now even if we set aside what is probably an anachronism (i.e., the identification of Mahāyāna with the selflessness of dharmas),[14] by stating that the core section of the first chapter was a sermon on the doctrine of selflessness, Schmithausen implies that it would have been recognized to take up its place among other sermons teaching this doctrine. Indeed, there are a number of well-known sermons that present the term "emptiness" as a synonym for "selflessness."[15] For example, the *Mahāmālunkyaputtasutta* of the *Majjhima Nikāya* states,

> Whatever exists therein of material form, feeling, perception, formations, and consciousness, he sees those states as impermanent, as suffering, as a disease, as a tumour, as a barb, as a calamity, as an affliction, as alien, as disintegrating, as void [*suññato*], as not self [*anattato*].[16]

If Schmithausen is correct and the purport of the *Perfection of Wisdom* is a version of selflessness, then we would have to understand it as an adaptation of the genre of selflessness sermons to suit the interests of bodhisattva groups.

The text assumes that the reader already knows that there are bodhisattvas and that the perfection of wisdom is a goal. Under this reading, the innovation of the sutra would lie in its identification of the perfection of wisdom with the realization of the doctrine of selflessness. Furthermore, *à la* Schmithausen, it becomes a sutra on the selflessness of all dharmas (presumably thereby becoming a Mahāyāna sermon on emptiness) only with the addition of the phrase "nor do I see a perfection of wisdom." The Non-Apprehension section under Schmithausen's reading would have become a full-fledged Mahāyāna text with the final interpolation of the Mahāyāna section that connects the image of the Great Vehicle to the preceding discussion of the indeterminacy of dharmas.

Schmithausen is on to something here, but exactly *how* Subhūti's non-apprehension would have been recognized as having anything to do with selflessness is not immediately obvious. Setting aside the ongoing debate about whether or not the Buddha is ever depicted as asserting that there is no such thing as a soul,[17] we can nevertheless agree that *anātman* (however one wants to interpret it) does play an important role in canonical texts. Yet even with this admission, not all sermons on selflessness are cut from the same cloth. Clearly, this section of the *Perfection of Wisdom* reads quite differently from the paradigmatic sermon on selflessness (e.g., the *Anattalakkhanasutta* of the *Saṃyutta Nikāya*). In the latter sutra and many like it, selflessness forms a conclusion that is the endpoint of a larger analysis of conditioned phenomena. Alternately, the doctrine of selflessness is treated as a kind of simple catechistic fact in the *Cūḷasaccakasutta* of the *Majjhima Nikāya*. There, a certain ascetic named Saccaka asks the monk Assaji how the Buddha's teaching is usually presented to his disciples. Venerable Assaji responds:

> This is how the Blessed One disciplines his disciples, Aggivessana, and this is how the Blessed One's instruction is usually presented to his disciples: "Bhikkhus, material form is impermanent, feeling is impermanent, perception is impermanent, formations are impermanent, consciousness is impermanent. Bhikkhus, material form is not self, feeling is not self, perception is not self, formations are not self, consciousness is not self. All formations are impermanent; all things are not self [*sabbe dhamma anattā*]."[18]

Clearly, Schmithausen's core pericope is not a simple statement about selflessness in the manner of the above sutras, since the doctrine is never explicitly mentioned by name. On the other hand, if the selflessness of all dharmas were indeed the hallmark of Mahāyāna (in contrast to any other form of Buddhism), then the *Cūḷasaccakasutta* would also have to be an early Mahāyāna text since it clearly states that all dharmas are devoid of *ātman*. This raises a pertinent question: if the core pericope of the *Perfection of Wisdom* had been meant to inculcate selflessness, why does it never use the word "self," "person," etc.?

Nominalism?

There are a number of other possibilities for the interpretation of this passage as an argument about selflessness. We might emphasize the fact that Subhūti does not see *any dharma* to be a bodhisattva, in which case the focus would be on the dharmas and we could take the passage as arguing for the merely nominal status of the bodhisattva (a variant on the selflessness theme). The classic formulation here is Vajirā Bhikkunī's famous analogy[19] of the word (*sadda*) "chariot" existing on the basis of its parts. In the *Perfection of Wisdom* passage, Subhūti asks, "What dharmas are (subsumed under the) *designation* 'bodhisattva'? I don't see an existing dharma (to be a) bodhisattva at all." There are a number of places in the canon that argue selflessness by way of a kind of nominalism, i.e., the self is just a name for an aggregation of parts (a.k.a. the *skandhas*). Lokakṣema's interlinear notes discussed in the previous chapter show that this was at least how he understood this passage. The problem with this argument is that the canonical term for "name" of a composite entity in these discussions is almost invariably *prajñapti*, or as in Vajirā Bhikkunī's discussion "word" (*śabda*). The *Perfection of Wisdom* passage uses *adhivacana* which, although sometimes treated as a synonym for *prajñapti*,[20] is usually reserved in the sutras for a kind of metaphorical or allegorical equivalence or epithet.[21] It is not clear, then, whether "Bodhisattva" as an *adhivacana* is to be understood as the *word* "Bodhisattva" or as the title "Bodhisattva." When it is used in a more technical sense, it seems to be more closely tied to mental function of conceptual attribution *per se* than the English term "designation." In the *Mahānidānasutta* of the *Dīgha Nikāya*, the term *adhivacana* appears to denote the identification that occurs when the mind encounters an object (this "contact-designation" – *adhivacana-samphassa*) as opposed to awareness derived from the contact between the senses and their objects (*paṭigha-samphassa*).

> By whatever properties, features, signs or indications the mind-factor is conceived of, would there, in the absence of such properties . . . pertaining to the mind factor, be manifest any grasping at the idea [*adhivacana*] of the body factor? 'No Lord'.
>
> Or in the absence of any such properties pertaining to the body-factor, would there be any grasping at sensory reaction [*paṭigha*] on the part of the mind-factor? 'No Lord.'[22]

The *Mahānidānasutta*, probably more than most other suttas, grounds old age sickness and death – epitomizing samsaric existence – in cognitive and verbal identifications associated with *adhivacana*.

> If consciousness did not find a resting-place in mind-and-body, would there subsequently be an arising and coming-to-be of birth, aging, death and suffering?' 'No, Lord." Therefore, Ānanda, just this, namely mind-and-body, is the root, the cause, the origin, the condition of consciousness. Thus far, then, Ānanda, we can trace birth and decay, death and falling to other states and being reborn, thus far extends the way of designation (*adhivacana-patho*), [of terminology – *niruttapatho*], of concepts (*paññatti-patho*) thus far is the sphere of understanding (*paññāvacaraṃ*), thus far the round goes as far as can be discerned in this life, namely to mind-and-body together with consciousness.[23]

Vasubandhu (fourth/fifth century) in his *Abhidharmakośabhāṣya* clarifies the distinction in a way that certainly seems to apply to the *Mahānidāna* passage.

> The contact of the eye, the ear, etc., have *sapratigha* organs for their support (*aśraya*); thus they are termed *pratigha sparśa* taking their name from their support. The sixth, the contact of the mental organ, is called *adhivacana samsparśa*. What is the meaning of the term *adhivacana*? *Adhivacana* is a name. Now name is the object (*alambana*) par excellence of contact associated with the mental consciousness. In fact it is said, "Through the visual

> consciousness, he knows blue; but he does not know, 'It is blue'; through the mental consciousness, he knows blue and he knows, 'It is blue.'[24]

Nominalist arguments showing the chariot (like the person) to be mere names rely on the fact that the item designated can be seen to be a "mere name" by virtue of its manifestly real, albeit multiple, parts. The mind makes identifications such as designating a visual stimulus as "blue" based on mental contact with that ocular sensation. It would be hard to argue that the relationship between the single designation blue and its presumably singular stimuli have the same relationship as that between the single designation "chariot" and its multiple parts. In the latter case, one can say the singular chariot is a mere word because its parts are multiple. It is harder to argue this is the case of the knowledge that something "is blue." Of course, Dignāga (480–540) will make precisely this case later on, but it would be hard to argue that the use of *adhivacana* here amounts to an argument about the merely nominal status of the Bodhisattva. It appears that when Subhūti says he does not see any dharma for the *adhivacana*, "Bodhisattva," he is saying that the idea bodhisattva does not find any objective support. But if this is the case, why single out the Bodhisattva? Why not just look around and say that you do not see anyone – Bodhisattva or otherwise?

Cessation of cognition

If this is a variety of *anātman* sermon, it is not exactly standard fare. Clearly, it displays many differences from the *Anāttalakkhanasutta*, but which of these differences are significant and which are accidental? If the current text is an adaptation or rejoinder to another set of texts, we will only be able to make sense of it if we place it back within that conversation. In other words, we need to find those differences that will refer us to the suite of texts in which this text was understood to belong.

I propose we begin by noticing that the core sutra revolves around Subhūti's "not seeing" (*sam+anu√paś*) and "not grasping" (*an+upa√labh*) the bodhisattva. Here, at least in the Pali, we do find *an+upa√labh* used in the context of the doctrine of selflessness in sutras such as the *Alagaddūpamasutta*.

> Bhikkhus, since a self and what belongs to a self are not apprehended as true and established [*saccato thetato anupalabbhamāne*], then this standpoint for views, namely, "This is self, this is the world; after death I shall be permanent, everlasting, eternal, not subject to change; I shall endure as long as eternity" would it not be an utterly and completely foolish teaching?[25]

This certainly seems to be teaching the doctrine of selflessness. But notice that unlike other texts that preach selflessness, the emphasis here is not that the self does not exist but that there is *no apprehension* of said self. This is a crucial distinction, because saying, "I don't see trees" is quite different from saying, "Trees don't exist." The wording in Saṅghadeva's Chinese translation of the same sutra is different from the Pali in a number of ways,[26] but for our purposes it will be sufficient to point out a passage slightly earlier than the one cited above which amplifies this point:

> Again, there are six standpoints for views. What are the six? Monks, that which has form in the past, in the future or in the present, whether internal or external, whether pure or impure whether profound or not profound, whether close or far, all that does not have a self, the self does not have that, it is not this spirit, Such is discerned and he knows it to be true. He who has this understanding, who has these concepts, who has this view that nothing has a self, that the self does not have anything, that I will be nothing, that I will not be, that all that is not self, that I am not that, and there is no self, discerns thus and knows it to be true, the one that has this view 見, if he sees 見, hears, cognizes or thinks, what is grasped or what is discerned, the thought that is cognized (所得所觀, 意所思念)[27] follows (him) from this world to that world, follows him from that world to this world, (namely:) that all are without self . . . (etc.).[28]

In this passage, like the Pali passage above, we have a number of views about the self that are "grasped" – and I think we can safely assume that Saṅghadeva's manuscript had something like *anu√grah* here. But Saṅghadeva has the verb for grasping followed immediately by another verb for seeing, 觀. Since 見 is used to translate both the noun "(speculative) viewpoint" as well as the verb "sees," the verb *guān* was chosen to denote a different sort of "seeing," (i.e., a view) that leads to rebirth.

Sam+anu √paś appears to be a technical verb whose idiosyncratic object is a kind of 'view' or conception. Saṅghadeva's translation choices should warn us to the dangers of translating *sam+anu √paś* simply as an optical exercise. Even in the Pali, the Buddha states that the self and what belongs to the self are not apprehended *as true and established*. He does not say that they are not apprehended at all. The same goes for seeing. When Saṅghadeva uses *guān* in contrast to *jiàn* in his translation, he is contrasting a "view" or what is optically "seen" to the recognition (in either sense of that word as either "acknowledgement" or as "recognizing" *x* to be *y*) of that cognitive event on some kind of meta-level.

Indeed, the vast majority of instances of the verb *sam+anu√paś* occurring in the Pali Canon are in the context of the mental state in which selflessness is realized. Again, in these instances, *sam+anu√paś* does not denote a simple seeing, but rather a seeing *x as* something *y*. The corollary is that when the practitioner ceases to regard in this manner, she attains liberation. Thus, in the *Mahānidānasutta* of the *Dīgha Nikāya*:

> And anyone who says: "Feeling is not my self, but my self is not impercipient, my self is of a nature to feel" should be asked: "Well, friend, if all feelings absolutely and totally ceased, [*sabbaso vedanāya asati vedanānirodhā api*] could there be [the thought]: 'I am this?'" "No Lord" . . .
>
> From the time, Ānanda, when a monk no longer regards [*na . . . samanupassati*] feeling as the self, or the self as being impercipient, or as being

> percipient and of a nature to feel, by not so regarding, he clings to nothing in the world; not clinging, he is not excited by anything, and not being excited he gains personal liberation, and he knows: "Birth is finished, the holy life has been led, done was what had to be done, there is nothing more here."[29]

This paragraph is missing from the *Dīrgha Āgama*, although the discussion leading up to it most likely represented *saṃ-anu-√paś* with constructions involving 計.[30] Better attested is a passage from the *Aṅguttara Nikāya*:

> [I]t is not possible sir, nor could it happen, that when one is free of the thought 'I am' and sees not [*na samanupassato*] within one the thought 'This I am,' the dart of doubt and questioning 'How, how?' can invade the heart and stay. It is not possible. Indeed, sir this is just the escape from the dart of doubt and questioning, I mean the complete rooting out of the conceit 'I am.'[31]

This passage is referenced in the *Saṅgītisutta*[32] and *Dasuttarasutta*.[33] The wording in *Dīrgha Āgama* is abbreviated with no equivalent to *na samanupassato*.[34] The passage is, however, well represented in Xuanzang's translation of the *Saṅgītiparyāya*.[35] Clearly in the *Perfection of Wisdom*, it is Subhūti's "not-seeing" in the sense of being bereft of the mental event of identifying anything as a bodhisattva. But whereas "self" is a view that one can relinquish in order to achieve liberation, the *Perfection of Wisdom* has Subhūti merely "not apprehending" *the bodhisattva* – which to the extent we can call it a "view" at all would hardly be a pernicious one.

Selflessness . . . but differently

While both of the canonical passages discussed above are ostensibly about the doctrine of selflessness, neither weighs in on whether something named a self or soul exists (as indeed few do). Rather, both are concerned primarily with the cessation of the mental event that registers the idea "self." Perhaps the emphasis of the *Perfection of Wisdom* passage is less on what Subhūti should not be seeing (i.e., the Bodhisattva) and more on the attenuation of the activity of making identifications in the first place. We could read it as something akin to or possibly an extension of *indriya saṃvara* or "restraint of senses" that is practiced at early stages of the path.[36] There, the practitioner is to restrain each sense from contacting its respective object. Though not stated explicitly the implication seems to be that the cessation of such seeing and grasping ends the ideas that provide the foundation of rebirth, resulting in liberation. We might even want to paraphrase this to say that when cognition is stopped there is no contact (*phassa*) between mind and sense to give rise to the expression (*adhivacana*) of "the bodhisattva." This is confirmed in the *Dīrgha Nikāya* passage quoted above whose phrase, "if all feelings absolutely and totally ceased (*sabbaso vedanāya asati vedanānirodhā*)," appears to be related to the "cessation of perception and feeling" (*saññaveditanirodha*) so common in the *Majjhima Nikāya*. Where this kind of objectless awareness is explicitly tied to the attainment of release is in a number of sutras in the *Saṃyutta Nikāya* such as one of the *cetanāsuttas* of the *Nidāna Saṃyutta:*

> Bhikkhus, what one intends, and what one plans, and whatever one has a tendency towards: this becomes a basis for the maintenance of consciousness. . . . [This becomes the basis for the links of dependent-origination tending toward old age, sickness and death etc.] But, bhikkhus, when one does not intend, and one does not plan and does not have a tendency towards anything, no basis exists for the maintenance of consciousness. When there is no basis, there is no support for the establishing of consciousness. When consciousness is unestablished and does not come to growth, there is no production of future renewed existence. . . . Such is the cessation of this whole mass of suffering.[37]

As we saw with Bhāviveka and Candrakīrti, in these passages the cessation of mental identification is the true end of the cognition of a self and in the last sutra, liberation is achieved by not having any object of awareness (cp. Candrakīrti's statement that "One wishing to teach the ultimate truth cannot teach explicitly for it is ineffable and not just a referent of consciousness.").[38] As such, emptiness would describe the panoply that the practitioner does *not* cognize and not a proposition or an ontological commitment to the absence of a self. As for our *Perfection of Wisdom* passage it remains unclear as to whether the Bodhisattva is to attenuate and eventually abandon all mental identifications or whether there is something specific about the Bodhisattva.

It is Subhūti's non-identification or non-cognition of the bodhisattva that is identified as the *Perfection of Wisdom*. I am not the first to suggest that non-cognition is the key to the *Perfection of Wisdom*. We saw the Dalai Lama alluding to a connection between emptiness and the noble truth of cessation in the second chapter. But this idea was also hinted at by Nalinaksha Dutt in an insightful, if passing, comment made in his *Mahāyāna Buddhism*.

> In the *Mūlapariyāyā-sutta* (i.e., the basic discourse on Buddhism) it is stated that a person regards earth as earth and establishes a relation with it e.g., in earth from earth, my earth etc. In the same way, he goes with the other four elements (*mahābhūtas*), the various gods as gods, the different kinds of meditation as meditation and establishes a relation with them as indicated above. Even an Arhant regards Nibbāna as Nibbāna and thinks that he has attained Nibbāna. Bhagavān Buddha or the Tathāgata, however, knows earth etc. but does not establish a relation with them (*paṭhaviṃ paṭhaviṃ na maññati*, etc.) because the Tathāgata is free from all ideas or conceptions while an Arhat is not, hence, this is the difference that exists between an Arhat and a Tathāgata. In other words, earth, water, meditation etc. are merely worldly phenomena with a fleeting existence and do not exist in unchangeable reality.[39]

Dutt is on to something here, but this reference alone does not explain everything going on with this passage. The *Mūlapariyāyāsutta* clearly has the Arhat not cognizing "earth as earth" in pretty much the same way that Subhūti says that the bodhisattva "should not think herself to be a bodhisattva." Nevertheless, whereas the *Mūlapariyāyāsutta* probably does belong to a suite of texts to which the *Perfection of Wisdom* alludes, it lacks other specific vocabulary employed by the *Perfection of Wisdom*. But more to the point, canonical passages stating that the noble disciple does not see a self invariably state this in reference to the disciple's *own self*. In the *Perfection of Wisdom*, Subhūti does not tell the Buddha that he does not see or grasp himself. He simply says that he neither sees nor grasps *someone else* - namely, the bodhisattvas.

The perfected as untraceable

There are, in fact, few canonical passages stating that someone else cannot be perceived. The one context in which the formula usually reserved for one's self is applied to another occurs in passages discussing the status of the Tathāgata. In this context we also find the verb *anupa√labh* used quite freely. For example, we find in sutras such as the *Anurādhasutta* or the *Yamakasutta* of the *Samyutta Nikāya* immediately after a discussion of how the self is seen neither in the aggregates nor apart from them the identical argument is applied to the Tathāgata. The argument concludes:

> But, friend, when the Tathāgata is not apprehended by you as real and actual in this very life [*diṭṭheva dhamme staccato thetato tathāgate anupalabbhiyamāne*], is it fitting for you to declare: "As I understand the Dhamma taught by the Blessed One, a bhikkhu whose taints are destroyed is annihilated and perishes with the breakup of the body and does not exist after death"? [Yamaka responds:] ". . . friend Sāriputta I have abandoned that pernicious view and have made the breakthrough to the Dhamma."[40]

The Chinese parallel in Baoyun's translation (there is no parallel in T. 100)[41] represents *anupa√labh* with "not knowing and not seeing" (不知, 不見). In context, it is possible that Baoyun simply translated *upa√labh* as "to know." Regardless, Baoyun's translation of this sutra is somewhat abbreviated and refers the reader to the *Yamakasūtra*. There we do find the Buddha explicitly said to be neither graspable nor designatable. The relevant phrase there is:

> It is like this, Yamaka, the Tathāgata sees the dharma truly and really like this. His state (住 *sthāna*) cannot be grasped (無所得 *anupalabhyate*) nor can it be designated (無所施設 *na prajñāpayati*). [Therefore] how can you say, "I know and explain what the Blessed One said, (*viz*) that upon the death of the arhat, he does not exist," as you have said now?[42]

These sutras provide a kind of "selflessness" justification for the indeterminable points set forth in sutras such as the *Poṭṭhapādasutta* of the *Dīgha nikāya*[43] that assert the indeterminability of the Tathāgata after death. The Pali version of the *Yamakasutta*, and the one that follows it, argue that if the Tathāgata cannot be grasped in any of the aggregates *in the present life* how much less can any person be grasped in the subsequent state? While that phrase is missing from the Chinese, the implication is certainly there, since the status of the arhat after death is what Yamaka is primarily interested in.

The wording here quite explicitly melds the standard *anātman* arguments found in the *Alagaddūpama* or *Mahānidānasuttas* quoted above to the indeterminate points of sutras like the *Aggivaccagottasutta*[44] – making connections that are not drawn out in the latter sutras. More importantly, in the *Yamakasutta* we have a clear case of the ideal state being one in which *another person* is not perceived or grasped – namely the arhat. Here, ungraspability becomes tantamount to 'indescribability' since the status of the Tathāgata after death is rather famously one of those points on which the Buddha would not speak in the *Poṭṭhapādasutta* of the *Dīgha Nikāya*. If this is the backdrop against which the Non-Apprehension section is to be read, then we are not justified in reading Subhūti's lack of perception as asserting the simple absence of the bodhisattva since "absence" is one of the four positions negated in the *Poṭṭhapādasutta*. In this regard, I should also mention the *Brahmanimantaṇikasutta* of the *Majjhima Nikāya*, which asserts that all who understand earth to be earth (etc. for the elements, heavens and gods) are within the domain of Brahmā. The sutra then introduces a discussion that is clearly meant to contrast with the one who knows earth as earth, although it is unclear whether it is uttered by the Buddha or Brahmā,[45] lauding the "unmanifest consciousness" (*viññāṇaṃ anidassanaṃ*) in which "earth as earth" is not perceived (*ananubhūtaṃ*). Thereafter, Brahmā tries to vanish from the Buddha's sight and is unable to. The Buddha, then, *does* vanish from Brahmā's sight and utters the stanza:

> Having seen fear in every mode of being
> And in being seeking for non-being,
> I did not affirm any mode of being,
> Nor did I cling to any delight [in being].[46]

The theme here in each of these sutras seems to be that the one who does not perceive beings is not themselves able to be perceived – even by Brahmā or the Lord of Death himself.[47] While this teaching is usually applied to the Tathāgata in the *Tripiṭaka*, it should be remembered here that Subhūti is speaking about *bodhisattvas* or "*tathāgatas-to-be*."

Hence, it is possible that our *Perfection of Wisdom* passage may be trying to hint that the Tathāgata's indescribability may also be predicated of the *tathāgata-in-potentia*, namely the bodhisattva. To further support this interpretation, we should note that there are other sutras in the Pali Canon suggesting that "not seeing" the

Tathāgata as we do in the Non-Apprehension section is tantamount to the eradication of all false views, an index of a degree of awakening itself. So, for instance, in the *Aggivacchagottasutta*, after establishing that the four possible views of the existence of the Tathāgata after death are "speculative views," the Buddha tells Vacca:

> '[S]peculative view' is something that the Tathāgata has put away. For the Tathāgata, Vaccha, has seen this: 'Such is material form, such its origin, such its disappearance . . . [repeated for each of the five aggregates].' Therefore, I say, with the destruction, fading away, cessation, giving up, and relinquishing of all conceivings, all excogitations, all I-making, mine-making, and the underlying tendency to conceit, the Tathāgata is liberated through not clinging. "When a bhikkhu's mind is liberated thus, Master Gotama, where does he reappear [after death]?" "The term 'reappears' does not apply, Vaccha." "Then he does not reappear, Master Gotama?" "The term 'does not appear' does not apply, Vaccha." "Then he both reappears and does not reappear, Master Gotama." "The term 'both reappears and does not reappear' does not apply, Vaccha." "Then he neither reappears nor does not reappear, master Gotama?" "The term 'neither reappears nor does not reappear' does not apply, Vaccha."[48]

This passage counters "false views" with what is presumably the correct view – namely that each of the aggregates has an origin (*samudaya*) and destruction (*atthaṅgama* – literally "gone home"). But the correct view is then said to result in "the destruction, fading away, cessation, giving up, and relinquishing of all conceivings, all excogitations, all I-making, mine-making, and the underlying tendency to conceit," in which, "the Tathāgata is liberated through not clinging." While we may want to interpret "all conceivings" here to simply mean wrong thoughts, the passage is certainly open to the interpretation that the cessation of all conceptualization will result in tathāgata-hood. Under this reading, the sermon is not merely advocating the adoption of a correct doctrinal standpoint or even advocating that one maintain "noble silence" on these points. Rather, the sutra tells us that because things are impermanent, the Tathāgata has destroyed all conceptions (*sabba maññitānaṃ khaya*). These thinkings (*maññita*) presumably refer to the same mental activity the bodhisattva is told not to engage in in the *Perfection of Wisdom* [i.e., "*na manyeta*"]. Furthermore, not only does this *Vacchagotta* passage connect the Buddha's lack of the four speculative views regarding the Tathāgata's post-mortem existence with his relinquishment of "all conceivings, all excogitations, all I-making, mine-making, and the underlying tendency to conceit," the passage immediately moves on to the monk whose mind is thus liberated. The implication is that the person who does not see him or herself in any of these four ways *either is, or is on its way to being likewise unseeable* in these four ways. This sutra has two variations in the *Saṃyukta Āgama*.[49] Unfortunately, both instances limit the discussion to the status of the Buddha and say nothing about the status of a disciple who does not perceive themselves this way. Nevertheless, at least in the anonymous *Bieyi za ahan jing* (T. 100), the whole passage including the famous simile comparing the Buddha after enlightenment to a flame going out revolves around the fact that neither the Tathāgata nor the flame can be *seen.*[50]

Were these passages the literary background against which the core of the *Perfection of Wisdom* was written? If they were, then we should read the Non-Apprehension section as attempting to recommend the cessation of the mental identification of the Tathāgata to the disciple on the way to that state – namely the bodhisattva who, in turn, will become equally unseeable. In this sense, we could even look at this passage in the *Perfection of Wisdom* as a kind of missing link between the sutras on the Indeterminable Points in the Chinese canon and some of the more developed versions in the Pali Canon.

I think we are close to discerning the intertextual elements at play in this passage. There remain, however, a few problems with this interpretation which force us to push on. The first is that all of the above passages deal with the so-called "indeterminate points" (*avyākṛtāṇi adhikaraṇāni*). But nowhere in the *Perfection of Wisdom* do we find this term used, nor do we find the idiosyncratic "tetralemma" formula applied to the bodhisattva in this passage. Only one section in the first chapter attempts to relate Subhūti's teaching to the elimination of false views,[51] but this elimination of views is in the context of dependent-origination, not the "indeterminable points."

There are two collections of sermons that eschew any and all identifications or propositions without using the tetralemma format: the *Aṭṭhakavagga* and the *Pārāyanavaggas* of the *Suttanipāta*. In his justly famous 1976 article, "Proto-Mādhyamika in the Pāli Canon?", Luis Gomez asserted that the rejection of all mental standpoints found in the *Aṭṭhakavagga*, probably had something to do with early Mahāyāna.

> The last two books of the *Suttanipāta*, *Aṭṭhakavagga* and *Pārāyanavagga*, respectively, constitute no doubt the oldest strata of the work and belong to the oldest of the Pāli texts. The significance of these passages cannot be exaggerated. In many ways they anticipate (rather than foreshadow) some of the key doctrines of the Great Vehicle and often help establish possible connections or smooth transitions from the Buddhism of the Nikāyas to the Buddhism of the Great Vehicle. One is tempted to discover here a common ground, unfortunately neglected by the Abhidharmist and long forgotten by the Great Vehicle.[52]

More to the point, Gomez goes on to argue that the unique features of this text – features that cut against the grain of what would later become Buddhist orthodoxy – gave rise to the distinct tradition that became the *Perfection of Wisdom.*

> It also seemed evident that the pronouncements made in this sutta could not be reduced to other, more common teachings of the Pāli Canon without doing some violence to the text . . . These passages strike the reader

> as some of the most explicit and representative statements of an extreme apophatic tendency found elsewhere in Buddhist literature. This tendency – or is it a contemplative tradition of some kind? – reappears later in the literature of the Perfection of Wisdom, and, even more patently, in the *Prāsaṅgika Mādhyamika* and in the various Ch'an lines.[53]

It is true, as Gomez points out, that even the earliest commentaries as well as the Chinese rendering appear to perform a certain violence to the text in order to wrench it in line with what would become standard doctrine. Where I part company with Gomez is that, while I will agree heartily that the *Aṭṭhakavagga* and the *Pārāyanavaggas* share certain thematic similarities with the core *Perfection of Wisdom*, the divergences in vocabulary are significant enough to prevent us from identifying either chapter as real intertexts.

The *Aṭṭhakavagga* has two primary themes: the cessation of all views and identifications (*diṭṭhi* or *saññā*), and non-reliance (*nissāya*) on anything. Take for example, these verses from the *Paramaṭṭhakasutta*:

> By him not even a minute notion (*saññā*) has been formed here in respect of what is seen, heard, or thought. How could anyone here in the world have doubts about that brahman, who does not adopt a view.
>
> They do not form (views), they do not prefer. Nor do they adhere to doctrines. A brahman is not to be inferred by virtuous conduct or vows. Gone to the far shore, such a one does not fall back (on anything).[54]

The key terms of the core *Perfection of Wisdom* section, on the other hand, are "not seeing" and "not grasping" (*na samanupaśati* and *anupalabhati*). While neither of these terms or derivatives thereof appear in the *Suttanipāta*, disengagement regarding "what is seen," (*diṭṭhe*) at least, features in five out of 16 of the sermons in the *Aṭṭhakavagga*. These sermons warn against either relying on (*nissāya* or *upanissāya*)[55] "what is seen, heard (vowed) or thought" or as in the above verses, against "mentally constructing" (*pakappitā*)[56] the same into a "cognition" (*saññā*), calculation (*saṃkhā*) or other mental proliferation (*papañca*). Thus, Subhūti's "not seeing" the bodhisattva is thematically close to the *Aṭṭhakavagga's* not forming a conception of "what is seen, heard or thought," even if it is not close idiomatically.

There is one passage in the *Pārāyanavagga* not discussed by Gomez that really does come close to what the *Perfection of Wisdom* is interested in. Like a number of other sermons in the canon such as the *Aggivacchagottasutta*,[57] the *Mogharājamāṇavapucchā* of the *Suttanipāta* presents the perfected person as unseeable – but unseeable because of a particular view:

> 'Twice I have asked the Sakyan', said the venerable Mogharāja, 'but the one with vision has not answered me. I have heard that the deva-seer does indeed answer the third time.'

> (There is) this world, the next world, the Brahma-world together with the devas. I do not know the view of you, the famous Gotama, (about these).
>
> I have come with a desire (to ask) a question to the one who has such excellent vision. What view of the world is one to have for the king of death not to see him?
>
> 'View the world as empty, Mogharāja, always (being) mindful. Destroying the view of one's self, one may thus cross over death. The king of death does not see one who has such a view of the world.'[58]

Here it is not just any view that would render the practitioner unseen by the Lord of Death but specifically seeing the "world as empty" (*suññato lokaṃ avekkhassu*), and the (corresponding?) absence of view of self. While the term "emptiness" is not used for Subhūti's lack of perception in the first chapter, it is applied to it at the beginning of the second chapter even if his lack of perception of self is not particularly thematic in the first chapter of the *Perfection of Wisdom*.

Fearlessness

If I am correct that Subhūti's non-perception of the bodhisattva was meant to be read against canonical texts promoting the extinction of the idea of a self through the cessation of all ideas, coupled with discussions of the perfected as unseeable or untraceable, then what do we make of the reported lack of fear which accompanies perfection of wisdom? Each case of Subhūti reporting that he neither sees nor apprehends a bodhisattva in the first chapter of the *Perfection of Wisdom* is framed by a statement that the bodhisattva who hears this one who is "not afraid . . ." (etc.) followed by what appears to be a string of similes for fear and depression. Such a bodhisattva should be known as someone who has reached the goal. Being afraid is not a hazard usually associated with teaching about selflessness.

Under a certain reading of the *Brahmanimantanikasutta*, we might take the non-manifesting consciousness to be the opposite of the fear that is inherent in being and non-being. But then why doesn't the *Perfection of Wisdom* simply say that the one who does not apprehend a bodhisattva is free from fear? Why the string of similes for fear? I suspect there is a string here because it is referencing a similar string found elsewhere. If we look for canonical passages in which a monk is said to be not afraid or distressed along with a list of synonyms with a cadence of "not *x*, not *x*, not *x*, not *x*," we find a few candidates in the Pali Canon. The most obvious ones, as has already been pointed out, are the *Aggivaccagottasutta* itself and the *Abyākatasutta* of the *Aṅguttara Nikāya*. In both we find the phrase, "Thus knowing, thus seeing, the learned Ariyan listener is not afraid, trembles not, wavers not, shakes not, nor falls into quaking concerning these points."[59] The phrase "is not afraid, trembles not, (etc.)" can also be found in the *Brahmāyusutta* of the *Majjima Nikāya*[60] and the *Ārakkasutta*[61] of the *Aṅguttara Nikāya*.

There is, however, one other passage that stands out as a possible model for the core passage. In Saṅghadeva's Chinese translation (completed in 397–98 CE) of the *Dhātuvibhaṅgasutta* of the *Madhyama Āgama* we find the Buddha saying:

> The Buddha told him: "Monk, the person has six elements (*dhātus*), six places of contact (*sparṣāyātana*), eighteen mental explorations (十八意行 presumably *manopavicāra*), and four stations (*adhiṣṭhāna*). When one abides (*sthitaṃ*) therein, one does not hear difficult or sad affairs. *Not hearing difficult or sad affairs the mind does not hate, does not get depressed, does not toil*, and *is not afraid*. Like this he is instructed, does not neglect 放逸 wisdom, and protects the real truths, and makes the full-moon (*uposatha*) day offering.[62]

and later

> Monk, the 'I' is a self-promotion 自舉. 'I will be' is also a self-promotion. 'I will neither be nor not be' is also a self-promotion. ''I will be form' is also a self-promotion. 'I will be formless' is also a self-promotion. 'I will be neither form nor formless' is also a self-promotion. 'I will be cognizant' is also a self-promotion. 'I will not be cognizant' is also a self-promotion. 'I will be neither cognizant nor non cognizant' is also a self-promotion. It [self-promotion] is vanity (是貢高 *darpita?*), it is arrogance. It is self-indulgence. Monks, if one is without this: [without] all self-promotion his mind is said to be at peace. *Monks, if his mind is at peace, it will not be angry, not be depressed, will not toil, will not fear*. Why? Because that monk accomplishes the dharma. He is not able to speak hatred again. If he doesn't hate then he is not depressed. Not depressed, he will not sorrow, not being sad, then he will not toil, not toiling he will not fear. Because not fearing then he will attain nirvāna. After birth is exhausted, after the *brahmacārya* is established after doing what is to be done, and not again desiring and he knows as it is.[63]

These two passages from Saṅghadeva come closer to the sequence of synonyms for fear in the core *Perfection of Wisdom* than any other sutra – especially when compared with the translations of Lokakṣema and Zhu Fonian. In the *Perfection of Wisdom*, the monk *who hears* the teaching of Subhūti not perceiving a bodhisattva should be known as being versed in perfection of wisdom in Vaidya's Sanskrit and should be known as studying it (當念作是學) and should be recognized as dwelling in it (當念作是住) in Lokakṣema and Zhu Fonian. The bodhisattva is established thus if the bodhisattva's mind does not tremble, become despondent, etc.

In Saṅghadeva's passage, we find the relevant pieces in a different order. Where the *Perfection of Wisdom* passage has the bodhisattva *hearing* of Subhūti's not-perceiving, Saṅghadeva's *Madhyama Āgama* passage has the monk *not hearing* pleasant and unpleasant affairs. In Lokakṣema and Zhu Fonian, the bodhisattva who hears of the non-perception and is *not negligent, afraid, nervous, in trouble* or *apprehensive* (five items) is one who should be known as one who has finished learning and as one who has achieved the standpoint. Saṅghadeva's passage has the monk who does not hear affairs as *not angry*, *nervous*, *troubled* or *trembling with fear* (four items.) Saṅgadeva's passage only has the four items relating to fear, but does have "*not negligent*" toward wisdom as one of the *adhiṣṭhāna*. In other words, when we compare the terms in Saṅghadeva's list to that of Lokakṣema and Zhu Fonian, we find that almost all of the key words are present, just slightly out of order. The only difference is that Lokakṣema and Zhu Fonian omit "hate" while doubling "fear." The monk in Saṅghadeva's passage achieves the state of non-conception "if he stands there."[64]

As mentioned above, the bodhisattva who hears of the non-perception and is not afraid, etc. should be known as accomplished in the standpoint, or in Vaidya's Sanskrit, " if he stands thus, this is his training" (*saced evaṃ tiṣṭhati, eṣaivāsyāvavādānuśāsanī*). The bodhisattva in the *Perfection of Wisdom* who hears this teaching and is not afraid, etc. is (in Vaidya's Sanskrit) to be known as schooled in the perfection of wisdom. In Saṅghadeva's passage the monk who accomplishes this state is said not to be negligent toward wisdom and as one who safeguards the truth.

The Pali parallel has been translated by Bhikkhu Bodhi. The sections parallel to those quoted above are as follows:

> Bhikkhu, this person consists of six elements, six bases of contact, and eighteen kinds of mental exploration (*manopavicāra*), and he has four foundations. The tides of conceiving do not sweep over one who stands upon these [foundations?] and when the tides of conceiving no longer sweep over him he is called a sage at peace. One should not neglect wisdom, should preserve truth, should cultivate relinquishment, and should train for peace.

And later,

> Bhikkhu, 'I am' is a conceiving; 'I am this' is a conceiving; 'I shall be' is a conceiving; 'I shall not be' is a conceiving; 'I shall be possessed of form' is a conceiving; 'I shall be formless' is a conceiving; 'I shall be percipient' is a conceiving; 'I shall be non-percipient' is a conceiving; 'I shall be neither percipient nor non percipient' is a conceiving. Conceiving is a disease, conceiving is a tumour, conceiving is a dart. By overcoming all conceivings, bhikkhu, one is called a sage at peace. And the sage at peace is not born, does not age, does not die; he is *not shaken and is not agitated [sic]*. For there is nothing present in him by which he might be born. Not being born, how could he age? Not aging, how could he die? Not dying, how could he be shaken? Not being shaken, why should he be agitated? So it was with reference to this that it was said: "The tides of conceiving do not sweep over one who stands upon these [foundations], and when the tides of conceiving no longer sweep over him he is called a sage at peace."[65]

In the Pali *Dhātuvibhaṅgasutta* we find that the sage who does not conceive of any of these things is neither "shaken, shaking with anger" (*na kuppati*) nor "desirous" (*na piheti*)[66] – possibly an allusion to two of the three root *kleśas*, desire and anger. At least as far as the list of "nots" goes, the Pali version appears to be farther from our *Perfection of Wisdom* than Samghadeva's Chinese.

If the *Dhātuvibhāṅga* was an important intertext in the authoring of the core section of the *Perfection of Wisdom* (and I think that it was), then it corroborates a hypothesis already set out by Daniel Stuart that early Yogācāra with its call to "mind-only" began with its enthusiasts reworking the same sutra and not with some independent "mind-only school."[67] The second chapter of Stuart's *Saddharmasmṛtyupasthānasūtra*, which appears to be an early Mahāyāna text foregrounding a mind-only doctrine, is quite explicitly an adaptation of the *Madhyama Āgama* version of the *Dhātuvibhaṅga*. But the *Dhātuvibhāṅga* also points us to the fact that non-cognition was already important in other early sources and was probably part of a suite of texts sharing the same concerns. The wording "not seeing" and "not apprehending" calls to mind those texts like the *Alagaddhūpamasutta* or the *Mūlapariyāyasutta* in which the practitioner does not acknowledge the existence of something, i.e., the self or "earth." Subhūti saying that he does not see a dharma for the *adhivacana* "bodhisattva" recalls the *Mahānidānasutta* in which the contact of the mind with the idea or identification is referred to as *adhivacana samphassa*, or mental contact with the concept. In the latter sutra, release is obtained when this contact ceases. The fact that it is the "bodhisattva" that Subhūti does not see also recalls sutras such as the *Yamakasutta* whereby the unseen bodhisattva is comparable to the Tathāgata or to an extinguished candle flame. By the same token, the phrasing of the Bodhisattva's lack of fear led us to similar sermons in which the practitioner is not to cognize something such as the idea "I am" (as in the *Dhātuvibhaṅga*) or "This is earth" etc. (as in the *Mūlaparyāyasutta* and the *Brahmanimantanikasutta*).

The suite of texts urging the pacification or attenuation of the cognitive activity of identification can be seen to take its place among a larger set of thematic suits such as those tracing suffering and rebirth to cognition (*saṃjñā*)[68] or mental proliferation (*prapañca*)[69] and showing the way out as the cessation of the same. So what kind of practice is this? The practitioner is clearly not supposed to entertain certain ideas. And yet, the cessation of certain ideas is not necessarily to be replaced by others. Is the practice being enjoined here simply that the bodhisattva should not entertain *certain* thoughts, i.e., simply don't think about the self or the bodhisattva or the element earth, etc., or is the bodhisattva to attempt to attenuate and ultimately to annihilate the very activity of conceptualization itself through ending the contact between mind and mental identifications? The latter could consist of something as simple as an extension of "guarding the sense doors" (*indriya saṃvāra*) to cover mental activity or it could indicate something more extreme such as the "cessation of perception and feeling" (*saṃjñāveditanirodha*) that forms the goal in a number of sermons of the *Majjhima Nikāya*. Indeed, we might suspect that guarding of the sense doors and the cessation of perception and feeling constitute two poles on a continuum of a certain type of practice staked out by these textual suites. But individually we would be hard-pressed to argue that the cessation of perception and feeling is the *telos* of each text. The cessation of *all* conceptualizations is not what the *Dhātuvibhaṅga* is aiming at – or at least this is how the *Aṭṭhakathā* on the *Dhātuvibhaṅga* states it when it glosses "the outflows of conception" (*maññāssavā*) with "outflows" of desire, pride and views.[70]

It would appear then both from the *Perfection of Wisdom* as well as from the canonical material itself that *samādhi* did not just designate the endpoint and culmination of efforts to stop mental activity, the term *samādhi* could refer to the entire continuum of effort beginning with the stopping of particular thoughts and ending with complete absorption; contrast for example the *Dhātuvibanga* or the *Devadahasutta* of the *Saṃyutta* Nikāya in which the ability to quell certain thoughts allows the mind to arrive at one-pointedness with the *Samādhisutta* of the *Aṅguttara Nikāya* in which presumably all cognitions cease. By framing Subhūti's "not seeing" with a statement echoing this passage, the *Perfection of Wisdom* seeks to color Subhūti's "not seeing" with the a *samādhi*-like flavor oriented toward cessation of cognitive activity.

Abhidharma *echoes*

There remain, however, some things that cannot be adequately explained by an appeal to the sutra section of the *Tripiṭaka*. For example, Schmithausen argues that Subhūti's statement that he sees neither the bodhisattva's dharma nor the word for the bodhisattva, that this is a typical nominalist argument for the absence of self. But when such arguments occur in the sutras, it is often presented quite independently of the practice of mental absorption or *samādhi*.

Is there any way to read this as saying something about practitioners of *samādhi* instead of about the nominal status of the self? I believe there is. What is so striking about the cadence of forms of the Non-Apprehension section is the repetition of his not seeing two items: the bodhisattva's *dharma* or the *word* that denotes bodhisattva (some places we get three items: the *bodhisattva*, the bodhisattva *dharma* and the bodhisattva *word*). Knowledge of object (*artha*), the dharma and the expression (*vyañjana/pratibhāna*, etc.) are the three consistent elements of a rather unstable list of "discriminations" (*pratisaṃvid/paṭisambhidā*) that one should cultivate in order to become a great preacher. In A.K. Warder's excellent discussion of the history of the term, he notes that the list probably coalesced from a description of Śāriputra's excellent preaching, despite the fact that it is Mahākoṭṭhita who is said to have been the most excelled at these discriminations.[71] Warder points out that items are added or removed from the list of discriminations over time, but three items remain constant: the meaning "*artha*", the *dharma* and the expression.

It is significant that in the Theravāda tradition, while these discriminations are attributed to such luminaries as Śāriputra, Mahākoṭṭhita and the Buddha himself, it is also assumed that one encounters monks and nuns possessing these discriminations in far more quotidian settings. Thus, Warder notes that in the Theravāda Vinaya (Vin vs. 197),

> [I]t is laid down that the nuns should not talk with a monk who has not attained the four discriminations . . . This is immediately followed by the

> statement that a monk should not be elected to a committee if he is not skilled in meanings, principles (ideas), language, expression and context.[72]

Indeed, nowhere in the Pali Canon are the four discriminations associated in any way with *samādhi*.

The idea that discrimination of *artha*, *dharma* and expression was important for preaching is, of course, also present in the Northern tradition. We find the four discriminations mentioned in the *Dīrgha Āgama*'s account of the *Saṅgītisūtra* (whereas it is absent from the Pali version), and it is similarly discussed in the *Ekottara Āgama* and the *Dharmagupta Vinaya*. In each of these cases, as in the Pali texts discussed above the four discriminations are merely said to enable excellent preaching and are qualities of the Buddha. They are not explicitly associated with states of mental absorption.

The case is quite the opposite when we turn to Northern *abhidharma* literature. If we look at the *Abhidharmahṛdaya* of Dharmaśreṣthin, we find a description of the highest stage of the fourth *dhyāna*. There we find three qualities of mind produced as a result of that state:

> 171 When one without attachment is by nature immovable, he achieves all concentrations. Through his power of concentration he can give rise to the uppermost fourth trance.
>
> When he produces qualities in his mind here, they are the qualities: knowledge resulting from resolve [*praṇidhijñāna*], absence of strife [*araṇa*], analytical knowledges [*pratisaṃvid*], etc. . . . Analytical knowledge; when the meanings and the *vyañjanas* of all dharmas are certain and beyond doubt, he is unhindered and fearless.[73]

From this passage we can see that already the fourth *dhyāna* had been divided up into multiple sub-levels. These are explained in more detail in the *Abhidharmakośabhāṣya* as being the fourth *dhyāna* cultivated in an inferior, middling and superior manner – with each level being itself subdivided into inferior, middling and superior. The highest level, then, would be the fourth *dhyāna* cultivated in the most superior manner of the superior level. Though there are many kinds of arhats who achieve their goals through different methods (faith, etc.) it is only the "unshakable" arhat – that is, incapable of regressing – that achieves this highest *dhyāna*. Among the qualities of knowledge achieved at this stage, the unshakable arhats acquire knowledge of the object (*artha*), its dharma and its verbal expression in addition to the *araṇa*-vihāra that we saw attributed to Subhūti. In other words, the unshakable arhat is the best preacher precisely *because* of attaining this highest level of absorption.

Indeed, we find the association between the four discriminations and the highest level of the fourth *dhyāna* as a common assumption of all Northern (and possibly Sarvāstivādin)[74] *abhidharma* texts. In all likelihood Dharmaśreṣṭhin set the theme of the three kinds of knowledge as a result of the highest level of the fourth *dhyāna* and subsequent Sarvāstivādin texts followed him.[75]

Conclusion: the perfection of wisdom

Our investigation into possible intertexts for the opening section of the *Perfection of Wisdom* will not be complete until we examine intertexts for the idea of "perfection of wisdom" itself, since it is clear that even in the core *Perfection of Wisdom* that the terms "bodhisattva" and "perfection of wisdom" are assumed by the text, not coined by it. So far, I have argued that the *Perfection of Wisdom* presents us with a perfection of wisdom that by all appearances is tantamount to a very high level of mental absorption. The question is whether, in so doing, the text is drawing on earlier definitions of perfection of wisdom or offering us a new definition. If the perfection of wisdom is being *re-defined* in this text, then what was its definition before?

In the Pali Canon, where admittedly the term does not receive the same emphasis that it does in Northern texts, we find perfection of wisdom used in two senses. The first is simply as a description of one who has mastered Buddhist doctrine. Thus, in the *Questions of King Milinda*, we find:

> And furthermore, O king, those of the Bhikkhus who carry in their hearts the words of the excellent knowledge that is immeasurable, who are free from bonds, whose goodness and fame and power and glory no man can weigh, who . . . keep the royal chariot-wheel of the kingdom of righteousness rolling on, who have reached perfection in [wisdom – *paññāpāramiṃ*] – such Bhikkhus are called, O king, "The Commanders of the Faith in the Blessed One's City of Righteousness."[76]

Here the term "perfection," as elsewhere in the *Questions of King Milinda*, appears to be a non-technical term. Elsewhere, the perfection of wisdom also comes up as one of the 10 perfections accomplished by a Buddha. Discussions of the perfection of wisdom as prerequisite for enlightenment are confined to the *Buddhapadāna*, the *Apadāna* and the *Theragātha*. In these works, we find it explicitly tied to the mastery of *samādhi*, although exactly which *samādhi* is never made explicit. For example, we find in the *Buddhavaṃsa* the statement, often repeated in the *Aṭṭhakathās*, that "having made your *samādhi* firm, go to perfection of wisdom, if you wish to attain Bodhi."[77] Beyond this simple statement, we get no information on the content or function of this perfect wisdom in these texts.

Similarly, the Sarvāstivādins appear to have vacillated between perfection of wisdom simply being the non-technical accumulation of learning and acumen cultivated in past lives and as a technical term for the highest states of *samādhi*. Although it is difficult to know for certain whether the discussion predates the *Perfection of Wisdom*, Xuanzang's translation of the *Mahāvibhāṣa* states:

> Just as when the bodhisattva was called Govinda and vigorously sought Bodhi, he was clever and the best at debating hard without opposition. The world all praised him. Just this is called the fulfillment of the perfection of wisdom.

> Or some say, from the sitting on the diamond throne [vajrāsana – i.e., where the Buddha sat when he became enlightened] to his entering the diamond-like *samādhi* [*vajrasamādhi*] which leads to the attainment of the highest state of sambodhi; this is called the fulfillment of *prajñāpāramitā*.[78]

It appears that by the time of Vasubandhu (third century?), only the latter definition of perfection of wisdom was in vogue, since we find perfection of wisdom defined exclusively as the knowledge gained in the diamond-like *samādhi* *(vajropamasamādhi)* in Vasubandhu's *Abhidharmakośa*[79] as well as in the slightly later *Abhidharmadīpa*[80] and in the works of Saṅghabhadra (a younger contemporary to Vasubandhu).[81] Thus, like the core *Perfection of Wisdom*, there are texts in both the Theravāda and Sarvāstivādin traditions that take the perfection of wisdom to be a state of *samādhi*.

We do need to exercise a bit of caution here, however. The identification of perfection of wisdom with the *vajropamasamādhi* only occurs in Xuanzang's translation of the *Mahāvibhāṣa*, not in the earlier two translations. By the same token, it is not clear to me when the *Buddhavaṃsa* and *Apadāna* were written, and in terms of vocabulary and content, they may well represent a later strata than most other canonical texts. All of this is to say that the connection of the perfection of wisdom to the practice of *samādhi* could just as easily be a response to the *Perfection of Wisdom* as a precursor to it.

Yoke Meei Choong has argued that the emptiness of the *Perfection of Wisdom in 8,000 Lines* begins to make sense if seen in light of *abhidharma* interpretations of high states of mental absorption and their place in these articulations of the Buddhist path. She observes that many of the key terms in the perfection of wisdom refer to absorptions *immediately prior to becoming an arhat*.

> At least this much is sure: that the steadfast irreversible liberation of the mind of an Arhat is preceded by a certain *samādhi*.
>
> MN I: 297f. shows that the liberated mind of the Arhat can have properties such as *appamāṇa*, *ākiñcañña*, *suññata* and *animitta* [immeasurableness, nothingness, emptiness and signlessness]. Given the fact that the state of mind in *samādhi* just before obtaining nirvana is perfected, it is conceivable that the liberated state of mind differs from the immediately preceding state of mind in *samādhi* only in that it is free from the *āsavas* or unwholesome factors. The fact that the immediately preceding *samādhi* is an experience of reality, has the characteristics of *appamana* etc. of the mental status of an arhant but not its being freed from the *āsavas*, results from the following considerations.
>
> Some teachings depict the liberating insight into the path, such that they appear in the lower meditation levels like *saṃjñāvedayitanirodha* [cessation of perception and feeling]. According to MN I: 435–436, it can first consist in the negative investigation and then in the insight which has nirvana as its object. The results from the negative investigation of nirvana as an object requires only the transformation of mind. The text says, if the practitioner

> lingers in this state (i.e. one in which the Nirvana is the object of contemplation), he can negate the inflows (*āsavas*). It is therefore clear that nirvana is an object of contemplation immediately prior to liberation. Although the section on nirvāṇa as object of investigation is missing in the Chinese translation (T. 26, p. 780a17–20), it finds its place in the later commentaries.

A bit further down, she continues:

> In the *Prajñāpāramitā* the *dharmas* are equated with nirvāna. The object of concentration in the three *samādhis* are therefore the aspects of nirvāna, and thus the object of concentration. In contrast to MN I: 435–6 and VisM, the three *samādhis* are not anticipated by the negative investigation, they have far more in common with *ānimitta samādhi* in *AK* (*Bh*); consistently the aspects of the Nirvāna as object. In paragraph (21), the way of looking at things in the three *samādhis*, ie the *Prajnaparamitā*, is equated with the immeasurable (*aprameya*). This shows that the three *samādhis* (or *prajñāpāramitā*) have the properties of immeasurableness etc. (but not of liberation from influxes) of the mental state of the Arhat. In chapter 3, §A.a it has been shown that the practice of absorption does not go beyond this experiential anticipation of liberation. The three *samādhis* of the *Prajñāpāramitā* must therefore indicate the absorption shortly before reaching arhatship, because the three *samādhis* of the *Prajñāpāramitā* have the properties (the emptiness, unmarked, and desirelessness measurelessness) of the *cetovimutti* [liberation of mind] of arhats, but not their freedom from the *āsavas*. In other words, the *Prajñāpāramitā* is an insight into the nature of phenomena, but not analytically, and has the properties of the mystical experience of an arhat.[82]

Choong's solution is brilliant and she may well be correct for some early communities. She argues that, in foregrounding emptiness, and referring to it as "perfection of wisdom," the eponymous text is describing the direct perception of nirvana that *abhidharma* treatises were placing immediately prior to the liberation from the outflows that constituted arhat-hood. As such, the text becomes a sustained argument for *not* becoming an arhat; i.e., remaining a bodhisattva.

I agree that the concentration foregrounded as the perfection of wisdom probably does have something to do with the *vajropamasamādhi*. The problem I have with this interpretation, at least as it applies to the first chapter,[83] is that her argument assumes the centrality of two ideas: the first being that "emptiness" was the motivating insight of the *Perfection of Wisdom* and the second is that the bodhisattva was understood as someone who did *not* become an arhat.

When we look at the first chapter of the *Perfection of Wisdom*, neither of these assumptions are at all apparent. The three *samādhis* of the emptiness, signlessness and wishlessness do not appear in the first chapter (as mentioned above, "emptiness" gets a cameo, although as something one should *not* be attached to). The meditation touted by the *Perfection of Wisdom* only gets referred to as "emptiness" in the second chapter. Nor is there any indication that the author or the audience assumed a bodhisattva to be someone who postponed enlightenment. If we can assume arhats to fall under the category of *śrāvakas* (and certainly a number of known arhats among the Buddha's immediate disciples, such as Śāriputra, etc. are known as "*mahāśrāvakas*") then the first chapter certainly appears to be of two minds about them. The core section, as noted above, states that the Perfection of Wisdom will benefit "*śrāvakas* and *pratyekabuddhas*," whereas later in the chapter we are told that the Perfection of Wisdom is *not* common to the *śrāvakas* and the *pratyekabuddhas*. I take this discrepancy to be an indication that the work is the fruit of multiple authors, but even if you don't, it would be difficult to argue that a strong distinction between the mind of the arhat and bodhisattva is a blanket and driving assumption behind the entire work.

To conclude this chapter, I would like to return to Riffarterre's observations on how we identify intertexts.

> [O]ne of the basic components of a text's literariness . . . is that the text is not simply a sequence of words organized as syntagms but a sequence of presuppositions. In literary writing every lexical element is the tip of an iceberg, of a lexical complex whose whole semantic system is compressed within the one word that presupposes it. To put it otherwise: the literary text is a sequence of embeddings with each significant word summarizing the syntagm situated elsewhere.

To the 21st-century English-speaker who approaches Conze's translation of the opening of the *Perfection of Wisdom* with no other background in early Buddhist literature, Subhūti's inapprehension of the bodhisattva appears incoherent and the Buddha's statement that his non-seeing is perfect wisdom appears to be a nonsequitur. But this is because it wasn't written for that reader. To paraphrase Riffaterre, the opening section of the *Perfection of Wisdom* is "a sequence of embeddings, with each significant word summarizing a syntagm situated elsewhere in the" *Tripiṭaka*. The lack of sense on the page is resolved when understood or recognized as a response or rejoinder to larger conversations about mental absorption and its relation to preaching and enlightening others. Read against the background of the above texts and concerns in the canon, we can provide a coherent reading of all parts of the Non-Apprehension section. Indeed, it is *only* against such a backdrop that the passage makes any sense. It is primarily concerned with Subhūti's not-seeing the bodhisattva, which keys both discussions of very high levels of mental absorption while simultaneously keying discussions of the indeterminability of the enlightened person. But the passage is equally concerned with the preaching that results from that meditation. The section is framed by the *prāṭimokṣa* (a day for purification, but also for preaching), the Buddha's charge to speak and the first dialogue between Śāriputra and Subhūti about the authority by which the Buddha's disciples preach. If the expectation of an enlightened monk was that through meditation they would have intimate knowledge of objects, their dharmas and the proper verbal expressions associated with them, then when the Buddha asks Subhūti to preach to the bodhisattvas about the perfection of wisdom, there is a kind of logic to Subhūti replying that he sees neither the object (the bodhisattva), the bodhisattva's dharma nor the expression for the dharma, since the not-seeing is descriptive of the state of perfect wisdom.

It is therefore *not* the case that the origins of this Mahāyāna sutra are "out of reach." Here, the precursors to this Mahāyāna sutra are simply known sutras and *abhidharma* discussions from the *Tripiṭaka* itself, adapted to the new context of the bodhisattva striving for perfect wisdom.

Notes

1 Jan Nattier uses this phrase in discussing the verbal origins of our sūtras as sermons that were "sūtrified" at a later date. While Nattier is careful to state that we cannot have direct access to this phase, she nevertheless leaves open the possibility that we can infer things about it. See Nattier (2003), pp. 13, 100, 191.
2 Harrison (1995), p. 56.
3 Bakhtin (1986), p. 89.
4 Eliot (1982), p. 37.
5 Riffaterre (1980), p. 625.
6 Ibid., p. 627.
7 Ibid., 626–627.
8 There has been a virtual mountain of scholarship done on this phrase. For a good recent summary, see Anālayo (2014a).
9 For a more theoretical discussion of 'keying' across interpretive frames, see Goffman (1974) esp. pp. 40–82.
10 Frow (2006), p. 2.
11 Conze (1958), pp. 1–2.
12 Schmithausen (1977), p. 45.
13 This article was written in 1977 when one could still use this word to describe Mahāyāna's "other". On the inappropriateness of the term, see Anālayo (2014b).
14 See chapter 2, note 17.
15 See Ven. Huifeng (2016), pp. 98–111.
16 Bodhi (1995), p. 540.
17 Cp. Pérez Remón (1980) and Harvey (1995). More recently see, Walser (2018).
18 M.N. I. 228. cp. T. 99, p. 35b1–5.
19 At S.N. 5.10.
20 The only instance I have been able to find is in the *Dhammasaṃgani*: 1313. *Katame dhammā adhivacanā? Yā tesaṃ tesaṃ dhammānaṃ saṅkhā samaññā paññatti vohāro nāmaṃ nāmakammaṃ nāmadheyyaṃ nirutti byañjanaṃ abhilāpo – ime dhammā adhivacanā. Sabbeva dhammā adhivacanapathā*. Dhs p. 226.
21 For example, in the *Jānusoṇisutta* of the *Saṃyutta Nikāya*, the Brahmin Janusoṇi comes out of a village mounted on a posh chariot, and Ānanda asks the Buddha if there is anything in Buddhism that merits the *designation* "the brahmin's vehicle." The Buddha's reply is that the Noble Eightfold Path can be designated the Brahmin's vehicle of Buddhism. See also *Majjhima Aṭṭhakathā* II. 10.
22 Walshe (1996), p. 225.
23 Ibid., p. 226.
24 Pruden (1988–1990), vol. II, p. 425.
25 M.N. p. 232; 1.138; cp. T.26, p. 764c15–27.

26 For an excellent treatment of this complex sutra, see Anālayo (2011), vol. 1, pp. 147–158.
27 The Pali omits "what is grasped, what is discerned," having instead: "*yampi taṃ diṭṭhaṃ sutaṃ mutaṃ viññātaṃ pattaṃ pariyesitaṃ, anuvicaritaṃ manasā tampi 'etaṃ mama, esohamasmi*" M.N. I. 135.
28 T. 26, p. 764c15–27.
29 D.N. Walshe pp. 227–228. (also S.N. 4.167/ 1233).
30 e.g. T. 1, p. 61c2–3, 夫計我者, 齊幾名我見, 名色與受, 俱計以為我.
31 AN 3.291/III. p. 210.
32 Walshe p. 501.
33 Ibid., p. 515.
34 cf. T. 1, p. 52a15.
35 T. 1536, p. 431a7–8, 我雖遠離我慢不觀見我我所.
36 E.g., D.N. I. p. 70.
37 Bodhi (2000), p. 576; S.N. II p. 65. For similar sutras, see Huifeng (2016), pp. 137–138.
38 Vose (2009), p. 214, note 2.
39 Dutt (1977), pp. 71–72.
40 S.N. 933/PTS 3.111.
41 See T. 99, p. 32c2ff.
42 T.99 31b1–4 如是, 焰摩迦! 如來見法真實如, 住無所得, 無所施設, 汝云何言: "我解知世尊所說, 漏盡阿羅漢身壞命終無所有." 為時說耶? See Anālayo Bhikkhu's translation of this passage at www.buddhismuskunde.uni-hamburg.de/pdf/5-personen/analayo/translations/sa05.pdf.
43 See Walshe, p. 164.
44 The simile of the indeterminability of the flame when extinguished in the *Aggivaccagottasutta* is often used to explain the doctrine of *anātman* in modern literature, despite the fact that in context the simile refers only to the enlightened one after death.
45 See Anālayo Bhikkhu (2017), p. 13
46 Bodhi (1995), p. 428.
47 See, e.g., the *Nivāpasutta*, MN. #25.
48 Bodhi (1995), p. 592.; MN i. 487.
49 T. 99, p. 244a24ff./T 100, p. 446a25ff.; T 99, p. 245c29ff./T. 100, p. 445b18ff.
50 T. 100, p. 445b4ff.
51 T. 224, p. 427b18; T. 225, p. 480c7; T. 226, p. 510b9.
52 Gómez (1976), p. 139.
53 Gómez, pp. 139–140.
54 Norman (1992), pp. 93–94.
55 Sn. 5.3, 9.5, 12.10, 13.7.
56 Sn. 5.7.
57 There are a number of sermons in which a monk dies (e.g. the *Vakkalisutta* (S.N. 22.87) or the *Channa* at S.N., 35.87) in which the Buddha declares that Mara cannot see where they went. The *Tissabrahmāsutta* of the *Aṅguttara Nikāya* (A.N. 7.56.) has Moggallāna say that the liberated one cannot be seen by gods or men. In addition to the *Mogharājasutta*, the idea of the perfected not being seen by the Lord of Death, also occurs at Dhp. vss.57; 92–93.
58 Norman (1992), p. 126.
59 Hare (2001), pp. 38–39; A.N. IV. 68. *Evaṃ jānaṃ kho, bhikkhu, sutavā ariyasāvako evaṃ passaṃ evaṃ abyākaraṇadhammo hoti abyākatavatthūsu. Evaṃ jānaṃ kho, bhikkhu sutavā ariyasāvako evaṃ passaṃ na chambhati, na kampati, na vedhati, na santāsaṃ āpajjati abyākatavatthūsu.*
60 M.N. 2.138
61 A.N. 2.120.
62 T. 26, p. 690b22–26

63 T. 26, p. 692a22-b5.
64 We find this conditional in the Pali as well as in Saṅghadeva's Chinese. Pali: "*yattha ṭithaṃ maññassavā* . . . . etc." ≈ Saṅghadeva: "若有住彼不聞憂慼事."
65 Bodhi (1995), pp. 1094–1095/ M.N. III. 246.
66 Bhikkhu Bodhi has "not agitated" for *na piheti* while the Pali-English Dictionary has, "[cp. Vedic *spṛhayati, spṛh*] . . . to desire, to long for" [s.v.].
67 See Stuart (2015), chapter 4.
68 E.g., the *Madhupiṇḍakasutta* of the *Majjhima Nikāya.*
69 A.N. II. 161; See discussion Ñāṇananda (1971), pp. 18ff.
70 *Majjhima Nikāya Aṭṭhakathā* 5.59.
71 Warder (1997)
72 Ibid., p. ix
73 Willemen (2006), pp. 203–204.
74 I am hesitant to ascribe hard and fast sectarian affiliations here.
75 There are long discussions of the four discriminations in the *prāntakoṭika* fourth *dhyāna* in the *Samyuktābhidharmahṛdaya*, the *Abhidharmakoṣabhāṣya* as well as in such Sarvāstivāda-inflected works as the *Mahāprajñāpāramitopadeśa.*
76 Davids (1894), p. 234. "*Ye kho te, mahārāja, bhikkhū aparimitañāṇavaradharā asaṅgā atulaguṇā [atuliyaguṇā (sī. pī. ka.)] atulayasā atulabalā atulatejā dhammacakkānuppavattakā paññāpāramiṃ gatā, evarūpā kho, mahārāja, bhikkhū bhagavato dhammanagare 'dhammasenāpatino'ti vuccanti.*"
77 *maṃ tvaṃ catutthaṃ tāva, daḷhaṃ katvā samādiya; Paññāpāramitaṃ gaccha, yadi bodhiṃ pattumicchasi.*
78 T. 1545, p. 892b16–19.
79 Cf. Pruden (1988–1990), vol. 2, p. 694, "At the moment of Vajropamasamādhi, immediately before Bodhi, he accomplished the virtues of dhyāna and prajñā"; Pradhana (1975), p. 156: "bodheḥ pūrva-samanantaraṃ dhyāna-prajñāpāramitayoḥ paripūrir vajropamasamādhau."
80 Jaini (1977), p. 194. Stuart (2015), p. 261.
81 T. 1562, p. 591c17–21 and a virtually identical discussion at T. 1563, p. 889a21–24.
82 Choong, 2006, pp. 64–65.
83 Here, it should be kept in mind that Choong's work is a thorough investigation of the "Emptiness Chapter" of the *Perfection of Wisdom in 8,000 Lines.*

8

PALIMPSEST II

Brahmanical writings on the *Tripiṭaka*

The importance of incoherence

In the previous chapter, we examined the intertextual heritage of the first half of the original kernel of the *Perfection of Wisdom in 8,000 Lines*. The present chapter completes this process by investigating possible intertexts for the remaining portion, namely the discussion on the "mind which is not a mind," or the "mind which is mindless." This section is, if anything, even more difficult to place than the section that led up to it. And yet the ability to place "mindlessness" within its proper literary world is just as crucial as the placement of Subhūti's "not-seeing" since, at first read, it makes little sense.

Again, following Riffaterre, I believe the most profitable approach will be to begin precisely with those points of the passage that resist easy interpretation and whose straightforward rendering appears incoherent. Here, I ask the reader to consider the first time they read this passage. Right after Subhūti tells Śāriputra that "the thought or mind [of the bodhisattva] should not think itself to be a bodhisattva" we come to what we would expect to be the punchline of the entire sutra. Why should it not cognize a bodhisattva? The answer is . . . *drumroll* . . . "that thought is no-thought"! (*tac cittaṃ acittaṃ*).[1]

< *sound of crickets chirping* >

OK, so that didn't make much sense. If Subhūti had said that the Bodhisattva's thought *does not* cognize itself to be a bodhisattva, it might make sense to say that it is not aware of it because bodhisattvas don't exist or because bodhisattvas are somehow insentient. But the optative here means that the Bodhisattva's thought *should not* cognize itself as a bodhisattva (i.e., some bodhisattvas might do so but they shouldn't) because *for all* bodhisattvas (good and bad) that thought is apparently already insentient.

Reading on, every version other than that of Lokakṣema and the *Split Manuscript* goes on to explain that, in Conze's translation, the "thought is no-thought since in its essential original nature thought is transparently luminous"[2] (*prakṛtiś cittasya prabhāsvarā*). Even if we go with Conze's translation this phrase does not help us much, since it is not immediately clear why a luminous awareness would not be aware.

From there, Subhūti and Śariputra engage in a short dialogue about the ontological status of the thoughtless thought. Again, from Conze:

Sariputra: That thought which is no thought, is that something which is?
Subhuti: Does there exist, or can one apprehend in this state of absence of thought either a 'there is' [*astitā*] or a 'there is not' [*nāstitā*]?
Sariputra: No, not that.
Subhuti: Was it then a suitable question when the Venerable Sariputra asked whether that thought which is no thought is something which is?
Sariputra: What then is this state of absence of thought?
Subhuti: It is without modification or discrimination [*avikārā . . . avikalpā acittatā*].[3]

This turn to ontology is also odd in context. We can recommend the cessation of thought, but what exactly does it mean to say that an "absence of thought exists" in the first place? And, honestly, why would I even care if my thought really existed or didn't exist?

If we attempt a straightforward grammatical reading of this passage, it is difficult to know exactly what to do with it. The term *citta* is the past passive participle of the verb √*cit*, a verb whose range of meanings include "to perceive," "to attend," "to notice" and "to know." *Citta*, then would be that which is perceived, attended to, noticed or known – i.e., a perception or thought or simply "attention." Given the context in which Subhūti has just said the bodhisattva's *citta* does not cognize itself to be a bodhisattva, I think Conze's translation of *citta* as "thought" works just fine. But if *citta* is "thought" then how do we interpret its negation, *acitta*? The question is whether to read the *a+citta* substantively as a *karmadhāraya* (a compound word in which the second is a noun and the first an adjective, e.g., "blueberry") compound (i.e., the thought "is a non-thought" or "is not a thought"), or to read it adjectivally as a *bahuvrīhi* (a compound in which both terms of the compound serve to modify another word in the sentence, e.g. "highbrow") compound as all Chinese translators read it (i.e., the thought is "thoughtless" or "thought-free"). Whichever way we read it, we are still left with a contradiction: either we are stuck with a thought that is not a thought or with a thoughtless thought. From the discussion in the last chapter, we might surmise (correctly, I think) that the passage has something to do with the attenuation of mental activity and concept formation, in which case *acitta* would mark the endpoint or goal of that attenuation. But while contextualizing *acitta* as a kind of meditative cessation might explain the general point being made, it cannot make sense of why the author chose to express it in this way. If this passage is to urge the bodhisattvas to practice the cessation of cognition, why not just say that? What is added by specifying that that there is a thought that is thoughtless? Though it might be possible to eat a "jumbo shrimp," it is not immediately obvious how to think a thoughtless thought. And why then inquire into the existence or non-existence of that thoughtlessness? Finally, why was thoughtlessness considered to be so important, and who was it that was so invested in thoughtlessness?

Technically there is nothing ungrammatical about the passage and yet the inherent and irreducible contradiction of the *citta* that is *acitta* renders any straightforward reading of it unintelligible. While a first read might dismiss this section (and indeed the *Perfection of Wisdom* as a whole) as a kind of Dadaist rant *avant la lettre*, there are too many technical features of this passage to write it off as mere obscurantism. If the author wanted the reader simply to wallow (or "bask" depending on your predilections) in the irrational, it would have been easier to stop at saying the thought is not a thought, or to multiply similar contradictory constructions on down the page ("the thought is not a thought, the bodhisattva is not a bodhisattva, the Buddha is not a Buddha, *Ceci n'est pas une pipe*," etc.). Instead, this passage offers us the luminosity of the mind and then addresses the issue of whether existence or non-existence can be found in the state without thought. All of this seems too calculated to be dismissed as intentional irrationalism. If the passage won't let us cast *Perfection of Wisdom* authors as mere purveyors of the irrational, then the onus is again on us to place it in the discursive world in which it made perfect sense.

Surely the use of the word *acitta* here is "grammatical" in the standard sense (i.e., via the idiolect). Its use is "ungrammatical" however in the context of Buddhist literature (the presumed sociolect). If, as Riffaterre argues, "[t]he text's ungrammaticality is but a sign of a grammaticality elsewhere, its significance a reference to meaning elsewhere," then, what corpus of literature must it be read against in order to be meaningful?

The context of *abhidharma* literature?

In the last chapter, we made sense of Subhūti's not-seeing and of the Bodhisattva's lack of fear by appealing to generically similar sermons in the *Sūtra Piṭaka*. If we try to make sense of *acitta* by the same procedure, we notice that the term is rare[4] in canonical sutras. *Acitta* and its related terms are predominantly negative in connotation,[5] meaning either "unconscious" or "negligent," similar to *acitti* in Vedic texts.[6] Hence, from the standpoint of sutra literature, if we were to assume *acitta* to mark the culmination of the call to "not cognize" we run into a problem. Even the sutras that advocate the cessation of cognition (whether *saṃjñā* or *maññita*), never refer to the resulting mental state as *acitta*. In the sutras, there is basically one state of cessation (*nirodha*): that which occurs at the culmination of a long series of increasingly rarified states of mental absorption, for example, in "the cessation of perception and feeling" (*saṃjñā-vedita-nirodha*).

The situation is different, however, in *abhidharma* literature. In Northern *abhidharma* literature there are two such cessations, although exactly how they are allocated and described is a bit unstable. Thus we have in the *Abhidharmahṛdayaśāstra*:

> Two attainments: the attainment without perception and the attainment of cessation. The term attainment without perception is used when, disgusted with birth and death, and having the notion that it means deliverance, the series of thoughts is suddenly broken off on the basis of the fourth trance. The term attainment of cessation is used when, disgusted with hardship and having the notion that it means tranquility, the series of thoughts is suddenly broken off on the basis of (the sphere of) neither perception nor non perception.[7]

So far so good. Willemen translates from Dharmaśreṣṭhin's text (T. 1550), in which the topic is the "two attainments" (the two *samādhis*). A slightly later work, also entitled *Abhidharmahṛdaya* (this one by Upaśānti; T. 1551) has an almost identical passage with the exception that these two *samādhis* are called "thoughtless *samādhis*" (無心定). So it is only in Northern *abhidharma* literature that we begin to get the term *acitta* explicitly used in association with high states of mental absorption and cessation. In the *Mahāvibhāṣa*, there are two versions of the state of neither perception nor non-perception that are referred to as the two thoughtless *samādhis*.[8] In the above example from Dharmaśreṣṭhin, the first attainment occurs subsequent to the fourth *dhyāna* while the second is one that follows the state of neither-perception-nor-non-perception. The fact that they are both *samādhis* appears to have resulted in the new nomenclature of "thoughtless samādhi" that comprise both of them, since in the second translation of the text the two absorptions are said to be "thoughtless *samādhis*."

These two "thoughtless *samādhis*" are mentioned in a number of other works as well. For example, the *Mahāvibhāṣa* gives us two versions of the state of "neither-perception-nor-non-perception": the first involving thought (*sacitta*) and the second thought-free (*acitta*).[9] So here at least we find *acitta* used in a positive sense to describe high levels of meditative absorption. However, it also appears that the mindless designation of this state was controversial. Whether the thought-free absorption is in the fourth *dhyāna* or in the state of neither-perception-nor-non-perception, there is considerable discussion of whether very high levels of absorption are "with thought" or "without thought." The question culminates in a debate between Vasumitra and another master[10] concerning whether the state of cessation is *sacitta* or *acitta*, a debate whose Sanskrit is preserved in the *Abhidharmakośabhāṣya* and *Vyākhyā*. This debate has been discussed extensively by Paul Griffiths in his book, *On Being Mindless*.

> The Bhadanta Vasumitra, on the other hand, says in the *Paripṛcchā*: 'This [i.e., the question of how mind arises from mindlessness] is a problem for one who thinks that the attainment of cessation is mindless; in my view, though, this attainment possesses mind [so there is no problem].' . . .

> The Bhadanta Ghoṣaka says that this is incorrect, since the Lord has said: 'Where consciousness exists there is contact, which is the conjunction of the three. Further, sensation, conceptualization and volition are conditioned by contact.' Hence, "[if consciousness does exist in the attainment of cessation as Vasumitra suggests] sensation and conceptualization could not cease therein."[11]

Although a bit obscured by Griffith's translation, what is at stake with the terms "with thought" (*sacitta*) and "without thought" (*acitta*), is the question of what can condition the resumption of thought after a period when it is absent. For Vasumitra, there is really no problem about the thought that conditions the resumption of thinking after cessation, since he believes that dharmas exist in the three time periods. The conditioning thought "exists" in the past and has causal efficacy from that vantage point. Hence, cessation is not devoid of (a conditioning) thought (i.e., it is *sacitta*). Ghoṣaka takes a more conventional stance to argue that "consciousness" (*vijñāna* understood here to mean *citta*) exists when there is contact between cognition (*saṃjñā*), feeling (*vedanā*) and awareness (*cetana*). When any one of the three is absent (or contact itself is absent) there is no sense in which "consciousness" can be said to exist. Conversely, if cognition and feeling cease (in *saṃjñāveditanirodha*) then there is no way we can say that the thought that is the combination of these three factors can be said to still exist.

In light of these discussions, I think it is reasonable to take the *acitta* of the *Perfection of Wisdom* as describing some kind of mental absorption on par with *nirodha*. And here it should be kept in mind the few instances in the *Nikāyas* where the state of the cessation of perception and feeling is said to be a state in which,

> it does not occur to him: 'I shall attain the cessation of perception and feeling,' or 'I am attaining the cessation of perception and feeling,' or 'I have attained the cessation of perception and feeling'; but rather his mind has previously been developed in such a way that it leads him to that state.[12]

The cessation described in sutras such as this necessitates a studied lack of self-awareness on par with the bodhisattva not conceiving him or herself to be a bodhisattva – the nonself-awareness of the mind in the *Perfection of Wisdom* passage thus being an index to the extent of its cessation and control of his concept formation. Indeed, the *Split Manuscript* version of this sentence has a variant that, although found in no other manuscript, is telling as to how at least one reader interpreted the sentence. Instead of "*tac cittaṃ acittaṃ*," ("this thought is thoughtless") the *Split Manuscript* has "*daṃtaṃ* [Skt. *dāntaṃ*] *taṃ cito acito*"[13] ("this restrained mind is thoughtless").

But, even if these Vaibhāṣika debates could be reliably dated to sometime prior to the *Perfection of Wisdom*, how far can we make sense of the wording of our passage in light of the Sarvāstivādin debates? In the *Mahāvibhāṣa*, we have a Vasumitra and Ghoṣaka debating whether *nirodha* can properly be described as *sacitta* or *acitta*. The terms *sacitta* and *acitta* are never applied to the word *citta* itself, and neither Vasumitra nor Ghoṣaka come close to claiming that any kind of thought is thought-free or that a thought is not a thought. Now, we might want to claim that thought is in reality a non-thought because (*a la* Nāgārjuna) it is dependently originated and hence does not exist essentially. But if that were the case, why not just say so? As it stands, the passage does not give us any indication it is going in that direction. More to the point, cessation can be thought-free, but for these Sarvāstivādin materials, thought can't be thought-free. Similarly, Buddhaghosa's *Visuddhimagga*[14] declares the person who has achieved *nirodha* to be "*acittako*," but not the *citta* itself. Thus, even though the term *acitta* becomes a technical term for a mental cessation in *abhidharma* literature, the technical sense it acquires in those discussions cannot really help us understand its use in the discussion in the *Perfection of Wisdom in 8,000 Lines.*

The context of other schools?

Outside of the Sarvāstivādin fold, there were some who thought that *citta*, or at least a "subtle" *citta* persisted in the state of cessation – and presumably not merely (as with Vasumitra) in the past. André Bareau refers to a discussion in Xuanzang's (seventh-century) translation of the *Mahāvibhāṣa* that mentions the Darṣṭāntikas and the Vibhajyavādins as holding precisely this opinion.[15] He also notes that Xuanzang's *Vijnaptimātratāsiddhi* attributes a similar opinion to the Sautrāntikas and the Theravādins that "mental consciousness" (*manovijñāna*) exists in *nirodha.*[16] We have to be careful with these doxographic references, not only because we cannot always be certain how old Xuanzang's manuscript in which we find them was, but also, as Collett Cox[17] has recently pointed out, doxographies can draw rather bold lines over terrain where there was in fact quite a bit of debate. Thus, while Xuanzang's *Vinjñaptimātratāsiddhi* maintains that the Theravādins believed mental consciousness still existed in cessation, Buddhaghosa (fifth-century author of the *Visuddhimagga*) himself, very much like Ghoṣaka, declares the one who becomes thoughtless (*acittako*) to have achieved cessation. Whatever the exact sectarian affiliation of these positions, we can nevertheless say that there were some who thought the state of cessation not to be completely devoid of cognition, but rather to be marked by a subtle awareness. That said, the terms of the debate in Xuanzang's translations of the latter texts do not stray from what we have already seen in his translations of the debate between Vasumitra and Ghoṣaka. The discussion concerns whether *nirodha* (or any of the proximate states of absorption) is *sacitta* or *acitta* (or "subtle" *citta*, 細心). No one discusses whether or not the *citta* is in fact *acitta.*

The context of luminous thought and varieties of unaware thought

So does this "thoughtless thought" make more sense when we add the phrase about the original luminosity of the thought? We have to be careful here, because this phrase is missing completely in both the *Split Manuscript* as well as in Lokakṣema's translation and that of Zhu Fonian. The *Da Mingdu Jing*[18] has the purified thought as "luminous" (淨意光明), but does not have anything corresponding to the word *prakṛti*. It is only in Kumārajīva's fifth-century translation that we have the full Sanskrit passage represented. Personally, I think it is possible that this phrase was not in the original, but was added piecemeal as an interpretive gloss which quickly became part of the text at some point beginning with the *Da Mingdu Jing*'s exemplar. However, whether it was original or interpretation, somebody early on understood this "thoughtless thought" to be luminous.

Conze translates the whole sentence as "That thought is no thought, since in its essential original nature thought is transparently luminous" (*prakṛtiś cittasya prabhāsvarā*). I see no reason to doubt that this was someone's paraphrase of the *Accharāsaṅghātavagga* of the *Aṅguttara Nikāya* where the Buddha says, "Luminous, bhikkhus, is this mind, but it is defiled by adventitious defilements" (*pabhassaram idaṃ, bhikkhave, cittaṃ. Tañ ca kho āgantukehi upakkilesehi upakkiliṭṭhaṃ*).[19] And indeed, if the word *prakṛti* is an interpellation into the first interpellation then without it the first would have looked very much like the Pali. It is likely that this phrase was added as a kind of explanation of the term *acitta*, since the adjective "luminous" (*pabha*) describes the unmanifest consciousness (*anidassana viññāṇa*) in the *Brahmanimantanikasutta* – hence, by association rendering the confusing term *acitta* (usually "negligent" or "stupid") intelligible as "unmanifest consciousness."[20]

But if someone wanted to gloss the "*cittaṃ acittaṃ*" with the *Accharāsaṅghātavagga* by way of the *Brahmanimantanikasutta*, we have to also be aware of the ways in which this would have been a somewhat strained reading of the former passage. Bhikkhu Anālayo has shown that while nonmanifesting consciousness may index a perfected state, canonical references to luminosity and to the luminous mind do not indicate a mind is free from defilements.[21]

When we turn to the *Aṅguttara Commentary* (*Aṭṭhakathā*), on the luminous mind passage, things get more interesting albeit somewhat less clear. The *Aṭṭhakathā* comments on this passage by quoting an unnamed text that says, "This *bhavaṅga-citta*, is also originally pure (*pakati-parisuddham pi*). When the (subsequent) *javana* moment arises, it is defiled with the defilement of desire, etc."[22] The commentary uses this unattributed (and unexampled) sentence to explain the mind of clear light from the original passage; hence we can understand the commentary to gloss the mind of clear light with the originally pure *bhavaṅga* mind.

It was the Theravādins, and only the Theravādins as far as anyone knows, who developed a series of "mind-moments" in the *Paṭṭhana*.[23] The sequence begins with a moment of mind called the *bhavaṅga citta* which is an inactive awareness taking as its object the dying thought moment of the previous life. When a series of mental events is over, this *bhavaṅga citta* becomes the cause of the resumption of the succeeding impulsion (*javana*) moments that not only have content, but are morally determining (i.e., they are good, bad or neutral). A number of such moments follow one another in sequence until the whole series collapses back into the original state of *bhavaṅga*. The *bhavaṅga* mind is "original" in the sense that it marks the beginning out of which the subsequent moments arise and it is "pure" because it is so far devoid of both content and moral determination.

If we were to interpret the *Perfection of Wisdom* passage in light of the Theravāda commentarial tradition, would it make more sense? This, of course, would assume that the mental sequence laid out in the *Paṭṭhana* was already fully developed and was already being used to comment on the *Accharāsaṅghātavaggo*, a text whose only exemplar is in Pali. If we are set to operate under this admittedly long set of conditions, we would have to understand the Subhūti's thought to be thoughtless because it is actually the *bhavaṅga* consciousness or the original non-cognizing cognitive substrate from which all cognitive content arises. It is a *citta* but one that would not register a "bodhisattva" because any such identification would be a *javana* consciousness, not the *bhavaṅga* itself. And yet, as Rupert Gethin emphasizes repeatedly, it is *not* the case that the *bhavaṅga* consciousness lacks an object and according to Gethin, "it is most definitely not *acittaka*."[24]

The problem is that while the cognition of a bodhisattva could not occur in the state of *bhavaṅga*, the Theravādins do not associate the *bhavaṅga* state with any kind of soteriological efficacy. We all have it. It determines who we are throughout our life and far from being an enlightened state, it is one of the things that ends when cessation is actually achieved. Peter Harvey writes:

> In the developed Theravāda theory, it is said that, in [*nirodha-samāpatti*], a person is '*citta*-less' (Vism. 708), with even *bhavaṅga-citta* 'ceased' (*niruddha*) (Asl. 283). This position is the same as taken in the Canonical Abhidhamma, which says that neither *citta* nor wisdom exist in cessation (Kvu. 519). The *Milindapañha* passage on *bhavaṅga* is rather more open-ended, for it says that, for a living person, *citta* is not 'functioning (*appavattaṃ*) in one of two circumstances: 'when it has become drowsy and entered *bhavaṅga*; and . . . when it has attained cessation' (Miln. 300). As this sees *citta* as not 'functioning' when *bhavaṅga* occurs, such a 'non-functioning' *citta* could also occur in cessation.[25]

Buddhaghoṣa explicitly states that the *bhavaṅga* itself ceases in *nirodha*. As mentioned above, cessation is only attained by the one who is *acittako*, and presumably this also means the cessation of the *bhavaṅga-citta*. While the *bhavaṅga* is the main factor present during sleep without dreams, it is something one falls into, not something to which one aspires. So, unlike dreamless sleep in the *Muṇḍaka Upaniṣad*, the *bhavaṅga* is not taken to be any kind of a higher state in Pali literature. The *bhavaṅga* mind serves to fill a gap in the system – the need to link unrelated consciousnesses and is emphatically not part of any mechanism to end defilements.[26] In other words, if we frame the statement that the thought is thought-free with the passage from the *Aṅguttara Nikāya* and its Theravādin interpretation by way of the *bhavaṅga citta*, then we would really have no way of explaining how such a state could be reckoned to be perfect wisdom.

If the *Perfection of Wisdom* sentence references the *Aṅguttara* passage, then it is somewhat slanted paraphrase, not a quote – and the shift is telling. In the Pali, "luminous" (*pabhāssara*) modifies "mind" (*cittaṃ*). The defilements are then said to not belong to the mind because they are "guests" (*āgantuka*) just passing through.[27] In the *Perfection of Wisdom* sentence, "clear light" is feminine (not neuter) and so refers to the word *prakṛti* (f.) rather than mind (n.). Hence, the whole Sanskrit sentence says, in my reading, "Why? Because this thought is thought-free. The original substance/nature (*prakṛti*) of thought is clear light."

Here we may be tempted to read *prakṛti* in a Sāṃkhyan vein as a kind of original substance that is contrasted to its manifestations. This reading would cohere with the statement a few lines down (which is missing in the *Split Manuscript* and in Lokakṣema but is in the *Da Mingdu Jing* and Zhu Fonian and all subsequent Sanskrit manuscripts, to the effect that the state of thoughtlessness is without mental activity or construction ("*avikāra*" and "*avikalpa*"). *Avikalpa* is a common term in Buddhist literature, but *avikāra* is far less common. It is, however, often applied to the original *prakṛti* in Sāṃkhya literature.[28]

The context of *acitta* neither existing nor not existing as anti-Brahmanical dependent-origination

The introduction of the term *prakṛti* renders the thoughtless thought to be a kind of "original" or even "foundational" consciousness that is in any case more fundamental than awareness as it is usually understood. But the thought-free thought is also framed (or perhaps was originally framed) by the dialogue about whether such a thought exists or not. The definitive answer by Subhūti is that in the thought-free state (*acittatā*), existence (*astitā*) and non-existence (*nāstitā*) can be neither found nor apprehended.

Now, the denial of both existence and non-existence immediately brings to mind discussions of dependent-origination. The *Kaccāyanagottasutta* of the *Saṃyutta Nikāya*,[29] for example, has the Buddha telling *Kaccāyanagotta* that right view is the middle between the two extreme views of "existence" and "non-existence" (*atthita/natthita*). The middle is then described as being the twelvefold chain of dependent-ordination whose ultimate foundation is ignorance (*avidyā*). The aim of the sutra is twofold. On the one hand, it presents interdependency or dependent-origination as the middle between the extreme views of eternalism and annihilationism. On the other hand, it presents ignorance (presumably here it is the embrace of the extremes of existence and non-existence) as the ultimate source for the entire causal chain. Destroy ignorance by relinquishing attachment to existence and non-existence and the rest crumbles.

But here the reference to the *acitta* being neither existent nor non-existent cannot be an allusion to dependent-origination. *Acitta* could in theory be a synonym for ignorance (*avidyā*), but this would not make sense in the context of the *Perfection of Wisdom*. To read *acitta* as ignorance or negligence would be to say that ignorance is perfect wisdom. So, if allusion to the chain of dependent-origination is not really a good fit for *acitta*, then perhaps the text uses the idea of the *acitta* as cessation to frame our reading of *avidyā* in canonical discussions of dependent-origination.

Indeed, later on in the first chapter of the *Perfection of Wisdom*, we find a pun between *avidyamāna* (not existing) and *avidyā* (ignorance). First Subhūti describes the bodhisattva's *samādhi* as not even registering that there is *samādhi* going on. Śāriputra then asks in what dharma the bodhisattva trains, to which the Buddha responds that the bodhisattva does not train in any dharma at all, because "[t]hey do not exist in such a way as foolish untaught, common people are accustomed to suppose." [He continues:] "As they do not exist, so they exist. And so, since they do not exist [*avidyamāna*], they are called . . . ignorance [*avidyā*]." What the pun foregrounds here is that the *avidyā* of the common person is their being aware (√*vid*) of dharmas. The bodhisattva is not aware of such things because they are non-existent (*avidyamāna*). The two, *avidyā* and *avidyamāna*, are however two sides of the same coin.

Joanna Jurewicz has done a remarkable job of showing how the first few links of dependent-origination, both as a concept and in their specific terminology, allude to and should be read against the backdrop of certain Brahmanical cosmogonies. She reads the fact that the 12 links begin with ignorance to allude and respond to *Ṛgveda* X. 129, the *Nāsadīyasūkta*, since the latter begins with the state of "the unknowable."

> The actual term *avidyā* does not appear in Vedic cosmogony. But the ability to cognize appears in it. Firstly, the pre-creative state of reality is identified with the state of being unknowable: the *Ṛgvedic Nāsadīya* describes it as the state in which neither *sat* nor *asat* exists. These notions have both ontological and epistemological meaning, so their negation means not only that neither being nor non-being exits in the pre-creative state but also that it is impossible to assert whether anything exists or does not exist. It is a state of total inexpressibility. Using the Buddha's term, one could call it pre-creative *avidyā*.
>
> . . . the *Nāsadīya* describes the manifestation of the creative power of the Absolute, called *tad ekam*, and then describes the appearance of darkness hidden by itself (*tama āsīt tamasā gūḷham*). In the *Ṛgveda*, darkness symbolizes the states which are characteristic for night, when no activity physical or mental takes place; cognition begins with the *vareṇyaṃ bhargas* of Savitṛ arousing thoughts (*RV* 3.62.10). The image of darkness which appears after the image of the creative manifestation should be interpreted as expressing the impossibility of cognition.[30]

Though I will delve into the *Nāsadīyasūkta* in depth below, for now let me take up Jurewicz' argument that "the Buddha" hews quite closely to Brahmaṇical cosmogonies in the articulation of the 12 links of dependent-origination in order to cast as simply ignorant the originating cosmic "mind"[31] that initially is not aware of anything prior to the first distinctions (*praketa* from *pra*+√*cit*) of thought. If the twelvefold chain of dependent-origination was formulated to undermine and denigrate Brahmanical cosmology, then the *Perfection of Wisdom* would have to be read as undermining this attempt to undermine. By declaring the thought which avoids the extremes of "existence and non-existence" to be the *acitta*, the *Perfection of Wisdom* not only casts its *acitta* as the antidote to foundational ignorance, but appears to return the state prior to cognition to a position of cosmic (if not cosmogonic) significance. If we substitute the *acitta* of the bodhisattva for *avidyā*, then we have to read the links of dependent-origination as leading back to a state of original, unconditioned noncognition, beyond which we can think of nothing prior. The *acitta*, like the Vedic "One" in Ṛg X. 129, is prior to (and the condition for) any possible distinction and thus a kind of Vedic/Buddhist *archē* (Greek, "origin" or "governing principle").

This reading of the *acitta* as both the apex of meditation as well as the foundational, pre-creative awareness prior to distinctions that was understood to be the font of the cosmos also helps us make sense of the statement that the thoughtless thought was the luminous *prakṛti* of the mind. Of course, as Jurewicz points out, light as a metaphor of cognition pervades early Brahmanical and yogic writings, (though the Vedic terms are *jyoti* and *tejas*, not *prabhā*).

Nevertheless, it does appear that here someone has attempted to drop a few breadcrumbs to lead us in the direction of Brahmanical thought. As mentioned above, the mind that does not apprehend either existence or non-existence is also said to be "*avikāra*" This term is generally confined to the Sāṃkhya tradition where it is used to describe the fact that the root primordial substance (*mūla-prakṛti*) remains unmodified (i.e., it remains *prakṛti*) despite its transformations into the 23 evolutes beginning with bare awareness (*buddhi*). If we attempt to read the *Perfection of Wisdom* passage in a Sāṃkhya register, the overall structure of this passage requires us to read the bodhisattva's awareness as an objectless awareness precisely because it resides in its original unmodified state. The *citta* is still in some sense the *acitta* from which it is derived. Here, it should be kept in mind that in Sāṃkhya, Puruṣa or Brahman[32] is characterized by knowing (*jñā*) while *citta* belongs to *prakṛti*. If the *acitta* is *avikāra* then it remains unmodified in its primal state in the midst of the operation of the mind and its senses, and potentially to be identified with the font of the cosmos itself.

Tempting as this interpretation might be, I see no warrant to read the *Perfection of Wisdom* as a Sāṃkhyan text – at least not in the developed form that we see in the *Sāṃkhyakārikā* – since the latter has radically dualist assumptions that are not apparent in the *Perfection of Wisdom*. Sāmkhya-inspired yoga texts such as Patañjali's *Yogasūtra* seek the cessation of mental activity (*cittavṛttinirodha*) as the final immobilization of *prakṛti* in order for the *puruṣa* to become manifest. One doesn't get the sense here that the *Perfection of Wisdom* seeks the cessation of cognition so that something *else* should appear (such as we find in the *Yogasūtra*'s "isolation" or *kaivalya* and in the *Visuddhimagga*'s treatment of nirvana).[33] Rather, in this passage, *acitta* is the perfection of wisdom, it is the goal and it is somehow manifest as *citta* itself.

The context of absence of mental construction (*avikalpa*)

The Sanskrit not only says that the thoughtless thought is without modification (*avikāra*), but also without mental construction (*avikalpa*). At this point, it might be objected that the solution has been right in front of our face all along. As discussed in Chapter 5, both Asaṅga and Bhāviveka characterize the Buddha's awakening to be "*nirvikalpa*" – a characterization that was adapted by Dharmakīrti and his Indic and Tibetan commenters to characterize "yogic perception."[34] Bhāviveka points out that the "unconstructed awareness" of the Buddha's mind is something that the śrāvakas already believe in and hence serves as common ground for Mahāyānists and their śrāvaka interlocutors. This seems about right. If Subhūti does not cognize "bodhisattva," is this absence of thought not the same thing as an awareness without mental construction (*nirvikalpa-jñāna*)? The statement that thoughtlessness is *avikāra* and *avikalpa* appears to be telling us explicitly that Bhāviveka is right, that Subhūti's non-apprehension is pointing directly to the unconstructed awareness of the Buddha that had been part of the Buddhist tradition all along.

The problem, of course, is that the phrase in question does not appear in Lokakṣema or in the *Split Manuscript*. For that matter, while the term "*vikalpa*" and its derivatives occur 60 times in the Sanskrit of the *Perfection of Wisdom in 8,000 Lines*, the equivalent term does not appear at all in Lokakṣema's translation. It does, however, appear in the *Da Mingdu Jing* and in Zhu Fonian's translation[35] and so appears to have been added as an important qualifier at some point early on.

But here we run into another problem. While from Bhāviveka's vantage point, the Buddha's mind can be said to be without mental construction, it is not at all clear when this idea became part of the Buddhist tradition or where it came from when it did. The term that Bhāviveka uses, "*nirvikalpa*," does not appear at all in the Pali Canon. The related term "*vikappa*" occurs often in the Pali *Vinaya*, but it is always used in the sense of "to assign" or "designate" something to somebody. Apart from that, there are very few instances where a form of "*vi√kḹrp*" is used in the technical sense of "mental construction" in the canon. In fact, the majority of instances are all from the same text, the so-called "book of eights" in the *Suttanipāta* and its commentary, the *Mahāniddesa*.

If we cast our net further, however, we come back to the three *cetana* ("volition") sutras in the dependent-origination (i.e., the *Nidāna*) section *Saṃyutta Nikāya* that do seem to fit the *Perfection of Wisdom* case:

> But, bhikkhus, when one does not intend [*ceteti*], and one does not plan [*pakappeti*], and one does not have a tendency towards anything [*anuseti*], no basis exists for the maintenance of consciousness [*ārammaṇametaṃ na hoti viññāṇassa ṭhitiyā*]. When there is no basis, there is no support for the establishing of consciousness. When consciousness is unestablished [*tad apatiṭṭhite viññāṇe* – i.e., when consciousness is *apratiṣṭha*] and does not come to growth, there is no production of future renewed existence. When there is no production of future renewed existence, future birth, aging-and-death, sorrow, lamentation, pain, displeasure, and despair cease. Such is the cessation of the whole mass of suffering.[36]

Here, when one does not mentally intend, construct or arrange, then consciousness (in context I think we can assume specifically mental consciousness here) has no intentional object whatsoever. When this occurs it is not that consciousness ceases, but rather it does not alight anywhere – it is a non-abiding consciousness (*apratiṣṭha-vijñāna*). And not being able to intend, construct or arrange, the links of dependent-origination that take consciousness as their condition are thereby undermined.

In saying that the state of thoughtlessness is *avikalpa* at the end of a dialogue in which it is stated that the thoughtlessness avoids the extremes of existence and non-existence would make perfect sense in light of this sutra that asserts the negation of *cetana* (from the same verb √*cit*) as well as *pra*√*kḷrp* to be key to the unraveling of dependent-origination. As the absence of *cetana* and as an objectless (*anālambana*) consciousness, this *vijñāna* comes close to what we would consider an "*acitta citta*" to be. Whoever inserted the word *avikalpa* after the discussion of thoughtlessness being neither existence nor non-existence appears to have been trying to make further links with canonical discussions of dependent-origination.

The unspoken assumption in these sutras, of course, is that consciousness (*vijñāna*), not ignorance, is the foundation of the links of dependent-origination. That formulation (i.e., omitting the first two links of ignorance and formations) is found in the *Mahānidāna* and *Mahāpadāna suttas* of the *Dīgha Nikāya*, but only rarely in any of the dependent-origination sermons of the *Saṃyutta Nikāya* (e.g., the *Naḷakalāpa* or "Sheaves of Reeds" Sutra). In both of these cases consciousness is not the sole foundation of the series like ignorance usually is. Rather, consciousness is said to be reciprocally dependent upon body and mind (or "name and form"). In other words, while the *cetana* sutras may be perfect to explain the *Perfection of Wisdom* passage as we find it in the Sanskrit, we appear to be in something of a canonical backwater here insofar as these sutras are quite idiosyncratic in their depiction of dependent-origination.

Nirvikalpa

While it may have been taken for granted that the Buddha's cognition was "*nirvikalpa*" or "devoid of mental construction" by the time of Asaṅga and Bhāviveka, it is not at all clear when this understanding developed. As mentioned above, the term *vikalpa* shows up sporadically in canonical texts. Nowhere, however, do we find the opposite "*avikalpa*" used, much less the term "*nirvikalpa*," and nowhere in the Pali Canon is the Buddha's awareness said to display an absence of mental construction using any form of the verb the verb √*kḷrp*. The closest equivalent we find in the canon are the terms for absence of mental proliferation, *aprapañca* and *niḥprapañca*, terms which have been exhaustively studied by Bhikkhu Ñāṇananda.[37]

Indeed, the terms *avikalpa* and *nirvikalpa* appear to have come on the scene slowly.[38] As mentioned above, the terms are scarce in the canon and just as absent from Brahmanical sources contemporary with the Pali Canon. It is not exactly clear when these terms started moving toward the center of Buddhist discourse, but Vasubandhu refers to a fairly well-elaborated system or typology of *vikalpas* in this *Abhidharmakośabhāṣya*[39] and also refers to the state of *avikalpa*, which is defined as being the absence of applied and sustained thought (*vitarka* and *vicāra*). It may well be that his use of *vikalpa* is roughly contemporary with that of Iśvarakṛṣṇa and Patañjali, both of whom use the term in their treatises.

In all of these treatises, however, *vikalpa* and its absence are something of a sideshow. In the *Abhidharmakośabhāṣya*, the state of *avikalpa*, while soteriologically desirable can hardly be said to be awakening itself. Vasubandhu identifies it with the feeling of "equanimity" experienced in the third *dhyāna* and above. It is decidedly not the state of mind in which nirvana is experienced, since that is achieved by three "knowledge faculties,"[40] not the cessation of knowledge. Similarly, although the *Abhidharmadīpa* does use the term *nirvikalpa*, like the *Abhidharmakośa*, it does not associate lack of *vikalpa* with the Buddha's liberating cognition.

The only text that I am aware of that foregrounds *nirvikalpa* (or a certain variety of it) as peculiar to the bodhisattva vehicle is the *Abhidharmasamucchaya* by Asaṅga. There, Asaṅga states that while there are ordinary "nondiscriminations" such as nondiscrimination in moments of contentment, only the bodhisattva's nondiscrimination is that which is devoid of mental proliferation. However, contrary to what we see in the *Perfection of Wisdom*, he explicitly states that the bodhisattva's nondiscrimination is not non-thinking, but simply the lack of mental construction about the cognitive object.

> What is the absence of discrimination (*nirvikalpatā*)? In brief, it is threefold: [1] non-discrimination in contentment (*santuṣṭinirvikalpatā*), [2] non-discrimination in the absence of error (*aviparyāsanirvikalpatā*) and [3] non-discrimination in the absence of vain speculations (*niṣprapañcanirvikalpatā*). One should consider these three kinds as pertaining respectively to the ordinary person (*pṛthagjana*), to the disciple (*śrāvaka*) and to the bodhisattva. The non-discrimination in the absence of vain speculations should not be understood either as non-thinking (*amanasikāra*), nor as surpassing thought (*manasikārasamatikrama*) nor as tranquility (*vyupaśama*) nor as nature (*svabhāva*) nor as mental construction concerning an object (*ālambane abhisaṃskāra*), but as lack of mental construction concerning an object (*ālambane anabhisaṃskāra*).[41]

While Asaṅga may be showcasing the term *nirvikalpa* here, the fact remains that his use of it is clearly subordinate to the much more clearly established term, *niḥprapañca*, understood as a variety of non-conceptualization of an object. This brings us back to the *Cetanasuttas* and their lack of mental construction as an objectless consciousness. But note that while objectless awareness was important for Asaṅga (coming as he does in the wake of the *Perfection of Wisdom*), there is really no indication that such awareness was important to other Buddhists, witnessing its absence in early developed *abhidharma* systems.

While the idea of an awareness devoid of intentional object or content does not rise to the status of *summum bonum* in the developed *abhidharma* systems that have come down to us, remnants of such an awareness can be found here and there in the canon. For example, in the *Kevaddhasutta* of the *Dīgha Nikāya* "a certain monk" in the Buddha's order asks Brahmā, "Where do the four great elements – earth, water fire and air – stop without remainder?"[42] The answer that the Buddha finally gives comes in the form of a verse:

> Unmanifest consciousness [*viññāṇaṃ anidassanaṃ*], endless [*anantaṃ*] and all luminous [*sabbatopabhaṃ*].
> Herein, water, earth, fire and wind are not established.
> Herein both long and short, small and great, pure and impure,
> And herein "name and form" stop [*uparujjhati*] without remainder.
> With the cessation of consciousness all this stops.

Now, as Bhikkhu Anālayo has shown, the original reading of this passage did not have "all-luminous" (*sabbato-pabhaṃ*) but "given up in every way" (*sabbato-pa(ja)ham*). Nevertheless, by the time of the *Dīrgha Āgama* translation, it appears that some form of *pabhā* was an acceptable reading.[43] This verse, which incidentally is quoted by Nāgārjuna in the *Ratnāvalī* in support of his own position, bears a number of affinities to the *cetana sutta* above. Here the four elements along with name-and-form (*nāma-rūpa*) are depicted as depending on consciousness. This consciousness, however, does not fit the usual description of the six consciousnesses as vision, audition, tactile sensation, olfactory sensation gustatory sensation and thoughts (i.e., mental sensation) insofar as it does not appear to have an object. Rather, it is the same unmanifest consciousness that we saw resulting in the Buddha's invisibility to even Brahmā in the *Brahmanimantanikasutta*. As mentioned above, the *Nidānasutta* of the *Dīgha Nikāya* ends its chain of dependent-origination with consciousness and name-and-form being reciprocally interdependent. Apart from the *Kevaddhasutta*, the maneuver in the rest of the *Dīgha* seems to aim explicitly at *not* having consciousness as the source of all things (thereby presumably avoiding unwanted Vedic resonances). And if we read the *uparujjhati* as "wholly destroyed" as Walshe does, then it would be difficult to maintain that this passage advocates for consciousness as either a source or a substrate. But is consciousness itself destroyed? Probably not. It is "stopped" or "stopped up" (*nirodha* from *ni*+ √*rudh* – to stop or to dam some flow). Sometimes *nirodha* can mean destroyed, but if we look at the parallel passage to the last two lines of the *Kevaddha* verse in the *Suttanipāta*[44] the metaphor is clearly the damming of a river, not its annihilation.

Peter Harvey points out that we might think passages such as this to advocate the annihilation of consciousness, given the fact that there are sutras such as the *Mahātaṇhāsankhayasutta* of the *Majjhima Nikāya* in which the Buddha argues that "without a condition there is no origination of consciousness." The Buddha goes on to say,

> "Just as a fire is reckoned as the particular condition dependent on which it burns – when fire burns dependent on logs, it is reckoned a log-fire . . . So, too, consciousness is reckoned by the particular condition dependent on which it arises. . . . Do you see, monks, 'from the stopping of that nutriment [*tad āhāra-nirodhā*], that which has come to be is subject to stopping'? 'Yes, Lord.' "[45]

Harvey argues that it is misleading and perhaps even anachronistic to read the "stopping" (*nirodha*) of the fire here as its destruction and subsequent absence.

> This passage might be seen as implying that, just as there is no latent, non-burning form of fire, so there is no latent form of discernment, apart from its six forms arising dependent on a sense-organ and sense object.
>
> We should not take our own ideas on the nature of fire, though, as those of the Indian cultural background against which the Buddha's hearers would have understood the above simile. In this culture, fire was seen as having a latent form. F.O. Schrader has pointed out the relevance of Upaniṣadic ideas of fire to Buddhist similes, asserting that such ideas illustrate 'the common Indian view . . . since the oldest times' (1904–05: 167). *Śvetāśvatara Upaniṣad* 1.13 talks of 'the form of fire when gone to its source (*yoni-gatasya*) is not seen and yet its seed is not destroyed'. As pointed out by Schrader (p. 167), *Śvetāśvatara Upaniṣad* IV.19 speaks of the God Maheśvara as 'a fire, the fuel of which has been consumed'. He attaches special importance to *Maitrī Upaniṣad* VI. 34.1 as 'it shows the image in question in connection with the Yoga philosophy which is known to have influenced the Buddha more than any other system' (p. 167–68). His translation of this runs: 'As fire from want of fuel comes to rest (*upasāmyati*) in its own place of birth, so, through the cessation of its motions, the thinking principle (*cittaṃ*) comes to rest in its own birth-place'. Thus, for the Upaniṣads, a quenched fire still exists in its source in a quiescent, latent form.[46]

Brahmanical intertexts and their implications

So where does all of this lead us? Our ur-*Perfection of Wisdom* culminated in the statement that the bodhisattva's thought is thoughtless (*acitta*). We tried to understand this "thoughtless" as a Sarvāstivādin technical term for one of the *samādhis* of cessation, then as a Theravādin reference to the intermediary (*bhavaṅga*) consciousness and then as an allusion to canonical discussions of the foundational awareness at the ground of all dependent-origination. While the *cittaṃ acittaṃ* paragraph certainly seems to resonate with portions of each of these contexts – and I do think that each of them shed some light on what the text is up to – the fact remains that we have explained pretty much everything except the wording. While the sense of this *acitta* is closest to the canonical "unmanifest consciousness" (*anidassana viññāṇa*), nowhere in any of the above discussions (or for that matter anywhere in Buddhist literature outside of Mahāyāna) do we find anything that comes close to the phrase "*tac cittaṃ acittaṃ*" of the *Perfection of Wisdom*. More to the point, in none of the discussions referred to above would the statement that the thought was thoughtless make the slightest bit of sense. As noted above, where the term *acitta* is used in early Buddhist sutra literature, it almost always means "stupid" or "negligent" or "in a stupor."

If a larger conversation in which a 'thoughtless thought' would be meaningful cannot be found in Buddhist literature, might we find an appropriate discursive and literary context for this phrase outside of what is usually deemed 'Buddhist literature'? There have been a number of points in our investigation where the wording of a passage or an idea has veered off in the direction of Brahmanical texts. What if the intertext we are looking for is in the Brahmanical corpus? This may seem odd, given that the prevailing assumption seems to be that Buddhism and Brahmanism are mutually opposed religions. But as I have argued in a recent publication,[47] there is simply no evidence that Buddhism was widely understood to be categorically different from Brahmanism in the early canon. Early Buddhist sutras appear to be far more interested in recruiting Brahmins *as they are* than in drawing borderlines that might exclude them or require them to "convert" (there is no real evidence of anything like late Christian conversion in early Buddhist texts). Furthermore, the distinction between Buddhism and Brahmanism, when it does appear historically, never reached the level of ubiquity that some scholars assume it did. This is for the simple reason that Buddhists *needed* Brahmins (especially those whose wealth was tied to their status as Brahmins) as patrons. Requiring them to renounce their caste status and the learning and ritual skills assumed to be behind it would have not only been unpalatable to the Brahmins but would have diminished the wealth of an important donor base for Buddhist monasteries.

Keeping in mind that people at different points in history would not have necessarily have been as invested in the same religious categories that we are, the first candidate for a Brahmanical intertext that comes to mind is one of the passages in the *Śatapatha Brāhmaṇa* commenting on the *Nāsadīyasūkta* of the *Ṛg Veda* (*Ṛg* X. 129). The third *brāhmaṇa* of the fifth *adhyāya* of the tenth *kaṇḍa*, begins as follows:

> Verily, in the beginning this was, as it were, neither non-existent nor existent; in the beginning this, indeed, as it were existed and did not exist: there was then only that Mind. Wherefore it has been said by the Ṛṣi (*Ṛg Veda* X, 129, 1) 'There was then neither the non-existent nor the existent'; for Mind was, as it were, neither existent nor non-existent.[48]

Here we have a discussion in Brahmanical literature that certainly appears to reflect the same themes as we find in the *Perfection of Wisdom*'s discussion of the status of the mind.

If the *Perfection of Wisdom* keys this discussion, it is important to notice that the *Śatapatha* is not just concerned with the ontological status of minds in general, it is concerned with the ontological status of the Mind that (as Jurewicz pointed out) is connected with the origins of the cosmos itself. Thus the knowledge that the mind is neither existent nor non-existent is a feature that connects the wise to the beginning when "that One" was neither existent nor non-existent, because it was prior to existence and non-existence. And indeed, Mind continues to be the connection between existence and non-existence (or so *Ṛg* X. 129 tells us) that the Vedic visionary poets or *kavis* see in their hearts. The problem is that, while the key term in the *Śatapatha Brāhmaṇa* is *manas*, the term in the *Perfection of Wisdom* is *citta*. Furthermore, while we do find an extended play on words connecting the "piling up" (*citta/citti/cayana*) of the fire sacrifice to the mind (*citta*),[49] nowhere in the *Śatapatha Brāhmaṇa* or any text of the Śukla Yajurveda branch, do we find the term *acitta* specifically used in any praiseworthy sense.

Brahmin boys were to begin memorizing Vedic materials from the time they were eight years old. Very few, however, would memorize all four vedas. Which works a boy would memorize would be determined by the Vedic "branch" or *śākhā* to which the family belonged. The *Śatapatha Brāhmaṇa* would have been the proprietary work of the Śukla branch of the Yajurveda and it assumes that branch's version of the root text —which likewise never uses the term *acitta* in a positive sense. In fact, there are only a limited number of Vedic Saṃhitās in which we do find the term *acitta* used in a positive sense that allows for speech and other activities. *Ṛg* I.152.5 is a possible candidate, although even it is ambiguous. Griffiths' old translation shows us youths wishing to praise the preceding riddles[50] as "*acittaṃ brahma*," a phrase which Griffiths translates as "mystery thought surpassing."[51] If Griffiths' is correct then this would be the one instance in the *Ṛgveda* in which *acitta* was used as something praiseworthy. Brereton and Jamison, however, interpret the *acitta* here in the usual sense of "unaware" or "ignorant" to modify "youths," not "*brahman*." Hence their translation reads, "(Though it cannot be) comprehended, the youths [= Maruts? Aṅgirasas? gods?] enjoy the formulation, as in (the presence of) Mitra and Varuna they hymn their ordinance."[52] Both translations are grammatically correct and which we choose depends on whether we think *acitta* is being used here to show the youths' inexperience or to laud the hymn's transcendence.

While there is no easy way to resolve this issue in the *Ṛgveda* itself, there are clear instances in the branches of the Kṛṣṇa Yajurveda in which *acitta* is used as a praiseworthy epithet. In two versions of the Yajurveda in the Kṛṣṇa branches, the *Maitrayaṇī* and *Kāṭhaka Saṃhitās*, we find a description of a celestial sacrifice done with Āryaman as the householder-patron (*gṛhaspati*), and then a number of priests in charge of different parts of the liturgy: a priest named "Great Oblation" (Mahāhavis) as the *hotṛ* priest, "Oblation of Truth" (Satyahavis) as the *adhvaryu* priest, *Acittapājā* as the *agnīdh* priest, *Acittamanas*[53] as the *upavaktṛ* priest, *Anādhṛṣya* and *Apratidhṛṣya* the two *abhigara* priests and Ayāsya as the *udgātṛ* priest.[54]

While this passage also appears in the *Śāṅkhāyana Śrāutasūtra* (a text of the Ṛg Vedic branch) it is only in the Maitrāyaṇī branch that the term *acitta* is continued to be used as a term describing an ultimate state or entity. Thus in the *Maitrāyaṇīya Upaniṣad* chapter 6 verse 19 we find:

> Elsewhere it has also been said: When indeed the *manas* [mind], having knowledge of the external has the goal of restraining the senses, and having entered into *prāṇa* [life-breath][55] he should thus abide as without *saṃkalpa* [constructed or intended thought]. Since, here from the *aprāṇa* [breathless] there arises the *jīva* [life] known as *prāṇa*, therefore *prāṇa* itself should restrain the *prāṇa* in the so-called *tūrya* [fourth and highest state]. Thus the text says:

> The *acitta* is in the midst of *citta* (*acittaṃ citta-madhyastham*), unthinkable, hidden and ultimate.
>
> There, *citta* should meditate on itself and (know) its subtle body [*liṅga*][56] to be without support.[57]

In context here the *acitta* in the second quoted verse is juxtaposed with the *tūrya* and *aprāṇa* of the framing prose section. As such we should, just as in the last chapter, read the *acitta* as the end result of the restraint of senses that is identified as a state devoid of mental construction or intention (*saṃkalpa*). In the current arrangement of the quoted verses, if not in the verses themselves, *acitta* is to be understood not as being knocked out, but as the mental state more subtle than that of sleep without dreams that lies in the midst of thought itself.[58]

Van Buitenen argues that this verse and the one that precede it are later interpolations.[59] That may be, but as H. W. Bodewiz points out, the interpolations into the *Maitrāyaṇīya Upaniṣad*, are not inserted randomly.[60] The discussion at the beginning of this paragraph about *jīva* being born into the world from the one without breath (*aprana*) is likely a reference to the creation story at the beginning of Śākāyāna's teaching at the beginning of the upaniṣad.[61] There, we are told that in the beginning Prajāpati was alone. Desiring company, he meditates (*abhidhyāyeta* – parallel to *nidhyāyeta* in 6.19) on himself to create offspring who are, nonetheless insentient, without life or breath. He then decides to enter them and takes the form of the wind (*vāyu*). He cannot enter them as one wind and so divides himself into five and becomes the five *prāṇas* of the offspring who are thereafter sentient.

If we read this story as Prajāpati becoming *prāṇa* in order to enliven beings, then in 6.19 the statement, "since, here from the *aprāṇa* there arises the *jīva* known as *prāṇa*" the *aprāṇa* must refer to Prajāpati himself, who – in the form of *prāṇa* – abides in each of us. The second half of the sentence justifies its recommendation for restraining the *prāṇa* in the *tūrya* on the fact that the *prāṇa* originally came from the *aprāṇa*. From here we can only assume that the restraint of *prāṇa* is some kind of return to its origin in Prajāpati. Since the quote about the *acitta* abiding in the midst of the *citta* was included to illustrate the point of the prose, we must assume the *acitta* to index the *aprāṇa*/original state of Prajāpati prior to creation in the prose section. In this case the pair *citta* and *acitta* should be read as similar to Nāgārjuna's *gata* and *agata* ["that which has been traversed already" and "that which has not yet been traversed"] with *acitta* meaning "that which has not [yet] been aware." Hence, just as we might translate the *aprāṇa* here as "prior to breath" or "before there was breath" we should translate the "*acitta*" that comes later not so much as "unthinkable" (as Griffith does at *Ṛg* I.152.5) but as "prior to thought" or that which precedes any possible thought.[62]

Even if we want to claim that this passage is an interpolation (which would be an odd objection, since the verse is clearly marked as a quotation from someplace else), the passage with its understanding of yoga is merely a restatement of a hymn quoted in an earlier section of the *Maitrāyaṇīya Upaniṣad* – one that

Van Buitenen does not consider to be interpolated into the earliest strata of the "Southern Manuscript." The hymn begins with a reference to a fire sacrifice and connects the fire to the mind in yoga:

S.M. 4.3
On this there are these stanzas:

1 Just as fire without fuel dies down in its hearth [*sva-yoni*], so does the mind [*citta*] die down in its hearth because of the cessation of its operations [*vṛtti-kṣaya*].
2 When the mind [*manas*] of one desirous of truth [*satyakāmin*] has died down it its hearth, and is no longer confused by the sense objects, these objects, which are slaves of karman, become untrue [*anṛta*].
3 For one should purify the mind with great effort; the mind is the saṃsāra: one becomes that which one has a mind to be [*yac cittas tan mayo bhavati*]; this is the everlasting secret.

Though the *Maitrāyaṇīya Upaniṣad* was probably not the first Kṛṣna Yajurvedin upaniṣad to read its yoga into the Piling the Fire Altar sacrifice,[63] the hymn here becomes a full-blown hymn to mind, though its vocabulary goes back and forth between *manas*, *citta* and *ātman*, treating the three as synonyms. It begins with the simile that likens the mind becoming pacified[64] "in its point of origin" to a fire that dies down "in its hearth" due to lack of fuel. The simile turns on the pun that "*yoni*" here can mean both "source/origin" as well as "hearth." The mind that has died down in its own origin is one whose operations (*citta-vṛtti*) have ceased and is no longer confused by sense objects. This is presented as the goal of the one who desires truth, and hence it is the origin of the mind in which all functions cease that is identified with truth (*satya*) and not its specific engagements which are said to be falsehoods (*anṛtāḥ*). The remainder of the hymn focuses exclusively on yoga.

4 For through the tranquility of the mind one kills off the act [*karma*], both good and evil; and, with tranquil spirit abiding in one's self [*prasanna ātma-ātmani sthitvā*], enjoys eternal bliss.
5 When a man's mind [*citta*] is as firmly attached to Brahman as it is to sense objects, who will then not be released from bondage?
6 The mind [*mano*] has been declared to be of two kinds, pure and impure. It is impure when it is touched with desire; pure when it is free from desire.
7 When a man, having made his mind [*manas*] perfectly stable, without either abeyance or projections, thereupon enters upon a state higher than that mind [*yāti amano-bhāvaṃ*], he reaches the supreme point [*tat paramaṃ padam = tūrya*].
8 The mind has to be kept in check until it has died down in the heart [*tāvan mano niroddhavyaṃ hṛdi*]; and knowledge of this is liberation [*etaj jñānaṃ ca mokṣaś*]; the rest is bookish proliferation.

9 The bliss, purified in highest concentration, that arises when the pure mind has been brought into the self [*samādhi-nirdhautam amalasya cetaso niveśitasya ātmani yat sukhaṃ bhavet*] cannot be described by words; it must be experienced directly through the inner organ [*tad antaḥ karaṇena gṛhyate*].

10 If a man's mind merges in the self [*evam antar gataṃ yasya manaḥ*], just as water is no longer distinguishable in water, nor fire in fire, nor space in space, then he is released.

11 The mind [*mana*] alone is man's cause of bondage and release; it leads to bondage when it is attached to sense objects, but to release when without objects; thus it is taught.[65]

In verse 4 we are told that the tranquility (or luminosity – *prasāda*) of the mind destroys karma. Van Buitenen then has "with tranquil spirit (*prasanna ātma*) abiding in one's self (*ātmani sthitvā*) enjoys eternal bliss." Since the *prasāda* modifies *citta* at the beginning of the sentence and then *ātman* in the second half, I think we are safe in identifying *ātman* with *citta* and *manas* in this case.

It is in verse seven that we really begin the parallel to the discussion of yoga from *Maitrāyaṇīya Upaniṣad* 6.19. There the *manas* becomes stable, neither manic nor depressed and then enters into a state of mindlessness (*amano-bhāvaṃ*), in which *amana* has to be read as a synonym for *acitta*. This state of mindlessness is then stated to be the *paramaṃ padaṃ*, or the final "fourth" ("*tūrya*" from "*catur*" meaning "four") step of Viṣṇu (a term often used in early Yogic texts for the ultimate state, e.g. *Kaṭha Upaniṣad*).[66] The following verse defines knowledge and release as occurring when the mind attains cessation in the heart. Verse 9 returns to the bliss which is purified in *samādhi*. Van Buitenen has it that this bliss occurs "when the pure mind has been brought into the self." While the *Maitrāyaṇīya Upaniṣad* is not shy about discussing *ātman*, I think the context of the immediately following verse requires us to read the *ātmani* here as a reflexive pronoun, "when the pure mind has been brought into itself."

In context, we should read this as the mind being mindless. The following verse states, "for the one whose mind enters inside [itself] (*antar-gataṃ*) [like] water in water or fire in fire or void (*vyoma*) in void can't be distinguished, so he is fully released." Here, just like water poured into water is no longer distinguishable, so too the mind returned to itself can no longer be distinguished.[67] Though it does not use exactly the same phraseology, this verse certainly prefigures the *acitta* in the *citta* of 6.19. Verse 11 rounds out the discussion by stating that bondage is when the mind has objects (*viṣaya*) and released when it "remembers [or attends to] the objectless" (*nirviṣayaṃ smṛtam*).

The hymn is tightly constructed around a few central themes. The mind in samsara is defined as that which is engaged with objects (verses 2, 5, 11) and subsequent desire for them. Release and knowledge occur when the mind has no objects (verses 2, 11), but more importantly when it returns to its source or to itself (verses 1, 2, 4, 9, 10). This abiding within its source is then identified with "mindlessness" (*amanas*, verse 7) and the highest state (the *paramaṃ pādaṃ*). It is also said to be attachment to *brahman* (verse 5). The last term, *smṛti*, is most often translated "mindfulness" in English translations of Buddhist texts, and indeed the term can simply refer to the cognition of or attention to an object. But the most straightforward rendering of the word is "memory." In yogic meditation, *smṛti* can be a practice of "remembering" or going back to an origin that is both historical and ontological.

Here, it is "the objectless" or mind itself as the font of all thought that is presented as brahman. As the ultimate source of samsara, this mind is also the source of creation (verse 3). Returning then, to *Maitrāyaṇīya Upaniṣad* 6.19, the *acitta* in the midst of the *citta* is the mind itself which is identified with *brahman*/Prajāpati. Returning to this primordial state is release. The *acitta* abides within the *citta* insofar as mind is always present to itself. When mind engages with objects, there is desire and torment in samsara. But when mind abides in mind *qua* mind, it can no longer be distinguished and is thus "mindless" (*acitta* or *amanas*). On the whole, then, we would have to say that, if nothing else, this verse along with the hymn to mind in the *Maitrayaṇīya Upaniṣad* come quite close in sentiment at least to the perfected nature of the "three natures" doctrine of Asaṅga.

This hymn, which appears in both the *Vulgate* and the *Southern Manuscript*, actually sheds a bit more light on *Maitrāyaṇīya Upaniṣad* 6.19 discussed above. While the *Vulgate's* discussion of yoga appears to refer back to Prajāpati's creation, with *acitta* referring to Prajāpati himself, the hymn from the *Southern Manuscript* is even more explicit about the connections between the fire sacrifice (possibly the *agnicayana*) and meditation and in addition gives us more context for our understanding of the thoughtless.

Does this background help make sense of the passage in the *Perfection of Wisdom*? I think that it does. While one might initially read expressions in the *Maitrāyaṇīya Upaniṣad* such as *aprāṇa* and *acitta* as ontological absences (i.e., as *karmadhāraya* compounds), in Maitrāyanī Brahmanic context *acitta* describes the *brahman* that is *prior to* awareness or thought. The force of the negation seems to be rather on a temporal priority, albeit an ongoing one. The yogic method in this upaniṣad, as is often the case in Brahmanic forms of meditation, is simply cosmogony in reverse – starting with the sensory panoply and ending up at the point of cosmic origin, which is *brahman* or Prajāpati himself. As such *acitta* is not exactly the negation of *citta*. The two do not cancel each other out, since the *acitta* exists in the midst of the *citta* as the presence of the origin within that which was originated. If we read the *tac cittaṃ acittaṃ* in light of these Maitrāyanī assumptions then the awareness (*cittaṃ*) that is not aware of the bodhisattva turns out to be "the *acittaṃ*," or that which is primordially prior to thought (i.e., the standpoint of Prajāpati). Indeed, as I have been arguing throughout this chapter, we can't make sense of this sentence except against the backdrop of the *Maitrāyaṇīya Upaniṣad*. Strictly within a Buddhist literary sociolect the mindless mind is "ungrammatical" in a way that it is not in the Brahmanical milieu. By the same token, we can't claim that the *Maitrāyaṇīya Upaniṣad* borrowed the mindless mind from the *Perfection of Wisdom*. We can appeal to the narrative of the *Maitrāyaṇīya Upaniṣad* to explain the mindless mind in the *Perfection of*

Wisdom but not the other way around. The statement of the mindless within the mind fits into the narrative logic of the upaniṣad quite organically – something we can't say for its somewhat abrupt occurrence in the *Perfection of Wisdom*.

We might now be able to account for the difference between the *Aṅguttara Nikāya* phrase and that of our text. The Pali has *pabhāssaram idaṃ bhikkhave cittam* ("this mind is clear") whereas the *Perfection of Wisdom* has *prakṛtiś cittasya prabhāsvarā*, "The original substance/nature (*prakṛti*) of thought is clear light." In other words while the *Perfection of Wisdom* may allude to something like the Pali here, it does so to emphasize that the state of *acittaṃ* is a clarity or luminescence that is *prakṛti*, original or primordial. Now, while I read this *prakṛti* to be something like "essence" or simply "nature," the early Chinese translators emphasize the sense of "source" or "origin." Starting with Kumārajīva,[68] this *prakṛti* is translated as 本 (meaning in this case "root" or "origin").

The reading of the bodhisattva's *acitta* as a kind of primordial (non-)awareness against the backdrop of Vedic literature then makes sense of Śāriputra's question about whether existence or non-existence can be apprehended in that state, and Subhūti's reply that they cannot. Read against the passage from the *Śatapatha Brāhmaṇa* referred to above, the Śulka Yajurvedins read "the One" in *Ṛg* X.129 to be a kind of cosmic Mind (albeit *manas*, not *citta*) that existed prior to being (*sat*) and non-being (*asat*). Here, Subhūti tells Śāriputra that in the state of *acittatā* there is neither an "it exists" nor an "it doesn't exist" – presumably because awareness is prior to (since it is the condition for) the possibility of recognizing anything as existing or not existing. Read in light of Brahmanical texts, then, this section of the dialogue becomes fully intelligible against the backdrop of technical cosmogonic debates (*brahmodya*) being held between sub-branches of the Yajurveda.

While scholars are fond of labeling the *Maitrāyaṇīya Upaniṣad* as "late,"[69] this characterization is rarely supported with much argument or any attempt to explain what "late" actually means here. The characterization of its belatedness can be traced to Paul Deussen, who opposed Max Müller and L. von Schroeder's characterization of the upaniṣad as early. The evidence Deussen gives for its belatedness is: 1) that it quotes from the *Chāndogya*, *Bṛhadāraṇyaka*, *Kaṭha*, *Śvetāśvatara* and *Praśna Upaniṣads*; 2) it refers to "the knowledge of all upaniṣads" thereby assuming an existing corpus of upaniṣads; 3) Śāṅkara never mentions this upaniṣad; 4) it refers to a heretical doctrines hostile to the Vedas (he assumes this to be Buddhism); and 5) it is not only influenced by Buddhism but includes "literal contacts (quotations) from the *Sāṃkhyakārikā*." He concludes, "[A]ll this makes the late character of the work indubitable."[70]

In context, what Deussen means by "late" is simply that the *Maitrāyaṇīya Upaniṣad* was written later than the upaniṣads he considers to be "early" (i.e., the *Chāndogya*, etc.) and sometime after the advent of Buddhism and the *Saṃkhyākārikā*. But since the advent of Buddhist orders presumably preceded discussions of the Mahāyāna distinction and since the dating of the "early" upaniṣads is hardly fixed, the "lateness" of the evidence he cites could still place it earlier than the *Perfection of Wisdom*. As mentioned above, the *Maitrāyaṇīya Upaniṣad* is clearly a composite text with some sections later than others (I am certainly willing to concede that the sections referring to the *trimūrti* of Brahmā, Viṣṇu and Śiva, the *cakras* and the deniers of *ātman*, etc., may have been added as late as the middle of the first millennium CE). The relevant question for the *Perfection of Wisdom* is: how early are the *early* portions of the upaniṣad? Jean Filliozat places the *Maitrāyaṇīya Upaniṣad* prior to the second century on the basis of apparent references to it in a work by Hippolytus,[71] and E. W. Hopkins points to quotations from it in the third chapter of the *Mahābhārata*.[72] Ellwood Welden has shown that the version of Sāṃkhya philosophy in the *Maitrāyaṇīya* indeed predates the *Sāṃkhyakārikā*.[73] More recently, Signe Cohen has reviewed all of the above arguments and has weighed in on its composition, adding her own linguistic and metrical analysis. She summarizes her findings as follows:

> The Southern recension (*SM*) of the *MtU* is a fairly unified Upaniṣadic text with a strong Sāṃkhya flavor. The Sāṃkhya philosophy presented there is not yet as systematic as that found in the *Sāṃkhyakārikās*, but more akin to the proto-Sāṃkhya of the *Śvetāśvatara Upaniṣad* and the *Mahābhārata*. The central theme of the text is the distinction between the two *ātmans, the higher ātman* and the *bhūtātman*. Based on the development of philosophical ideas and on the linguistic features of the text, it is reasonable to assume that the Southern recension of the *MtU* was composed after the *Kaṭha* and *Śvetāśvatara Upaniṣad*, but perhaps before the *Praśna* or *Māṇḍūkya Upaniṣads* . . .
>
> I would therefore suggest that the textual history of the *MtU* developed as follows: The original *MtU* consisted of 1.2–4.3 [the section from the *SM* I quoted above] and chapter 7 of the text of the Vulgate. This is the text that has been transmitted in the Southern recension. Sections 1.1, 4.4–4.6, and chapters 5 and 6 are later interpolations that were added as the text was transmitted in the Maitrāyaṇīya school. Some of the older interpolated passages have preserved typical Upaniṣadic *sandhi*, whereas others are more modern both in form and content.[74]

Again, there is nothing in any of this to suggest that the *Maitrāyaṇīya Upaniṣad* in some form could not have existed before the first century CE – and thus no chronological reason to assume that the *Maitrāyaṇīya Upaniṣad* borrowed from the *Perfection of Wisdom*. But more to the point, the *acitta citta* is an organic part of the *Maitrāyaṇīya Upaniṣad*, whereas its use in the *Perfection of Wisdom* is abrupt and quite frankly "ungrammatical" in the sociolect of early Buddhist sutra literature.

If I am correct that the Mindlessness section of the *Perfection of Wisdom* assumes both familiarity and competency with specifically Yajurvedin discussions of yoga and of *brahman* qua Prajāpati (the latter being referred to as both *nirātman* and as *śūnya* "empty")[75] then we may also have an answer as to why Subhūti does not see the bodhisattvas. His "not seeing" is part of his withdrawal of all awareness back into its source, a yogic attempt to directly experience that which has ultimate and absolute ontological and epistemological priority: brahman *qua* emptiness understood as that which is prior to (and empty of) any possible conceptual distinctions whatsoever.

Once we see the opening section of the *Perfection of Wisdom* to describe a kind of meditation in which conceptualization is brought back into its cosmogonic source on par with yogic meditations of the Kṛṣṇa Yajurvedin branches, I think we can make more sense of the parts of the expanded *Perfection of Wisdom in 8,000 Lines* that Orsborn identifies as being central to its chiastic structure. Orsborn identifies chapter 16 and Dharmodgata's sermon in the middle of the Sadāprarudita section to be structurally (and therefore thematically) central to the text. The topic of the first is "suchness" (*tathatā*) and the topic of the latter is the Buddha himself or the "Tathāgata." I would like to return to my argument from Chapter 6 that the iterations after section G of the ur-sūtra were attempts to bring the teachings of the ur-sūtra in line with a budding Buddhist "orthodoxy" that was heading in a different direction. While, as Orsborn points out, there were certainly sutras in the early canon that held up emptiness (or signlessness) as a thing[76] – even an ultimate thing – the Brahmanical tradition had developed (or was developing) an idea of an ultimate cosmic font or foundation that was also in some sense personal. Most of the Upaniṣads treat *brahman* as a kind of impersonal force, but as we have seen, the *Maitrāyaṇīya Upaniṣad* assumes this *brahman* to be Prajāpati, just as the *Kauṣītaki Upaniṣad* has the seeker enter into a long conversation with *brahman* represented anthropomorphically as sitting on a throne.[77] Canonical Buddhism had an ultimate (whether emptiness or nirvana), just not as a person. The developed *Perfection of Wisdom* takes Subhūti's non-perception in the beginning, applies it to the epithet "Great Vehicle" in the first chapter to say that the Mahāyāna of Buddhism neither comes nor goes. This theme of "neither coming nor going" (a phrase applied to nirvana in the *Udāna*)[78] is then applied to "suchness" (*tathatā*, an epithet occurring in the canon that can apply to either "Buddhist" or "non-Buddhist" ideas of the ultimate)[79] in chapter 16.[80] The sectarian ambiguity of *tathatā* (in contradistinction to, say "nirvana") would have served our Buddhist Brahmins well when they got to the Dharmodgata sermon, which takes the argument about the neither coming nor going of *tathatā* from chapter 16 and applies it to the "Tathāgata." The latter is now said to be the "thusness" (the *tathatā* of *Tathāgata*) that neither comes nor goes (the *agata* of the Tath*āgata*).[81] *Voilà*, we have a version of the Buddha that is, arguably, the functional equivalent of the Kṛṣṇa Yajurvedin *brahman* – *śūnya*, *nirātman*, timeless and yet still the Tathāgata of Buddhist discourses with whom a sovereign might identify. And here it should be kept in mind that it is the last chapter of the *Perfection of Wisdom in 8,000 Lines* and its discussion of the Tathāgata that was the inspiration for subsequent Mahāyāna discussions of the *dharma-kāya* of the Buddha.[82]

Once we place the core *Perfection of Wisdom* within larger discussions within the Maitrāyaṇīya Yajurveda branch, other things attract our attention as well. As mentioned above, in addition to the Maitrāyaṇīya version of the Yajurveda, there are a number of other Yajurveda recensions. The *Vājasaneyī Saṃhitā* (both Mādhyandina and Kaṇva versions), the *Taittirīya Saṃhitā* and the *Kaṭha Saṃhitā* (both *Kaṭha* and

Kapiṣṭala-*Kaṭha* versions) each begin with the identical sentence, which presumably would have been the first to be memorized by boys of the Yajurveda branches:

> *iṣe tvorje tvā vāyava sthopāyava stha devo vaḥ savitā prārpayatu śreṣṭhatamāya karmaṇe*

The only outlier for this sentence is the *Maitrāyaṇī Saṃhitā*, which has:

> *iṣé tvā* ***subhūtāya*** *vāyáva sthopāyava stha devo vaḥ savitā prārpayatu śreṣṭhatamāya karmaṇā*

The *Maitrāyaṇī Saṃhitā* is the only one with the word "*subhūtāya*" in the first line. Though I do not believe that there is enough evidence to say that "Subhūti" in the *Tripiṭaka* was to be read as a Maitrāyaṇī Brahmin, the choice of Subhūti as the main interlocutor of a sutra that lauds the ideal mind as an *acittaṃ cittaṃ* may well have been a wink at those in the audience who came from this particular branch.

We might have a similar wink later in the first chapter of the *Perfection of Wisdom*, when the topic of mindlessness comes up again. In the Sanskrit, immediately after Sariputra reminds us that the Buddha has declared Subhūti to be the best at the *araṇavihāra*, Pūrṇa Maitrāyaṇī-putra, comes from out of nowhere and asks a question about the great armor, the *mahāsattva*, and the Mahāyāna. Subhūti then engages in a conversation with the Buddha about these three topics as if Maitrāyaṇīputra had never spoken. Near the end of the section, Subhūti does respond to Maitrāyaṇīputra's second question about the suchness of form being neither bound nor freed by saying the form of an illusory man is neither bound nor freed and in Lokakṣema's Chinese, Subhūti and Maitrāyaṇīputra exchange a few words. Subhūti concludes by saying, "This is the great armour, the great non-armour of a bodhisattva, a great being, who is armed with the great armour, who has set out in the great vehicle, who has mounted the great vehicle,"[83] after which, we are told, Maitrāyaṇīputra abides in noble silence (usually the sign of assent). The discussion of the Great Vehicle continues between Subhūti and the Buddha as if Maitrāyaṇīputra weren't there, focusing more specifically on the ontological status of the great vehicle. Maitrāyaṇīputra chimes in one last time to say, "This Elder Subhūti, when asked about perfect wisdom, fancies that the great vehicle is something that can be pointed out."[84] Subhūti (again, ignoring Maitrāyaṇīputra) asks the Buddha if he has spoken of the Mahāyāna without transgressing against Perfection of Wisdom, to which the Buddha says that he has pointed out the great vehicle in agreement with Perfection of Wisdom.

It seems to me that the character of Maitrāyaṇīputra was interpolated here (albeit quite early, since this passage appears in all versions) since the entire dialogue would proceed quite nicely if all of his lines were erased. So why Maitrāyaṇīputra? It may be that he gets his cameo here because he was known for his likening of the Buddhist path to a "relay of chariots," (*Rathavinīta*) in the *Majjhima Nikāya* sutra of the same name, and indeed, the appearance of Maitrāyaṇīputra here and his exit later in the chapter brackets the entire discussion of the Great Vehicle. But we can also look at his appearance and his question about the *mahāsattva* as a natural continuation of the discussion between Śāriputra and Subhūti concerning the *mahāsattva*'s non-attachment (*asakta/asatta*) that precedes the discussion of the armor and the vehicle. Sariputra and Subhūti give reasons why the *mahāsattva* is so called, each ending with the refrain, "There, (the *mahāsattva*) is neither attached nor invested in the mind" (*tatrāpi citte asakto 'paryāpannaḥ*). After three repetitions, Subhūti's final reason (again, present in all versions) for the *mahāsattva*'s unattachment is that the mind is "mindless," *acittatva*. The Sanskrit here has a coda to the *tac cittaṃ acittaṃ* section from earlier, complete with the *araṇavihārin* sentence, although this paragraph seems only to have been inserted around the seventh century.[85] In all early versions, Maitrāyaṇīputra's name would occur immediately after the sentence about mindlessness.

Signe Cohen has quite ably demonstrated that the names of Vedic sages were used as a kind of code for the different Vedic branches, especially in the *Yajurveda Upaniṣads*,[86] and she argues that one variation of the Maitrāyaṇī branch name, Maitreyī,[87] is used as the name of one of Yajñāvālkya's wives in the *Bṛhadāraṇyaka Upaniṣad* and is code for the perceived relationship between the Vājasaneyī branch and the Maitrāyaṇī.[88] It is pretty clear that the variant "Maitrāyaṇī," the name of Maitrāyaṇīputra's mother, was an established name for a Vedic sage or *ṛṣi* since it is clearly stated to be a Brahmin lineage or *gotra* name in the *Aṅgulīmālasutta*.[89] For its part, Maitrāyaṇīputra himself is invariably coded as an über-Brahmin in Buddhist sources; so again, the association with this particular branch is not much of a stretch.[90]

That a Maitrāyaṇī Brahmin might be ordained as a Buddhist monk may be surprising to some today, but is certainly not without other examples. In the seventh-century *Harṣacārita of Baṇa*, King Harṣa tells us,

> "I have heard there is a gentleman, a childhood friend of the deceased Grahavarman of auspicious name, who was a Maitrāyaṇī and who, in spite of the threefold (knowledge), was a descendent of Brahmins who dwelled in the unarisen wisdom in the doctrine of the Well-Gone One and who as a youth donned the Buddhist robes."[91]

Whether one translates *vihāya* as "distancing himself from" as Cowell and Thomas do or "in spite of" as I have, we have in Baṇa's work the depiction of an ordained Maitrāyaṇī Brahmin Buddhist who wears Buddhist robes and practices a form of Buddhism that is coded as a form of Perfection of Wisdom (its *samādhi* being the "unarisen wisdom" *vidva-anutpanna-samādhi*). What is more important here is that Divākaramitra, the Maitrāyaṇī Brahmin, continues to be referred to as a Brahmin even after ordination (just like Aṅgulimāla and Maudgalyāya in the canon).[92] Even as late as 1879, Von Schroeder notes that "even now Maitrāyaṇīya Brahmana's who live at the foot of the Vindhyas at Bhaḍgaon, do not eat with those other Brahmaṇa's; the reason may have been the early Buddhist tendencies of many of them."[93]

On the other hand, that such a monk would seek proximity to a king should not be surprising at all if we look at what these Yajurvedic lineages were up to. The institution of the *brahmodya*, or debate about the ultimate origins of things, appears to have been held not only at the center of large-scale *śrauta* rituals (a kind of Vedic sacrifice conferring, among other things, levels of status upon the sacrificer) but in the courts of kings as well.[94] Not all performances of *śrauta* rituals were for kings (e.g., Brahmins could perform them for themselves), but when they were performed by monarchs, we can say that for all intents and purposes *śrauta* rites like the "Piling of the Fire Altar" (*agnicayana*) or the "Horse Sacrifice" (*aśvamedha* - a larger rite that incorporated the *agnicayana*) were essentially coronations. As such these rituals identify the chief patron (in this case the monarch) with Prajāpati himself, so when the priests debate about the foundation of the cosmos, they are debating about the cosmic status of the person they are about to install as the head of state. We can surmise that one of the purposes of such debates was to enable the king to select his court priests; i.e., the priest who could argue that he had direct knowledge of that which was most ultimate would be in charge of legitimating the king's rule.

Participation in these debates about the ultimate was not just the concern of "Brahmanical religion." Some Buddhists, at least, saw themselves as participating in these debates. The *Abhidharmadīpa* refers to its discussion of dependent-origination (which is itself all about the issue of cosmogony) as "*brahmodya*."[95] It is not incidental then, that Nāgārjuna (possibly a Śukla Yajurvedin himself),[96] tells a king in the *Ratnāvalī*,

> ask the Sāṃkhyas, the followers of Kaṇṇada, Nirgranthas, and the worldly proponents of a persona and aggregates, whether they propound what passes beyond "is" and "is not."
>
> Thereby know that the ambrosia of the Buddhas' teaching is called profound, an exclusive doctrine passing far beyond "is" and "is not."[97]

The Taittirīyas, another early branch of the Kṛṣṇa Yajurveda, apparently succeeded in securing the position of court priest at Kausāmbī as early as the reign of Puṣyamitra (ca. 150–50 BCE)[98] and remained in the area long enough to become the court priests of the Vākāṭakas.[99] If the Vākāṭaka priests were Taittirīyan, and their Gupta rivals in the fourth century were, as Michael Willis has argued, Maitrāyaṇīyas,[100] we can assume that the latter had been maneuvering to achieve this kind of placement in royal courts for some time. Indeed, the establishment of Yajurvedic lineages as dynastic priests by the fourth century may go a long way to explain the increase in visibility of Mahāyāna Buddhism during the Gupta Dynasty.

So, while Subhūti's "not-seeing" and "not-apprehending" along with the rest of the sections discussed in the last chapter can be understood against the background of a certain set of sermons in the *Tripiṭaka*, the section beginning with the statement "that thought is thoughtless" can only be fully understood against the literary background of the *Maitrāyaṇīya Upaniṣad* where its discussion is a more organic fit.

This is not at all to say that the *Perfection of Wisdom in 8,000 Lines* is *really* a "Brahmanical" text instead of a "Buddhist" one. Similar to what Rick Altman has pointed out regarding film genres, the judgment of whether or not something is "Buddhist" or "Brahmanical" is the work of the critic who surveys a range of works looking for common features.[101] But critics are often different people than producers. Producing a text requires a markedly different engagement with genres than the critical ascertainment of genre categories. The producer of a text is interested in saying something that has not been said elsewhere, and the author is quite free to draw on whatever generic elements are deemed to be most promising for the intended audience. While the apparent "generic mixing" we see in this text (and there is also good reason to understand this as not mixing at all), could be simply a matter of creative expression, in the current context I would suspect that innovation was introduced to meet a need of its intended audience. And since the most surprising innovations require Brahmanical competencies to understand, I think we can assume these needs to be those of a community of Brahmin Buddhists. But this chapter has also shown that at least the ideas of the mindless mind (if not the wording) contained in this passage are also found in the *Tripiṭaka* – albeit in relatively unused parts of it. Thus, if the *Perfection of Wisdom* is drawing on ideas and wording from the *Maitrāyaṇīya Upaniṣad*, then it is continuing a trend that had already begun in the canon itself. The *Perfection of Wisdom* thus becomes a "revolution" only in retrospect. From the vantage point of its authors, it was what their group had been doing all along.

Notes

1 Conze (1958), p. 2.
2 Ibid.
3 Ibid.
4 The only example I was able to find was in the *Abhisamāyakathā* of the *Paṭisambhidāmagga* (Psm. 2.214).
5 See Stede and Rhys Davids (1997) *acittikata* and *acittaka* S.v.
6 E.g., ṚV. IV.2.11; Cp. Monier-Williams, s.v.
7 Willemen (2006), p. 267.
8 T. 1546, p. 332b1ff.
9 T. 1545, p. 774c20ff.
10 Whom the *Abhidharmakośa* identifies as Ghoṣaka.
11 Griffiths (1986), pp. 67–70. Pruden, vol. I, p. 231; Pradhan pp. 72–73. This appears to refer to the discussion at T. 1545, p. 774a22ff, although Ghoṣaka is not named there.
12 Bodhi (1995), pp. 399–400 = MN #44, I. 301. Similar statements are made about the one who does not conceive of themselves as doing x sort of thing at S.N. 5.2, 22.47, 22.101, 28.9 and 41.6. A great many more references could be added if one considers the sutras in which one who reaches the goal is said to have overcome "I making, my making and the underlying tendency to conceit."
13 Falk and Karashima (2012), p. 34. I would like to thank Joe Marino for pointing this out to me.
14 Ñānamoli (1975), p. 831; Warren (1950), p. 609.
15 Bareau (1955), pp. 164, 172; T. 1545, p. 774a14ff.; Harvey (1995), p. 164.
16 Bareau, 159, 240
17 Cox (2009).

18 T. 225, p. 478c21.
19 Bodhi (2012), p. 97.
20 For an excellent discussion on the luminous consciousness, see Anālayo (2017).
21 Anālayo (2017), p. 29.
22 A.A. 1.61.
23 For an excellent discussion of *bhavaṅga*, see Gethin (1994).
24 Ibid, p. 14.
25 Harvey (1995), p. 164.
26 Ibid., p. 166
27 Anālayo argues that this is nonsensical on its surface because it would entail that defilements could exist independently of the mind. For this reason, he argues that the idea of the adventitious defilements migrated from a metaphor for the purification of gold to that of the mind. This makes sense to me, but it does not change the fact that once the current reading came on the scene, it was open to the reading that defilements could somehow not belong to the mind.
28 E.g., the *Yuktidīpika* on *Sāṃkhyakārikā* II.3 describes *mūlaprakṛti* as, "*sā ca avikṛtir avikāra-anutpādy ety arthaḥ.*" See Sastri (2009), p. 64.
29 S.N. 12.15.
30 Jurewicz (2000), pp. 81–82.
31 See Brereton (1999).
32 It appears that *brahman* was the technical term for the ultimate in Sāṃkhya in some circles in the first and second century CE since Aśvaghoṣa's *Buddhacarita* presents it this way. See, Larson (1989).
33 Ñāṇamoli (1975), p. 703.
34 On Yogi Pratyākṣa and later Mahāyāna thought, see Dunne (2006), Dreyfus (1997), pp. 412–415, and MacDonald (2009).
35 T. 225, p. 479a1 (as 無為) and T. 226, p. 508c22 (as 無造).
36 Bodhi (2000), p. 578; S.N. II. pp. 65–66; cp. T. 99, p. 100a23-b10.
37 Ñānananda (1971).
38 Bhikkhu Anālayo has, however, pointed out to me that the *Suttanipāta*, and especially the Aṭṭhavagga chapter, does have a lot of references to mental construction and may well be the inspiration of these ideas in later literature.
39 Pradhana (1975), p. 22.
40 The faculty that knows that the seeker does not know (*anājñātamājñāsyāmindriya*), the faculty of one who is wise (i.e., one who has just found out *ājñātāvīndriya*) and the faculty of one who is characterized by such knowledge (the *ājñātāvin* who has knowledge that defilements are destroyed [*kṣayajñāna*] and knowledge that they will no longer arise [*anutpādajñāna*]). See Pruden (1988), vol 1, pp. 162–163; Pradhana (1975), p. 42.
41 Rahula (1971), p. 176.
42 Cp. Walshe' translation (1996), p. 177.
43 Anālayo (2017), pp. 18–20.
44 i.e., S.N. verse 1043.
45 Bodhi and Nanamoli (1995), pp. 351–352.
46 Harvey (1986), p. 156.
47 See Walser (2018).
48 Eggeling (1882), vol. 4, p. 255. ŚB. 10.5.3. *neva vā idam agre 'sad āsīnneva sadāsīt| āsīdiva vā idamagre nevāsīttaddha tanmana evāsa|| tasmādetadṛṣiṇābhyanūktam| nāsadāsīnno sadāsīttadānīmiti neva hi sanmano nevāsat|| tadidam manaḥ sṛṣṭamāvirabubhūṣat||* (Gippert, 1997).
49 At 6.3.1ff, see Eggeling, vol. 3, p. 127ff.
50 See Renou (1949), pp. 12–13, in which he states that this *acittam brahma* refers to the preceding verses understood to be a *brahmodya* or debate about *brahman*.
51 Griffith (1973), p. 102.

52 Jamison and Brereton (2014), vol. I, p. 330.
53 *Acittapājā* and *Acittamanā* are changed to *Acutyapājā* and *Acutyamanā* respectively at *Taittirīya Āraṇyaka* 3.5.1; Mitra (1864), pp. 288–289.
54 See Schroeder (1881), p. 78–79; Amano (2009), p. 335. My thanks to Professor Amano for sending me her personal digitized version of portions of the *Maitrāyaṇī Saṃhitā*.
55 Taking here, with Van Buitenen, the SM *prāne* instead of V. *prāṇo*.
56 Following Rāmatīrtha's commentary here. He takes *liṅga* in its Sāṃkhya sense as the form that the soul or *jīva* takes. In this passage, the mind is to see that even this subtle manifestation is without basis. See Rāmatīrtha (1913-1919) p. 132
57 Van Buitenen (1962), p. 112: *athānyatrāpy uktam - yadā vai bahir vidvān mano niyamyendriyārthāṃś ca prāṇe (V: prāṇo) niveśayitvā niḥsaṃkalpas tatas tiṣṭhet... [aprāṇād iha yasmāt saṃbhūtaḥ prāṇasaṃjñako jīvas tasmāt prāṇo vai] . . . turyākhye dhārayet prāṇam iti / evaṃ hy āha - acittaṃ cittamadhyastham acintyaṃ guhyam uttamam / tatra cittaṃ nidhyayeta tac ca liṅgaṃ nirāśrayam /*
58 This assumes, of course *tūrya* here to be sleep without dreams as in the *Muṇḍaka Upaniṣad*. It may refer to the *tūrya brahman* of Atharvaveda VII.1.1.
59 Van Buitenen (1962), p. 48. For his hypothesis on the history of the text, see his entire first chapter.
60 Bodewitz (1973), p. 279.
61 Mait.U. II.6.
62 Rāmatīrtha, however, does not make this connection. For him, what is meant by the *acitta* is "the objectlessness of all sense faculties" (*sarvendrayāviṣaya*). His interpretation may stem from the fact that he takes the *Maitrāyaṇī* to be a composite work. While I agree that it is, the contribution of different authors does not preclude the possibility that the contributing authors were aware of what they were contributing to. Cowell (1913), p. 132.
63 See the opening verse of the *Śvetāśvatara Upaniṣad*'s second chapter: "*yuñjānaḥ prathamaṃ manas tatvāya savitā dhiyaḥ.*" The entire discussion of seated yoga meditation appears to be a kind of commentary on the phrase that is uttered aloud at the very beginning of the agnicayana sacrifice. Cp. The verbatim phrase at *Mānava Śrautasūtra*. 6.1.1.5; Gelder (1985), p. 142.
64 It should be noted here that verbs associated with √*śām* "to pacify" are used in the Vedic sacrificial context to refer to the suffocation of an animal.
65 Van Buitenen (1962), pp. 132–133; p. 105.
66 *Kaṭha Upaniṣad* 3.9.
67 Indeed, one wonders if Nāgārjuna's *Dhātuparīkṣa* (chapter 5 of the *Mūlamadhyamakakārikā*) with its investigation of the relation between space (*ākāśa*) and its characteristics (*lakṣaṇa*) was somehow inspired by this passage.
68 While the phrase about the luminosity of the mind is present in all exemplars except for Lokakṣema and the *Split Manuscript*, it appears that there were two stemma lines of this sentence – one that had the word *prakṛti* and one that did not. The *Da Mingdu Jing*, Zhu Fonian, one of Xuanzang's translations and *Dānapāla* don't have any equivalent of *prakṛti* here (see T. 225, p. 478c21–22; T. 226, p. 508c16–17; T. 220, p. 763c18; and T. 228, p. 587b15). But Kumārajīva, Xuanzang's other translation and of course the Sanskrit edition do (see T. 227, p. 537b14–15 and T. 220, p. 866a10).
69 E.g., Wood (1992), p. 67; Nakamura (2004), p. 285.
70 Deussen (1990), vol. 1, pp. 328–329.
71 Filliozat (1945), esp. pp. 76ff.
72 Hopkins (1902), pp. 33ff.
73 Welden (1914).
74 See Cohen (2008), pp. 264–265.
75 See *Maitrāynṇīya Upaniṣad* 2.3.
76 Huifeng (2016), pp. 140–143.

77 *Kauṣītaki Upaniṣad* 1.6.
78 Ud. 8.1. See Walser (2005), pp. 175–183.
79 We find *tathatā* used as the ultimate spiritual destination, usually in the dative and often with some kind of verb of motion. Thus, at *Dīgha Nikāya* II.64 we find it used in the context of someone striving for the self (*āttan*) assumed to exist in the next world. The seeker says that "this not being suchness (*atathaṃ*)" s/he will "accrue to suchness" "*tathattāya upakappessāmī*" (*tathatta* here meaning the soul). Similarly, we have *tathatta* used for nirvana at *Dīgha Nikāya* I.175 where other ascetics are to be told, "The ascetic Gotama roars his lion's roar, in company and confidently, they question him and he answers . . . and are satisfied with what they have heard, they behave as if they are satisfied, they are on the path of truth . . . (lit. "they enter into thusness," *tathattāya ca paṭipajjanti*)" [Walshe, 1996, p. 156].
80 Orsborn does a good job discussing the textual history of this section and its relevance to the whole. Orsborn (2012), pp. 284ff.
81 Again, see Orsborn's excellent treatment of the textual history of this passage. Ibid., pp. 231ff.
82 See Makransky (1997), chapters 3 and 12.
83 Conze (1958), p. 9.
84 Ibid, p. 10.
85 It only appears in one of Xuanzang's translations, at T. 220, p. 766b27ff.
86 Cohen (2008), pp. 72–85.
87 The Upaniṣad itself is known as either the *Maitrī Upaniṣad* or as the *Maitreya Upaniṣad*. For the variations on the name of both the Upaniṣad and the Vedic branch, see Van Buitenen (1962), pp. 21–23.
88 Cohen, pp. 82–83.
89 The Pali (M.N. II. 100) has Aṅgulimāla's father's *gotra* as Garga and his mother's as Maitrāyaṇī. The 鴦崛髻經 (T.119, p. 511b16–17), apparently unaware of *gotras*, has Aṅgulimāla state that his name is Garga and his mother's is Maitrāyaṇī.
90 See Senart (1882–1897), pp. 3.337ff. and the "Mantāṇiputtapuṇṇattheravatthu" in the *Aṅguttara Aṭṭhakathā* vol. I, pp. 199ff.
91 Comp. Cowell and Thomas (1993), p. 233; Bronkhorst (2011), 184.
92 For Moggalana and Aṅgulimalla being referred to as "Brahmin" after their ordination, see: S.N. 40.1–9 and M.N. II, p. 104.
93 Von Schroeder (1879), p. 30.
94 See Black (2007), chapter 2.
95 Jaini (1977), p. 277.
96 Cp. *Vigrahavyāvartanī* vs. 49; Westerhoff (2010), p. 34 and *Śatapātha Brāhmaṇa* 6.1.2.26; Eggeling (1882), vol. 3. p. 107 vs. 26.
97 Hopkins (1998), p. 102; cf. Hahn (1982), p. 26.
98 Sharma (1960), pp. 15 and 126.
99 Willis (2009), p. 188.
100 Ibid, 187–219.
101 Altman (1999), p. 38; Walser (2015), pp. 356–357.

9

PLACING EARLY MAHĀYĀNA

Piecing together what has been said in the past few chapters, what can we conclude about the understanding of Mahāyāna from the core section of the *Perfection of Wisdom in 8,000 Lines*? The first thing to notice is that the sutra was primarily about the practice of attenuating or ceasing conceptualization, not just during meditation but all the time. We might think that it would be difficult for Subhūti to talk about the fact that he did not perceive any bodhisattvas if his mind in fact was "mindless," but as we have seen from the *Brahmanimantanikasutta* even when the Buddha is identified with the *anidassana viññāṇa*, he can be heard even when not seen. This sermon, then is not just about stopping the mind, it is about such stopping rendering the bodhisattva invisible to gods and even to death itself. In the second chapter, this practice becomes associated with the term "emptiness" by way of the "emptiness *samādhi*." But we should probably not interpret the emptiness intended here to be necessarily understood as a proprietary doctrine of "Buddhism." It could very well be that it was prestigious as a Buddhist attainment precisely because these ideas were already prestigious as a *yogic* attainment. Whether one was a Buddhist or a non-Buddhist may have been less important at the time than the degree of yogic attainment one could claim.

But why would "emptiness," or for that matter, the mind prior to any conceptualization have been regarded as prestigious across sectarian boundaries at that time? Although the terms "empty" and "emptiness" are used in early Buddhist discourses, we don't really get a sense of why, for instance, one of the gates to liberation should be emptiness. Commentaries often take emptiness in these contexts to be a synonym for selflessness, but then we have the awkward situation in which the three marks of samsara are "suffering, impermanence and selflessness" while gates of liberation are "emptiness, signlessness and wishlessness." With selflessness being asserted as identical to emptiness, this would make samsara none other than nirvana long before Nāgārjuna. Since, signlessness and wishlessness are mental states, it would make sense to distinguish emptiness as a mental state devoid of an awareness of selves (akin to the *Perfection of Wisdom*'s *acitta*) from an awareness of the selflessness of phenomena (granting, of course, that the two are related).

We get the sense that ideas like the cessation of conceptualization and emptiness are imbued with a degree of prestige in Buddhist texts, but we are left without a sense of why they are prestigious. The discussion of emptiness and mindlessness seem to have a more natural home in Brahmanical works such as the *Maitrāyaṇīya Upaniṣad* where both are indicators of a primordial and cosmogonic foundation of everything – a foundation to which the practitioner may return in meditation and ultimately in liberation. But for this to be the case, mind (more specifically mind *prior to thought*) has to be posited as having cosmogonic potency. We find an argument made for such a primordial mind beginning in the *Ṛg Veda* and carried out in the Brāhmaṇas and Upaniṣads of the Yajurveda.

Placing the *Perfection of Wisdom* in the early Mahāyāna suite

The *Perfection of Wisdom in 8,000 Lines* was not the only early Mahāyāna sutra to deploy precisely these elements. As a matter of fact, once we begin to look for the themes of non-perception and *acitta*, we notice what appears to be a suite of sutras dealing with the same themes. I see no reason to delve further into the interrelations between these texts to figure out which was first, because texts are very rarely simply composed – they are revised. In other words, to discern a sequence of when the texts in the suite of early Mahāyāna sutras were composed we would have to assume that we could assign the composition of any of these texts to discrete and contrasting moments. This would mean that these texts were not revised in response to feedback both from the social network of the author(s) as well as from other works written in response to the initial work. It is far more likely that the texts that we have fall into identifiable textual suites composed in concert – i.e., composed, performed and revised in an ongoing, tandem response to one another.

The one text that I do think it is fair to say marks the early threshold of our Mahāyāna suite is the *Saddharmasmṛtyupasthānasūtra*, studied exhaustively by Daniel Stuart.[1] Although Stuart's work has received scant attention so far, it seems clear to me that his work is one of the best so far in wrestling with the very early origins of Mahāyāna. The *Saddharmasmṛtyupasthānasūtra* itself appears to have been composed over a long period of time, but the second chapter does seem to represent a very early form of Mahāyāna. By "early" I mean that the second chapter is a text that stays very close to canonical wording. It never mentions the "Mahāyāna" and while later chapters do discuss a number of named bodhisattvas, nowhere in any of the chapters does it refer to ordinary Buddhist practitioners as "bodhisattvas" in the manner of the *Perfection of Wisdom in 8,000 Lines*. And yet it presents an early argument for everything being "mind-only." By straddling canonical texts and early Yogācāra thought it may prove to be a kind of "missing link" in the evolution of the latter. For our purposes, there are several aspects of this text that bear remarkable affinities to the core section of the *Perfection of Wisdom in 8,000 Lines.* First and foremost, the *Saddharmasmṛtyupasthānasūtra,* like the *Perfection of Wisdom in 8,000 Lines* appears to be an outgrowth of the *Saddhātuvibhaṅgasūtra* of the *Madhyama Āgama* – albeit the former admittedly hews far closer to the wording of the *Madhyama Āgama* version of the *Saddhātuvibhaṅga* than the *Perfection of Wisdom.* In both cases, however, it is the canonical discussion of the six elements and especially the emphasis on the mind that ceases to conceptualize any element that was compelling to our Mahāyāna authors. Furthermore, Stuart points out that the *Saddhātuvibhaṅgasūtra*

> is unique in the *āgamic* record [to the extent that] . . . it describes a practice of raw insight meditation – in other words, discernment (*prajñā*) – in which a practitioner attains to the highest spheres of meditative experience *without ever departing from the application of such insight* [emphasis mine].[2]

Stuart also shows (following Yoshimichi Fujita)[3] that the emphasis on the perfection of wisdom (*prajñāpāramitā*) that we find in early Mahāyāna circles was probably derived from the term *prajñādhiṣṭhāna,* "foundation of wisdom," that we find in the *Saddhātuvibhaṅgasūtra.* If the *Perfection of Wisdom in 8,000 Lines* posited mindless mind as a kind of non-conceptual mental substrate prior to thought, then the *Saddharmasmṛtyupasthānasūtra* similarly interpolates a "mind element" as the substrate of any possible mental event.

> 2.9 Now what is the mind-element? The mind-element is conjoined with the twelve sense spheres. One experiences the [visual] object that is experienced by eye-consciousness by way of mind-consciousness (*manovijñāna*). In this way ear[-consciousness], nose[-consciousness], tongue[-consciousness], body[-consciousness] and mind-consciousness (*manovijñāna*) have their origin in the mind-consciousness element (*manovijñānadhātu*), and are rooted in the mind.[4]

The interpellation of a mind-element (*manovijñānadhātu*) that is distinct from mental awareness (*manovijñāna*) into the *Saddhātuvibhaṅga Sutra*'s discussion of the six elements introduces an element that opens quickly to the idea of an original mind element anticipating the later Yogācāra's "storehouse consciousness" (*ālayavijñāna*). According to Stuart:

> A consequential development of mentalist doctrine can be seen when the text presents a theory of mind that posits the mind-element (*manodhātu*) as a mediating factor of all sense-consciousness, and the mind-consciousness element (*manovijñānadhātu*) as an originary source or basis for those sense-consciousnesses. This mentalist project gets developed further when the monk of the text discerns the faculty of perception (*saṃjñā*), seeing it as a fundamentally constructive element of the mental process, and largely

> responsible for building an individual's experience of the so-called external world of materiality. These developments present us with evidence of what might be described as an emergent *vijñānavāda* or *cittamātra* (mind-centered or mind-only) theoretical framework, and the most explicit assay in this direction can be found in the fifth stage of our text, when a monk sees and understands that all sense objects are nothing but cogitation (*kevalaṃ saṅkalpamātrakam eva*). In a somewhat enigmatic development, the text also subsumes the entire world of material sense phenomena within the *dharmāyatana* ["sphere of dharma"], an additional philosophical thrust in the direction of an idealistic framework of thought. This philosophical project is perhaps most sharply apparent in the seventh stage of the text, where we find a depiction of mental action as the fundamental creative force behind the entire flow of existence (*saṃsāra*), a philosophical position figuratively represented by a metaphorical description of the mind as a master painter who uses colors, brush, and palette to create the world of experience.[5]

Here, in a kind of proto-Mahāyāna text, we find an attempt to draw an "an originary source or basis" out of (or interpolate one into) a canonical text. It is not at all clear that any version of the *Dhātuvibhaṅga* had a non-cognizing "mind" as a substrate for the phenomenal world. But the *Saddharmasmṛtyupasthānasūtra* and the *Perfection of Wisdom*'s reworking of the *Dhātuvibhaṅga* does. It should be noted, however, that while I contend that the *Perfection of Wisdom* was circulated in Brahmin Buddhist communities and was understood not only to be about personal liberation but to access the power of the original cosmic substratum of the primordial, empty mind, the *Saddharmasmṛtyupasthānasūtra* presents Brahmins (and especially their aversion to eating cows)[6] as "outsiders" 外道[7] and is also critical of those (like Nāgārjuna?) "who loiter at the king's gate, employing [dishonest] stratagems."[8] It is certainly possible that the *Saddharmasmṛtyupasthānasūtra* was not circulated in Brahmanical communities. I would not, however, go so far as to say that a text that reprimands monks for becoming adjuncts to the royal court is somehow therefore "apolitical," any more than anyone would understand a senator who accuses her opponents of "playing politics" to be apolitical herself. As we will see in the next chapter, the situation is likely to have been much more complicated.

More contemporary to our *Perfection of Wisdom* are the texts that do mention Mahāyāna and/or bodhisattvas found among the Late Han Dynasty and early Three Kingdoms Period Chinese translations. Here we find a number of other sutras that stand out as having the greatest doctrinal affinity to *Perfection of Wisdom*. The most obvious examples are the *Wen shu shi li wen pu sa shu jing* (*Mañjuśrī's Inquiry Concerning the Office of the Bodhisattva Sūtra*, T. 458), the *Kāśyapaparivarta*, the *Vimalakīrtinirdeśa*, the *Ajātaśatrukaukṛtyavinodanāsūtra*, the *Vajracchedikā* and the **Tathāgatajñānamudrāsamādhi* (T. 632), and now the text from Bajaur that has been the focus of a recent work by Andrea Schlosser and Ingo Straugh.[9] But this list is by no means exhaustive, since texts translated much later bearing some of the same characteristics may have been written much earlier in India.[10]

Mañjuśrī's Inquiry Concerning the Office of the Bodhisattva Sūtra

Doctrinally, the sutra that comes closest thematically to our early *Perfection of Wisdom* is *Mañjuśrī's Inquiry Concerning the Office of the Bodhisattva Sūtra* (文殊師利問菩薩署經, T. 458) although structurally it has far more in common with the *Kāśyapaparivarta*. The sutra opens with a dialogue between Buddha and Śāriputra in which the latter asks how the bodhisattva should "don the great armor," a phrase that appears parallel to "mounting the Great Vehicle" in the *Perfection of Wisdom*. Like the early *Perfection of Wisdom*, it does not make a sharp distinction between the attainment of the bodhisattva and that of the arhat since it describes the bodhisattva's donning of the great armor as being filled with the aspiration to establish everyone in arhatship.[11] Śāriputra then goes on to the main topic of the sermon, the "Office of the Tathāgata" 怛薩阿竭署.[12] He explains to Śāriputra, "A Tathāgata has four things: What are the four? The first is to arouse the thought/mind. The second is to achieve non-retrogression. The third is to sit under the Bodhi tree. The fourth is to fulfill the Buddha dharmas. These are the four."[13] Here we have the production of a thought (notice that it is not referred to as "*bodhicitta*" here) that leads to the next stage called (as in the core *Perfection of Wisdom*) "irreversibility." Only after attaining the latter state can the Bodhisattva sit under the Bodhi tree and attain all Buddha dharmas. The production of thought deals with a concern for all sentient beings that we did not find in the *Perfection of Wisdom*, but the stage of non-retrogression does have a strong parallel to the latter text:

> The office of non-retrogression is that which is done for all: delighting in nothing he seeks this stage, the stage of pacification 安隱地, the stage that is aware of nothing 無所想地, and the stage of firmness (*dhruva*?). This is for the Buddha dharma the foundation realm (*bhūtakoṭi*?). Therefore it is said to be the second mark.[14]

The remainder of the sutra is structured as follows: the dialogue with Śāriputra occupies first 18% of the sutra, followed by discussions with a number of other luminary monks (Subhūti and Mahākāśyapa are there, although the longest section is devoted to Raṣṭrapāla). Finally, the remaining 58% of the sutra is devoted to dialogues between the Buddha and "500 Brahmins" (in actuality only 32 are mentioned).

The non-cognition that marked the stage of irreversibility is the recurrent and dominant theme of the initial dialogue with Śāriputra, and in its iterations with Brahmins we get a better sense of what early communities thought this meditation was. As we saw in the *Perfection of Wisdom*, it is a kind of non-conceptualization characterized as a "seeing which is not seeing." For example:

> Buddha said to Śāriputra, "The dharma of form is the Buddha dharma. Feelings, ideas, samsara [sic. *samskāra*?] and the dharma of consciousness

> [i.e., the five aggregates] are the Tathāgata's dharmas. According to the teaching of this office, all dharmas are without attachment.[15] Once there is no attachment to any dharma, there will be no awareness of either being or nonbeing. This is according to the teaching. After being attached to neither being nor nonbeing, you should follow the rootless teaching . . . The official 署者 is neither past nor future but manifests in the present. Thus, the official sees everything and does not see anything."
>
> Śāriputra asked the Buddha, "How is it said to be seeing?" [Buddha replies:] "No obstruction and no obscuration is complete seeing. This is the Tathāgata's office." "Why is it said to be not seeing anything?" "It is said to be so because he does not see any place where they (the dharmas) enter in. Therefore it is not seeing. This is the Tathāgata's office. But the office is neither associated with emptiness, nor non-cognition (*asaṃjñā*) nor absence of aspiration, nor non-perception, nor non-apprehension. Equal to extinction 寂 then, this office is pure. The officer is without the ability to grasp long and short and the officer has no assistance. The officer is not able to attain assistance. The officer is without differences. This, as an office, is devoid of that which accompanies re-birth. This is said to be the office of the Tathāgata."[16]

There is a lot going on in this section and it certainly appears that this sutra is every bit as rich as the *Perfection of Wisdom in 8,000 Lines* itself. For the time being, let me point out that "the office of the Tathāgata" is the teaching that does not attach to/discriminate dharmas. Like the state of mindlessness in the *Perfection of Wisdom*, this mental state goes so far as to not even be cognizant of presence or absence. It is a seeing which is a non-seeing since it is not obstructed by anything while at the same time not recognizing anything whatsoever.[17] We would expect the sutra to reveal that this is the teaching of emptiness, or non-perception, but it is careful to state that the seeing which is non-seeing is not associated with any of the terms that we would expect – since any of these identifications would distinguish it from something else. Why should we seek out this office? Because, its absence of mental activity is equal to nirvana (indicated by 寂 here) itself.

Śāriputra is not the only one to receive the teaching of the office of the Tathāgata. A striking feature of this sutra is the amount of it devoted to preaching this doctrine to Brahmins. The Brahmin section begins with 500 Brahmins arriving where the Buddha is. The Buddha asks why they have come. In turn, each of them relates to the Buddha the omens/visions and or voices that led them to the Buddha that day. Each of them was doing something that we would expect a Brahmin to be doing: preparing a sacrifice, giving alms, going to market, purchasing incense, doing astrology and meditation. In each case, the vision or voice connects the Brahmanical activity to some standard Buddhist teaching and tells the Brahmin to seek out the Buddha in order to learn about the Tathāgata's office. Each of the Brahmins seems to think this is a pretty good idea and so they all arrive and relate the story of the omen that brought them here.

Curiously, although each of the Brahmins is sent to learn about the Tathāgata's office, few of them actually hear the teaching itself. In fact, of the 32 Brahmanical dialogues, only four actually hear what the teaching of the Tathāgata's office is: a Brahmin called *Mahākāruṇa, one called *Anukāliya, and a third and fourth whose names are more problematic, 阿禾真 (*Āhūcī?) and 沙竭末 (*Sāgaramati?). For example, Mahākāruṇa is caught bathing in preparation for a fire sacrifice when Buddha, complete with all major marks and minor characteristics, appears in the air before him.

> The Buddha said, "Since you sacrifice in the fire of dharma, this is inappropriate. Why? Because it arises and is extinguished." I asked: "I didn't cause this extinction. Why should I extinguish it?" The Buddha replied, "Don't conceive of a person, don't conceive of a self, don't conceive of a life-force, don't conceive of existence or non-existence, don't conceive of unity, don't conceive of a middle between the two and do not conceive any ideas. This is a fire that cannot be extinguished but it destroys itself. This fire is able to be aware[18] of the true nature/self-immolation[19] that yet does not use fuel.[20]

The next to actually receive instruction about the Tathāgata's office is the Brahmin named Anukāliya or Anukalyāṇa (阿耨迦惟延).

> There was another Brahmin named Anukāliya who said to the Buddha, "I went outside of the city and sat under a tree. My mind became stabilized as if in meditation (*dhyāna*), I saw the four directions pervaded with a great light. I saw incalculable Buddhas. They said, "You should not sit in meditation like this." Then I asked the Buddhas, they said, "There is nothing that arises and nothing that ceases. This is the meditation by which one may attain vision. Without having seen this serves as vision. Thoughtless, [var. *acitta citta* 無心心] how will one fixate the thoughts 繫? Why? His mind is devoid of thought; hence it is considered to be meditation (*dhyāna*). This is the dharma called the Tathāgata's office. [You] should follow Śākyamuni Buddha and should ask to this learn his dharma." This was my original omen." The Buddha said, "You should learn it, just as it was taught [in the omen]."[21]

There are a few important points to make about this sutra. First of all, while we might expect these passages to criticize Brahmanical practices in order to win the Brahmins over to Buddhism, it is not at all clear that this is what is going on here. True, the apparitional Buddha does tell Mahākaruṇa not to do the fire sacrifice, but he is not criticized for causing suffering or because the sacrifice is ineffectual.[22] Rather, in the case of Mahākaruṇa, the Buddha tells him that since he sacrifices into the fire of dharma (already), he should not do the fire sacrifice. In other words, the physical fire sacrifice is already beneath his practice since it is subject to production and extinction. A better fire sacrifice is the internal fire sacrifice in which the mind ceases to consume the fuel of cognitive objects. It would certainly appear that the teachings these Brahmins are given here was one that certain groups of Brahmins in the first century were already invested in. Conversely, if we are to take the Buddha's request for Mahākaruṇa to stop sacrificing as a criticism of sacrifice itself, then we would also have to take the Buddha's request that Anukāliya to stop meditating as a criticism of meditation. So, if we keep in mind that Subhūti, Pūrṇa Maitrāyaṇīputra and Śāriputra are all Brahmins themselves then (in addition to being marked by Hitchcockesque Mañjuśrī cameos),[23] we have a correlation between a certain kind of meditation and dialogues with and amongst Brahmins in the earliest strata of Mahāyāna texts.

But perhaps an even more important observation is the fact that we have here a sutra with manifest Brahmanical interests clearly talking about the same meditation as we find in the core *Perfection of Wisdom*. We find here the seeing which doesn't see, not cognizing any dharma and mindlessness used in ways that are virtually identical to what we find in the opening section of the *Perfection of Wisdom in 8,000 Lines*. And yet, there is no indication that the practices here were understood to have anything to do with something called "perfection of wisdom." The text is certainly aware of the six perfections. They are listed at p. 440a5–9. But when the text comes to describe the perfection of wisdom, it merely glosses it as "having heard much" 多所聞 (i.e., one becomes a "learned" *bāhuśrūtīya* monk). In other words, the key features of the core *Perfection of Wisdom* that were also thematic among other early Mahāyāna texts[24] were the meditations involving a non-seeing seeing, non-cognition or the mindless mind.[25] The association of these features with *Perfection of Wisdom*, or even Mahāyāna then, appears to have been the (unique?) innovation of the early *Perfection of Wisdom*. Similarly, while there are certainly early texts like the *Saddharmasmṛtyupasthānasūtra* and the *Vimalakīrtinirdeśa* that do not appear to privilege a Brahmanical perspective, both the *Perfection of Wisdom* and *Mañjuśrī's Inquiry* do, insofar as they present only those criticisms of Brahmins that are also found in Brahmanical texts and they present doctrines that are not significant variations on what Vedic practitioners already believed. Hence it is significant that both texts use the term *acitta* in a way that is consistent with literature of the Maitrāyaṇīya branch of the Yajurveda. Indeed, one wonders whether the mention of compassionate thought that sets one out on the path culminating in cessation of cognition was an attempt to hearken back to the *brahmavihāras* – a set of graded meditations beginning with compassion and ending with equanimity, onto which a number of sutras add meditation on nothingness, emptiness and signlessness.[26] The *Mettāsahagatasutta* has a group of wanderers object that when the Buddha teaches this sequence, they do not understand how it is any different from what they have been doing all along.[27] And indeed, we do find four of the *brahmāvihāras* mentioned at *Yoga Sūtra* 1.33. Though I wouldn't want to argue that this sequence was understood to be the exclusive domain of Brahmins, it does seem to have been understood to not be exclusive property of Buddhists.

Placing the early *Perfection of Wisdom*

So, if some of the very earliest Mahāyāna texts interested in the mindless concentration that led to the Mahāyāna ontologies of emptiness and mind-only had their provenance in Buddhist Brahmin communities, is it possible to locate any of these communities in a specific social and geographical context? I will leave it to other scholars to do the spade work for other texts, but given the work we have done so far on the core section of the *Perfection of Wisdom in 8,000 Lines*, I think we can begin to triangulate a location and social context for its composition and early circulation.

Let's return to the term *bodhicitta*, which certainly appears to have been a ghost word produced at some point by an inadvertent eye-skip and applied retroactively to the compassionate thought with which one begins the path. If the original had been the equivalent of the Sanskrit *bodhisattvena cittaṃ na manyeta* then how do we explain the current Sanskrit *bodhicittena*, which, as I mentioned, is already reflected in the third-century *Da Mingdu Jing*? Schmithausen suggests haplography from *bodhisattvena cittena* (as reflected in Kumārajīva's 菩薩心)[28] to the *bodhicittena*. I believe he is correct, but if so then Kumārajīva's manuscript would have preserved the intermediate phase between the earliest manuscripts (which would have had *citta* in the nominative) and the *bodhicitta* of the *Da Mingdu Jing* for this sentence. In other words, how do we explain a sentence change from ***bodhi**sattvena* ***cittaṃ*** *na manyeta* to ***bodhi**sattvena* ***cittena*** *na manyeta*, in order for the haplography to produce the current **bodhicittena** *na manyeta*?

The first possibility is that the manuscript had *cite* instead of *cito* and that the *cite* then coalesced with the following *na* to create something like *citeṇa*. Since *te* and *to* in Kharoṣṭhi are usually quite distinct, it is unlikely that we are dealing with a simple misreading here. Now it might be possible to read *cite* as locative here, something like "By the bodhisattva it is not considered in his mind," or even if we take *bodhisattvaś citte na manyeta* as a reading,[29] and take the verb as a passive, then we might translate: "A Bodhisattva ought not be conceptualized in the mind." But since *no* translator renders mind as locative here,[30] I think this reading is unlikely.

Another possibility is that the early manuscript somehow preserved a variant nominative declension (sometimes seen in Aśokan inscriptions) ending in - *e* rather than in - *aṃ*. If this had been the case, then the manuscript would have read something like *bodhisattvena citte* (nom.) *na manyeta*. The *citte na* would have been misread as *cittena* and then coalesced with the prior *bodhisattena* to make *bodhicittena*. But in order for this to have been the case, the original would have had to have the nominative of *citta* as *citte*. Nominative declensions in - *e* were relatively common in Aśokan edicts, but were replaced by - *o* or - *u* in the Northwest and by - *aṃ* or simply - *a* to the South by the second century BCE.[31] Of course, like a lot of these morphological changes, there are always a few stray inscriptions that preserve older forms.[32] In literary texts, the final - *e* termination for neuter nouns is prevalent in Ardhamāghadī, but rare in Gāndhārī manuscripts.[33] Though manuscripts contemporary with the Gāndhārī materials have not been recovered from the South, the absence of a neuter, nominative - *e* ending in inscriptions makes it unlikely that the original had a *cite ṇa*.

A more likely solution (and I have to thank Stephen Hodge for this solution) is that the *anusvāra* at the end of the *cittaṃ* was somehow mistaken for an - *e*.

With the *aṃ* read as an *e*, a scribe could very easily have read: *cittaṃ na manyeta* as *cittena manyeta*. If this had been the case, it would not have taken long for another copyist to recognize that there needs to be a "not" before *manyeta* and (re)insert another "*na*"; making *bodhisattena cittena* [na] *manyeta*. This change may even be attested in the Gilgit manuscript where the corresponding passage of the *Perfection of Wisdom in 25,000 lines* preserves the reading of "*tena bodhicittena mantavyām*." (i.e., without the corrected "*na*").[34]

There are two Kuṣāṇa-period Brāhmī script forms of the medial "– *e*." The dominant form throughout South India from Karle to Kuda to Nagarjunakonda appears simply as the top line of the letter extending horizontally to the left. Even as far north as Bamiyan, this form is the only form of the medial – *e* attested in the Schøyen manuscripts, though it is also found in other Northern early Brāhmī manuscripts from the Turfan oasis such as the *Spitzer Manuscript*. The other version of the – *e*, however, consists of a short stroke extending either vertically or arcing slightly to the left from the top of the consonant. This form of medial – *e* is limited to Kuṣāṇa inscriptions from Sarnath and Mathura but can also be found in Turfan documents. Since both types of – *e* can be found in the *Spitzer Manuscript*,[35] it appears that either style of – *e* could be used somewhat arbitrarily by the same copyist in the region around Qizil at some point in the first few centuries CE.

The *Schøyen Manuscript* of the *Perfection of Wisdom*, on the other hand, uses only the horizontal form of the – *e*, making confusion between the – *e* and the *anusvāra* out of the question.[36] While we do not have a large sample of very early Brāhmī from this area, to the extent that the *Schøyen* scribes' handwriting was representative the mistake was unlikely to have occurred transcribing a Brāhmī manuscript in the area around Bamiyan.

Not all writers of Brāhmī, however, made such a clear distinction between the medial – *e* and the *anusvāra*. The copyist of the first drama published in Lüder's *Bruchstücke Buddhistischer Dramen* (1911) makes his – *e* above the letter and far shorter than the – *i*, making it look much more like the *anusvāra*, which in turn tends to slant to the right much like the – *e*. If we compare the – *te* of 4b2 with the *taṃ* and *ṭṭe* of 7b2, it is easy to see how idiosyncratic penmanship might make the confusion between the two much more likely.

One could imagine if the *-e* had been made as a short diagonal stroke (or if there had been an ink-skip) it could easily be confused with an *anusvāra*, especially if the previous copyist was in the habit of making shorter or curved *anusvāras*.

Given that a reading of *tenāpi bodhisattvena cittaṃ na manyeta* both makes more sense than *tenāpi bodhisattvena cittena na manyeta* and is supported by Lokakṣema and Zhu Fonian, I suggest that it constitutes the original reading of this passage. The former reading produced the latter by a copyist mistaking *cittaṃ na* for *cittena* while copying a Brāhmī manuscript. The same mistake would not have been made in Kharoṣṭhī where the medial – *e* and the *anusvāra* could not have been confused. This conclusion already provides us with some constraints since Kharoṣṭhī appears to have been the preferred alphabet in the Afghanistan/Pakistan area in the first century and before.

4b

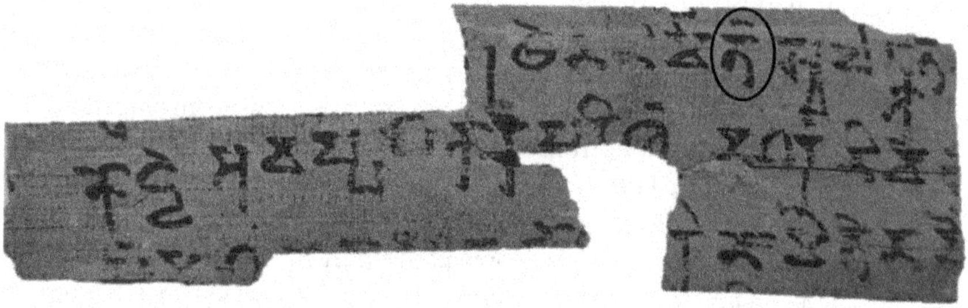

7b

FIGURE 9.1A Lüder's *Bruchstücke Buddhistischer Dramen*[37]

4b2.. [ṭ]ṭh. [a]cchariyaṃ – du[ṣṭa] . . . , = peśśeti ajja *te* dāśīputta mimena pa[l] . . . to – tato vaṭi[y] . . . ; 7b1–2 rūthena nirmi*taṃ* svalaṅkṛta ko*ṭṭe* avappapākārapa[r]ikhaṃ nagaraṃ nive[s] . . .

Mistaken sounds

We have now explained how *cittaṃ* may have become *cittena* and have a hypothesis that the current "*bodhicitta*" was produced by a haplography of the local equivalent of *bodhisattvena cittena*. But if the alteration from *cittaṃ* to *cittena* had occurred in the North (in Gāndhārī, this would have been *cito* to *citeṇa*), the next step – the haplography from *bodhisattvena cittena* to *bodhicittena* could not have occurred there. An eye-skip from – *tveṇa* to – *teṇa* in Kharoṣṭhī is a bit hard to swallow since the postconsonantal - *v* at the base of the - *t* is usually quite visible and would be hard to miss (just as the – *i* on top of the *c* in *cito*). The eye-skip is much more plausible if we are dealing with a dialect that was not Gāndhārī. Schmithausen had argued for a Middle Indic original based on a pun found later in the chapter to the effect that the *mahāsattva* is called *mahāsattva* because s/he is "not attached" (= Skt. *asakta* but the pun works better as Middle Indic, *asata*).[38] Schmithausen is correct, but "Middle Indic" is a broad category and his solution does not really rule out a Gāndhārī original, since the - *kt* consonant cluster is almost always assimilated to - *t* (Richard Salomon gives the examples of *bhatu* = *bhaktam* and *bhuta* = *bhuktam*[39] from Gāndhārī manuscripts). The haplography of *bodhisattvacitta* to *bodhicitta*, however, would require the former to have been "*bodhisatacita*" (without the - *v*) and the latter, in turn is a feature of Middle Indic Prakrits. In Middle Indic Prakrits the - *tv* is usually assimilated to - *ta*, for example, we find the Sanskrit *sattva* rendered as *sata* at Karle in the Western Deccan as well as Dhānyakaṭaka and Nāgārjunakoṇḍa in the Eastern Deccan.[40] In later literary languages the coalescence of *tv* into *tt* becomes a characteristic feature of Ardhamāghadī as well as Jain Māghādī and Śaurasenī.[41] Even when the language is mixed as in such as Pali[42] or the *Patna Dharmapada*, the - *t* of *satva* appears in literature even when it is not in inscriptions.[43]

If the language of the manuscript had been one of these dialects, the copyist would not expect to see a sub-linear - *v* and the similarity of the endings of *bodhisatena* and *citena* could easily lead to the haplograph *bodhicitena*. On the other hand, the assimilation of - *tv* into - *t* is *not* found in the North or Northwest.[44] In both the Kharoṣṭhī Gāndhārī of the *Split Manuscript* as well as in the Kuṣāṇa Brāhmī of the *Schøyen Manuscript* of the *Perfection of Wisdom*,[45] we find *bosisatva*[46] and *bodhisatva* respectively - with the latter having - *v* written prominently below the - *t*.[47] Thus, we can assume that the original community that produced the copyist mistake leading to *bodhicitta* was not in the North since the *Split* and *Schøyen* manuscripts hail from the Gandhāra region.

The haplography could thus have occurred with an original manuscript written in a Deccan Prakrit or at least south of Mathura. This dialect would account not only for the haplography *bodhisatena citena* to *bodhicitena*, but also for the *asakta/asata* pun that occurs later on in the chapter.[48] As indicated above the coalescence of - *tv* into - *t* is not a feature of Northern dialects during the time period we are interested in. *Sattva* is regularly represented as "*satva*" in inscriptions from Sarnath to Mathura on up to Gandhāra.

If I am correct that the latter haplography would have had to occur in a Southern dialect, we would have to explain how the text was produced in Turfan, was transmitted to Gandhāra and then to a Middle Indic–speaking area where the haplography occurred and then re-transmitted north for Kang Sengui's school to translate this variant into Chinese by the third century. While I am sure that stranger things have happened, I think parsimony dictates that we adopt the simpler solution - that the original had been circulated in Middle Indic and in Brāhmī (where the copyist errors occurred) where both the original and the flawed versions were subsequently transmitted north into Gāndhārī/Kharoṣṭhī while continuing to be circulated in Brāhmī by the end of the second century. Perhaps coincidentally, this follows the trajectory of the *Perfection of Wisdom* outlined in the 10th chapter of the current *Perfection of Wisdom in 8,000 Lines* itself, which states that it will appear in the South and migrate to the North. For what it is worth, all versions of the text state that, "In northern India, there will be very many *bodhisattvas*. However, there will be only a few among them who will study the *Prajñāpāramitā*."[49]

Subhūti's *araṇavihāra*: preaching or penetration?

The evidence so far suggests that the earliest communities to circulate the *Perfection of Wisdom* (or at least the initial core of the text) were not in a Gāndhārī-speaking/Khāroṣṭhī-writing area, but were farther south. This limits the provenance of the text somewhat (actually, not much) and limits its chronology hardly at all. We can, I think, do much better if we now turn our attention to Schmithausen's second objection to the Mindlessness section. Concerned that the "therefore" after the statement of Subhūti's attainment of the *araṇavihāra* makes no sense, he argues that *Subhūti*'s accomplishments in a state of meditation (the *Abhidharmahṛdaya* places it in the fourth dhyāna) cannot be the reason for the bodhisattvas' attainment of irreversibility.

To explain how this may not have been a problem for our author, I will discuss a passage from the Old Khotanese *Vajracchedikā Sūtra*, in which the *araṇavihāra* was explicitly stated to be a concentration that stopped the defilements in someone else. If, however, we trace the development of and provenance of this doctrine, it turns out that the interpretation of the *araṇavihārin* that shows up in that version of the *Vajracchedikā* is regionally specific and not some pan-Indic understanding of the state. It will be thus worth our while to delve into the development of the idea of the *araṇavihāra* and what it meant to different Buddhists in different places.[50]

It turns out that the term *araṇa-vihārin* has been a stumbling block for readers of the text all the way back. The term should be easy enough. It is a compound coined from "*araṇa*" and "*vihārin*." While some technical terms seem to catch on almost as soon as they are coined, this one apparently did not – Buddhaghosa, for instance, is aware of the term, but does not think it important enough to include in his *Visuddhimagga*. For those who did use the term, it was generally agreed that the term described something that Subhūti was good at, but there appears to have been some confusion as to what exactly it was.

The problem is that both term *araṇa* and the term *vihārin* are ambiguous. The term *áraṇa* is a fairly common term in Vedic literature, found mainly in the *Ṛg* and *Athārva Vedas* and in references to these in later *Brāhmaṇa*, *Śrauta* and *Gṛhasūtras*. In these contexts, the term usually means "stranger" or "foreigner," though sometimes it appears to have the connotation of "outsider/enemy." The term *araṇya* ("wilderness") is derived from this sense of the "outside" and while the sense of "stranger" is virtually unknown outside of Brahmanical circles,[51] its derivative *araṇya* is common for "wilderness" or "forest" in later literature and comes to be associated with the special power of religious specialists. *Araṇa* as "forest" is the idea behind the genre of *āraṇyaka* or meta-commentaries on Vedic rituals, and can also be seen in the special status afforded the "*araṇī*," or two sticks that are drilled to produce fire. The latter are praised as the ultimate source from which the god Agni arises as well as that to which he returns if the owner of the fires must travel for some reason. The return of Agni to his source becomes a model for the "internalization of the fires" in the body of the *brahman* that, in turn, forms the theoretical basis for both renunciation as well as for later rituals such as the *prāṇāgnihotra* or offering into the fire of the breath.[52]

It is probably due to its association with various forms of renunciant religiosity that Subhūti's attainment was understood in some circles as being an *araṇya-vihārin* – the term used in the *Perfection of Wisdom in 100,000 Lines*[53] and the probable source of the *Da Mingdu Jing*'s translation, "one who travels in mountains and swamps" (山澤行 = *araṇya* as wilderness). Of course, how we understand the first term determines how we read the second. If the first term is read as "forest" then it is only natural to read *vihārin* as "dweller." Thus, Subhūti is said to be an "*aranyavihārin*."

When the term *araṇa* appears elsewhere in Buddhist literature, it inevitably does so as a technical term denoting an accomplishment whose primary exemplar is Subhūti. By the time this literature was written, the Vedic usage of *araṇa* as "foreign" had fallen into disuse, and the Buddhists appear to be coining a new term in their *araṇa*. This usage can be traced back to a single source: the *Araṇavibhaṅgasutta* of the *Majjhima Nikāya*. This sutra is a riff (or *vaipulya*) on the Buddha's so-called "First Sermon" on the Four Noble Truths.

The sermon begins with the Buddha saying that he is going to give an exposition on *araṇa*. He then states that there are two extremes: that of sense pleasure and self-mortification. He states that he teaches a "Middle Way" between these two extremes that leads ultimately to nirvana. So far, the Buddha has done little more than to quote the first sermon delivered at Varanasi. The tripartite structure of the first sermon (i.e., the two extremes and the middle) becomes the paradigm for the next instruction that one should neither extol nor disparage (two extremes) others but rather teach only the dharma (the Middle Way). The next topics are bipartite, not tripartite. The monks are instructed to avoid sense pleasures and seek pleasure in themselves in the meditative absorptions. The last three items each govern speech. One should neither utter covert speech, nor sharp speech nor speak hurriedly. Finally, one should neither insist on the local language nor override normal usage. All of the above topics are said to be the "exposition of *araṇa*."

The sutra labels the extremes to be avoided as "*saraṇa*" (i.e., "with *raṇa*"), which forces us to read *araṇa* as the negation of *raṇa*. Although the term *araṇa* does not appear anywhere in Buddhist or non-Buddhist literature except with reference to this sutra, its putative opposite, *raṇa* is quite common. The latter term is derived from √*raṇ*, meaning "delight or pleasure" and by extension, "battle (as an object of delight)."[54] Thus *raṇa* can be read bivalently to denote both "sense pleasure" as well as "battle" or "conflict," with *a-raṇa* being the lack of either. Indeed, this is how the term *araṇa* is most often translated into Chinese; 無諍 meaning "non-dispute."

The whole sermon ends with the Buddha stating, "Therefore, monks, you should train yourselves thus: 'We shall know the dharma with *raṇa* and we shall know the dharma without *raṇa*, and knowing these we shall travel the path to *araṇa*.' Now, monks, Subhūti is a clansman who has entered upon the path of *araṇa*." As Bhikkhu Anālayo has noted, the Chinese *Madyama Āgama* inserts a verse stating that Subhūti is one who has really practiced true emptiness, and having renounced all this, he abides in tranquility (*śamatha*).[55]

On the whole, this sermon appears to be treating two very separate phenomena, and the discrepancy in the sermon falling under the single rubric of *araṇa* may be a result of ambivalent interpretations of the *araṇavihāra* as well as of Subhūti's attainments. On the one hand the topic of avoiding sense pleasure and self-mortification, as well as the topic of seeking pleasure internally (*adhyātma*) promotes both detachment from the world of the senses as well as the practice of meditative absorption. On the other hand, the remaining topics: censure and blame, covert speech, sharp speech, hurried speech or overly formal speech appear to have less to do with the practitioner's attainment of the goal than it does with perfecting one's instruction to *others* such that conflict or ill will does not arise in them.

To bring these topics together under one rubric, the sermon plays on both meanings of the term *raṇa*. The states of absorption in the meditative topics can be said to be *araṇa* in the sense that they are the negation of (worldly) "delight," while proper speech can also be said to be "*araṇa*" in the sense that it can assuage conflict. The sermon thus turns on an equivocation (one might more charitably call it a "pun") between two different senses of *araṇa* – one applied to inner cultivation and the other applied to the training of others.

In its original language, the term *araṇavihara* could (if somewhat awkwardly) accommodate both senses, that is until one tacks on the word *vihārin* to the end of it. If we read *araṇa* as "without (sensual) pleasure" and take it as the sutra does to be perfected through the levels of absorption or *jhānas*, then we should read the term *vihāra* to be a state of meditation or *samādhi* on the model of the *brahma-vihāras*,[56] which are first and foremost about internal development. Thus in Dānapāla's translation of the *Perfection of Wisdom in 8,000 Lines* as well as in both of Xuanzang's translations, Subhūti is said to be the best at "the *araṇa samādhi*."[57] This interpretation of Subhūti as one skilled in absorption may well be the inspiration behind the statement in the *Madhyama Āgama* that Subhūti truly practices emptiness, as well as the Buddha's praise of him at *Udāna* 6.7 and 71.10 for his accomplishments in a version of "not thinking" (here *avitarka*) meditations as well as in the formless concentrations.

One development that opens the door for later commentators to bring together the *araṇaviharin* as meditator with *araṇaviharin* as preacher is the identification of *raṇa* with defilements in general. Under this reading, *araṇa* can be the absence of sense pleasure (= the *kleśa* of *rāga*) just as much as it is the absence of strife (= the *kleśa* of *dveṣa*). This not only appears to be what is behind the standard Tibetan translation of *nyon mongs pa med pa*[58] for *araṇa*, but also forms an essential part of later interpretations of the term. Thus in *Paṭisambhidāmagga* we find the *araṇavihāra* synonymous with the removal of "obscurations" (*nivāraṇa*):

> Abiding without conflict: in what sense abiding without conflict? It removes the hindrances by means of the first *jhāna*, this it is an abiding without conflict. It removes applied thought and sustained thought by means of the second *jhāna* [on up to "neither perception nor non perception].[59]

While the *Paṭisambhiddhamagga* does not connect the *araṇavihāra* with teaching, we see an expansion on this logic in the *Aṅguttara Aṭṭhakathā*.

> In the third (sentence) "*araṇavihārin*," (means) "abiding in the state without affliction (*nikklesa-vihārinaṃ*)". "*Raṇa* "(dispute), is called the torments (*kilesa*) of passion etc. With their absence, the abiding in afflictionlessness is called *araṇavihāra*. For those of whom such is the case, they are *araṇavihārin* (i.e., they abide in *araṇa*). Of these dwellers in *araṇa*, the Elder Subhūti is the best. Some others, say *aranāvihāra* is the destruction of *āsavas* [i.e. moral defilements]. Moreover, by this Elder, this title was obtained due to his teaching of the doctrine (*dhamma*). Other monks teach the doctrine and then assign praise or blame or yell. The Elder, however, teaches the doctrine the without exceeding the limit of instruction set by the Teacher. That's why he became "the foremost of those who abide in *araṇa*."[60]

We find this sense of the *araṇavihārin* as proper teacher preserved, if in a somewhat vestigial form, in statements in the *Ekottara Āgama* to the effect that not only does Subhūti practice absorption in emptiness, but he excels in explaining it as well.[61]

In all of these examples from Theravādin literature, what is telling is what is *not* here. Nowhere in all of the Southern Theravāda literature is the *araṇaviharin* credited with eliminating the defilements in *somebody else* through meditation, nor is there any indication from any of these sources that their authors were even aware of such an interpretation even to disagree with it.

But what is absent from Southern discussions of the *araṇavihāra* is commonplace in Northern *abhidharma* literature and in texts known to have come from the far North. These texts apparently sought to smooth over the discrepancy between two senses of *araṇa* in the sermon by casting the *araṇavihāra* as a state of meditation in which one person attained a state of absorption which destroyed the *kleśas* in another person. The *Abhidharmahṛdaya* in particular defines the *araṇavihāra* as follows:

> Absence of strife (*araṇa*): when he wants to arrange that strife does not arise in someone else's mind, it does not arise.[62]

The *Saṃyuktabhidharmahṛdaya* does not come out and state that the *araṇa samādhi* stops the defilements of others in so many words, but it does go into a lengthy description of how one possessed of this knowledge would be the most effective at saying or doing just the right thing to end that person's defilements.[63] Toward the end of this section, Dharmaśrī tells us that the ones who develop this state are, "such [persons] as Buddha and the *śrāvakas* who develop the *pāramitās*."[64] In all these sources, the *araṇavihāra* is a knowledge developed in the fourth level of meditation (the fourth *dhyāna*) that eliminates the defilements in others as well as the self. By this definition, it is actually makes perfect sense for Śāriputra to say that

Subhūti's *samādhi* of the *araṇavihāra* is the reason why *the bodhisattvas* should be considered irreversible – because Subhūti's *samādhi* affects other people's minds.

The testimony of the two texts above demonstrates not only that some held the *araṇavihāra* to be a concentration capable of destroying defilements in someone else, but that this idea was known reasonably early in the Northwest where Dharmaśrī was writing. Though we have to be careful about claiming absolutely that this was exclusively a Sarvāstivāda doctrine, it does appear in Xuanzang's translation of one of their core *abhidharma* texts, the *Jñānaprasthāna*, with a follow-up in his translation of the *Mahāvibhāṣa*.[65] This passage is, however, missing in the earlier translations of the same texts. Whether it was a doctrine exclusive to the Sarvāstivādins, it was a doctrine that they nevertheless adopted at some point.

That this was how *Perfection of Wisdom* advocates understood Subhūti's *araṇavihāra* can be demonstrated from the "Old Khotanese version" of the *Vajracchedikāsūtra*:

> By the Venerable Exalted One the defeat of the *kleśa* [i.e., greed, hate and delusion] enemies has been declared in my case to be splendid, the foremost of all. If I had wrapped myself with affection in the arhat wisdom, the Venerable Exalted One would not have prophesied of me: "he is the highest *araṇāvihārin* of all, who in the *araṇa*, resplendent in absorption, reaches the defeat of the *kleśas* in a different train of thought" (*haṃdarye saṃttāña = anyasmin saṃtāne*).[66]

Stopping the defilements in someone else's mind makes sense if "dwelling in *araṇa*" has something to do with preaching. But here and in the above *abhidharma* materials, we have someone "who in the *araṇa*, resplendent in absorption, reaches the defeat of the *kleśas* in a different train of thought." What can the suppression of *kleśas* in someone else possibly have to do with my *samādhi*? Nothing, of course, unless I can somehow enter into their mind.

Emptiness, Brahmin nuns, *tulkus* and the power of possession

This may seem odd to the casual reader of Buddhist literature . . . but then again, not that odd. Meditations that allow the yogi to enter into another person is one of the Six Yogas of Naropa, and at least in the Mahāmudrā tradition of the Kagyupa, the practice of transference or *'pho ba* (**saṃkrānti*) is the meaning of *mahāmudra* itself.[67] The fact that a Kagyupa would identify the yogic power of transference with the attainment of *mahāmudrā* is particularly significant since it was precisely this ability that allowed the Kagyupa lama Karma Pakshi (1204/6–1283) to become the first reincarnate lama or *tulku*. And it may well be that modern Tibetans see the authority of their tulkus to lie more in their ability to remember their past incarnations than in any association with the dharma-body of the Buddha. But yogic penetration was not just a medieval Tibetan thing. In the *Saṃyutta Nikāya*, a nun named Uppalavaṇṇā appears to have been quite good at it. At *Saṃyutta* Nikāya 5.5 Māra basically threatens her with rape. She comes back with a verse saying, in effect, that if he even thinks of doing so she will penetrate him every which way 'til Sunday before he even knows what is happening. Wisely, he leaves her alone. Bhikkhu Bodhi translates her verse as follows:

> Though a hundred thousand rogues
> Just like you might come here,
> I stir not a hair, I feel no terror;
> Even alone, Mara, I don't fear you.
>
> I can make myself disappear
> Or I can enter inside your belly.
> I can stand between your eyebrows
> Yet you won't catch a glimpse of me.
>
> I am the master of my mind,
> The bases of power are well developed;
> I am freed from all bondage,
> Therefore I don't fear you, friend.[68]

If tales of possession by Buddhist monks (or in Uppalavaṇṇā's case, one seriously badass nun) are rare, they were *du jour* in yogic circles, as David Gordon White has discussed extensively in his brilliant *Sinister Yogis*. It may well be that for the authors of the *Perfection of Wisdom*, the bodhisattva being *Buddhist* was not the emphasis of the text but rather the bodhisattva being a *Buddhist yogi*.

One of White's examples is, I think, particularly interesting in light of the Buddhist Brahmanical intersections that we have already found in the *Perfection of Wisdom*. The *Mokṣadharma Parvan* of the *Mahābhārata* records a dialog between another, equally badass "nun" (*bhikṣukī*) named Sulabha (who also happens to be a Brahmin) and King Janaka of Videha (the great-great grandfather of King Bṛhadratha to whom the *Maitrāyaṇīya Upaniṣad* is taught[69]), whose mind she had just penetrated.[70] He, of course, objects at being penetrated by someone of a different caste. She responds that he, as a yogi himself, should not object since, "With Yatis, among all orders of men, the custom is to pervade the empty, *to dwell in the empty*. What harm then have I done?"[71]

Here, we have a confluence of two factors (the yogic powers to possess another, coupled with a meditation on emptiness) which also appear to be related in the *Perfection of Wisdom in 8,000 Lines*. Of course, the term *araṇavihāra* is only used in Buddhist texts, but it may well have been coined by a Yajurvedic Brahmin contingent within Buddhism – which may be why the term did not really catch on in the way intended. The only other place in Brahmanical literature where I can find parallel yogic penetration of someone else's mind along with references to emptiness as a spiritual goal mentioned is the *Maitrāyaṇīya Upaniṣad*,[72] which I have already noted has a number of intersections with the *Perfection of Wisdom*.

There is, thus, ample reason to think that the "therefore" (*atas*) that so disturbed Schmithausen actually turns out to not be a problem if we assume the author to be familiar with these Northern, possibly Sarvāstivādin *abhidharma* materials. Though there are others who might argue otherwise, I am doubtful that the term *araṇavihāra* was in Lokakṣema's manuscript (one would have to make a case that he, like Zhu Fonian after him, translates it with 空身慧, which hardly seems like a slam-dunk case to me). What is clear is that this passage does appear in the *Da Mingdu Jing* and so is probably another case in which there was more than one manuscript line. If so the *araṇavihāra* reference would have been part of the text circulated in Middle Indic and was not immediately transmitted to Gāndhārī-speaking regions.

Putting it together

Here we have a puzzle. If the *Da Mingdu Jing* contains the *bodhicitta* phrase, then it reflects copyist mistakes that could have only occurred in a Southern dialect, while also being the only early exemplar to have *araṇavihārin* represented – a feature which assumes an audience familiar with knowledge that, as far as I can tell, was circulating in Buddhist circles only in the Gandhāra/Kashmir region. Furthermore, the text that *does* eventually appear in Gāndhārī, Lokakṣema's manuscript as well as that of Zhu Fonian (this word is missing from the *Split Manuscript*) *doesn't* contain the reference to the *aranavihāra* – a doctrine which could only have come from there – but rather has Subhūti excelling at bodily witnessing of emptiness 空身慧 (which actually *does* clash with the "therefore" that follows).

At this point, I think we can piece these clues together to come up with a narrative for the composition of this text and a solution to the mystery. I propose that if we take all of these factors into consideration, we should plot the composition and early circulation of the *Perfection of Wisdom in 8,000 Lines* at a time and place where there was:

a) contact between the Sarvāstivāda ideas circulating in the Northwest and authors further south
b) contact between users of Middle Indic Sanskritized Prakrit and Gāndhārī, and
c) contact between users of the Kharoṣṭhī script and users of Brāhmī script.

If the composition had occurred precisely in this zone of contact, I see no reason at all to posit lengthy periods of time between the composition of this passage and its development, translation and transmission to Gandhāra and then to China. We could be talking about a period of a decade just as easily as a century. By way of a hypothesis, I propose the Mathura area as the place of its composition, since after 29 CE, we start to see the introduction of Kharoṣṭhī script in numerous inscriptions along with the continued use of Brāhmī.[73] As Harry Falk has shown, it appears that Rajuvula brought the Kharoṣṭhī script with him along with a number of Sarvāstivādin monks when he was forced out of Jammu in 29 CE. According to Falk:

> Rajuvula's reign came to an end through Gondophares' presence in Jammu. His defeat at the hands of Gondophares necessitated the settlement of his family in Mathura. This may have taken place around AD 29 or somewhat later. When the family moved south from Jammu, they brought along clerks writing Kharoṣṭhī and monks of a certain affiliation [i.e., Sarvāstivāda]. The fleeing party would also have rescued the Buddhist relics from the monastery of their patronage and would have re-installed them in their new location at Mathura as soon as possible. The Mathura lion should, therefore, have been inscribed rather shortly after the re-location.... Mentions of Sarvāstivādins are very rarely found in inscriptions at Mathura and, apart from the Lion, only about a century later. It stands to reason that the lion documents the first influx of Sarvāstivāda monks into Mathura, and we also surmise that this introduction occurred when the family of Rajuvula/Śoḍāsa to move from the Jammu area down south to Mathura. They brought their "family" Buddhist group with them, as they did with the script they were wont to use, Kharoṣṭhī, alien to the local culture. We can also presume that these new arrivals were regarded as a threat by the Mahāsaṅghikas. On the other hand, the imported Sarvāstivādins were too few in number to overtake the Mahāsaṃghikas in importance, even with royal patronage. Three times we read on the lion of the Sarvāstivādins as donees and three times *ācārya* Buddhadeva appears as their head.[74]

If the *Perfection of Wisdom in 8,000 Lines* had been written by a Sarvāstivādin monk in Mathura, in Brāhmi script, it would have to have been after 30 CE when the Sarvāstivādins arrived with the king and before 147 CE, which is the outside date provided by the C_{14} dating of the *Split Manuscript*. Given that there seems to have been only one such monastery at this time (the Sarvāstivādin monastery referred to in the Lion Capital inscription), the author would most likely have been an incumbent of Buddhadeva's "*guhavihāra*" or cave monastery outside of Maṭ (i.e., in close proximity to the palace).[75]

Of course, while we know that the *araṇavihāra* interpretation that appears in the *Perfection of Wisdom in 8,000 Lines* was used by Sarvāstivādins and that they may have brought this interpretation with them, we have no reason to believe that this doctrine was particularly contentious. We also have no pressing reason to believe that it was not adopted by other monasteries throughout the region – other than the fact that the idea apparently did not spread too far, since the Theravādins were unaware of it. The author may have been a monk living somewhere else in the region, but he would still have had to have written it after the influx of Northwestern monks to the Mathura area in 29 CE. The various additions and accretions to the text would have occurred in this region over a period of up to a century – plenty of time for all the changes and variations to have occurred if we are not postulating huge distances for the text to travel in order to accumulate all these changes.

Conclusion

Now much of the above argument will, I am sure, make serious philologists apoplectic (try deep breaths into a paper bag or a glass of Sauvignon blanc . . . it helps). They will correctly observe that there are just too many moving parts and too few surviving samples of handwriting to raise my conclusions anywhere near the level of "proof." It would be really nice to have something more solid to hang our hat on. I, for one, really like radiocarbon dating. As someone who spends his days squinting into the murky darkness for any trace of authors who have been dead for millennia, there is something reassuring about the concreteness of isotopic half-lives. The C_{14} date of the *Split Manuscript* tells us that it was completed sometime between 47–147 CE (about 81.1% certainty). Unless, of course, it wasn't. In that case it was definitely completed between 25–43 CE (14.3% certainty).[76] Then again, there is still the slight (4.6%) remaining chance (even disregarding the possibility of sample contamination) that it was completed some other time. This kind of uncertainty around even the most concrete artifact of early Mahāyāna may cause some to throw up their hands at the prospects of knowing anything at all about the sutra itself much less about the origins of Mahāyāna in general, to deride the whole historical enterprise and to stick to the happy certainties of "Buddhist philosophy." Those that do will content themselves with the idea that we simply do not know the origins and social context of the *Perfection of Wisdom*. But degrees of probability (or degrees of uncertainty) are simply a part of historical research and if the lingering uncertainty disappoints our expectations it is not a sufficient reason to abandon the project. The conclusions that are derived from historical research should, rather, be treated as hypotheses whose truth then becomes a matter of the use to which they are put by other scholars.

So, like a C_{14} date, I will state definitively that the core portion of the *Perfection of Wisdom* was probably written near Mathura in the second half of the first century . . . unless it wasn't. What I have done here is to identify points within the text of the *Perfection of Wisdom in 8,000 Lines* that need to be taken into account together in order to triangulate a place and date of composition. While my tentative conclusion that the author was a Sarvāstivādin monk residing at Buddhadeva's Guhavihāra outside of Maṭ between 30 and 147 CE may seem ridiculously precise for those who are used to dealing with early texts, I am actually more interested in the points of triangulation than the place itself. If one of my points turns out to be false, then my results will have to be adjusted accordingly. For instance, if someone wants to make an argument that the pronunciation of *sata* for *satva* is not relevant for the scribal errors that have been pointed out, then we would also have to consider Turfan as a place of composition and adjust the date to when Sarvāstivādin *abhidharma* ideas arrived (pretty early I would think). But then again, one would also have to address the question of why we find the slanted medial - *e* in Turfan in the first place. Did it originate there or was it adapted from the style that coming into vogue in Central India? Again, if it turns out that this particular interpretation of the *araṇavihārin* is not specifically tied to the North or to Sarvāstivāda, then we will have to explain why the Theravādins appear to have never heard of this interpretation of it, and will have to adjust the source of the *Perfection of Wisdom* accordingly. On the contrary, if these points hold up and central India somewhere between Mathura and Sarnath can be taken as a reasonable place of origin for the *Perfection of Wisdom in 8,000 Lines*, then we need to begin connecting the ideas and phraseology of this text to the considerable political, social and economic details that we know about this region at this time.

Notes

1 Stuart (2015).
2 Stuart (2015), p. 127.
3 Fujita (2009).
4 Stuart (2015), p. 119.
5 Ibid., p. 111.
6 T. 721, p. 28c23.
7 E.g., Ibid., p. 30b20.
8 Stuart (2015), p. 239.
9 Schlosser (2016) and Strauch (2010).
10 One thinks here of a number of sutras included in the Ratnakūṭa collection (T. 310) whose translations are included in Chang (1996), such as #46 "Mañjuśrī's discourse on the Pāramitā of Wisdom. # 36, "How to Kill with the Sword of Wisdom." etc.
11 T. 458, p. 435b16–17.
12 Exactly how to translate *shu* 署 here is a bit of a head-scratcher. In Han Dynasty texts, it tends to mean "office" or "government position," and so I have chosen the most straightforward translation. But there is still some question in my mind as to what is intended here. After a lot of back and forth on H-Net Buddhism, the scholars I consulted could not come to any agreement. Seishi Karashima suggested that since 署 can mean "office" and by extension the signature or stamp of the office, so that it should be translated as "*mudrā*". However, 印 seems to have been the preferred translation of *mudrā* in Lokakṣema's circles (see, e.g. T. 418, pp. 919b6ff.) Others questioned whether the term *mudrā* was used in this sense this early. Dan Lusthus and Chuck Muller suggested "teaching" or "teach" while Paul Harrison translates it as "*cārita*." Harrison (1993), p. 161. It seems to me that an original of *adhikaraṇa* or *nāmadheya* would cover most of the meanings of 署 as title or office. But *adhikaraṇa* also tends to mean "dispute" in Buddhist texts. For this reason, I am sticking to the primary dictionary definition from Mathews (1943) and will leave it to whoever eventually translates the text to make a definitive judgment.
13 T. 458, p. 435b21–2 怛薩阿竭署者有四事. The pattern of declaring that there are a certain number of "issues" (事) and then enumerating them is the primary structure of the *Kāśyapaparivarta*, in which the character 事 consistently translates "dharma."
14 T. 458, p. 435b26–29.
15 無所著. Although "non-attached" is the most straightforward rendering, it is also possible that this translates *avikalpa* – "non-constructed awareness," which might even work better in context. See Karashima (2010), p. 516.
16 T. 458, pp. 435c29–436a12.
17 Later on, the Buddha states that this seeing of non-seeing is the non-duality of mind: "There is nothing seen and no seeing. What is seen does not produce two thoughts. Aware without grasping, this awareness is nothing made and is not something that arises" Ibid, pp. 436b1ff.
18 Taking the variant reading of 令 as 念.
19 The translator appears to be punning on 自然, which commonly means "nature" or is the standard translation of "*svabhāva*" and yet the Chinese *ran* is also literally, "to burn."

20 T. 458, p. 438b14–25.
21 T. 458, p. 439a1–10.
22 However, the Brahmin at 439c26ff is told to not engage in a sacrifice involving suffering. Instead, each of the six perfections is said to be a better sacrifice for him.
23 cf. T. 224, p. 425c8, T. 458, p. 435b08, T. 474, pp. 525b18ff. T15n0626, p. 389a17ff.
24 See for example: T. 418 p. 908b27-c1; T. 417, 899c4–7; T. 350 p. 190c20–23 and192a13ff. T. 626, p. 389c5ff. and 393a09–10; T. 474 p. 519c20–22. Most importantly, we find this same teaching in the "Blackie Brahmin sutra" T. 583, p. 967c4–6.
25 It may be that the recent Bajaur manuscript contains some of these same themes, although the key term in that manuscript appears to be *avijñāpti*, not *acitta*. See, Schlosser, 195, 201, 205.
26 See for e.g. S.N. 41.7 and 46.54.
27 See Bodhi (2000), p. 1608: "We too, friends, teach the Dhamma to our disciples thus: . . . dwell pervading the entire world with a mind imbued with loving kindness . . . compassion, altruistic joy . . . equanimity . . . without ill will." For important discussions on this sequence with other references, see Huifeng (2016), pp. 111–113 and Pande (1995), pp. 528–529.
28 T. 227, p. 537b14, also found in one of Xuanzang's translations T. 220, p. 866a10.
29 I am aware, of course, that the original would not have been in Sanskrit. I am merely using Sanskrit here to provide a reference point between languages – assuming that more readers will be familiar with Sanskrit than Gāndhārī. When the peculiarities of the local dialect are a significant departure from the Sanskrit, I will note it accordingly.
30 Reading Lokakṣema's入中心 as reflecting *citte* is, I think, too much of a stretch. (cf. T. 224, p. 425c25).
31 Mehendale (1948), p. 238.
32 Mehendale mentions two exceptions, one from Nasik and one from Sañci, in which a neuter singular nominative noun has an – *e* termination. See pp, 87 and 173 respectively.
33 I could find no instances of neuter nominatives ending in – *e* in the *Anavatapta Gāthā*, the Gāndhārī *Saṃyuktāgama* fragments, either of the two versions of the Gāndhārī *Dharmapada* or the Rhinoceros Horn Sutra. See the indices to Salomon (2000, 2008); Lenz, Glass, and Dharmamitra(2003) and Glass and Allon (2007). There are a total of three neuter instrumentals ending in – *e* in known Gāndhārī texts – two in the Gāndhārī fragments of the *Samyukta Āgama* and one in the *Anavatapta Gāthā* fragments of the Senior Collection. That said, none of these are *citta*. The term *citta* is well attested in these texts, and its nominative is always represented as either *cito* or *citu* – never *cite*.
34 Verboom (1998), "Appendix 4," p. 6. Technically, there is nothing to rule out *tena bodhicitte na mantavyām*, but then we are left with an idea occurring "in the *bodhicitta*," which is weird.
35 See Franco (2004), vol. 1, pp. 53, 4b line 2 and 57, 8a+263a line 2.
36 Sander (2000), 5 verso, the bottom line has several clear examples.
37 Lüders (1911), plate I.
38 Schmithausen (1977), pp. 51–53.
39 Salomon and Glass (2008), p. 119.
40 Mehendale (1948), pp. 81 and 129.
41 Schwartzschild (1956), p. 113.
42 See von Hinuber (1982).
43 The – *tv* is clearly represented in the word *bodhisatva* in several Kuṣāna-era inscriptions from Mathura. See Falk (2012), pp. 501–503.
44 Mehendale (1948), p. 168.
45 See Sander (2000).
46 e.g., Falk and Karashima (2012), p. 32.
47 e.g., Sander (2000), pp. 38 ff.; plates on p. 245 verso, line 4.
48 As Schmithausen points out. Schmithausen (1977), p. 52.
49 Karashima (2013), p. 180.

50 For a somewhat dated, though still astute full-length treatment of this concept, see Walleser (1917) and for an excellent and more recent discussion, see Huifeng (2016), pp. 116–118.

51 It is completely absent from the Epics, the Purāṇas, *dharma śāstra*, dramatic literature and early lexicographical works such as the *Amārakośa*.

52 See for example, *Mānava Śrautasutra*, 1.6.3, Patrick Olivelle (1992), pp. 86–89, and Bodewitz (1973).

53 Ghoṣa (1902), p. 502.

54 Monier-Williams, s.v.

55 See Anālayo (2011), vol. 2, p. 796, note 190; T. 26, p. 703c11. 此行真實空 捨此住止息

56 This interpretation can be found in the *Petavatthu Aṭṭhakathā*, p. 230. In the *Theragātha Aṭṭhakathā*, it is explained immediately after a description of Subhūti's accomplishments in the *araṇavihāra* that when he goes from house to house begging for morsels of food, he concentrates on kindness (*mettajhāna*) and for that reason he is said (as he is at A.N. I.) to be worthy of *dakṣinā* (offerings/sacrificial fees).

57 Dānapāla T. 228, p. 587b24: 誠如佛說，汝於無諍三昧行中最勝第 Xuanzang I: T. 220, p. 763c26:佛說仁者住無諍定最為第一 Xuanzang II: T. 220, p. 866a18–19: 善哉! 誠如所說. 佛說仁者住無諍定最為第一.

58 See Mahāvyutpatti, p. 617–618, # 1125,

59 Warder (1997), p. 94.

60 Aṅguttara Aṭṭhakathā, p. I. 220; See Walleser (1917), p. 26.

61 Anālayo (2011), vol. 2, 796, note 190. See also, e.g., T. 202, p. 396a7–8.

62 Charles Willemen (2006), p. 204; T. 1550, p. 825c15–6 不諍者。欲令他意不起諍.

63 See Bart Dessein (1999), pp. 429–430; T. 1552, p. 922c21–23a17.

64 T. 1552, p. 923a16–17佛及波羅蜜諸聲 聞等. 得無諍滿而不數入(為令眾生因惱得度故有時不入無諍三昧也). Discussions can also be found in the *Abhidharmakośabhāṣa*, Kośa, 4. vs. 56ff.; 7. vs. 35ff., and Jaini (1977), p. 392, vs. 511.

65 See, T. 1544, p. 1017b26ff and p. 1018a27–29 and commentary at T. 1545, p. 898a13ff.

66 Hoernle (1988), pp. 280; 252–253. This interpretation also appears in Haribhadra's commentary on the *Aṣṭa* passage, see Vaidya (1960), p. 293.

67 Kragh (2015), p. 321.

68 Bodhi (2000), pp. 225–226.

69 White (2009) p. 143. White goes on to point out that the *Maitrāyaṇīya Upaniṣad* is the only upaniṣad to mention this kind of yogic penetration, as the teacher Śākāyana teaches Bṛhadratha from inside the latter's heart.

70 See discussion at White (2009), pp. 141–145; one wonders whether the subtext of the statement about not penetrating one of another caste was meant to reflect rules of consanguinity.

71 MBh. 12.308.168 *niyamo hy eṣa dharmeṣu yatīnāṃ śūnya-vāsitā| śūnyam āvāsayantyā ca mayā kiṃ kasya dūṣitam||*

72 See discussion in White (2009), pp. 89–96, 140 and 145.

73 There are, of course, a few stray Khāroṣṭhī inscriptions (some of which are bi-script) that were etched in Bihār and Uttar Pradesh, but these were most likely inscribed by or for travelers from the Northwest. See Konow (1969), pp. 177–179.

74 Falk (2011b), p. 132.

75 Ibid., pp. 132–133.

76 Falk (2011a), p. 20.

10

ON SITES AND STAKES

Meditation on emptiness and imperial aspirations

I began this genealogy with a discussion of the 14th Dalai Lama, noting the ways in which the Mahāyāna doctrine of emptiness and the Dharma Body, drawing on a long Tibetan precedent, provided an image for those attending dharma talks and tantric initiations of a cosmic apex upon which to model a new Tibetan constitution. I also argued that there were a number of factors at play in the 20th century that eventually rendered the political importance of Mahāyāna for the legitimation of sovereign authority superfluous – a countercurrent that would eventually overwhelm and occlude the formerly political stream of Mahāyāna authorizations. At present, the countercurrent appears to have won the day; in 2011 the Central Tibetan Administration has accepted the Dalai Lama's renunciation of any future political role regarding the Tibetan people and has again declared that the very institution of the Dalai Lama will end with him. By the end of the 20th century, it had become difficult for anyone to see the political implications of the image of emptiness for political sovereignty. In the second chapter, I went back to the 16th and 17th centuries to show just how important Mahāyāna in its tantric and Zen forms were to two of the most powerful Qing Dynasty emperors (emperors whose dominion spanned Tibetan, Chinese and Mongolian-speaking peoples). I showed that the ideas of emptiness and the ultimacy of mind were crucially important not only as a way to frame the Qing dynast as emperor, but to consolidate Qing rule with Mongolian Buddhists, Tibetan Buddhists and Chinese Confucian scholars. The fourth chapter went on to argue that emptiness and to some extent mind were important components of "internal colonialism" or, if you prefer, "nation building" within China historically insofar as the images of emptiness and primordial mind coded authority. The coded image proved to be authoritative not only across "religions" but allowed for the absorption of independent populations and cults into the imperial regime. The fifth chapter, then, went on to show how each of these processes was operative in India right up until the late 19th century. Through a discussion of Maitrīpa and Bhāviveka, I then showed that the *Perfection of Wisdom* – and especially its first chapter – stood out as prototypical of Mahāyāna, and that those who objected to Mahāyāna thought that it came too close to the Brahmanical thinking referred to as "*vedānta*."

The remainder of the chapters preceding the present one examine the core section of the *Perfection of Wisdom in 8,000 Lines* and the question of its origins. I argue that the original core was primarily concerned with the bodhisattva attaining the complete cessation of conceptual processes, and that emptiness was understood to describe this state in which no identifications could be made. I showed that its teaching of non-conceptualization appears to be a kind of riff on canonical sutras such as the *Dhātuvibhaṅga* – a feature shared with other early or proto-Mahāyāna works such as the second chapter of the *Saddharmasmṛtyupasthānasūtra*. I then showed that certain elements, while having affinities with canonical texts, appear to also be influenced by Vedic thought, especially that of the Kṛṣṇa Yajurveda Maitrāyaṇī branch and their particular articulation of *brahman*/Prajāpati as empty. The *Perfection of Wisdom*'s resulting articulation of the ultimate as emptiness on the one hand and (in later chapters) as the Tathāgata on the other, turns out to be a kind of Maitrāyaṇīya Buddha-centric version of *brahman*. Nor was the *Perfection of Wisdom* the only early Mahāyāna text to display these kind of Brahmanical affinities. Given that association with Brahmanism was precisely one of the objections registered against Mahāyāna in later generations, it seems likely that those most interested in emptiness and non-conceptualization identifying themselves with Mahāyāna early on were in fact Brahmins who saw in Buddhism the fulfillment of the Vedic promise embodied in the Brahmin, the so-called "matted-haired ascetics" or *jaṭila* and the yogis. But if we broaden our purview from an exclusively Buddhist domain to one that also encompasses a Brahmanical literary domain, we have to shift our interpretation of what early Mahāyāna would have meant at the time.

Having identified this early social and geographical milieu, what should we do with it? I certainly do not want to be accused of having identified this set of concerns in order to establish an "authentic" Mahāyāna. I am not arguing that forms of Buddhism that seek a cessation of mind resting in itself are authentic while those that reject reflexive awareness, Brahmanism or the foundationalism implicit in Vedic cosmogonic myths are somehow not. To do so would be to take a normative stand on a long history of Buddhist debates, and that is clearly above my paygrade. Rather, what I am arguing here is that the political and cosmogonic articulations of early Yajurvedin Brahmin Buddhists in the opening of the *Perfection of Wisdom* alluding to discussions of the primordial Prajāpati or *brahman* as a cosmogonic "emptiness" and the unmanifest source "prior to thought" form a kind of legitimate problematic, setting out the parameters of what *can be* debated in later Mahāyāna. The *Perfection of Wisdom* presents us with a non-perception and non-apprehension as perfect wisdom and then tells us that the bodhisattva's mind does not apprehend anything because "that mind is mindless." Now clearly the subsequent developments of this Mahāyāna will see interpretations of these points heading off in very different trajectories. But my point is that these are trajectories or genealogies *of precisely this problematic*. And returning to Stuart Hall's discussion of encoding and decoding, this is what we should expect to see. The Buddhist Brahmins of the first and second century had a set of concerns and literary capital that were radically different from those of Tsongkhapa, Mazu, Bankai or Alan Watts. When each of the latter decode Mahāyāna discussions of emptiness and mind, they do so within the codes bequeathed to them by their immediate teachers and environments. And yet, despite the fissiparous effects of time we find that the doctrines of emptiness, the luminous mind, or the Buddha mind are as important within Buddhist debates of the 21st century as they were in the first century. So, am I saying that the Yogācāra doctrine of mind-only is somehow the same as the Madhyamaka doctrine of emptiness? To say that the two are the same or different would similarly be to take a normative stance on something that in fact was long debated. Śāntarakṣita thought Madhyamaka and Yogācāra were compatible, Candrakīrti did not. Sakya Pandita thought that awareness was naturally self-reflexive, Tsongkhapa did not. *Tathāgatagarbha* texts reify emptiness as a thing (much like some early canonical texts reify the "signless" into an object to be observed)[1] while most Buddhist logicians (apart from the Jonangpa) reject the idea that emptiness serves as a kind of cosmogonic foundationalism. Then too, most tantric and some Zen authors manage to sneak emptiness back into the cosmic position in one way or another, either as the "Sovereign All-Creating Mind" or the "Primordial Foundation" of the Dzogchen,[2] the *Mahāmudrā qua Prajñāpāramitā* of the Kagyupa[3] or the Mind from before the cosmic eon of Hongzhi.[4] The point of tracing out a genealogy is *not* to identify some unchanging essence that persists, but to identify the horizons of persistent questions or debates. Mahāyānists may debate whether the centerpiece of Mahāyāna is mind or emptiness (and what exactly each of those means), but they are not debating about the existence or possibility of, say, an "unmoved mover." There are definitely disagreements, but the bounds and the boundaries of the debates determine the boundaries of the tradition. The suite of early Mahāyāna texts may (returning to Hall) have encoded a set of concerns about mind and authority then current among first-century Kṛṣṇa Yajurvedins, but these texts were taken out of the social milieu of the communities that had the proper literary capital to decode them in the way they were encoded. It was pretty easy for Tsongkhapa, etc. to assume that Mahāyāna had nothing to do with the Vedic tradition, because they didn't know any Brahmins.

Shifting contexts, shifting interpretations

I would like to conclude what has been a rather lengthy study with a few meditations on what it would look like to read early Mahāyāna materials as part of a larger political project that included Brahmanical Upaniṣads more broadly. We might venture that we would now have to look at the *Perfection of Wisdom* as a variety of yoga, but does that really tell us much that we didn't already know? The core section of the *Perfection of Wisdom* describes a cessation of conceptualization in which the practitioner is said to not be seen. It seems that what is being offered here simply a "personal salvation" – ostensibly arhatship – thus rendering the aspirant invisible to death. Alternately, we could say it is offering the aspirant access to the *araṇavihāra* – the yogic meditation that grants its user the power to penetrate and control the minds of others.

If we confine our understanding of the *Perfection of Wisdom* to Buddhist canonical intertexts, then, yes: the *Perfection of Wisdom* offers its practitioners arhatship, a few yogic powers but little else. However, if we open the discussion of emptiness and mind up to Brahmanical intertexts then we are forced to recognize ways in which the yogic practices that engaged these same ideas of emptiness and the mindless mind were already well ensconced in the large-scale *śrauta* sacrifices that were becoming vogue in Indian royal courts that begin to appear in the archaeological record around the second century BCE. I will be arguing that the courtly connection would not have been lost on anyone raised in a Brahmin village and taught to memorize Brahmanical texts from the age of eight onward in the first century CE. In this social milieu, a Brahmin Buddhist could not help but recognize yogic practices as aspiring to a direct experience of the ultimate, foundational reality (whether reified or not was hardly the issue) *and for that reason* to be the ground of all political authority.

Returning the doctrines of emptiness and mind of early Mahāyāna sources to the arena of political *ideology* illuminates Mahāyāna's social and political embeddedness and the relationship of the image of emptiness to the exercise of power. In the following I would like to think through the role of the yogi (whether Buddhist or non-Buddhist) as part of the "ideological state apparatus." As Louis Althusser once noted, "[T]he Ideological State Apparatuses may be not only the stake, but also the site of class struggle, and often of bitter forms of class struggle."[5] Althusser argues that we have to separate "state power" from "state apparatuses" – the latter being those institutions and mechanisms through which the state exercises power. According to these definitions, state *power* can be seized or lost by particular factions without the apparatus itself changing at all. The tricky part of Althusser's argument is that he argues that an institution can be understood as "private" and yet still be functionally a "state apparatus." This will require some explanation.

The state exercises its power most visibly through what Althusser calls its "repressive state apparatuses," such as the military or the judiciary. If we look at the state as a kind of industry, then the exercise of authority would be the state's "product," but we can't explain the exercise of authority through a description of the repressive apparatuses alone. As he points out, "in order to exist, every social formation must reproduce the conditions of its production at the same time as it produces, and in order to be able to produce."[6] In order for the state to exercise its power it must simultaneously *reproduce* the conditions that make possible the exercise of that power. It is the role of ideology to ensure the reproduction of the conditions for production, a process that is necessarily extrinsic to the exercise itself. Althusser gives the analogy of a factory:

> The reproduction of the material conditions of production cannot be thought at the level of the firm, because it does not exist at that level in its real conditions. What happens at the level of the firm is an effect, which

> only gives an idea of the necessity of reproduction, but absolutely fails to allow its conditions and mechanisms to be thought.
>
> A moment's reflection is enough to be convinced of this: Mr X, a capitalist who produces woolen yarn in his spinning-mill, has to 'reproduce' his raw material, his machines, etc. But he does not produce them for his own production – other capitalists do: an Australian sheep-farmer, Mr Y, a heavy engineer producing machine-tools, Mr Z, etc., etc.[7]

If we are really to understand the state's exercise of power, we cannot think of the regime as a self-contained or self-sufficient agent. The state may be responsible for the production of certain effects (the effects of power), but it cannot secure the reproduction of the means of this production all by itself. In order for the ruling faction to be *recognized* as ruling (in order for the threat of the repressive apparatuses to be "correctly" *interpreted*), the competencies to properly interpret as well as an array of dispositions (i.e., the disposition to obey superiors and to command subordinates) must be reproduced throughout the domain. It is necessary that the ideological state apparatuses reproduce these competencies and dispositions across the realm in order for the state to function at all. Althusser's primary examples of ideological state apparatuses are religious institutions and schools, although he also mentions families and courts. Crucial to our argument, he points out that ideological state apparatuses necessarily display a relative autonomy *vis-à-vis* the state. Even when they vociferously maintain their "private" or non-state status, these public assertions in no way obviate their contribution to the reproduction of the conditions of state authority. Here, Althusser references Gramsci to point out that the state is the condition of the possibility of the distinction between "public" and "private" to begin with.[8]

Buddhist monasteries and Brahmanical ashrams were not political in the sense of exercising administrative control of sizable populations in early India. They were, however, "ideological state apparatuses" to the extent that they disseminated and inculcated dispositions to centralized authority in the form of a mythological monogenesis of cosmic power. As vying ideological state apparatuses, the competing ideologies of ultimacy become both the site and the stake in the struggle for who gets to authorize state power. We should expect, then, the privilege of being designated or being able to designate the legitimating ideology to be one of the central stakes in the articulation of any ideological formulation. In this book, I have argued that emptiness and the primordial mind prior to conceptualizations were already beginning to be understood as the foundation of state ideology by the time of the *Śatapatha Brahmaṇa* and the *Maitrāyaṇīya Upaniṣad* (around the first century CE), and as such we find that meditation had already become a mechanism for the reproduction of this state ideology probably even before the *Perfection of Wisdom* was composed.

This interpretation runs counter to much of the literature on Buddhism, which treats meditation as a purely internal, non-political and psychological "experience." I do not deny that the practices of *samādhi* or *vipassanā* are technologies of self-cultivation. But in this, I think that (after the 20th century) we have been too steeped in the liberal theory coming out of Locke and Mill that renders religion to be a domain that belongs properly and *exclusively* to the internal and therefore *private* sphere. The legacy of these thinkers on American thought in general and on religious studies in particular has made it a bit difficult for us to see private meditation as having political repercussions. Suffice it to say that there is no reason to assume that our view was necessarily shared by our pre-modern South Asian authors, nor should we assume that even when meditation *was* understood to be a private affair that everyone would have understood this "private" use to contradict its importance for the "political." Indeed, as a number of recent publications amply demonstrate, the practice of meditation can be politically quite potent – precisely *because* it is understood as independent of politics. *Vipassanā* in Burma has become the preferred practice of what Ingrid Jordt[9] calls the "mass lay meditation movement," while *samādhi* is the primary practice of the Weikzas in the same country.[10] Both consider their respective practices to epitomize Buddhism, and neither lends much credence to the other. And yet, both the mass lay *vipassanā* meditation movement and the Weikzas' *samādhi* practices can be seen as a response to the loss of the Burmese monarchy, and both constitute a set of practices that legitimate or constrain the exercise of political power – albeit it in very different ways.

So what would these meditations and their realizations have meant politically in the first century? In other words, what were the political stakes of such meditations? I would like to begin with the observation that each touted object of meditation was already thoroughly political, since each meditation even in its most private moments is determined by its antagonism to its competitors. Looking at Buddhist texts alone, we see that absorptive meditations often come in a series of more and more attenuated concentrations. While there is not enough space to argue it here, there is reason to believe that there were different and competing configurations of these stages leading to the ultimate *samādhi* – with stages such as the meditation on the "sphere of nothingness" (*akiñcanāyatana*) sometimes accentuated as "ours" and sometimes accentuated as "theirs." Either way, the stages the meditator is to traverse *en route* to the ultimate goal are marked by the practices of known competitors.[11] Hence, competition with other schools of meditation and the triumphalism of a particular absorption is written into the very fabric of the meditations themselves. The absorption of nothingness, consciousness, the cessation-of-perception-and-feeling or emptiness were promoted precisely because each was at one point understood as the reality *non plus ultra*. *Samādhi* meditations were thus *always* private and *at the same time* they fossilize a record of previous debates over what is ultimate. One might say that the practice of stages of *samādhi* inscribes the intersectarian combat onto the private psyche – thereby raising the stakes of the fight in the process.

The *Uṇṇābhabrāhmaṇasutta* and the *Bṛhadāraṇyaka Upaniṣad* on cosmic foundations

The hierarchy of meditations leading to a *non plus ultra* (which thereby stops an otherwise infinite regress) is perhaps most explicitly demonstrated in the

Uṇṇābhabrāhmaṇasutta of the *Saṃyutta Nikāya*.[12] There, a Brahmin named Uṇṇābha asks the Buddha the following question: "[A]s these five [sense] faculties have different domains, different resorts, and do not experience each other's resort and domain, what is it that they take recourse in? And what is it that experiences their resort and domain?"[13] Bhikkhu Bodhi translates *paṭisaraṇa* as "to take recourse in," taking it as a form of Skt. *prati-* √*śṛ*. And indeed *paṭisaraṇa* is used most often in the Pali Canon in the sense of "refuge." In this sermon, however, we should keep in mind that the Buddha is addressing a Brahmin and that while *pratiśaraṇa* does not appear in early Brahmaṇical texts, *pratisaraṇa* (coming from *-prati* √*sṛ*) does. The latter, which would be indistinguishable from the former according to Pali phonetics, means either "leaning" or "resting upon" as well as "the streaming back (of rivers)."[14]

Thus, when Uṇṇābha notes that each of the five sense faculties have their own domain and do not register the domain of another sense faculty, we may want to read this in light of (presumably later) Nyaiyāyika and Vaiśeṣika discussions of the senses residing in the substrate of the soul.[15] The Buddha's reply, however, appears to have more affinities with the Sāṃkhya here (see *Nyāya Sūtra* 1.1.12) since he states that the five sense faculties depend on/return to "mind" (*mano*). Uṇṇābha then asks what the mind depends on/returns to. The Buddha answers that it is "mindfulness" or "memory" (P. *sati*/ Skt. *smṛti*) that mind depends on/returns to. Uṇṇābha then asks what it is that "memory" depends on/returns to. The Buddha replies that it is liberation (*vimokkha*). Uṇṇābha then asks what it is that liberation depends on/returns to. The Buddha replies that it is nirvana. When Uṇṇābha inquires what it is that nirvana depends on/returns to, the Buddha replies:

> You have gone beyond the range of questioning, brahmin. You weren't able to grasp the limit to questioning. For, brahmin, the holy life is lived with Nibbāna as its ground (*ogadha*; literally, one "becomes immersed" or "disappears" in Nibbāna), Nibbāna as its destination (*parāyaṇa*), Nibbāna as its final goal (*pariyosāna*).[16]

In this conversation with a Brahmin, we have Uṇṇābha and the Buddha engaged in a discussion, the structure of which (as in the *Nyāya Sūtra* but also in Aristotle's *On the Soul*) is typically employed to point to the ultimate substrate of the phenomenal person – i.e., the soul. But in the discussion here it is certainly *not* the case that the Brahmin asserts that such an ultimate substrate exists while the Buddha argues that it does not. On the contrary, the Buddha affirms that there is a series of such substrates, forming a kind of foundational regress whose limit is nirvana. The Brahmin is delighted to now know what the limit is and walks away satisfied with the Buddha's answer. There is no indication that he takes refuge in the Buddha or ceases any of his Brahmanical ritual obligations. Later the Buddha says that if he were to die that day he would attain liberation.

The logic here, if not the actual details, is not only similar to the *Nyāya Sūtra* passage (which again is presumably later than the *Uṇṇābha* sutra itself) but also strikingly similar to what we find in two sections of the Śukla Yajurvedin *Bṛhadāraṇyaka Upaniṣad* (which is likely to be earlier than the sutra). Both sections record debates between the Śukla Yajurvedin sage Yājñavalkya and the Ṛgvedin sage Gargī.[17] In the first (B.U. 3.6), Gargī asks him, "[S]ince this whole world is woven back and forth on water, on what, then, is water woven back and forth?" Yājñavalkya responds that it water is woven upon air. She then questions him on what air is woven upon, to which Yājñavalkya replies that it is "the intermediate regions." The two go back and forth describing a series of ever more subtle foundations, traversing the worlds of the Gandharvas, the worlds of the sun, the worlds of the moon, the worlds of the stars, the worlds of the gods, the worlds of Indra, of Prajāpati and finally the worlds of *brahman*. Similar to the Buddha, with this last question Yājñavalkya stops the series:

> At this point Yājñavalkya told her: 'Don't ask too many questions Gargī, or your head will shatter apart! You are asking too many questions about a deity about whom one should not ask too many questions. So, Gargī, don't ask too many questions!" Thereupon Gargī Vacaknavī fell silent.[18]

This passage is similar to the Buddha's discussion in its exploration of progressively more fundamental foundations. It differs from the Buddha's discussion in that the Buddha never threatens Uṇṇābha with violence. The *Saṃyutta Nikāya*'s discussion between the Buddha and the Brahmin is understood to be on friendly terms, unlike the rank competition between the Ṛgvedin and Yajurvedin Brahmins in the *Bṛhadāraṇyaka Upaniṣad*.

The competitive atmosphere becomes even more apparent in the second iteration of the contest between Gargī and Yajñāvālkya at *Bṛhadāraṇyaka Upaniṣad* 3.8. There Gargī begins by addressing the other Brahmins in the audience, saying, "Distinguished Brahmins! . . . I am going to ask this man two questions. If he can give me the answers to them, none of you will be able to defeat him in a theological debate (*brahmodya*)." She goes on, "I rise to challenge you, Yājñavalkya, with two questions, much as a fierce warrior of Kāśi or Videha, stringing his unstrung bow and taking two deadly arrows in his hand, would rise to challenge an enemy. Give me the answers to them!" She again asks what the things above the sky and below the earth as well as the things referred to as past, present and future are woven on. Similar to the last discussion, Yājñavalkya responds that they are woven onto space. However, instead of going into a longer series starting with the world of the Gandharvas, he argues (in what is perhaps a distant echo of Anaximander) that space is woven back and forth upon "the imperishable."

> This is the imperishable, Gārgī, which sees but can't be seen; which hears but can't be heard; which thinks but can't be thought of; which perceives but can't be perceived. Besides this imperishable, there is no one that sees, no one that hears, no one that thinks and no one that perceives.[19]

To this Gargī proclaims, "Distinguished Brahmins! . . . You should consider yourself lucky of your escape from this man by merely paying him your respects. None of you will ever defeat him in a theological debate (*brahmodya*)." Clearly in both this as well as in the previous section of the *Bṛhadāraṇyaka Upaniṣad* we have a dialogue between two learned interlocutors attempting to outdo one another in laying out the ultimate foundation or ground that undergirds and underwrites all contingent things. The ultimate ground can be arrived at through discussion, but cannot be surpassed by discussion. However, where the discussion between the Buddha and Uṇṇābha was amicable, the discussion between Gargī and Yajñāvalkya is contentious. More to the point, the genre placement here is specifically that of a "debate" – with two contestants each seeking victory in front of an audience of other competitors who witness the success or failure of the two contestants.

Key to the *Sitz im Leben* is Gargī's characterization of the debate as *brahmodya*. *Brahmodya*, or *brahmavāda* ("discussing brahman") are usually just rendered as "debates about *brahman*" or even "theological debates," and even though there was no rancor, I believe the *Uṇṇābhabrahmanasutta* to fall into the same genre. But to call them "theological debates" misses something of their social significance. I will grant that some *brahmodya*, like the Gargī debate in the *Bṛhadāraṇyaka Upaniṣad* example, are represented as freeform debates taking place in some non-specific location or perhaps in the court of a king (such as that of Janaka elsewhere in the *Bṛhadāraṇyaka*). However, the paradigmatic *brahmodyas* were scripted sets of questions and answers with prearranged victors taking place during a major sacrifice such as the paradigmatic *brahmodya* that occurs immediately before the climactic suffocation of the horse in the *aśvamedha* (Horse Sacrifice) coronation rite. According to the *Mānava Śrautasūtra* of the Maitrāyaṇīyas, the following exchange occurs immediately after the anointing of the horse and right *before* the binding of the horse for suffocation and the kindling of the sacrificial fire:

> The *hotṛ* and the brahman interrogate each other with question and response, on either side of the post facing the fire, with the verses: "Who moves alone? Who too is born again? What is a remedy for the cold? What is the large receptacle? The Sun moves alone. The moon is born again. The fire is the remedy for the cold. The earth is the large receptacle. *What was the first notion?* What was the great age? Who was the tawny one? Who was the smooth one? Heaven was the first notion. The horse was the great age. The night was the tawny one. The ewe was the smooth one." (Emphasis mine)[20]

The *Taittirīya Saṃhitā* has the identical set of verses but reverses the two sets of questions starting with the question about the "first notion" or better yet "that which is prior to thought" (*pūrvacitta*), followed by the questions beginning "Who moves alone?" This may have been the original ordering of the verses, since this order also occurs in the *Baudhāyana Śrautasūtra*,[21] which Fushimi argues is among the earliest *śrautasūtras*[22] (or at least the earliest to deal with the Horse Sacrifice), and also in the *Āpastamba Śrautasūtra* of the Taittirīyas.[23] Finally, the *Āpastamba* account also differs from the *Mānava Śrautasūtra* by the fact that it concludes with the terse statement that, "They accept the victory of the Brahman at the end."[24]

Despite the fact that the "debate" is scripted and its winner is predetermined, the declaration of victory in the *Āpastamba Śrautasūtra* was a declaration made to an audience – namely those members of the court and their allies who were invited to witness the sacrifice. It was a public and ritual declaration, displaying that the very same priest who held authority over other priests in the ritual and who ultimately coronates the king is the same one who directly knows the ultimate ground of the cosmos – i.e., *that which is prior to even thought itself*. Indeed, I believe that in the *Maitrāyaṇīya Upaniṣad's acitta brahman* (i.e., *brahman* [in whom there is yet] "no thought"), we have a Kṛṣṇa Yajurvedin explanation of the compound "*pūrvacittaṃ*" – a line that would have been uttered in hundreds of such coronation ceremonies over the past two millennia.

Thus, when we find a struggle between different religious groups to identify and articulate that which is most ultimate, one possible prize would have been the right for one's lineage to occupy the site where the Brahmana priest sits near the sacrificial stakes (*yūpa*) during the Horse Sacrifice.[25] Of course, as in the *Uṇṇābhabrāhmaṇa* case, or even that of Gargī, *brahmodya* debates could take place anywhere. But the prototype would have been the *brahmodya* during the Piling of the Fire Altar or Horse Sacrifice. Thus the site of philosophic battle also happened to be its "stakes" (sorry – I couldn't resist the pun).

This seat would have not only a position of highest prestige and authority, but eventually would have also been tied to lucrative land grants and tax immunities. Though I will have much more to say about these passages and the connections of meditation to coronation in a subsequent publication, suffice it to say here that the first question in the debate at the centerpiece of the Horse Sacrifice is "what is *prior to thought*." This is precisely what both the Buddha and Uṇṇābha as well as Gargī and Yajñavalkya are each trying to arrive at.

Liturgically speaking, the *brahmodya* (whether or not they were actually "debates") amounted to a public display of knowledge – not only about the ultimate font of the cosmos, but about the archaic origins of the sacrifice itself (and perhaps more importantly, of its patron). The *brahmodyas* as liturgical element are thus self-referential, albeit a legitimating self-reference. Since the *brahmodya*, along with the layered sacrificial platforms referenced in discussions of yoga, were key features of rituals of coronation, the ability to claim knowledge of an ultimate ground of legitimation (i.e., one that could not be trumped by a competing priesthood through debate or meditation) should be seen as a desiderata *of the court*. So instead of understanding Buddhists as eschewing the contest between Brahmanical groups to propose an unassailable royal ideology, I am arguing that early Mahāyāna was an attempt by one group of Brahmins to *win* the contest. While it is doubtful (though I am sure stranger things have happened) that an ordained Buddhist monk would have been called on to perform a ritual like the Horse Sacrifice,[26] it should be remembered that many dynasts did not have to perform these sacrifices. The mere fact that an ancestor had performed it would be sufficient for the dynasty to be authorized. But in order to extend the legitimating effect of the ritual, the court would have to maintain an expert who somehow embodied the cosmic and/or mythological truth on which the ritual was grounded. Both yogis and monks could embody and therefore signify the cosmic right to rule through displays of meditation on (and hence direct, unmediated knowledge) that truth.

The Horse Sacrifice

If our group of Mahāyāna Brahmins was active in the first and second centuries CE, they would have been interested in a kind of court ritual that (in the form that we now have it) might have only been around for about 200 years. As such, the image of emptiness or primordial mind touted by our early Mahāyānists would have been developing in tandem with this new form of political liturgy. It will be worth a bit of a detour to examine how the ritual worked and how ideas of emptiness and mind might have come into play within it.

The earliest record of a historical king performing the Horse Sacrifice was Puṣyamitra, who performed several in the second century BCE.[27] But as G. R. Sharma has demonstrated, he probably also performed a *puruṣamedha* or "human sacrifice" employing Taittirīya priests at Kauśambi.[28] In the first century BCE Hāthīgumphā inscription (l. 6), the Jain King Khāravela declares that he performed the "Royal Unction" or *rājasūya*.[29] His contemporary Śri Satkarṇi and his wives (esp. Nāganika) performed the Horse Sacrifice, presumably to legitimate and inaugurate their rival Sātavāhana Dynasty.[30] The Horse Sacrifice may well have also been performed by Cāntamūla I of the Ikṣvākus, possibly in the citadel at Nāgārjunakoṇḍa.

Of course, not every dynasty or king was installed with such as ceremony. Not a few kings (Rajuvula included) designated today as "Śāka" or "Kuṣāna" would have come closer to Achaemenid court practices and rituals. But it was the practice of Persian and Persian-inflected court cultures from the Ptolemies in Egypt to the Kuṣanas in India to legitimate their rule through visible patronage of *local* political theologies[31] – regardless of their own inaugurating religion. Thus, Kaṇiṣka may have been coronated with legitimating reference to Ahura Mazda, but in order to rule in India, the gods legitimating his reign had to simultaneously be understood as the gods who legitimated local authorities – as witnessed by the interlinear "translation" of Zoroastrian gods into their Indic "equivalents" in the Rabatak inscription.[32] Though there is no evidence of a royal sacrifice at Mathura, the time period that we have been looking at for the composition of the early *Perfection of Wisdom in 8,000 Lines* was precisely the time at Mathura when Buddhism, Brahmanism and Jainism were rising in visibility while beginning to absorb the local tutelary divinities (*yakṣas* and *nāgas*) cults that had been dominant prior to the first century.[33] By the third century, the ideology of ultimacy set forth in the Vedas and the *śrautasūtras* was on prominent display in an inscribed stone replica of a sacrificial post, recording the performance of a 12-day *sattra* (a sacrifice only for priests) by a certain "Drōṇala . . . of the Bhāradvāja [sic] gotra."[34] If kings chose not to access this legitimating authority by performing major *śrauta* sacrifices themselves, perhaps they sought its closest equivalent by patronizing Buddhist (or Buddhist Brahmin) virtuosos who had direct knowledge of its underlying principle.

Later on, the Horse Sacrifice was so important for the Gupta Dynasty that several of the early dynasts from Skandagupta on issued coins displaying the name of the emperor on one side and a picture of his chief wife holding a needle standing next to a horse.[35] If Buddhists objected to these Horse Sacrifices, they must have done so quietly. Puṣyamitra was certainly not very beloved by later Buddhist generations, but the Sātavāhanas who performed a number of them and the Ikṣvākus (or at least their queens) were. Puṣyamitra is taken to task by later Buddhist authors for many things, but neither Puṣyamitra nor any of these other dynasts are criticized by Buddhist authors for performing the Horse Sacrifice.

The reason for this silence may be that there was always a prominent contingent of Brahmin Buddhists who understood Buddhism to be very much a part of the culture of philosophical inquiry into ultimate authority that was being played out in the royal courts as part of the legitimation of sovereign rule. So instead of looking to Buddhism and Brahmanism as two distinct religions competing for the personal commitment of private citizens, we might have an easier time explaining how these religions came to take on the features that they did if we understand their formation within a court sacrificial culture that was undergirded by the prominent display of philosophical debate. In other words, as infrequently as these major sacrifices would have been performed, in early Indian court culture philosophy and sacrifice would have been understood to complement one another. We saw in the *Uṇṇābhasutta* that canonical Buddhist texts (or at least those circulating among Brahmin communities) were no stranger to these *brahmodya*. Today, the conventional wisdom seems to be that Buddhism was anti-ritual or at least anti-sacrifice. If so, then early Buddhist authors certainly knew a lot of very specific details about the Vedic *śrauta* sacrifices.[36] More to the point, while there are sutras critical of the performance of *śrauta* sacrifices, there are others in which the Buddha refuses to judge sacrifices or even on occasion condones aspects of Brahmanical ritual culture.[37] Since there are, by my count, only nine sutras (out of over 5,000)[38] in the Pali Canon that criticize the violence performed in these major sacrifices, we can assume that it would be quite possible for early monks and nuns to ignore or simply not emphasize this aspect of canonical teaching – especially if they, like Nāgārjuna, had close patron-client relations with a sovereign whose line was so authorized.

The ways that Buddhist authors drew on the legitimating authority of these rites becomes a bit clearer when we get into the details of the coronation rites employed at the time. I will discuss a few key features of the Horse Sacrifice as the culturally paradigmatic and prototypical example of the construction of sovereign power,[39] although it should be kept in mind that large-scale sacrificial rituals such as the Horse Sacrifice were composite rites that included other rites (such as the Piling of the Fire Altar or *agnicayana* and numerous *pravargya* rites) in full.

The Horse Sacrifice is a yearlong rite in which a horse is sent running followed by an army (in the *Mānava Śrautasūtra* of the Maitrāyaṇīyas, the army is to consist of 100 armored sons of the king's bed).[40] Wherever the horse goes, the patron/sovereign declares that territory to be his domain. Significantly, according to the *Āpastamba Śrautasūtra*, the military conquest is also an ideological conquest of the branch of Brahmins chosen to orchestrate the sacrifice. As the army progresses we are told,

> Whomsoever born as a Brahmin they meet, they should ask him "How much do you know of the Aśvamedha?" Having conquered him who does not know they may put (in front of the horse having forcefully taken from him) the food (fodder) and drink.[41]

In short, the territory conquered by the military was simultaneously understood to be the territory dominated by the ideology of the priestly lineage chosen to orchestrate the sacrifice.

The king's authority within the rite clearly draws on the performance of a very martial masculinity, highlighted by the army as well as the slaughter of many (oh so many) animals when the horse returns. Particularly important for Buddhist/court relations are the ways in which the king's (hyper)sexual masculinity are framed throughout the sacrificial year. On the one hand, the king's sexual fertility is highlighted by the fact that the 100 sons are "of his couch." But having established his fertility by the parading of the army of his offspring (anyone who is a parent to even one son will be suspicious that the number 100 is rank hyperbole here), other portions of the ritual aim to put into high relief that his virility is indexed by the superhuman fecundity that he is *not* using. In the *Kātyāyana Śrautasūtra*[42] we are told that he is to sleep every night for a year on the sacrificial platform (a rather public setting) between the thighs of his favorite wife observing (and presumably being observed practicing) celibacy all the while. Indeed the theme of seminal retention pervades the rite. In all versions, the horse is not to have sex for a year (making, at least, in the Śukla Yajurveda version, the king's penis parallel to that of the horse).[43] But perhaps the most memorable portion of the sacrifice[44] is the point where the horse is suffocated and the chief queen has either actual[45] or implied[46] sex with the then tumescent, dead horse. The *Mānava Śrautasūtra* has the queen state, "May I procure pregnancy,"[47] and yet she (in all versions) has just censored the horse for not satisfying her. While all of this is going on, the king is standing by and watching.

One suspects that the overt and very public (there appears to be quite a few members of the court in attendance) performance of sex with the horse serves several purposes simultaneously. Probably the most important purpose of this spectacle was to provide a very visible demonstration of which queen was chief queen and which queens were subordinate. Royal polygamy was essential to cement alliances, but would have been problematic in determining dynastic succession in which there can only be one heir apparent. The Horse Sacrifice foregrounds one and only one wife as the chief queen so that her subsequent son (framed here as the son of a stallion) will already be known as the legitimate successor. If primogeniture were the key to the succession of authority, it would have been important to frame the superlative qualities of not only the father but the mother as well. The queen is presented here not only as chosen by the king, but as having superhuman sexual capacities[48] insofar as she can have sex with a horse. But the prodigious sexuality of the queen also frames or highlights the sex that the king is *not* having. If the queen's feminine virtuosity is demonstrated by her ability to engage a mate of superhuman proportions, then the king's *über*-masculinity is publicized by his demonstrated (superhuman) seminal retention. How does one demonstrate an absence? Through a jarring juxtaposition with its opposite, namely sex.

Piling the Fire Altar and legitimation regress

If the Horse Sacrifice frames the founding dynastic couple in terms of superhuman fecundity, the rite itself is grounded in the legitimating authority of hoary antiquity. This is not immediately apparent in the script of the Horse Sacrifice itself, but comes out in the details of the *agnicayana* ritual that forms a part of the Horse Sacrifice (and thus is abbreviated in the *Śrautasūtra* descriptions of the latter). The *agnicayana* or "Piling of the Fire Altar," like the Horse Sacrifice that comes to incorporate it, was a rite of kingship. Theodore Proferes points out that:

> According to the *Śatapatha Brāhmaṇa* (9.3.4.8–9) one should perform first the Rājasūya, [royal unction] in order to become king (*rājan*), while one should perform the Vājapeya ["drink of strength" rite] after it, in order to become a supreme king (*samrāj*). The Agnicayana is to be performed, then, only after one has performed a Rājasūya and a Vājapeya, because the unction of the Agnicayana surpasses the unction of the other and transforms the great king into "the Whole", which includes being king and being supreme king.[49]

As discussed in Chapter 8, the *Śatapatha Brāhmaṇa* begins its commentary on the *agnicayana* with a creation account that (adapting the *Nāsadīyasukta,* Ṛg X.129)[50] opens with the phrase, "In the beginning there was nothing." This "nothing" turns out to be the seven Ṛṣis, who combine to form Puruṣa of the *Puruṣasukta* (Ṛg X.90). In this account, however, instead of the cosmos being fashioned out of the dismembered parts of Puruṣa, Puruṣa emits the different parts of creation from himself and is thereby spent to the point of disintegration.

> 6.1.2.12. Having created creatures he, having run the whole race, became relaxed; and therefore even now he who runs the whole race becomes indeed relaxed. From him being thus relaxed, the vital air went out from within. When it had gone out of him the gods left him.
>
> 13. He said to Agni, 'Restore me!' – 'What will then accrue to me?' said he. – 'They shall call me after thee; for whichever of the sons succeeds (in life), after him they call the father, grandfather, son, and grandson: they shall call me after thee, – restore me, then!' – 'So be it!' so (saying) Agni restored him: therefore, while being Prajāpati, they call him Agni; and verily, whosoever knows this, after him they call his father, grandfather, son, and grandson.

and later:

> 26. Now that father (Prajāpati) is (also) the son: inasmuch as he created Agni, thereby he is Agni's father; and inasmuch as Agni restored him, thereby Agni is his (Prajāpati's) father; and inasmuch as he created the gods, thereby he is the father of the gods; and inasmuch as the gods restored him, thereby the gods are his fathers.
>
> 27. Twofold verily is this, – father and son, Prajāpati and Agni, Agni and Prajāpati, Prajāpati and the gods, the gods and Prajāpati – (for) whosoever knows this.[51]

As a frame-story, this account of the *śrauta* sacrifice by which a man and his wives become authorized with sovereign authority grounds the sacrifice in the very fabric of the cosmos itself and its creation out of nothing. Drawing on an amalgam of themes pulled largely from the *Puruṣasukta* (*Ṛg* X. 90) the *Hiraṇyagarbhasukta* (*Ṛg* X. 121) and the *Nāsadīyasukta* (*Ṛg* X.129), the *Śatapatha Brāhmaṇa* casts the sacrifice, and by extension the sacrificer's dominion in terms of "becoming one with everything."[52] As Prajāpati, the sacrificer is identical not only with the extent of the cosmos but with its very advent. As father of all offspring, his is a preeminence that cannot be preempted.

As mentioned above, the Horse Sacrifice with its *agnicayana* was performed to inaugurate a dynasty. Subsequent dynasts were not expected to perform the rite since they merely had to reference the fact that they were descended from the founder of the dynasty who did perform the rite. By definition, the beginning of a dynasty has to establish the authority of the dynast *de novo*. Pragmatically speaking, the beginning of a dynasty is by definition the moment when there is no prior authority from which the authority of the upstart lord can be derived. The *Śatapatha Brāhmaṇa* rather cleverly transforms this awkward moment in which the dynasty has no history and its law no precedent into a moment of (cosmic) creation – which likewise had nothing preceding it. In so doing, the current regime is presented as having (and needing) no prior authorization because it precedes all other possible authority. The upstart dynasty thus becomes the ancestor of them all precisely because it has no precedent.

Unlike the *Puruṣasukta*, the *Śatapatha Brahmaṇa* is not content merely to ground the sacrifice in some primordial father-son-father strange loop. It simultaneously keys the *Nāsadīyasukta* of the *Ṛg Veda* (*Ṛg* X. 129) in order to articulate the ground of the sacrifice in such a way that it is impossible to even think of that which precedes it. The *Chandogya Upaniṣad* (a Sāmaveda Upaniṣad) gets grumpy about those who think that in the beginning there was nothing. As I will argue in a later publication, I think that there is good reason to believe that it was the Yajurvedins, and especially the Taittirīyas, with whom the Chandogyas were arguing. But it is in the *Nāsadīyasukta* itself that we find an early attempt to preempt both those who held that the first thing was Being and those who held it was Non-being by stating that, "The non-existent did not exist, nor did the existent exist at that time."[53] The "One" that existed and on which the cosmos and the sacrifice are founded was that which existed prior to existence and non-existence. So what could possibly exist prior to existence and non-existence? The answer which is implicit in the *Nāsādīyasukta* and, as Joel Brereton shows, is made explicit in the *Śatapatha Brāhmaṇa* treatment of this verse in the "Secrets of the *Agnicayana*" section, begins:

> Verily, in the beginning this (universe) was, as it were, neither non-existent nor existent; in the beginning this (universe), indeed, as it were, existed and did not exist: There was then only that Mind.
>
> Wherefore it has been said by the Ṛṣi [Vedic sage/Vedic author] (*Ṛg-veda* X. 129.1), 'There was then neither the non-existent nor the existent'; for Mind was, as it were, neither existent nor non-existent.'[54]

Here, it is Mind that is prior to existence and non-existence, since mind is the condition for the distinction between existence and non-existence. For our purposes, the really interesting part of the *Nāsadīyasukta* occurs in the third verse, which describes the first moment of creation. MacDonnell translates it as, "That which, coming into being, was covered with the void, that One arose through the power of heat."[55] The sticky point is the word that MacDonnell translates as "coming into being," *ābhū*. According to Brereton:

> in 3c there appears something called an *ābhú*, a term that, like the object it describes, is resolutely indeterminate. The semantic and grammatical functions of the word are unclear-it has been translated as an adjective, as an abstract noun, or as a concrete noun -but more significantly, it has two possible derivations. It could be from *a* (privative) + *bhū* and thereby describe something "not become," or it could be related to *ā* + *bhū* "come into being." Thus, the word could imply non-existence, or it could imply just the opposite, a coming into existence. The context surely favors the more usual derivation from *ā* + *bhū* "come into being." In 2c, the One suddenly emerged, and therefore we would expect there to be a something at the corresponding position in 3c. On the other hand, in vs. 3 the *ābhú* is described as concealed in emptiness, just as darkness is hidden in darkness in line *a*. As the core and the covering in line *a* are both forms of darkness, so those hearing the hymn could have imagined the core and covering in line *c* to be forms of emptiness. For this interpretation, a meaning "empty" for *ābhú* would be more appropriate. Thus the possibilities for interpreting *ābhú* as something "coming into being" and as something "empty" make this a word which embodies the ambiguous situation the verse describes, a state hovering between non-existence and existence.[56]

If we are faced with a choice as to whether to interpret *ābhū* as non-existence or as coming-into-being then, presumably, so were early interpreters of this hymn. A Yajurvedin Brahmin might wish to take 3c as describing a state in which "*that which was non-existent was concealed in emptiness*" – a construction that echoes the "darkness hidden by darkness, in the beginning" of 3a. The first act of creation, then, would occur in the transition from 3c to 3d. If we take the *yat/tad* as a relative correlative construction, then the second half of verse 3 reads, "The non-existent [one] which was concealed by emptiness; that one was born through the power of tapas." The point here is worth emphasizing. Here we have the original non-existence on the very verge of creation described as a "non-existent concealed by emptiness" (*tuchyéna-ābhv ápihitaṃ yád āsīt*). It has been one of the central concerns of this book to show that Brahmin Buddhists would have understood themselves to have been in competition with other Brahmins to prove that they had direct access to (and direct knowledge of) precisely this One mind/emptiness. It was in the context of the rising *śrauta* sutras that this originary emptiness/Mind would have been very publically operationalized in the form of an inaugural sacrifice.

Buddhist Brahmins

We should not get too concerned that the term for emptiness is *tuchya* instead of *śūnya*, since the former term seems to have gone out of vogue in Sanskrit by the time of the *Upaniṣads*, largely to be replaced by the latter as witnessed by early lexicons such as the *Amarakośa* that list *śūnya* as a synonym for "*tuccha*".[57] Moreover, it appears that later Vedic specialists began to associate the term *śūnya* with the point of cosmic origin spelled out in the *Nāsadīyasukta* rather than with Buddhism. The *Maitrāyaṇīya Upaniṣad* is perhaps the earliest text to use the term *śūnya* to describe both the unmanifest *brahman* (or *brahman prior* to manifestation) and the soul of one who has realized *brahman*.[58] But even a non-Maitrāyaṇīya such as Sāyaṇa (writing in 13th-century Vijaynagar) glosses "non-existence" (*asat*) as "*śūnyaṃ*" in his sub-commentary on the *Taittirīya Brāhmaṇa*'s commentary on the *Nāsadīyasukta*.[59]

In context, then, emptiness, just like Mind and "neither existence nor non-existence," was put forth (especially by Buddhist and non-Buddhist Brahmins of the Kṛṣṇa Yajurveda schools) as an attempt to posit an ultimate ground ("*brahman*") or origin of creation that could not be outstripped insofar as it preempts any attempt to think what could come before it. The idea of this primal *brahman* frames and grounds not only the king/patron, but also the priests who sought to inaugurate these dynasties from at least the time of Puṣyamitra onward. The vanishing point of Vedic cosmogony (vanishing, insofar as it retreats beyond both existence and non-existence) thus came to be understood as the ultimate ground of proximate authority.

Thus, "the debates about the foundation" of the cosmos (*brahmodya*) that we find in the court of Janaka in the *Bṛhadaraṇyaka Upaniṣad* and elsewhere were NOT idle speculations on the origins of things to satisfy the whimsy of idle curiosity. The fact that the king was ultimately the judge determining who won the debate suggests that such matters were crucial to his position – a suggestion confirmed by the fact that at the apex of the activity of the yearlong Horse Sacrifice, immediately before the suffocation of the horse[60] and the subsequent activity with the queen, all action stops and the Brahmins sit down and have a (usually scripted) debate about the origin of things and the secrets of the sacrifice. At the conclusion of the *brahmodya*, the *Āpastamba Śrautasūtra* at least tells us the *brahmana* priest is said to win.[61] Rivalries between priestly lineages (with their proprietary solutions to the regress problem) could map onto rivalries between kingdoms once a priestly lineage was adopted in the court as either the court *ṛtvij* or *purohita* – as happened in the fourth century when the imperial Guptas began patronizing the Maitrāyaṇīyas possibly due to the prevalence of the Taittirīyas among the Vākāṭakas to the south.[62]

On power and reproduction

Why do we find these intersections between yogic absorptions and political sacrifices? And if meditation is ultimately political, then why is it so often presented as a personal, private activity taking place far from human habitation in caves or under the roots of trees? Wouldn't the institution of the forest monk, so central to several discussions of early Mahāyāna, contradict the importance of these meditations for the court? If the king is to be crowned with legitimating reference to an idea of cosmic origin, why is it important to have a group of priests meditating on it in caves far away from the court? The most obvious answer is the risk of ritual failure. The growing body of literature on ritual failure suggests that not only was the failure of ritual to achieve its stated or intended goals *not* considered an aberration, but the fact of failure was necessary in order for its success to carry weight. As Webb Keane has pointed out, what is often at stake in ritual is for the framing of the ritual actors to be properly recognized. Failure, then, would be the misrecognition of the ritual and its statements by the target audience. In this case, the ritual of coronation of the king seeks to ground its sacrifices in the sacrifice of Prajāpati and the cosmic One/Mind prior to existence or non-existence. Ritual success would be for the king's authority to in fact be recognized as grounded in cosmic origins.

There are, however, many ways this ritual and its liturgical elements could be misrecognized. One concern that shows up in a number of upaniṣads is that a priest's ritual utterances might be understood to be mere words, uttered with no understanding whatsoever.[63] Any middle-schooler can tell you that "$E=mc^2$." But without being able to derive it, these words are merely the parroting of adult speech. The middle-schooler may be correct in her utterance, but have no authority in uttering it due to a lack of mathematical expertise and intimate knowledge of working with the formula. In the case of the *śrauta* sacrifices, the risk is that the audience (the court, the public, etc.) might misrecognize the ritual as being mere flowery or poetic words with no substance or truth behind them. Meditation, then, would be the liturgical equivalent of being able to personally derive $E=mc^2$, or in this case, demonstrating a direct and personal knowledge of the statements one utters in the ritual. Granted, there is still risk involved. The audience may see the priest or members of the priestly lineage going off to caves or secluded spots to sit still for hours, but no one can know whether or not the yogi is actually meditating or composing a grocery list. But when enough people are seen to practice the way that the texts such as the *Śvetāśvatara Upaniṣad* recommends, the chances that any individual yogi would be recognized to be directly experiencing a transcendent reality would be greater than if no one meditated at all.

But when we get to multiple yogis within the Yajurveda lineages practicing meditation, aren't we are moving away from the sacrificial platform itself and moving into the private domain? Here is where Althusser is particularly helpful. According to Althusser, ideology is not merely about the construction of power; it is also about the *reproduction* of the means of production of power. We are now ready to get more specific about what is reproduced with religion. Authority must be recognized in order to exist, but the recognition (as opposed to the misrecognition) of authority is not automatic. The cultural competencies to recognize the signs of legitimacy and authority must be actively disseminated and inculcated into the populace to be ruled.

The biggest obstacle to achieving this goal is distance and topography. The Horse Sacrifice may frame the king and queen's martial and gendered power quite forcefully, but it nevertheless does so only *locally*. No matter how far the army roams, the fact remains that most of the ritual action of the coronation would have taken place within a relatively miniscule area in comparison with the dominion it lays claim to. The problem, then, is not so much how to *produce* the structures of legitimation but how to *reproduce* and thus naturalize them across a wide geographical area and up into the harder to reach higher elevations. If I claim to be coronated by the legitimating authority of the Big Begonia in the Sky, it is not enough for the coronating priest to wax eloquent about it in a 100 x 100 ft. room filled with my family members. The people whom I rule from Des Moines to Lubbock, Texas have to *already* believe that: a) there is a Big Begonia in the Sky and that b) it is something that meaningfully confers monarchial rule, in order to: c) successfully assert that I have the mandate of the Big B. The task of the priesthood is to spread the legitimating ideology and the corresponding dispositions toward obedience *independent of any potentially undermining connection to the regime to be legitimated*, and to ingrain the idea of its legitimacy among the general public long before performing any coronation of a particular individual. Skandagupta could mint and circulate coins commemorating his Horse Sacrifice, only because he could assume that the general public *already* had the cultural competencies to recognize that the horse, the naked queen and the needle had something to do with his legitimacy.

The various legitimating features of the Horse Sacrifice could not simply be replicated across the realm by coins. It was the religious apparatuses of the various priesthoods that inculcated the competencies necessary to recognize monarchial authority among the populace across the empire. For example, the king's seminal retention could hardly have been recognized as a display of authoritative hyper-masculinity unless the subject population was already prepared to read it as such. Think about it. If a US president announced that he was going to retain his semen for a year, it is doubtful that his subsequent approval rating would show him much love. On the contrary, celibate masculinity had to *already* be a thing before any king could tap into it – and making it a thing would have to involve a propaganda campaign that would probably never be complete. Somebody had to continuously exert effort to inculcate the "proper" dispositions to celibacy across the target populations and constituencies. I am arguing that this would have been facilitated by the practice and display of temporary and full celibacy by religious practitioners everywhere from urban to remote reaches of the empire.

Now, we might want to see the stricture of celibacy as a merely personal remedy for the nuisance of sexual desire, but by the logic that legitimated the sovereignty of the major dynasties after the second century BCE, celibacy was *not* about the ending of sexual desire. First of all, celibacy is not obviously the opposite of sexual desire – on the contrary, it takes little imagination to see how sexual desire might be more of a problem for celibates than for married folk. Rather, in light of the logic of the Horse Sacrifice, we may now want to think of celibacy as the demonstration of a kind of hyper-masculinity – one exampled in the sovereign and trumped only by the monk who is celibate for life.

Sovereign echoes: on manhood and celibacy, on thrones and crowns

So what evidence is there for Buddhist monasteries inculcating the dispositions toward power and authority that were being deployed in the royal court and its sacrifices? In an article discussing the rule for the rehabilitation of a monk who has sex, Shayne Clarke compares the setting for this rule in the *Mahāsāṅghikavinaya* to that of the *Mūlasarvāstivādavinaya*. The case in question concerns a certain monk Nandika, who was renowned for his intense practice of meditation. In the Mahāsāṅghika version of the story,[64] seeing Nandika's accomplishments, a female member of Māra's retinue took the form of a beautiful woman and attempted to seduce Nandika. Nandika could resist for only so long and eventually jumped up from meditation to chase after her. What follows is somewhat less than intuitive:

> The goddess quickly departed. Nandika chased her to the Jetavana moat. In the moat (or pit) there was a dead royal horse (塹中有王家死馬). The goddess went to where the dead horse was and hid her form so she was invisible. Then, Nandika, ablaze with lustful thoughts, thereupon had sex with the dead horse. His lustful thoughts having been assuaged, he thereupon reflected this, I have been exceedingly bad and [have acted] contrary to the Dharma of a *śramaṇa*. With faith have I left home [for the religious life,] but I have committed a *pārājika* offense [i.e., the class of the most grievious monastic offenses]. I have worn the Dharma-robes and eaten food donated in faith by other people.[65]

Nandika breaks the first *pārājika* rule not by just having sex, but by having sex with a dead horse floating in a moat or a pit. When he comes to his senses, his regret is simply that he had sex. Apparently, the fact that he had sex with a large animal carcass floating in presumably less than potable water did not significantly add to his overall discomfort. One feels here that the same point could have been made (as it is in the *Mūlasarvāstivāda* parallel) by Nandika simply having sex with the goddess or some other person.

So why the sex with the dead horse? And why is it a *royal* horse floating in a moat? Couldn't the point have been made with just any old horse carcass? This passage really only makes sense against the backdrop of the Horse Sacrifice and the framing of the King's celibacy within it. If the Horse Sacrifice constituted the liturgical construction of power *par excellence*, then it should not be surprising to see subsidiary institutions such as monasteries attempt to replicate the structures of authority legitimating the dynasties in which they find themselves. Thus, when Nandika commits the first *pārājika* offense and has sex, he is no longer hyper-masculine *like the sovereign at the Horse Sacrifice*, but his gender is rather deliberately mis-recognized and inverted to that of the queen, who does have sex with the dead horse. While the queen's gender virtues may be augmented by this association, power is always gender-specific and reading Nandika as the queen only highlights his distance from the masculine power of the king. Thus, the Buddhists in embracing celibacy were not thereby resisting some universal Brahmanical order, but were rather disseminating and naturalizing its mark of sovereignty so that it might be universally recognized when the king performs it in the legitimation of his rule.

The situation with celibacy is parallel to the Buddhists' dissemination of the idea of the *uṣṇīṣa* as a kind of crown[66] or of the royal throne. As I have argued at length elsewhere,[67] the throne (especially the 'lion throne') was introduced to India by Vima Kadphises in the second or third century CE as one of his signs of sovereignty. Yasuhiro Tsuchiyama has argued that the throne was not originally part of the ritual paraphernalia of the Atharvan coronation ceremony but was introduced in the ancillary literature of the Maitrāyaṇīya Yajurvedins, such as the *Mānava* and the *Vārāha Śrautasūtras*.[68] Buddhists also adopted the throne not only into their stories of the Buddha and eminent monks but also as a pulpit in monasteries throughout the land. By the Gupta Dynasty, the *vinayas* or Buddhist monastic codes assume every Buddhist monastery would have had a lion throne from which Buddhist sermons would have been delivered. The presence of a religious authority evangelizing his sect's proprietary blend of ultimate truth in cities and villages across the sub-continent would have reproduced and disseminated the idea of the authority of "the throne" so that when kings sat on them, the public would already know how to correctly "decode" its significance, and more importantly: authority.

The fact that religious virtuosi and texts from time to time make a display of being distinct or indifferent to political concerns and stakes is not really an argument that they were not essential to the exercise of political authority. The function of ideological state apparatuses is to reproduce the signs of sovereignty and the competencies to properly recognize them. To do so, however, religious institutions must simultaneously inculcate a misrecognition of their political valence. If the lion throne in the monastery were not *independently* established as an authorizing frame of authority, then it would do little to contribute to the recognition of the king's authority. If, however, a strong distinction is *not* made between the monastic lion throne and the king's throne, then every abbot in the land would in fact contest the king's authority when preaching a sermon. But the fact of the matter is, that while religions reproduce the capacity to recognize sovereign power, they simultaneously inculcate the misrecognition of or taboo concerning the identification between the religious and the political. Christians may pray to "the Lord," but few of them think of "Lord" as a political term – despite the fact that it obviously is. The activity of praying to "the Lord" can authorize "lords" of estates,[69] if and only if the direct connection between the two is misrecognized.

Of course, Buddhists were not the only ones attempting to disseminate the competencies to properly decode monarchial authority and probably most Indian dynasts welcomed all the help they could get. From one point of view, Brahmin priests were so successful in propagating the idea of Vedic-based ritual and the liturgical construction of status through education of the top three castes that they almost taught their way out of a job. There arose a class of educated laity who were capable of performing their own household rituals, based in part on Vedic models and in part on local customs. In performing their own private and domestic echoes of Vedic rites, the laity across the domain were reproducing and internalizing the cultural competencies necessary to decode the royal ritual down to its most subtle nuances. This, of course, was great from the standpoint of the need to inculcate recognition of the king. It wasn't so great for the hereditary priesthood since it lent credence to the idea that anyone with a Vedic education had the authority to perform a ritual.

Who or what would authorize these rituals? Matthew Sayers[70] points out that during this time the role of the Brahmin was slowly changing from *śrauta* priest to that of a guest at domestic sacrifices. This shift is particularly evident in the funeral ceremonies, which fall under the *śrauta* rites in the *Mānava Śrautasūtra* but are householder rites in the *Gṛhasutras* of other Vedic branches. In particular, he notes that if a householder wished to establish his dead relatives as ancestors and then feed them regularly, he would have to perform certain regular sacrifices. These self-performed rituals would have been legitimated by a Brahmin guest at the rite who would then confirm to the ritual audience that the ancestors had indeed been fed. What enabled the Brahmin guest to place his imprimatur on the ritual? It was not just his Brahmin caste status, but his *learning*. The *Gṛhasūtras* assert that it is not enough for the Brahmin to simply be a Brahmin by birth: the efficacy of the sacrifice was indexed to the learning of the Brahmanical guest.

With the advent of the *Gṛha* version of the *piṇḍa* or "rice ball" ceremony and its stress on feeding a meal to a learned Brahmin guest, we have every reason to assume that Brahmin Buddhists were qualified to sit as "guests" (i.e., the embodiment of the sacrificial fire) at these rituals, and indeed they would have been obligated to do so at the very least for their own relatives. But if the emphasis was on knowledge as a ritual qualification and less on birth, then the door was open for monks of other castes to argue that knowledge *trumped* or even *defined* the Brahmin caste (i.e., a learned Kṣatriya monk could be a "true Brahmin" while a Brahmin-born dunce would not be). As such, non-Brahmin monks might want to claim the right to be guests at such sacrifices for reasons of livelihood or prestige. This may be why the *Arthaśāstra* has to explicitly forbid anyone to go to a Buddhist monk for funeral services.[71] The new trend in householder rites, then, opened the door for non-Brahmin religious professionals such as Buddhist monks to muscle in on what was quickly becoming a Brahmin-dominated ritual trade. And, indeed, this is exactly what we see in the numerous sermons in the *Tripiṭaka* that attempt to "redefine" the word "Brahmin." These sermons serve to recommend the inclusion of non-Brahmin monks as guests of these sacrifices.[72] Of course, there had always been at least a theoretical opening within Brahmanism itself for Kṣatriyas to become Brahmins. Viśvāmitra was originally a Kṣatriya who (in contrast to Triśaṅku) was transformed into a Brahmin *ṛṣi*, and the *rājasūya* rite originally had the king appropriating both the Brahma power and the Kṣatra power, leading Harry Falk to conclude that originally the king had been his own priest in this ritual and that the need of the *purohita* was only added later.[73]

What is often missed in discussions of how the Buddha redefines the word "Brahmin" to mean one who is learned, virtuous, etc., is that this redefinition would not have been particularly significant to Buddhists *who were already Brahmin*. Whether ordained as a Buddhist monk or not, a Brahmin Buddhist would have been eligible to be a guest at the ritual and their Buddhist learning about the ultimate emptiness or Mind would have only added prestige and gravitas to the ritual.

Buddhist *brahmodyas* as court debates

In one sense, the Brahmin Buddhist monk – especially if he were a Mahāyānist – would have been the ideal authority to have in the court. He would have had the caste prestige of being born a Brahmin. Furthermore, he would have championed an ideology of the ultimate on par with competing Brahmin groups while also providing a bridge to monastic practitioners of other castes who belonged to his sect (and who possibly meditated on the same object). It seems quite likely that Nāgārjuna would have been precisely this kind of Brahmin Buddhist monk. Kumārajīva's *Life of Nāgārjuna*, the earliest biographical account,[74] states that Nāgārjuna was born a Brahmin in South India. While it is common for biographers of this generation to ascribe the highest caste (the best education, etc.) to their subjects, in this case it probably also happens to be true. As Schohei Ichimura[75] has pointed out, Nāgārjuna was the first Buddhist we know of to write in proper Sanskrit, and he is doing so at a time when everybody other than Brahmins are writing in forms of Prakrit. Moreover, a knowledge of Paninian grammar and of the theories of Sanskrit grammarians is necessary to understand his philosophy.[76] It is significant then, that in his *Ratnāvalī* letter to a king, he portrays Buddhist philosophy as that which passes beyond the ideas of the ultimate set forth by competing schools.

> 1.61 Ask the Sāṃkhyas, the followers of Kaṇaḍa, Nirgranthas, and the worldly proponents of a person and aggregates, whether they propound what passes beyond "is" and "is not".

> 1.62 Thereby know that the ambrosia of the Buddha's teaching is called profound, an exclusive doctrine passing far beyond "is" and "is not."[77]

Why should the king care about these concerns? Because if the king was a Śātavāhana, his dynasty would have been inaugurated with a Horse Sacrifice (or two, or three), and therefore his own rule would have been to some extent legitimated by reference to the same sacrifice – a sacrifice whose proper performance was understood to turn on the profundity of one's knowledge of the font of the cosmos. Nāgārjuna is presenting Buddhism as providing precisely this legitimating knowledge/expertise. Nāgārjuna's Buddhism has already disseminated the idea of that which is beyond "is" and "is not," so that the ideology that imbued the Horse Sacrifice some two centuries prior would be understood as still immediate and relevant (and thus still legitimate). In being acknowledged and maintained at the court, Nāgārjuna's Buddhist and Brahmanical lineage would be granted legitimacy as that which was recognized to authorize the state. In other words, the benefit between religious virtuosi and the sovereign would have been entirely mutual.

The Mahāyāna genealogy from the Vedas to the sutras to Tantra to Zen

At this point, it would seem that we are a long, long way from the Barnes & Noble where this journey began. There, in some of the works currently marketed in the Religion and Self-Help section, I remarked on a tendency to cast Buddhism in general and Mahāyāna in particular as apolitical. At this point, I would like to conclude by pointing out that any statement about what the category "Buddhism" is or is not will necessarily be normative and not descriptive. In particular, claims about an apolitical Buddhism in the 20th century have usually been championed by those whose political careers depended on the silence of the monks as a moral political voice. Ananda Abeysekara has pointed to Jayawardene's condemnation of political monks in order to silence a major source of opposition to his political policies.[78] One does not have to use too much imagination to see exactly the same motivation behind exactly the same rhetoric used by the Burmese Junta to clamp down on monastic protests to their human rights abuses prior to 2012.

But even if we put conscious political activism aside, anyone concerned that Buddhism or "emptiness" did not play a role in the legitimation of sovereignty need only look at early works of Buddhist "Tantra," where the "imperial metaphor" and deliberate misrecognition of sovereignty becomes deafening. For example, the *Sarvatathāgatatattvasaṃgraha* begins with a paragraph that is all about sovereignty and marks of sovereignty:

> Thus have I heard. At one time the Lord, who had accomplished the most excellent knowledge of the *samaya* of adamantine empowerment [*vajra adhiṣṭhāna*] of All the Tathāgatas, who had obtained consecration [*abhiṣekha*] as the Dharma-king of the three realms . . . with the gemmed

> diadem of All the Tathāgatas, who had realized the mastery of the yoga of the knowledge of the omniscient one of All the Tathāgatas . . . was residing in the Great Maṇi (Jewel) Hall within the palace of the king of the Akaniṣṭha Heaven, a place frequented by all the Tathāgatas. [This palace] was variously adorned, with bells large and small and silken banners swaying in the gentle breeze, and it was bedecked with chaplets of pearls . . . and the like.[79]

Similarly, the *Vairocanābhisaṃbodhisūtra* begins:

> Thus have I heard. At one time the Bhagavān (Lord) was residing in the vast adamantine palace of the Dharma realm empowered by Tathāgatas, in which all the *vajradharas* had all assembled; the great pavilion [comparable to] the king of jewels, born of the Tathāgata's faith-and-understanding, play, and supernatural transformations, was lofty, without a center or perimeter, and variously adorned with great and wondrous jewel-kings, and the body of a bodhisattva formed a lion throne.[80]

Perhaps not incidentally, the bodhisattvas making a royal throne for Vairocana with their bodies echoes an earlier discussion of a coronation rite in the *Aitareya Brāhmaṇa* in which various gods use their bodies to form an equally four-legged throne for the one being anointed.[81] To find the connection of the imperial opening of the *Vairocanābhisaṃbodhisūtra* with *Perfection of Wisdom*, one need only read on a few more pages where the echoes of the core section of the latter are patent:

> The Buddha said, ". . . Lord of mysteries, what is *bodhi*? It means to know one's mind as it really is. Lord of Mysteries, this is *anuttarā samyaksaṃbodhi* . . . and there is not the slightest part of it that can be apprehended. Why? [Because] Bodhi has the characteristic of empty space, and there is no one to comprehend it, nor is there any understanding of it. Why? Because *bodhi* has no [differentiating] characteristics. Lord of Mysteries, all dharmas are without characteristics. That is to say, they have the characteristic of empty space" . . . Lord of Mysteries, it is in one's own mind that one seeks *bodhi* and omniscience. Why because its original nature is pure. The mind is neither within nor without, nor can the mind be apprehended between the two.[82]

On being initiated into the mandala, the initiate joins one of the Tathāgata families within the court of Vairocana in his palace along with the retinue of that family. Of course, a lot more could (and has)[83] been said about the political resonances of Buddhist tantra. But the point is that Buddhist engagement in legitimating royal authority and the appeal of the doctrines of emptiness and mind-only to accomplish this has been right in front of us all along. It is only because "tantric studies" have been relegated to something of an academic subdiscipline that scholars have not always seen it. I suspect that this is more of our problem than theirs. As Sam van Schaik and Jacob Dalton[84] suggest, there may have been more far more conversation and cross-pollination between Tibetan speaking-practitioners of Mahāmudrā or Mahāyoga Tantra and their Chan counterparts at Dunhuang in the eighth/ninth century than between scholars of Tantra and scholars of Zen in the modern academy.

Notes

1 Shi Huifeng discusses a tendency (albeit a minor one) in early sutras to reify the absolute as an object of attention. For example, he notes a slight shift from a signless concentration in some sutras to attending to "the signless" in others. Hence: "A definition of the signless which makes it an actual object appears in the statement of "directing attention to the signless" in MN 43 *Mahāvedalla*, as a supplement together with the negative "non-attention to all signs," . . . The sense of nibbāna as a reified object can also trace legitimacy from passages in *Udāna* 8:1–4 which indicate such a definition of nibbāna, particularly Ud 8:3 . . . These few suttas were often cited by Sthavīra schools as definitions of nibbāna par excellence. However, such reified phrasing seems to be actually the exception, rather than the rule, in the Pāli suttas . . . Wynne sharply criticizes the idea that this *Udāna* passage is the original Buddhist position, saying that 'this description of nirvāṇa corresponds exactly to the early Brahmanic ideas (Wynne 2007:100). I concur." (See, Huifeng, 2016, pp. 140–141). Wynne holds that the reified nirvana is not the original Buddhist position because it is Brahmanical. I also concur that it may well be Brahmanical, but for that reason it also corresponds to the original position of a community of early Buddhists.
2 *Kun byed rgyal po or gdod ma'i gzhi* respectively. See Karmay (2007), pp. 175ff.
3 On *mahāmudrā* as a kind of reified emptiness or Perfection of Wisdom see Hatchell (2014), pp. 46, 114–115, 167 and 189.
4 Schlütter, p. 152.
5 Althusser (1971), p. 147.
6 Ibid. p. 128.
7 Ibid., p. 129.
8 Ibid., p. 144.
9 Jordt (2007).
10 See Turner, et al. (2014).
11 The *Aryaparyeṣanasutta* with its discussion of Aḷara Kālāma and Udraka Rāmaputta is probably the best Buddhist example of this phenomenon.
12 S.N. 48.42; no parallels.
13 Bodhi (2000), p. 1687
14 Monier-Williams (1986) s.v.
15 e.g., Vātsyāyana's commentary on *Nyāya Sūtra* 1.1.10 and Uddyotkara's commentary on N.S. 1.1.14.
16 Bodhi (2000), p. 1668.
17 See, Cohen (2008), pp. 72–76 for an excellent discussion.
18 Olivelle (1996), pp. 40–41.
19 Ibid.
20 Gelder (1963), p. 263; verse quoted from the *Maitrāyaṇī Saṃhitā* 3.12.24ff.
21 See Baudhāyana Śrautasūtra, 15. 28. 232: vs. 15–20.
22 Fushimi (2007), p. 1.
23 *Āpastamba Śrautasūtra* 20.19.7 abbreviates the whole exchange with, "*kiṃ svid āsīt pūrvacittir ity etasyānuvākasya pṛṣṭāni hotuḥ pratijñātāni brahmaṇaḥ*."
24 Ibid., 20. 19: 6–8; Thite (2004), vol. 2, p. 1219.
25 Note, however, that since the Horse Sacrifice was usually performed only once at the beginning of a dynasty, the "right of place" would have been the real stake of these debates, not actual attendance at the sacrifice – though I see no reason to doubt that

there may well have been Buddhist monks who were happy to preside over such sacrifices, despite the handful of sutras in which the Buddha condemns them.

26 Śaṅkarācarya, in the introduction to his *Bṛhadāraṇyaka Upaniṣad Bhāṣya*, argues that meditation on *brahman* is a substitute for the Horse Sacrifice for one who knows. See, Madhavananda (1993) p. 4.
27 See Sahni (1929).
28 Sharma (1960).
29 Though Sircar contests this reading on the grounds that Kharavela was a Jain. See text and notes in Sircar (1965), p. 215, note 8.
30 Lüders (1913), #1112.
31 See Strootman (2014) and Basu (2001 and 2006).
32 Sims-Williams (1996), p. 79. The phenomenon of the translation of deities in various cultural encounters was widespread over the ancient Near East and especially in the Levant. See Smith (2008).
33 See Singh (2004).
34 Lüders (1913), #149a.
35 Kulkarni (2006).
36 See Falk (1988).
37 e.g., A.N. 3.59, 5.41, 10.177.
38 D.N. 5, 23, M.N. 51, S.N. 3.9, A.N. 4.39, 4.40, 4.198, 7.47, 8.1.
39 For an excellent summary of the history and geographical distribution of these sacrifices, see Voegeli (2012).
40 MŚS. 9.2.1.30.
41 Thite, 1186; ĀpŚS XX.5.15–16.
42 KŚS 20.1.17.
43 Later tradition has it that the Buddha's penis is sheathed "like a horse." See, e.g. T. 1509, p. 251c26–29. Bernard Faure also points out that the Buddha's horse penis figures prominently in some later tantric meditations. See Faure (1998), pp. 60–61 and 281.
44 The best treatment of this part of the sacrifice that I am aware of is in Jamison (1996), pp. 65–110.
45 ĀpŚS XX. 18.4.
46 MŚS 9.2.4.14–15.
47 The implication is that the son born to such a queen will be stallion-like. The best example of this line of thinking is that of the *Rāmāyana* in which Rāma is born to King Dasarātha and Kausalyā only after the performance of the *aśvamedha*.
48 We may think of this ritual as degrading of the chief queen's womanhood, but when you consider depictions of the literary and historical women who performed this rite there, is simply no evidence that they had anything other than a superlative (and chaste) reputation as virtuous women after having done so.
49 Proferes (2007), p. 119.
50 The connection between the *Nāsadīyasukta* is more explicit at ŚB 10.5.3.3.
51 Eggeling (1882), vol. 3, pp. 150–154; ŚB. 6.1.2.12, 13, 26, 27.
52 Proferes, pp. 142ff.
53 Brereton (1999), p. 250.
54 Eggeling, 1882, vol. 4, pp. 374–375.
55 MacDonnell (1917), p. 209.
56 Brereton (1999), p. 253.
57 *Amarakośa*, 273.6. *Tuccha* is, however, still used in Pali alongside *sūñña*.
58 M.U. 2.4, 6.31, 7.4.
59 On TB.2.8.9.4c; Mitra (1862), p. 924.
60 It occurs afterwards in the ĀpŚS 20.19.6.ff.
61 ĀpŚS. 20. 19.8.
62 Willis, pp. 188ff.

63 See C.U. 2.22.1.

64 Only the *Mahāsaṅghikas* mention the moat or the fact it is a royal horse. The story does, however appear in other *vinayas*: e.g. in the *Dharmaguptavinaya* T. 1428, p. 809a8, and also at p. 972b11ff.; in the *Sarvāstivādavinaya* T. 1435, p. 2c29ff and 425a14ff.; the *Mahīśāsakavinaya* (T. 1421, p. 182c9ff.) cf. also T. 1463, p. 813a3ff.

65 Clarke (2009), p. 11; T. 1425, p. 232b1–6. Note that technically the horse carcass floating in the moat would have been from the Piling of the Fire Altar sacrifice that is part of the Horse Sacrifice, and is not the horse with whom the chief queen has sex. The latter is roasted and eaten. The author seems to have taken some poetic license here.

66 See Falk, 2012a.

67 Walser (2009).

68 Tsuchiyama (2005), pp. 72–73.

69 The "imperial metaphor" has long been a topic among Sinologists and provides another context for this phenomenon. See Feuchtwang (1992).

70 See Sayers (2013).

71 Egge (2002), p. 136, note 110, "*śakyājīvakādīn vṛṣalapravajitān devapitṛkāryeṣu bhojayataḥ śatyo daṇdaḥ*." Arthaśāstra 3.20.16, cited in PV Kane, *History of Dharmaśāstra* I: 219. Other texts exclude Buddhist monastics from the rites without mentioning them by name. BDhS. 2.15.5 asserts that when a person wearing ochre clothes makes a sacrifice or accepts a gift at a rite for gods or ancestors, the oblation does not reach its intended recipient. *Manu* 3.150–166 gives a long list of persons to be excluded from the *śraddha*, including atheists, those who have not studied the Veda, those who have forsaken the fires, and those who revile the Veda."

72 There are quite a few sermons mentioning qualifications of those worthy of gifts or worthy of being fed at a sacrifice. See, SN 7.8, 7.9, AN 2.55, 5.175, 6.2, 6.3, 6.4, 6.93, 7.18, 7.46, 9.10, 10.16, 10.177, and Snp 1.4.

73 See Falk (1984).

74 Corless (1995).

75 Ichimura (1992).

76 Bhattacharya (1980).

77 Hopkins (1998), p. 102; Hahn (1982), p. 26, "sa-sāṃkhy-aulūkya-nirgrantha-pugdala-skandha-vādinam / pṛccha lokaṃ yadi vadaty asti nāsti vyatikramam || 1.61 dharmayautakam ity asmān nasty astitva vyatikramam | viddhi gambhīram ity uktaṃ buddhānāṃ śāsanāmṛtam || 1.62"

78 Abeysekara (2002), pp. 97ff.

79 Giebel (2001), p. 19.

80 Giebel (2005), p. 3.

81 See Keith (1920), p. 329.

82 Giebel (2005), p. 6.

83 See, e.g., Davidson (2002).

84 Van Schaik and Dalton (2004).

BIBLIOGRAPHY

Abeysekara, Ananda. *Colors of the Robe: Religion, Identity, and Difference.* Columbia, SC: University of South Carolina Press, 2002.

——. "Religious Studies' Mishandling of Origin and Change: Time, Tradition, and Form-of-Life in Buddhism." *Cultural Critique* 98 (Winter, 2018): 22-71.

Agrama, Hussein Ali. *Questioning Secularism: Islam, Sovereignty, and the Rule of Law in Modern Egypt.* Chicago: University of Chicago Press, 2012.

Allan, Sarah. "On the Identity of Shang Di 上帝 and the Origin of the Concept of a Celestial Mandate (Tian Ming 天命)." *Early China* 31 (2007): 1–46.

Allon, Mark. *Buddhist Manuscripts Vol. 1.* Manuscripts in the Schøyen Collection 1; Oslo: Hermes Publications, 2000.

Althusser, Louis. "Ideology and Ideological State Apparatuses." In *Lenin and Philosophy, and Other Essays*, 127–188. London: New Left Books, 1971.

Altman, Rick. *Film/Genre.* London: BFI Publications, 1999.

Amano, Kyoko. *Maitrāyaṇī-Saṁhitā I-II: Übersetzung Der Prosapartien Mit Kommentar Zur Lexik Und Syntax Der älteren Vedischen Prosa.* Münchner Forschungen Zur Historischen Sprachwissenschaft; Bd. 9; Bremen: Hempen, 2009.

Anālayo, Bhikkhu. "The *Brahmajāla* and the Early Buddhist Oral Tradition." *Annual Report of the International Research Institute for Advanced Buddhology at Soka University* 17 (2014a): 41–61.

——. "The Hīnayāna Fallacy." *Journal of the Oxford Centre for Buddhist Studies* 6 (2014b): 9–31

——. *A Comparative Study of the Majjhima-Nikāya.* Taipei, Taiwan; New York: Dharma Drum; Chan Meditation Center [North American distributor], 2011.

——. *The Genesis of the Bodhisattva Ideal.* Hamburg: Hamburg University Press, 2010.

——. "The Luminous Mind in Theravāda and Dharmaguptaka Discourses." *Journal of the Oxford Centre for Buddhist Studies* 13 (2017): 10–50.

Apple, James B. "An Early Bka'-Gdams-Pa Madhyamaka Work Attributed to Atiśa Dīpaṃkaraśrījñāna." *Journal of Indian Philosophy* 44, no. 4 (2015): 619–725.

Bakhtin, Mikhail. *Speech Genres and Other Late Essays* [Translation of: Ėstetika slovesnogo tvorchestva.]. Edited by Vern McGee, Michael Holquist, and Caryl Emerson. Austin: University of Texas Press, 1986.

Ballantyne, James Robert. *Vedānta-Sāra*. Madras: The Christian Literature Society for India, 1898.

Banerjee-Dube, Ishita. "Religion, Power and Law in Twentieth Century India." *History Compass* 13, no. 12 (2015): 621–629.

Bankei, and Norman Waddell. *The Unborn: The Life and Teachings of Zen Master Bankei, 1622–1693*. Rev. ed. New York: North Point Press, 2000.

Bareau, Andre. *Les Sectes Bouddhiques Du Petit Vehicule*. Paris: Publications De L'ecole Française D'extrême-Orient, Ecole francaise d'Extreme-Orient, 1955.

Baums, Stefan and Andrew Glass. "A Dictionary of Gāndhārī." https://gandhari.org/n_dictionary.php.

Basu, Chandreyi. "Patronage and Representation at the Huviska Vihara, a Kusana-Period Monastery in Mathura." *Studies in History* 22, no. 2 (2006): 157–179.

——. "Redefining the Nature of Cultural Regions in Early India: Early India: Mathura and the Meaning of "Kusana" Art (1st–3rd Centuries AD)." Ph.D. diss. University of Pennsylvania, 2001.

Beal, Samuel. *Si-Yu-Ki. Buddhist Records of the Western World*. Popular ed. New York: Paragon Book Reprint Corp., 1968.

Behera, Subhakanta. "Jagannath and Alekh: A Study in Juxtaposition." *Economic and Political Weekly* 32, no. 33/34 (1997): 2096–2097.

Bergen, Benjamin K. *Louder Than Words: The New Science of How the Mind Makes Meaning*. New York, NY: Basic Books, 2012.

Bhattacharya, Kamaleswar. "Nāgārjuna's Arguments against Motion: Their Grammatical Basis." In *A Corpus of Indian Studies: Essays in Honour of Professor Gaurinath Sastri*, edited by Arthur Llewellyn Basham, 85–95. Calcutta: Sanskrit Pustak Bhandar, 1980.

Black, Brian. *The Character of the Self in Ancient India: Priests, Kings, and Women in the Early Upaniṣads*. SUNY Series in Hindu Studies. Albany: State University of New York Press, 2007.

Bodewitz, H. W. *Jaiminīya Brāhmaṇa I, 1-65. Transl. And Commentary with a Study Agnihotra and Prāṇāgnihotra*. Leiden: Orientalia Rheno-Traiectina, 1973.

Bodhi, Bhikkhu. *The Connected Discourses of the Buddha: A Translation of the Saṃyutta Nikāya; Translated from the Pāli by Bhikkhu Bodhi*. Boston: Wisdom Publications, 2000.

——. *The Numerical Discourses of the Buddha: A Translation of the Aṅguttara Nikāya*. Boston: Wisdom Publications, 2012.

Bodhi, Bhikkhu and Bhikkhu Nanamoli. *The Middle Length Discourses of the Buddha: A New Translation of the Majjhima Nikāya*. Teachings of the Buddha. Boston: Wisdom Publications, 1995.

Böhtlingk, Otto and Rudolph Roth. *Grosses Petersburger Wörterbuch*. Petersburg: n.l., 1868.

Bokenkamp, Stephen R., and Peter S. Nickerson. *Early Daoist Scriptures*. Berkeley: University of California Press, 1997.

Boltz, Judith. *A Survey of Taoist Literature, Tenth to Seventeenth Centuries*. Berkeley, CA: Institute of East Asian Studies, 1987.

Boretz, Avron Albert. *Gods, Ghosts, and Gangsters: Ritual Violence, Martial Arts, and Masculinity on the Margins of Chinese Society*. Honolulu: University of Hawai'i Press, 2011.

Bourdieu, Pierre. "Censorship and the Imposition of Form." In *Language and Symbolic Power*, edited by Pierre Bourdieu and John B. Thompson, 137–162. Cambridge, MA: Harvard University Press, 1991.

Brassard, Francis. *The Concept of Bodhicitta in Śāntideva's Bodhícaryāvatāra*. McGill Studies in the History of Religions; Albany, NY: State University of New York Press, 2000.

Breen, John, and Mark Teeuwen. *A New History of Shinto*. Hoboken, NJ: Wiley, 2010.

Brereton, Joel P. "Edifying Puzzlement: *Ṛgveda* 10. 129 and the Uses of Enigma." *Journal of the American Oriental Society* 119, no. 2 (1999): 248–260.
Bronkhorst, Johannes. *Buddhism in the Shadow of Brahmanism.* Leiden: Brill, 2011.
——. *Buddhist Teaching in India.* Boston: Wisdom Publications, 2013.
Brook, Timothy. *The Chinese State in Ming Society* London: Routledge Curzon, 2005.
——. *Praying for Power: Buddhism and the Formation of Gentry Society in Late-Ming China.* Cambridge, MA: Council on East Asian Studies, Harvard University and Harvard-Yenching Institute, 1993.
Brose, Benjamin. *Patrons and Patriarchs: Chan Monks and Regional Rulers during the Five Dynasties and Ten Kingdoms.* Honolulu: University of Hawai'i Press, 2015.
Bstan-'dzin-rgya-mtsho Dalai Lama, X. I. V. "The 14th Dalai Lama's Nobel Lecture." www.dalailama.com/messages/acceptance-speeches/nobel-peace-prize/nobel-peace-prize-nobel-lecture.
——. *Buddha Heart, Buddha Mind: Living the Four Noble Truths.* New York: Crossroad Pub. Co., 2000.
—— and Jeffrey Hopkins. *Advice on Dying and Living a Better Life.* New York: Atria Books, 2002.
Buitenen, Johannes Adrianus Bernardus van. *The Maitrāyaṇīya Upaniṣad: A Critical Essay, with Text, Translation, and Commentary.* Disputationes Rheno-Trajectinae; Gravenhage: Mouton, 1962.
Cardwell, Edward. *Documentary Annals of the Reformed Church of England: Being a Collection of Injunctions, Declarations, Orders, Articles of Inquiry, &C. From the Year 1546 to the Year 1716.* Oxford: Oxford University Press, 1839.
Central Tibetan Administration. "Constitution of Tibet." www.tibetjustice.org/materials/tibet/tibet2.html.
Chan, Timothy Wai Keung. *Considering the End: Mortality in Early Medieval Chinese Poetic Representation.* Leiden: Brill, 2012.
Chang, Chen-chi. *A Treasury of Mahāyāna Sūtras: Selections from the Mahāratnakūṭa Sūtra.* Delhi: Motilal Banarsidass, 1996.
Chavannes, Édouard. *Le T'ai Chan: Essai De Monographie d'un Culte Chinois. Appendice: Le Dieu Du Sol Dans La Chine Antique.* Paris: Musée Guimet, 1910.
Choong, Yoke Meei. *Zum Problem Der Leerheit (Śūnyatā) in Der Prajñāpāramitā.* New York: Lang, 2006.
Choudhury, Kamal Narayan. "A Critical Study of the Assamese Mystic Poets of the Romantic Age." Ph.D. diss. University of Gauhati, 1997.
Chua, Ying "Tantra in China." In *The Circle of Bliss: Buddhist Meditational Art.* Huntington, John C., and Dina Bangdel, pp. 45-50. Serindia Publications, 2003.
Clarke, Shayne. "Monks Who Have Sex: *Pārājika* Penance in Indian Monastic Buddhism." *Journal of Indian Philosophy* 39 (2009): 1–43.
Cohen, Signe. *Text and Authority in the Older Upaniṣads.* Brill's Indological Library. Leiden: Brill, 2008.
Cole, Allan. "Schisms in Buddhism." In *Sacred Schisms: How Religions Divide*, edited by J.R. Lewis and S.M. Lewis, 61–82. Cambridge: Cambridge University Press, 2009.
Conze, Edward. *Abhisamayālaṅkāra: Introduction: And Translation from Original Text with Sanskrit-Tibetan Index by Edward Conze.* Serie Orientale Roma. Rome: Is. M.E.O., 1954.
——. *Aṣṭasāhasrikā Prajñāpāramitā.* Calcutta: The Asiatic Society, 1958.
Corless, Rodger. "The Chinese Life of Nāgārjuna." In *Buddhism in Practice*, edited by Donald Lopez, 525–531. Princeton: Princeton University Press, 1995.
Cowell, Edward B. *The Maitri or Maitrāyanīya Upanishad.* Calcutta: Asiatic Society, 1913.

Cowell, Edward Byles, and Frederick William Thomas. *The Harsa-Carita of Bana*. Delhi: Motilal Banarsidass, 1993.

Cox, Collett. "What's in a Name? School Affiliation in an Early Buddhist Gāndhārī Manuscript." *Bulletin of the Asia Institute* 23 (2009): 53–63.

Dasgupta, Surendranath. *A History of Indian Philosophy*. Vol. 3, London: Cambridge University Press, 1940. repr. Delhi: Motilal Banarsidass, 1997.

Davidson, Ronald M. *Indian Esoteric Buddhism: A Social History of the Tantric Movement*. New York: Columbia University Press, 2002.

Davis, Edward. *Society and the Supernatural in Song China*. Honolulu: University of Hawai'i Press, 2001.

Dayal, Har. *The Bodhisattva Doctrine in Buddhist Sanskrit Literature*. Delhi: Motilal Banarsidass, 1975.

De Bary, William Theodore, Irene Bloom, Wing-tsit Chan, Joseph Adler, and Richard Lufrano. *Sources of Chinese Tradition: Volume 1*. New York: Columbia University Press, 1999.

——. *Sources of Chinese Tradition: Volume 2: From 1600 through the Twentieth Century*. New York: Columbia University Press, 2010.

Dean, Kenneth. *Lord of the Three in One: The Spread of a Cult in Southeast China*. Princeton, NJ: Princeton University Press, 1998.

——. "Transformations of the *She* (Altars of the Soil) in Fujian." *Cahiers d'Extreme-Asie* 10 (1998): 19–75.

Dessein, Bart. *Saṃyuktābhidharmahṛdaya = Heart of Scholasticism with Miscellaneous Additions*. Delhi: Motilal Banarsidass Publishers, 1999.

Deussen, Paul, V. M. Bedekar, and Gajanan Balkrishna Palsule. *Sixty Upanisads of the Veda*. Delhi: Motilal Banarsidass, 1990.

Dhole, Heeralal. *A Manual of Adwaita Philosophy, the Vedantasara of Paramhansa Sadananda Jogindra: With an Introductory Memoir on Matter and Spirit*. Calcutta: Heeralal Dhole, 1888.

Douglas, Mary. *How Institutions Think*. Syracuse, NY: Syracuse University Press, 1986.

Dreyfus, Georges B. J. *Recognizing Reality: Dharmakīrti's Philosophy and Its Tibetan Interpretations*. SUNY Series in Buddhist Studies. Albany: State University of New York Press, 1997.

Duara, Prasenjit. *Culture, Power, and the State: Rural North China, 1900–1942*. Stanford, CA: Stanford University Press, 1988.

——. "Knowledge and Power in the Discourse of Modernity: The Campaigns against Popular Religion in Early Twentieth-Century China." *The Journal of Asian Studies* 50, no. 1 (1991): 67–83.

Dubois, Joël André-Michel. *The Hidden Lives of Brahman: Śaṅkara's Vedānta through His Upaniṣad Commentaries, in Light of Contemporary Practice*. Albany, NY: SUNY Press, 2014.

Duff, Tony. *The Illuminator Tibetan-English Dictionary*. Tibetan Dictionaries, Text and Software. Fully ed. new elect. ed. ed. [s.l.]: Padma Karpo Translation Committee, 2000.

Dunne, John. "Realizing the Unreal: Dharmakīrti's Theory of Yogic Perception." *Journal of Indian Philosophy* 34 (2006): 497–519.

Dutt, Nalinaksha. *Mahāyāna Buddhism*. Delhi: Motilal Banarsidass, 1977.

——. *The Pañcaviṁśātisāhasrikā Prajñāpāramitā*. Calcutta: Calcutta Oriental Press, 1934.

Dyczkowski, Mark. *The Aphorisms of Siva: The Siva Sutra with Bhaskara's Commentary, the Varttika*. Albany: SUNY Press, 1992.

Eaton, Richard Maxwell. *The Rise of Islam and the Bengal Frontier, 1204–1760*. Comparative Studies on Muslim Societies; 17. Berkeley: University of California Press, 1993.

Ebrey, Patricia Buckley. *Confucianism and Family Rituals in Imperial China: A Social History of Writing about Rites*. Princeton, NJ: Princeton University Press, 1991.

Eckel, Malcolm David. *Bhāviveka and His Buddhist Opponents*. Harvard Oriental Series; V. 70. Cambridge, MA: Harvard University Press, 2009.
Edgerton, Franklin. *Buddhist Hybrid Sanskrit Grammar and Dictionary*. Delhi: Motilal Banarsidass, 1985.
Egge, James R. *Religious Giving and the Invention of Karma in Theravāda Buddhism*. Curzon Studies in Asian Religion. Richmond: Curzon, 2002.
Eggeling, Julius. *The Śatapatha-Brāhmaṇa According to the Text of the Mādhyandina School*. Sacred Books of the East, 2nd Series, Vol. Xli. Oxford: At the University Press, 1882.
Eliot, T. S. "Tradition and the Individual Talent." *Perspecta* 19 (1982): 36–42.
Elverskog, Johan. *Buddhism and Islam on the Silk Road*. Philadelphia: University of Pennsylvania Press, 2010.
——. *Our Great Qing: The Mongols, Buddhism and the State in Late Imperial China*. Honolulu: University of Hawai'i Press, 2006.
Falk, Harry. "Small-Scale Buddhism." In *Devadattiyam: Johannes Bronkhorst Felicitation Volume*, edited by Voegeli François and Johannes Bronkhorst, 491–517. Bruxelles: Peter Lang Pub. Inc., 2012.
——. "The 'Split' Collection of Kharoṣṭhī Texts." *Annual Report of the International Research Institute for Advanced Buddhology at Soka University* 14 (2011a): 13–25.
——. "Ten Thoughts on the Mathura Lion Capital Reliquary." In *Felicitas: Essays in Numismatics, Epigraphy and History in Honour of Joe Cribb*, edited by Joe Bhandare Shailendra Garg Sanjay Cribb, 121–141. Mumbai: Reesha Books International, 2011b.
——. "Vedische Opfer Im Pali-Kanon." *Bulletin d'études indiennes* 6 (1988): 225–254.
——. "Die Legende von Śunaḥśepa vor ihrem rituellen Hintergrund." Zeitschrift der Deutschen Morgenländischen Gesellschaft 134, no. 1 (1984): 115–135.
Falk, Harry, and Seishi Karashima. "A First-Century Prajñāpāramitā Manuscript from Gandhāra – Parivarta 5 (Texts from the Split Collection 2)." *Annual Report of the International Research Institute for Advanced Buddhology at Soka University* 16 (2012): 97–169.
Farquhar, David. "Emperor as Bodhisattva in the Governance of the Ch'ing Empire." *Harvard Journal of Asiatic Studies* 38, no. 1 (1978): 5–34.
Faure, Bernard. *The Red Thread: Buddhist Approaches to Sexuality*. Princeton, NJ: Princeton University Press, 1998.
Feuchtwang, Stephan. *The Imperial Metaphor: Popular Religion in China*. London: Routledge, 1992.
Filliozat, Jean. "La Doctrine Des Brahmanes D'apres Saint Hippolyte." *Revue de l'histoire des religions* 130 (1945): 59–91.
Flynn, Dennis O. and Arturo Giráldez. "Born with a Silver Spoon: The Origin of World Trade in 1571." *Journal of World History* 6, no. 2 (1995): 201–221.
Franco, Eli. *The Spitzer Manuscript: The Oldest Philosophical Manuscript in Sanskrit*. Denkschriften/Österreichische Akademie Der Wissenschaften, Philosophisch-Historische Klasse; Bd. 323; Beiträge Zur Kultur- Und Geistesgeschichte Asiens; Nr. 43; Wien: Verlag der österreichischen Akademie der Wissenschaften, 2004.
Fronsdal, Egil. *The Dawn of the Bodhisattva Path: The Early Perfection of Wisdom*. Berkeley, CA: Institute for Buddhist Studies and BDK America, 2014.
Frow, John. *Genre*. London; New York: Routledge, 2006.
Fujita, Yoshimichi. "The Bodhisattva Thought of the Sarvāstivādins and Mahāyāna Buddhism." *Acta Asiatica* 96 (2009): 99–120.
Fushimi, Makoto. "Baudhayana Śrautasūtra: Development of the Ritual Text in Ancient India." Ph.D. diss. Harvard University, 2007.
Gach, Gary. *The Complete Idiot's Guide to Buddhism, 3rd Edition*. London: DK Publishing, 2009.
Garfield, Jay. *Engaging Buddhism: Why It Matters to Philosophy*. Oxford: Oxford University Press, 2015.

Gelder, Jeanette Maria van. *Mānava Śrautasūtra Belonging to the Maitrāyaṇī Saṃhitā (English Translation)*. New Delhi: International Academy of Indian Culture, 1963.

——. *The Mānava Śrautasūtra Belonging to the Maitrāyāṇī Saṃhitā (Sanskrit Edition)*. Sri Garib Das Oriental Series; No. 31–32. Delhi: Sri Satguru Publications, 1985.

Gelek, Geshe Drakpa. "Dissolution and Emptiness Meditation in the Kālacakra Six-Session Guru Yoga Sādhana." In *As Long as Space Endures: Essays on the Kālacakra Tantra in Honor of H.H. The Dalai Lama*, edited by Edward Arnold, 449–457. Ithaca, NY: Snow Lion Publishers, 2009.

Gethin, Rupert. "*Bhavaṅga* and Rebirth According to the Abhidhamma." In *The Buddhist Forum*, edited by Tadeusz Skorupski and Ulrich Pagel, 11–35. London: School of Oriental and African Studies, 1994.

——. *The Buddhist Path to Awakening*. Oneworld Classics in Religious Studies. 1st South Asian ed. Leiden: E.J. Brill, 1992.

Ghoṣa, Pratāpacandra. *Çatasāhasrikā-Prajñā-Pāramitā: A Theological and Philosophical Discourse of Buddha with His Disciples*. Calcutta: Asiatic Soc., 1902.

Giebel, Rolf W. *Two Esoteric Sutras*. Bdk English Tripiṭaka; 29-Ii, 30-Ii. Berkeley, CA: Numata Center for Buddhist Translation and Research, 2001.

——. *The Vairocanābhisaṃbodhi Sutra*. Bdk English Tripiṭaka; 30-I. Berkeley, CA: Numata Center for Buddhist Translation and Research, 2005.

Gippert, Jost. TITUS edition of "White Yajur-Veda, Śatapatha-Brāhmaṇa (Mādhyandina-Recension), on the Basis of the Edition byAlbrecht Weber, the *Çatapatha-Brāhmaṇa in the Mādhyandina-Çākhā* with Extracts from the Commentaries of Sāyaṇa, Harisvāmin and Dvivedānga, Berlin 1849/Repr. Varanasi 1964 (Chowkhamba Sanskrit Ser., 96) Entered (Books 1–11, 13–14) by H.S. Anantanarayana (Supervisor W.P. Lehmann), Austin, Texas, 1971; Reedited by J.R. Gardner, Iowa, 1998; Book 12 Entered by Makoto Fushimi, Kyoto/ Harvard 1999; Corrections by Matthias Ahlborn; Titus Version by Jost Gippert, Frankfurt a/M, 4/21/2012" http://titus.fkidg1.uni-frankfurt.de/framee.htm?/index.htm.

Glass, Andrew, and Mark Allon. *Four Gāndhārī Saṃyuktāgama Sūtras: Senior Kharoṣṭhī Fragment 5*. Gandhāran Buddhist Texts; V. 4; Seattle: University of Washington Press, 2007.

Goffman, Erving. "Footing." In *Forms of Talk*, 124–159. Philadelphia: University of Pennsylvania Press, 1981.

——. *Frame Analysis: An Essay on the Organization of Experience*. Cambridge: Harvard University Press, 1974.

Gokhale, V. V. "Masters of Buddhism Adore the Brahman through Non-Adoration." *Indo-Iranian Journal* 5, no. 4 (1962/12/01 1962): 271–275.

Goldstein, Melvyn. "The Circulation of Estates in Tibet: Reincarnation, Land and Politics." *The Journal of Asian Studies* 32, no. 3 (1973): 445–455.

Goldstein, Melvyn C, and Gelek Rimpoche. *A history of modern Tibet*. Berkeley: University of California Press, 1991.

Gómez, Luis O. "Proto-Mādhyamika in the Pāli Canon." *Philosophy East and West* 26, no. 2 (1976): 137–165.

Goossaert, Vincent. "1898: The Beginning of the End for Chinese Religion?" *The Journal of Asian Studies* 65, no. 2 (2006): 307–335.

Greenwood, Kevin. "Yonghegong: Imperial Universalism and the Art and Architecture of Beijing's 'Lama Temple'." Ph.D. diss. University of Kansas, 2013.

Griffith, Ralph T. H. *The Hymns of the Ṛgveda*. New rev. ed. Delhi: Motilal Banarsidass, 1973.

Griffiths, Paul. *On Being Mindless: Buddhist Meditation and the Mind-Body Problem*. La Salle, IL: Open Court, 1986.

Grupper, Samuel Martin. "The Manchu Imperial Cult of the Early Ch'ing Dynasty." University Microfilms, Ph.D. diss. Indiana University, 1979.

Guojia, wenwuju gu wenxian, yanjiushi. *Mawangdui Hanmu Boshu*. Beijing: Wenwu, 1980.

Guzy, Lidia. "From Non-Brahmin Priests of the Goddess to Ascetics of the God Alekha." *Baessler-Archiv* 53 (2005).

Haas, Ernst and Gisela Minke. "The Kālacakra Initiation." *The Tibet Journal*, 1.3/4, (Autumn 1976), pp. 29-31.

Hahn, Michael and Yukihiro Okada. *Nāgārjuna's Ratnāvalī*. Bonn: Indica et Tibetica Verlag, 1982.

Hakeda, Yoshito S. *The Awakening of Faith*. New York: Columbia University Press, 1967.

Halbfass, Wilhelm. *India and Europe: An Essay in Understanding*. Albany, NY: State University of New York Press, 1988.

Hall, Stuart. "Encoding and Decoding." In *The Cultural Studies Reader*, edited by Simon During, 97–112. London; New York: Routledge, 1993.

Hare, Edward M. *The Book of the Gradual Sayings (Anguttara-Nikāya) or More-Numbered Suttas. 4, (the Book of the Sevens, Eights and Nines)/Transl. by E. M. Hare*. Translation Series/Pali Text Society 26. Repr. ed. London: Pali Text Soc., 2001.

Harrison, Paul. "The Earliest Chinese Translations of Mahāyāna Buddhist Sūtras: Some Notes on the Works of Lokakṣema." *Buddhist Studies Review* 10 (1993): 135–178.

——. "Searching for the Origins of the Mahāyāna: What Are We Looking For?" *The Eastern Buddhist* 28, no. 1 (1995): 48–69.

Harvey, Peter. *The Selfless Mind: Personality, Consciousness and Nirvāṇa in Early Buddhism*. Surrey: Curzon Press, 1995.

——. "'Signless' Meditations in Pāli Buddhism." *Journal of the International Association of Buddhist Studies* 9, no. 1 (1986): 25–52.

Hatchell, Christopher. *Naked Seeing: The Great Perfection, the Wheel of Time, and Visionary Buddhism in Renaissance Tibet*. New York: Oxford University Press, 2014.

Hazra, Rajendra Chandra. *Studies in the Upapurāṇas*. Calcutta: Sanskrit College, 1963.

Heinrich, Lüders. *Bruchstücke Buddhistischer Dramen*. Berlin: G. Reimer, 1911.

Hikata, Ryusho. *Suvikrāntavikrāmi-Paripṛcchā Prajñāpāramitā-Sūtra*. Kyoto: Rinsen, 1953.

Hixon, Lex. *Mother of the Buddhas: Meditation on the Prajnaparamita Sutra*. Kolkata: Alchemy, 2004.

Hobbes, T. *Hobbes's Leviathan; Harrington's Ocean; Famous Pamphlets [A.D. 1644 to A.D. 1795]*. G. Routledge and sons, 1889.

Hoernle, A. F. Rudolf. *Manuscript remains of Buddhist literature found in Eastern Turkestan: facsimiles with transcripts, translations and notes*. Delhi, India: Sri Satguru Publication, 1988.

Hopkins, Edward Washburn. *The Great Epic of India: Its Character and Origin*. New York: C. Scribner's Sons, 1902.

Hopkins, Jeffrey. *Buddhist Advice for Living & Liberation: Nāgārjuna's Precious Garland*. Ithaca, NY: Snow Lion Publications, 1998.

Huifeng, Shi (= Matthew Orsborn). *Old School Emptiness: Hermeneutics, Criticism & Tradition in the Narrative of Sunyata*. Kaohsiung City, Taiwan: Fo Guang Shan, Institute of Humanistic Buddhism, 2016.

Hutton, Eric L. *Xunzi: The Complete Text*. Princeton: Princeton University Press, 2014.

Ichimura, Shohei. "Re-Examining the Period of Nagarjuna: Western India, Ad 50–150." *Journal of Indian and Buddhist Studies (Indogaku Bukkyogaku Kenkyu)* 40, no. 2 (1992): 1079–1083.

Illich, Marina. "Selections from the Life of a Tibetan Buddhist Polymath: Chankya Rolpai Dorje (Lcang Skya Rol Pa'i Rdo Rje), 1717–1886." Ph.D. diss. Columbia University, 2006.

Jaini, Padmanabh. *Abhidharmadīpa with Vibhāṣāprabhāvṛtti*. Patna: Kashi Prasad Jayaswal Research Institute, 1977.

——. "On the Ignorance of the Arhat." In *Paths to Liberation: The Mārga and Its Transformations in Buddhist Thought*, edited by Robert E. Buswell and Robert M. Gimello. 135–145. Honolulu: University of Hawaii Press, 1992.

Jamison, Stephanie W. *Sacrificed Wife/Sacrificer's Wife: Women, Ritual, and Hospitality in Ancient India*. New York: Oxford University Press, 1996.

—— and Joel P. Brereton. *The Rigveda: The Earliest Religious Poetry of India* New York: Oxford University Press, 2014.

Janousch, Andreas. "The Emperor as Bodhisattva: The Bodhisattva Ordination and Ritual Assemblies of Emperor Wu of the Liang Dynasty." *University of Cambridge Oriental Publications* 54, no. 1 (1999): 112–149.

Jha, Mahāmahopādhyāya Gaṅgānātha, ed. *Manu-Smṛti with the 'Manubhāṣya' of Medhātithi*. Allahabad: Asiatic Society of Bengal, 1932.

Jiang, Yonglin. *The Great Ming Code: Da Ming Lü*. Seattle: University of Washington Press, 2005.

Johnson, Wallace. *The T'ang Code*. Princeton, NJ: Princeton University Press, 1979.

Jordt, Ingrid. *Burma's Mass Lay Meditation Movement: Buddhism and the Cultural Construction of Power*. Athens: Ohio University Press, 2007.

Jorgensen, John. "The 'Imperial' Lineage of Ch'an Buddhism: The Role of Confucian Ritual and Ancestor Worship in Ch'an's search for legitimation in Mid-Tang dynasty." *Papers on Far Eastern History* 39 (1987) pp. 89–133.

Jurewicz, Joanna. "Playing with Fire: The Pratītyasamutpāda from the Perspective of Vedic Thought." *Journal of the Pali Text Society* 26 (2000): 77–103.

Kane, P. V. *History of Dharmaśāstra: (Ancient and Mediaeval Religious and Civil Law). Vol I.* Poona: Bhandarkar Oriental Reserch Institute, 1930.

Kantorowicz, Ernst Hartwig. *The King's Two Bodies: A Study in Mediaeval Political Theology*. Princeton, NJ: Princeton University Press, 1957.

Kanxi Emperor. *Kangxi Zidian*. 1850.

Karashima, Seishi. *A Critical Edition of Lokakṣema's Translation of the Aṣṭasāhasrikā Prajñāpāramitā*. Bibliotheca Philologica Et Philosophica Buddhica. Tokyo: International Research Institute for Advanced Buddhology, Soka University, 2011.

——. *A Glossary of Lokaksema's Translation of the aṣtasāhasrikā Prajnāpāramitā*. Tokyo: International Research Institute for Advanced Buddhology, Soka University, 2010.

——. "Was the *Aṣṭasāhasrikā Prajñāpāramitā* Compiled in Gandhāra in Gāndhārī?" *Annual Report of the International Research Institute for Advanced Buddhology at Soka University* XVI (2013): 171–188.

Karmay, Samten Gyaltsen. *The Great Perfection: (Rdzogs Chen): A Philosophical and Meditative Teaching in Tibetan Buddhism*. Leiden: Brill, 2007.

Keane, Webb. *Signs of Recognition: Powers and Hazards of Representation in an Indonesian Society*. Berkeley: University of California Press, 1997.

Keith, Arthur Berriedale. *Rigveda Brāhmaṇas: The Aitareya and Kausītaki Brāhmanas of the Rigveda*. Cambridge, MA: Harvard University Press, 1920.

Kimura, Takayasu. *Pañcaviṃśatisāhasrikā Prajñāpāramitā. Ii-Iii*. Tokyo: Sankibo Busshorin Pub. Co., 1986.

King, Richard. *Early Advaita Vedānta and Buddhism: The Mahāyāna Context of the Gauḍapādīya-Kārika*. Albany, NY: SUNY Press, 1995.

Khunu Rinpoche. *Vast as the Heavens, Deep as the Sea: Verses in Praise of Bodhicitta*. Simon and Schuster (2012).

Konow, Sten. *Central Asian Fragments of the Ashṭādaśasāhasrikā Prajñāpāramitā and of an Unidentified Text, 1942*. Calcutta: Archaeological Survey of India, 1942.

——. *Kharoshṭhī Inscriptions, with the Exception of Those of Aśoka*. Corpus Inscriptionum Indicarum, V. 2, Pt. 1; Corpus Inscriptionum Indicarum; V. 2, Pt. 1. Varanasi: Indological Book House, 1969.

Korom, Frank. "The Bengali Dharmarāj in Text and Context: Some Parallels." *Journal of Indian Philosophy* 32 (2004): 843–870.

Kragh, Ulrich. *Tibetan Yoga and Mysticism: A Textual Study of the Yogas of Naropa and Mahāmudrā Meditation in the Medieval Tradition of Dags Po*. Tokyo: The International Institute for Buddhist Studies, 2015.

Kulkarni, Prashant. "Aśvamedha: The Yajñā and the Coins." In *Mahāsenasiri: Riches of Indian Archaeological and Cultural Studies; (a Felicitation Volume in Honour of Dr. I. K. Sarma)*, edited by P Chenna Reddy; Inguva Karthikeya Sarma, 493–519. Delhi: Sharada Publishing House, 2006.

Kulke, Hermann. *Kings and Cults: State Formation and Legitimation in India and Southeast Asia*. New Delhi: Manohar Publishers, 1993.

——. "Legitimation and Town Planning in the Feudatory States of Central Orissa: Ritual Space in India: Studies in Architectural Anthropology." *Art and Archaeology Research Papers* 17 (1980): 30–40.

Lai, Ming-chiu "Legitimation in Qin-Han China: From the Perspective of the Feng and Shan Sacrifices (206 B.C.–A.D. 220)." In *The Legitimation of New Orders: Case Studies in World History*, edited by Yuansheng Liang, 1–26, Hong Kong: Chinese University Press, 2007.

Lakoff, George. "The Contemporary Theory of Metaphor." In *Metaphor and Thought* edited by Andrew Ortony. Cambridge: Cambridge University Press, 1992.

Lancashire, Ian. "A Brief History of the Homilies." (1997). www.library.utoronto.ca/utel/ret/homilies/elizhom3.html.

Lancaster, Lewis. "An Analysis of the *Aṣṭasāhasrikāprajñāpāramitāsūtra* from the Chinese Translations." Ph.D. diss. University of Wisconsin, 1968.

Landaw, Jonathan and Stephan Bodian. *Buddhism for Dummies*. Hoboken, NJ: Wiley, 2011.

Larson, Gerald James. "An Old Problem Revisited: The Relation between Sāṃkhya, Yoga and Buddhism." *Studien zur Indologie und Iranistik* 15 (1989): 129–146.

Lempert, Michael. *Discipline and Debate: The Language of Violence in a Tibetan Buddhist Monastery*. Berkeley: University of California Press, 2012.

Lenz, Timothy, Andrew Glass, and Bhikshu Dharmamitra. *A New Version of the Gāndhārī Dharmapada and a Collection of Previous-Birth Stories: British Library Kharoṣṭhī Fragments 16 + 25*. Gandhāran Buddhist Texts; V. 3. Seattle: University of Washington State, 2003.

Lessing, Ferdnand. *Yung-Ho-Kung, an Iconography of the Lamaist Cathedral in Peking, with Notes on Lamaist Mythology and Cult, Volume One*. Reports from the Scientific Expedition to the North-Western Provinces of China under the Leadership of Dr. Sven Hedin. Stockholm 1942.

Lindtner, Chr. *Nagarjuniana: Studies in the Writings and Philosophy of Nāgārjuna*. First Indian edition. ed. Delhi: Motilal Banarsidass Publishers, 1987.

Lopez, Donald S., Jr. *Prisoners of Shangri-La: Tibetan Buddhism and the West*. Chicago: University of Chicago Press, 1998.

Lüders, Heinrich. *Bruchstüke Buddhistischer Dramen*. Berlin: G. Reimer, 1911.

——. *A List of Brahmī Inscriptions from the Earliest Times to About A.D. 400 with the Exception of Those of Aśoka*. Calcutta: Superintendent Government Printing, 1913.

MacDonald, Anne. *Knowing Nothing: Candrakīrti and Yogic Perception*. Vol. 64. Wien: Verlag der Österreichischen Akademie der Wissenschaften, 2009.

MacDonnell, Arthur Anthony. *A Vedic Reader for Students*. Oxford: Clarendon Press, 1917.

Madhavananda, Swami. *The Bṛhadāraṇyaka Upaniṣad with the Commentary of Śaṅkarācārya*. Calcutta: the Advaita Ashrama, 1993.

Makransky, John. *Buddhahood Embodied: Sources of Controversy in India and Tibet*. Albany: State University of New York Press, 1997.

Marx, Karl, C. J. Arthur, and Friedrich Engels. *The German Ideology: Part One, with Selections from Parts Two and Three, Together with Marx's 'Introduction to a Critique of Political Economy'*. 2nd ed. London: Lawrence & Wishart, 2004.

Mathews, R. H. *Mathews' Chinese-English Dictionary*. Rev. American ed. Cambridge, MA: Harvard University Press, 1943.

McDermott, Joseph. *The Making of a New Rural Order in South China*. Cambridge, United Kingdom: Cambridge University Press, 2013.

McHale, Shawn. *Print and Power: Confucianism, Communism, and Buddhism in the Making of Modern Vietnam*. Honolulu: University of Hawai'i Press, 2004.

McRae, John. *The Northern School and the Formation of Early Ch'an Buddhism*. Honolulu: University of Hawaii Press, 1986.

Mehendale, Madhukar Anant. *Historical Grammar of Inscriptional Prakrits*. Poona: Deccan College, Postgraduate and research Institute, 1948.

Mehrotra, Rajiv. *Essential Dalai Lama*. New York: Viking, 2005.

Meulenbeld, Mark. *Demonic Warfare: Daoism, Territorial Networks, and the History of a Ming Novel*. Honolulu: University of Hawaii Press, 2015.

Mitra, Rājendralāla. *The Taittiriya Aranyaka of the Black Yajur Veda*. Calcutta: Asiatic Society of Bengal, 1864.

Mitra, Rájendralála, ed. *The Taittiriya Brāhmaṇa of the Black Yajur Veda: With the Commentary of Sayanacharya*. Calcutta: Asiatic Society of Bengal, 1862.

Mohanty, Lenin, ed. "Odisha Reference Annual – 2014." Edited by Information & Public Relations Department. Bhubaneswar: Government of Odisha, 2014.

Monier-Williams, Monier, et al. *A Sanskrit-English Dictionary Etymologically and Philologically Arranged with Special Reference to Cognate Indo-European Languages*. Delhi: Motilal Banarsidass, 1986.

Moyn, Samuel. *The Last Utopia*. Cambridge, MA: Harvard University Press, 2012.

Mueggler, Erik. *The Age of Wild Ghosts: Memory, Violence, and Place in Southwest China*. Berkeley: University of California Press, 2001.

Murti, T.R.V. *The Central Philosophy of Buddhism: A Study of the Mādhyamika System*. London: George Allen and Unwin, 1955.

Nakamura, Hajime, Trevor Leggett, and Sengaku Mayeda. *A History of Early Vedānta Philosophy. Part Two*. 1st ed. Delhi: M. Banarsidass, 2004.

——. *A History of Early Vedānta Philosophy*. Vol. 1, Delhi: Motilal Banarsidass, 1983.

Ñāṇananda, Bhikkhu. *Concept and Reality in Early Buddhist Thought: An Essay on 'papañca' and 'papañca-Saññā-Saṅkhā.'* Kandy: Buddhist Publication Society, 1971.

Ñāṇamoli, Bhikkhu. *The Path of Purification – Visuddhimagga*. Kandy: Buddhist Publication Soceity, 1975.

Nance, Richard. "Review of Walser, Joseph, Nāgārjuna in Context: Mahāyāna Buddhism and Early Indian Culture." (2006). www.h-net.org/reviews/showrev.php?id=11329.

Nattier, Jan. *A Few Good Men: The Bodhisattva Path According to the Inquiry of Ugra (Ugraparipṛcchā)*. Honolulu: University of Hawai'i Press, 2003.

——. *A Guide to the Earliest Chinese Buddhist Translations: Texts from the Eastern Han* 東漢 *and Three Kingdoms* 三國 *Periods* Tokyo: Soka University, The International Research Institute for Advanced Buddhology, 2008a.

——. "Who Produced the Da Mingdu Jing 大明度經 (T225)? A Reassessment of the Evidence." *Journal of the International Association of Buddhist Studies* 31, no. 1–2 (2008b (2010)): 295–338.

Nedostup, Rebecca. "Religion, Superstition and Governing Society in Nationalist China." Ph.D. diss. Columbia University, 2001.

Nicholson, Andrew J. *Unifying Hinduism: Philosophy and Identity in Indian Intellectual History*. New York: Columbia University Press, 2010.

Nietzsche, Friedrich, and W. Kaufmann. *On the Genealogy of Morals and Ecce Homo*. Knopf Doubleday Publishing Group, 2010

Nobili, Roberto de, and Svarimuthu Rajamanickam. *Roberto De Nobili on Indian Customs*. Palayamkottai: De Nobili Research Institute, 1972.

Norman, K. R., and Society Pali Text. *The Group of Discourses (Sutta-Nipāta)*. Oxford: Pali Text Society, 1992.

Obermiller, Eugéne, and Haracarana Siṅgha Sobatī. *Prajñāparamitā in Tibetan Buddhism*. Delhi: Book Faith India, 1999.

Olivelle, Patrick. *Saṃnyāsa Upaniṣads*: Hindu Scriptures on Asceticism and Renunciation. Oxford: Oxford University Press, 1992.

——. *Upaniṣads*. New York: Oxford University Press, 1996.

——. *Manu's Code of Law*. New York: Oxford University Press, 2004.

Orsborn, Matthew Bryon (= Shi Huifeng). "Chiasmus in the Early *Prajñāpāramitā*: Literary Parallelism Connecting Criticism & Hermeneutics in an Early Mahāyāna Sūtra." Ph.D. diss. University of Hong Kong, 2012.

Pagel, Ulrich. *The Bodhisattvapiṭaka: Its Doctrines, Practices and Their Position in Mahāyāna Literature*. Tring, UK: Institute of Buddhist Studies, 1995.

Pande, Govind Chandra. *Studies in the Origins of Buddhism*. 4th rev. ed. Delhi: Motilal Banarsidass Publishers, 1995.

Pankenier, David W. "A Brief History of Beiji 北極 (Northern Culmen), with an Excursus on the Origin of the Character Di 亲." *Journal of the American Oriental Society* 124, no. 2 (2004): 211–236.

Patnaik, Tandra. *Śūnya Puruṣa: Bauddha Vaisṇavism of Orissa*. New Delhi: D.K. Printworld, 2005.

Perdue, Peter C. *China Marches West: The Qing Conquest of Central Eurasia*. Cambridge, MA: Belknap Press of Harvard University Press, 2005.

Pérez Remón, Joaquín. *Self and Non-Self in Early Buddhism*. The Hague: Mouton, 1980.

Pine, Red. *The Zen Teaching of Bodhidharma*. New York: North Point Press, 1989.

Pittman, D.A. *Toward a Modern Chinese Buddhism: Taixu's Reforms*. Honolulu: University of Hawai'i Press, 2001.

Powers, John. *Introduction to Tibetan Buddhism*. Ithaca, NY: Snow Lion Publications, 1995.

Pradhāna, Prahlāda. *Abhidharmakośa-Bhāṣyam*. Patna: K.P. Jayaswal Research Institute, 1975.

Pregadio, Fabrizio and Lowell Skar. "Inner Alchemy (*Neidan*)." In *Daoism Handbook*, edited by Livia Kohn, 464–497. Leiden: E.J. Brill, 2000.

Proferes, Theodore Nicholas. *Vedic Ideals of Sovereignty and the Poetics of Power*. New Haven, CT: American Oriental Society, 2007.

Pruden, Leo. *Abhidharmakośabhāṣyam of Vasubandhu*. Berkeley, CA: Asian Humanities Press, 1988–1990.

Puett, Michael J. *To Become a God: Cosmology, Sacrifice, and Self-Divinization in Early China*. Cambridge, MA: Published by the Harvard University Asia Center for the Harvard-Yenching Institute, 2002.

Qvarnström, Olle. "Hindu Philosophy in Buddhist Perspective: The *Vedāndatattvaviniścaya* Chapter of Bhavya's *Madhyamakahṛdayakārikā*." Plus Ultra, 1989.

Rahula, Walpola. *Le Compendium De La Super-Doctrine (Philosophie) (Abhidharmasamuccaya) D'asaṅga*. Paris: École Française D'Extrême-Orient, 1971.

Rai, Mridu. *Hindu Rulers, Muslim Subjects: Islam, Rights, and the History of Kashmir*. Princeton, NJ: Princeton University Press, 2004.

Rāmatīrtha., *Maitri or Maitrāyaṇīya Upaniṣad: with the commentary of Rāmatīrtha*. E.B. Cowell, Satīśa Candra Vidyābhūṣaṇa, eds. Calcutta: Asiatic Society of Bengal, 1913-1919.

Ramble, Charles. "Sacral Kings and Divine Sovereigns: Principles of Tibetan Monarchy in Theory and Practice." In *States of Mind: Power, Place and the Subject in Inner Asia*, edited by David Sneath, 129–149. Bellingham, WA: Western Washington University Center for East Asian Studies, 2006.

Raz, Gil "'Conversion of the Barbarians' [Huahu 化胡] Discourse as Proto Han Nationalism." *The Medieval History Journal* 17, no. 2 (2014): 255–294.

Renou, Louis. "Sur La Notion De Brahman." *Journal Asiatique* 237 (1949): 7–46.

Rhys Davids, T. W. *The Questions of King Milinda/Part 2 [Books 4-7]*. Sacred Books of the East, Ed. F. Max Muller; V. 36. Oxford: Clarendon Press, 1894.

Riffaterre, Michael. "Syllepsis." *Critical Inquiry* 6, no. 4 (1980): 625–638.

Robinson, Richard H. *Early Mādhyamika in India and China*. New York: Samuel Weiser, 1978.

Roemer, Stephanie. *The Tibetan Government-in-Exile: Politics at Large*. London: Routledge, 2008.

Ruegg, David Seyfort. "On the Authorship of Some Works Ascribed to Bhavaviveka/Bhavya." In *Earliest Buddhism and Madhyamaka*, 59–71. Leiden: E.J. Brill, 1990.

Sahni, Daya Ram. "A Sunga Inscription from Ayodhya." *Epigraphia Indica* 20 (1929): 54–58.

Salomon, Richard. *A Gāndhārī Version of the Rhinoceros Sūtra: British Library Kharoṣṭhī Fragment*. Seattle [u.a.]: University of Washington Press, 2000.

Salomon, Richard, and Andrew Glass. *Two Gāndhārī Manuscripts of the Songs of Lake Anavatapta (Anavatapta-Gāthā): British Library Kharoṣṭhī Fragment 1 and Senior Scroll 14*. Gandhāran Buddhist Texts; V. 5; Seattle: University of Washington Press, 2008.

Sander, Lore. "Fragments of an Aṣṭasāhasrikā Manuscript from the Kuṣāṇa Period." In *Buddhist Manuscripts*, edited by Jens Braarvig, 1–53. Oslo: Hermes Publishing, 2000.

Sastri, Suryanarayana. *Sāṃkhyakārikā of Īśvarakṛṣṇā: Text, Translation and Commentary - Yuktidīpikā*. 1st ed. Delhi, India: Bharatiya Kala Prakashan, 2009.

Sayers, Matthew R. *Feeding the Dead: Ancestor Worship in Ancient India*. Oxford: Oxford University Press, 2013.

Schipper, Kristofer Marinus, and Franciscus Verellen. *The Taoist Canon: A Historical Companion to the Daozang* = [道藏通考]. Chicago: University of Chicago Press, 2004.

Schlosser, Andrea. "On the Bodhisattva Path in Gandhāra: Edition of Fragment 4 and 11 from the Bajaur Collection of Kharoṣṭhī Manuscripts." Ph.D. diss. Free University of Berlin, 2016.

Schlütter, Morten. *How Zen Became Zen: The Dispute over Enlightenment and the Formation of Chan Buddhism in Song-Dynasty China*. Studies in East Asian Buddhism; No. 22. Honolulu: University of Hawai'i Press, 2008.

Schmithausen, Lambert. "Textgeschichtliche Beobachtungen Zum 1. Kapitel Der Aṣṭasāhasrikā Prajñāpāramitā." In *Prajñāpāramitā and Related Systems: Studies in Honour of Edward Conze*, edited by Lewis Lancaster and Luis Gomez, 35–80. Berkeley: University of California Berkeley, 1977.

Schopen, Gregory. "Archaeology and Protestant Presuppositions in the Study of Indian Buddhism." *History of Religions* 31, no. 1 (1991): 1–23.

——. "The Phrase '*Sa Pṛthivīpradeśaś Caityabhūto Bhavet*' in the *Vajracchedikā*: Notes on the Cult of the Book in Mahāyāna." *Indo Iranian Journal* 17, no. 3–4 (1975): 147–181.

Schroeder, Leopold von. *Maitrāyaṇī Samhitā*. Leipzig: F.A. Brochaus, 1881.

——. "Ueber Die *Maitrāyaṇī Samhitā* Ihr Alter, Ihr Verhältniss Zu Den Verwandten Cākhā's, Ihre Sprachliche Und Historische Bedeutung." University of Dorpat, 1879.

Schuessler, Axel, and Bernhard Karlgren. *Minimal Old Chinese and Later Han Chinese: A Companion to Grammata Serica Recensa*. Honolulu: University of Hawai'i Press, 2009. Ebook

Library http://public.eblib.com/choice/publicfullrecord.aspx?p=3413409 JSTOR www.jstor.org/stable/10.2307/j.ctt6wqtzt

Schwarzschild, LA. "Some Forms of the Absolutive in Middle Indo-Aryan." *Journal of the American Oriental Society* 76, no. 2 (1956): 111–115.

Schwieger, Peter. *The Dalai Lama and the Emperor of China: A Political History of the Tibetan Institution of Reincarnation*. New York: Columbia University Press, 2015.

Seiwert, Hubert Michael, and 西沙馬. *Popular Religious Movements and Heterodox Sects in Chinese History*. Leiden: Brill, 2003.

Shapin, Steven. *A Social History of Truth: Civility and Science in Seventeenth-Century England*. Chicago: University of Chicago Press, 1994.

Sharf, Robert. "Buddhist Veda and the Rise of Chan." In *Chinese and Tibetan Esoteric Buddhism*, edited by Yael Bentor and Meir Shahar, 85–120. Leiden: Brill, 2017.

——. "Mindfulness and Mindlessness in Early Chan." *Philosophy East and West* 64, no. 4 (2014): 933–964.

Sharf, Robert H. *Coming to Terms with Chinese Buddhism: A Reading of the Treasure Store Treatise*. Honolulu: University of Hawai'i Press, 2002.

Sharma, G. R. *The Excavations at Kauśāmbī (1957–59) the Defences and the Śyenaciti of the Puruṣamedha*. Allahabad: Department of Ancient History, Culture & Archaeology, University of Allahabad, 1960.

Shastri, Mahamahopadhyaya Haraprasad. *Advayavajrasamgraha*. Baroda: Oriental Institute, 1927.

Shên, T., and S. Liu. *Tibet and the Tibetans*. Stanford, CA: Stanford University Press, 1953.

Shue, Vivienne. *The Reach of the State: Sketches of the Chinese Body Politic*. Stanford, CA: Stanford University Press, 1988.

Silk, Jonathan. "What, If Anything, Is Mahāyāna Buddhism?" *Numen* 49, no. 4 (2002): 355–405.

Sims-Williams, Nicholas. "A New Bactrian Inscription of Kanishka the Great." *Silk Road Art and Archaeology: Journal of the Institute of Silk Road Studies* 4 (1996): 75–142.

Singh, Jaideva. *The Doctrine of Recognition: A Translation of Pratyabhijñāhṛdayam*. Delhi: Motilal Banarsidass, 1998.

——. *Vijnanabhairava, or, Divine Consciousness: A Treasury of 112 Types of Yoga*. Delhi: Motilal Banarsidass Pub, 2003.

Singh, Upinder. "Cults and Shrines in Early Historical Mathura (C. 200 BC – AD 200)." *World Archaeology* 36, no. 3 (2004): 378–398.

Sircar, Dineschandra. *Select Inscriptions Bearing on Indian History and Civilization. Vol. 1, from the Sixth Century B.C. To the Sixth Century A.D.* 2nd ed., rev. & enl. ed. Calcutta: University of Calcutta, 1965.

Smith, Mark S. *God in Translation: Deities in Cross-Cultural Discourse in the Biblical World*. Tübingen: Mohr Siebeck, 2008.

Snellgrove, David L. *Hevajra Tantra: A Critical Study*. 2nd ed. ed. Hong Kong: Orchid Publishers Group UK, 2010.

Staunton, George Thomas. *Ta Tsing Leu Lee: Being the Fundamental Laws and a Selection from the Supplementary Statutes of the Penal Code of China*. London: s.n., 1810.

Stede, William and T.W. Rhys Davids. *Pali-English Dictionary*. Delhi: Motilal Banarsidass, 1997.

Strauch, Ingo. "More Missing Pieces of Early Pure Land Buddhism: New Evidence for Akṣobhya and Abhirati in an Early Mahāyāna Sūtra from Gandhāra." *The Eastern Buddhist* 41, no. 1 (2010): 23–66.

Strootman, Rolf. *Courts and Elites in the Hellenistic Empires: The Near East After the Achaemenids, BCE. 330 to 30 BCE*. Edinburgh: Edinburgh University Press, 2014.

Stuart, Daniel Malinowski. *A Less Traveled Path: Saddharmasmṛtyupasthānasūtra. Chapter 2: Critically Edited with a Study on Its Structure and Significance for the Development of Buddhist*

Meditation. Vienna: China Tibetology Publishing House Austrian Academy of Sciences Press, 2015.

Taixu. *Lectures in Buddhism*. Paris: [Imp. Union], 1928.

Tatz, Mark. "*Tattva-Ratnāvalī*-the Precious Garland of Verses on Reality." In *Researches in Indian History, Archaeology, Art and Religion: Prof. Upendra Thakur Felicitation Volume*, edited by Kumudamani G. and K. Kuppuram, 491–513. Delhi: Sundeep Prakashan, 1990.

Thite, Gaṇeśa Umākānta. *Āpastamba-Śrauta-Sūtra: Text with English Translation and Notes*. Delhi: New Bharatiya Book Corporation, 2004.

Tsong-kha-pa, Blo-bzang-grags-pa. *The Great Treatise on the Stages of the Path to Enlightenment*. Ithaca, NY: Snow Lion Publications, 2000.

Tsuchiyama, Yasuhiro. "Abhiṣekha in the Vedic and the Post-Vedic Rituals." In *From Material to Deity: Indian Rituals of Consecration*, edited by Shingo Einoo, 51–93. New Delhi: Monohar Publishers & Distributors, 2005.

Turner, A., K. Crosby, P. Pranke, J. Schober, B.B. de la Perriere, N. Foxeus, K. Tosa, et al. *Champions of Buddhism: Weikza Cults in Contemporary Burma*. Singapore: NUS Press, 2014.

Vaidya, P. L. *Aṣṭasāhasrikā Prajñāpāramitā: With Haribhadra's Commentary Called Āloka*. Darbhanga: Mithila Institute of Post-Graduate Studies and Research in Sanskrit Learning, 1960.

Van Schaik, Sam. *Tibet: A History*. New Haven: Yale University Press, 2011.

—— and Jacob Dalton. *Where Chan and Tantra Meet: Tibetan Syncretism in Dunhuang*. na, 2004.

Verboom, Arie Willem Cornelis. "A Text-Comparative Research on the Perfection of Discriminating Insight in Eight Thousand Lines, Chapter 1." Ph.D. diss. Leiden, 1998.

Voegeli, Francois. "Progress Report for the Snf Project 'Vedic Places of Worship: A Study of Their Layout and Spatial Organisation', 1st Year (Nov. 2011–Nov. 2012)." Lausanne: IASA – Université de Lausanne, 2012.

Von Glahn, Richard. *The Sinister Way: The Divine and the Demonic in Chinese Religious Culture*. Berkeley: University of California Press, 2004.

von Hinüber, Oskar. "Pali as an Artificial Language." *Indologia Taurinensia* 10 (1982): 133–140.

Vose, Kevin. *Resurrecting Candrakīrti: Disputes in the Tibetan Creation of Prāsaṅgika*. Studies in Boston: Wisdom Publications, 2009.

Walleser, Max. *Die Streitlosigkeit Des Subhūti: Ein Beitrag Zur Buddhistischen Legendenentwicklung*. Heidelberg: Carl Winter's University Press, 1917.

Walser, Joseph. "The Classification of Religions and Religious Classifications: A Genre Approach to the Origin of Religions." *Culture and Religion* 16, no. 4 (2015): 345–371.

——. *Nāgārjuna in Context: Mahāyāna Buddhism and Early Indian Culture*. New York: Columbia University Press, 2005.

——. "On Buddhists and Their Chairs." In *Scriptural Authority, Reason and Action: Proceedings of a Panel at the 14th World Sanskrit Conference, Kyoto, September 1st–5th, 2009*, edited by Vincent Eltschinger and Helmut Krasser, 49–70. Wien: Verlag der Österreichischen Akademie der Wissenschaften, 2009.

——. "The Origin of the Term 'Mahāyāna' (the Great Vehicle) and its Relationship to the Āgamas." *Journal of the International Association of Buddhist Studies* 30, no. 1–2 (2007 (2009): 219–252.

——. "Abhidharma" In *Buddhist World*, edited by John Powers. London: Routledge (2015).

——. "When Did Buddhism Become Anti-Brahmanical? The Case of the Missing Soul." *Journal of the American Academy of Religion*, 86.1, (March 2018) pp. 94–125,

Walshe, Maurice. *The Long Discourses of the Buddha: A Translation of the Digha Nikāya*. Boston: Wisdom Publications, 1996.

Ward, Jean Elizabeth. *Book of Odes*. Lulu Enterprises Incorporated, (lulu.com) 2008.

Warder, A.K. and Bhikkhu Ñāṇamoli. *The Path of Discrimination (Paṭisambhidāmagga).* Oxford: Pali Text Society, 1997.
Warren, Henry C. *Visuddhimagga of Buddhaghosâcariya.* Cambridge, Mass: Harvard University Press, 1950.
Weirong, Shen. "Tibetan Buddhism in the Mongol Yuan China (1206–1368)." In *Esoteric Buddhism and the Tantras in East Asia,* edited by Charles Orzech and Richard Payne, 539–549. Leiden: Brill, 2011.
Welch, Holmes. *The Practice of Chinese Buddhism, 1900–1950.* Cambridge: Harvard University Press, 1967.
Welden, Ellwood Austin. "The Sāṃkhya Teachings in the Māitrī Upaniṣad." *The American Journal of Philology* 35, no. 1 (1914): 32–51.
Welter, Albert. *The Linji Lu and the Creation of Chan Orthodoxy: The Development of Chan's Records of Sayings Literature.* Oxford: Oxford University Press, 2008.
——. *Monks, Rulers, and Literati: The Political Ascendancy of Chan Buddhism.* New York: Oxford University Press, 2006.
——. *Yongming Yanshou's Conception of Chan in the Zongjing Lu: A Special Transmission within the Scriptures.* New York: Oxford University Press, 2011.
Westerhoff, Jan. *The Dispeller of Disputes: Nāgārjuna's Vigrahavyāvartanī.* Oxford: Oxford University Press, 2010.
White, David Gordon. *Sinister Yogis.* Chicago: University of Chicago Press, 2009.
Whitney, William Dwight. *A Sanskrit Grammar: Including Both the Classical Language, and the Older Dialects, of Veda and Brāhmaṇa.* Leipzig: Breitkopf and Härtel, 1879.
Willemen, Charles. *The Essence of Scholasticism: Abhidharmahṛdaya. T 1550.* Delhi: Motilal Banarsidass Publications, 2006.
Williams, Duncan. "Registering the Family, Memorializing the Ancestors: The Zen Temple and the Parishoner Household." In *The Other Side of Zen: A Social History of Sōtō Zen: Buddhism in Tokugawa Japan,* 13–38. Princeton, NJ: Princeton University Press, 2005.
Williams, Paul. *Mahāyāna Buddhism: The Doctrinal Foundations.* London: Routledge, 2009.
Willis, Michael D. *The Archaeology of Hindu Ritual: Temples and the Establishment of the Gods.* Cambridge: Cambridge University Press, 2009.
Wood, Thomas E. *The Māṇḍūkya Upaniṣad and the Āgama Śāstra: An Investigation into the Meaning of the Vedānta.* Delhi: Motilal Banarsidass, 1992.
Wootton, David. *Divine Right and Democracy: An Anthology of Political Writing in Stuart England.* Indianapolis: Hackett Publishing Company, 2003.
Wu, Jiang. *Enlightenment in Dispute: The Reinvention of Chan Buddhism in Seventeenth-Century China.* Oxford: Oxford University Press, 2008.
Wynne, Alexander. *The Origin of Buddhist Meditation.* London: Routledge, 2007.
Yat-Sen, Sun. "中华民国临时约法." 1912.
Yongzheng (雍正). 雍正御制佛教大典 [*Yongzheng yu zhi fo jiao da dian*]. Beijing: Zhongguo she hui ke xue chu ban she, 2003.
Zito, Angela. "City Gods and Their Magistrates." In *Religions of China in Practice,* edited by Donald Lopez, 72–81. Princeton, NJ: Princeton University Press, 1996.
——. "City Gods, Filiality, and Hegemony in Late Imperial China." *Modern China* 13, no. 3 (1987): 333–371.

INDEX

abhidharma 92, 141, 181–182, 192–195, 237–238
Abhidharmadīpa 184, 203, 217
Abhidharmahṛdaya 182, 192–193, 237
Abhidharmakośa 167, 182, 184, 193, 202–203
Abhidharmasamucchaya 203
Abhisamayālaṃkāra 195
abhiṣekha 19, 269
acitta 83, 116, 118, 143, 148, 190–218, 223, 228–229, 255
Altar for Baleful Spirits (*litan*) 厲壇 90
Althusser, Louis 249–250, 264
Aṅguttara Nikāya 170, 177, 181, 196–197, 237
An Shigao 83
araṇavihāra 141, 144, 154, 182, 215–216, 234–242
arhat 11, 114, 131–132, 136, 151, 154, 171, 173, 182, 184–186, 226, 238, 248–249
Asaṅga 12, 65, 200, 203, 211
ātman 59, 120–122, 142, 149, 150, 164, 166, 173, 209–210, 213–214

Bakhtin, Michael 160–161
Bhāskara 107, 109–111, 118
bhavaṅga citta 327–328, 329, 344
Bhāviveka 108, 111–123, 171, 200–202, 246
bodhicitta 5, 10, 12, 15, 19, 36, 59, 117–118, 123, 143–149, 154, 226, 230, 232–233, 240
Bodhisattvapiṭaka 153, 157
bodhisattvas 12, 13–15, 18, 132, 152–154, 173, 175
brahman 9, 99, 100, 103, 104, 120–122, 209, 211, 213–214, 247, 253, 255
Brahmanism 5, 9, 94, 99, 100–101, 105–111, 118–123, 199–202, 206, 247
brahmavihāra 385
Brahmins 101, 103, 176, 206–207, 215–216, 225–229, 239, 244n24, 247, 249, 252–253, 257–258, 267–269
brahmodya 122, 212, 217
Buddha Bodies; *dharma-kāya* 16, 17–18, 25, 28, 35, 57–58, 112, 122, 214; *mirmāna-kaya* 16, 17, 57; *sambhoga-kāya* 16, 28; *svabhāva-kāya* 38n47; *tulku* 17, 25, 28, 36, 57, 238
Buddhist Brahmins 9, 109–111, 216, 221n92, 225, 229–230, 247–249, 255–257, 262–263, 267–269

Cakrasamvara Tantra 53–54, 57
Candrakīrti 108, 116, 171, 248
Caodong 64
celestial pole 51, 73–79, 84, 89
Central Tibetan Administration 8, 22, 23, 25, 29, 32, 36
cessation 15–19, 64–65, 106, 113, 116, 123, 168–171, 174, 181, 191–198, 204, 223, 229, 247; Cessation of Perception and Feeling (*saṃjñāveditanirodha*) 170, 180, 184, 192, 194, 251
Chankya Rolpai Dorje 54, 56–58, 67

City God 城隍神 49–53, 61, 85, 89–90
compassion 5, 6, 11, 12, 14, 17, 18–20, 36, 39n66, 123, 148, 154, 229
Confucianism 45–53, 61–62, 73, 77, 85–91, 105

Dahui Zonggao 64, 66
Dalai Lama (Fourteenth) 11–39; Fifth Dalai Lama 23, 30, 55; Thirteenth 29
Daoism 41, 46, 48, 51, 73, 77–93
De Nobili 110–111
Dhātuvibhaṅga 178–181, 225, 247
Di 帝, 76–85
Dignāga 116, 168
Dīgha Nikāya 53, 138, 167, 169, 173, 202–204
Dong Zhongshu 51
dzogchen 19, 21, 248

Ekottara Āgama 182, 237
encoding/decoding 74, 84, 247, 248

Feng and *Shan* (封 and 禪) Sacrifice 81–84
Four Noble Truths 14–17, 106, 115, 162–163, 235

Ganden-Phodrang 23
Gandhāra 106, 233, 240
Gelukpa 19–20, 21, 54–58
Guhyasamājatantra 37n17, 53

Han Dynasty 79, 81, 83, 85, 225
Haribhadra 130, 149
Hevajratantra 19, 53–55, 58, 69n46
Hongwu, Emperor 90–91
Hongzhi 64–66, 248
Horse Sacrifice 9, 217, 255–269
Huizong, Emperor 89, 91
Human Rights 20–23, 31, 36, 38n32

Jagannāth 102–105, 124n21

Kagyupa 20, 21, 57, 100, 105, 238, 248
Kālacakra tantra 21, 31–39n59, 53
Kangxi, Emperor 51, 56, 62
Kāśyapaparivarta 153, 225, 226, 243n13
Khunu Rinpoche 19
kōan 64–65
Kṣatriya 101, 267, 268
Kublai Khan 54–58, 69n40, 70

Laṅkāvatāra Sūtra 67
Linji 63–65

Madhyama Āgama 178, 180, 224, 236
Mādhyamika 3, 12, 19, 106, 107–111, 116, 117, 118, 123, 138, 149, 176, 248
Mahābhārata 104, 125n58, 213, 239
mahāmudrā 20, 21, 100, 105, 238, 248, 271
Mahāvibhāṣa 141–142, 156n36, 183–184, 193–195, 238
Mahāyāna sect 9
Mahima Dharma Sampradaya 100–105
Maitrāyaṇīputra 133, 151–152
Maitrāyaṇīya (branch of Yajurveda) 9, 207–229, 239, 245n69, 247, 250, 254–255, 257, 262–263, 266
Maitrīpa 105–111
Majjhima Nikāya 120, 138, 165–166, 170, 173, 180, 189 n 68, 204, 215, 235
Mānava Śrautasūtra 254, 257–258, 266–267
maṇḍala 24, 33, 51–53, 58, 92, 270
Mañjuśrī's Inquiry Concerning the Office of the Bodhisattva Sūtra 226–229
Mao Zedong 21, 36
Mathura 9, 231, 233, 240, 241–242, 256
Mazu 63, 94, 248
mind-only (Yogacara) 3, 9, 10, 12, 15, 42–44, 66–67, 94, 106, 116–119, 137, 180, 223–224, 229, 248, 270
Ming Dynasty 62, 72, 81, 85, 90

Nāgārjuna 6, 12, 19, 21, 115, 120, 122, 149, 154, 194, 204, 208, 217, 220n67, 222, 225, 257, 268–269
Nehru, Jawaharlal 22–23, 31
Nietzsche 6
Nyingmapa 19, 21

Orissa 100–105

Pakpa 54–57, 70n49
Pangu 81–82
Paṭisambhidamagga xi, 218n4, 236
Patsab 108
Piling the Fire Altar (*agnicayana*) 209, 259
prabhāsvarā 191, 196, 212
Prajāpati 9, 121, 208, 211, 213–214, 217, 247, 253, 259–260, 263
prāṇāgnihotra 235
prāsaṅgika 108, 176
primal ancestors 78
pūrvacitta 254–255

Qingyuan Weixin 63

Ratnaguṇasaṃcāyagāthā 144, 150, 155n17
Ratnāvalī 122, 204, 217, 268

"Religion" 5, 27, 28, 34–37, 40–49, 51, 72, 79, 84, 93, 99, 100, 257, 264, 267
Ṛgveda 110, 122, 199, 206–207, 223, 253, 260–261
Rite of the Three Altars 92

Sacrificial Registry (*sidian* 祀典) 46–47
Sadāprarūdita 131, 133–134, 214
Saddharmasmṛtyupasthānasūtra 180, 223–225, 229, 247
Sāṃkhya 120, 122, 126n92, 197, 198, 200, 212–213, 217, 219n32, 252
Saṃyutta Nikāya xi, 134, 138, 166, 171–172, 174, 198, 201–202, 238, 252–253
Sarvāstivāda 189n75, 238, 240–242, 265
Sarvatathāgatatattvasaṃgraha 59, 93–94, 269
Śatapatha Brāhmaṇa 346, 347, 358, 423, 441–443
selflessness (*anātman*) 17–20, 106, 108, 113, 115, 123, 141–142, 149–151, 164–166, 168–170, 173, 177, 222, 223; *dharma-nairātmya vs. pudgala-nairātmya* 17, 37n16
Shang Dynasty 72, 75–80, 95n11
she altar 社 85–86, 88, 91–92
Shenhui 84
Śiva 106, 109–110
Song Dynasty 49, 62, 64, 66, 78, 86, 87–89, 91–92
sovereign all creating mind (*kun byed rgyal po*) 20, 248
Suttanipāta 175–176, 201, 204, 219n38

Taixu 42–46
Tang Dynasty 49, 59, 66, 84–86, 92, 94
tathatā 112, 138, 149, 151, 214, 221n79
Tsongkhapa 5, 19, 36, 58, 248

Vairocanābhisaṃbodhisūtra 270
Vajracchedikāsūtra 225, 234, 238
vajropamasamādhi 16, 92, 112, 184–185
Vasubandhu 17, 37n16, 42, 65, 167, 184, 202–203
Vedānta 109, 118–121
Vimalakīrtinirdeśa 225, 229
Visuddhimagga 195, 200, 234

Yat-sen, Sun 41, 45, 93
yoga 9, 36, 200, 205, 208–211, 229, 238, 248, 255
Yongming Yanshou 66, 78, 84
Yuan Dynasty 41, 55–59, 82, 89

Zen 11–12, 42, 60–68, 83–84, 91, 94, 100
Zhou Dynasty 51, 77–81, 84–87
zong 宗 66–67, 71n86, 78–80, 84, 86–96
zongjiao 宗教 42, 47, 71n86